UNSOLVED CASES

UNSOLVED
CASES

Edited by Lorrie Mack, Lesley Riley
and Frank Smyth

St Michael

Acknowledgements

Photographs were supplied by Agencia Ansa, Associated Newspapers, Associated Press, Aviation Photographers International, BBC Hulton Picture Library, Catt Wilson Literary Agency, Clara Calvi, Colorific, Arnold Desser, John Fairfax, John Hillelson Agency, Imperial War Museum, Jean Justice, Kobal Collection, Howard Kohn, Peter Lofts (Ramsay & Muspratt), London Express, Tony Lopez, National Portrait Gallery, National Trust, News of Australia, New Scotland Yard, Oklahoma Publishing, Barrie Penrose, The Photo Source, Popperfoto, Press Association, Rex Features, Patrick Scale Books, Spectrum, Frank Spooner, Syndication International, Times Newspapers, John Topham Picture Library, U.P.I.

Chapter opening photographs specially taken by Helen Pask.

The publishers would like to thank the following authors for contributing to this book: Paolo Filo della Torre 138-145; Sandy Fawkes 152-157; Paul Foot 42-50, 138-145; Werner Forman 14-19; Art Gatti 74-83; Fred Goerner 174-181; Rodney Hallworth 8-13; Brian Innes 112-121; Philip Jacobson 66-73; Robert Kimball 36-41; Phillip Knightley 164-172; Jack Lodge 20-27; Peter McKay 58-65; Irene Matthews 52-57; John Penrose 182-189; Chapman Pincher 94-104, 106-111, 122-128; Colin Simpson 146-151; Frank Smyth 84-93; Linda Sonntag 158-163; Alan Stewart 130-137; Clare Taylor 28-35.

This edition first published for Marks and Spencer plc
in 1986 by Orbis Book Publishing Corporation Limited
A BPCC plc company
Greater London House, Hampstead Road, London NW1

Printed in Italy

Contents

Introduction

In the tidy world of fiction the mystery is always solved, the murderer is unmasked, justice triumphs. Real life is somewhat different. Death occurs in such strange circumstances that the law is unable to decide whether it is a case of murder or accident. People disappear off the face of the earth, creating mysteries that defy solution. Sometimes murderers get away with it. And, often enough to be disturbing, the State sometimes punishes the innocent and ignores the guilty.

This book examines some of those recent cases that can only be labelled "UNSOLVED". Where, for example, is Lord Lucan? After a sensational coroner's court hearing in London in 1974 it was accepted that the dashing British peer had killed his children's nanny and tried to slaughter his wife. But there was no murder trial because Lucan was never found.

Marilyn Monroe died a sad, tragic figure, and the official report was unequivocal: an overdose of barbiturates, taken deliberately or accidentally. But it was not long before questions were being asked. Why did the post mortem find no trace of the drugs in Marilyn's digestive tract? Why were the police not notified until several hours after the body had been found? Who visited Marilyn that night? Was it the attorney general, Robert Kennedy?

Doubt about the official version of Marilyn Monroe's death surfaced quickly but in other cases it has taken years. Bruno Richard Hauptmann, a German immigrant, went to the electric chair in the United States in 1936 for the kidnap and murder of Charles Lindbergh jnr, the baby son of the famous American aviator. There was general satisfaction; the nation's honour had been vindicated. Then, nearly 50 years later, new investigations suggested that Hauptmann was innocent.

In the Drummond murder case, the police again had no doubt about the killer. Sir Jack Drummond, a well-known British scientist, his wife, and their ten-year-old daughter were all found dead at their road-side camping site in the south of France in 1952. A nearby farming family, the Dominicis, were immediate suspects and when one member of the family accused his father, the inquiry appeared closed.

But then the Dominicis began to change their stories with such bewildering rapidity that the police case fell apart. In the end, the father, Gaston, was sentenced to death, but President Charles de Gaulle later granted him clemency. No motive was ever established and today the file still remains open.

So, too, does the file for the Australian scientist Dr Gilbert Bogle and his friend, Mrs. Margaret Chandler, whose bodies were found in bizarre circumstances on a river bank in a Sydney suburb on New Years Day, 1963. No one has ever been charged with their murders and the theories about their deaths range from an attack by agents of a foreign secret service to an accidental overdose of LSD.

The way the bodies were arranged was proof that whether Bogle and Chandler died accidentally or were murdered, a third party was afterwards on the scene. Yet no one has come forward, no motive has ever been established, and despite the most exhaustive scientific tests, even the cause of death has never been discovered.

There was at first no mystery about the death of Edith Morrell. Officially this Eastbourne widow had suffered a stroke, but the police had other ideas. Mrs. Morrell's doctor, John Bodkin Adams, specialised in treating wealthy, elderly women, many of whom died suddenly after leaving Dr Adams large sums in their wills. When, after a lengthy investigation, the police arrested him, he said, "Murder? I don't think you could prove it was murder. She was dying in any event."

At his Old Bailey trial in 1957, the jury found him not guilty, but the police remained convinced that Adams had practised not euthanasia but murder.

In Karen Silkwood's case there was not even a suspect. Karen was driving to a meeting with a New York Time's reporter in 1974 to discuss safety issues at the plutonium plant where she worked. Her car veered off the road and crashed into a concrete culvert killing her instantly. Death by accident, or murder by persons unknown?

And when the famous American flyer, Amelia Earhart, sent an SOS message on the last lap of her flight around the equator in 1937, where was she? Over the ocean, and the sea claimed her, say some. About to force-land on a Japanese-occupied island, say others, and the Japanese executed her as a spy.

In a world that has become smaller because of amazing advances in communications and technology, it is still possible for people to vanish. With all our medical and scientific resources it is still possible for people to die without apparent cause. With all the checks and balances of our legal systems, it is still possible for the guilty to go free and for the innocent to suffer.

Yet, although all the cases in this book are unsolved they may not always remain so. Publication provokes information. Somewhere, someone reading these stories may hold a fragment of the puzzle that enables the authorities to change the label on the yellowing file from UNSOLVED to CASE CLOSED.

PHILLIP KNIGHTLEY

1
Guilty as charged?

Society can function only within a framework of law that protects the innocent and punishes transgressors, but sometimes the process goes badly wrong. This chapter examines some notorious cases where justice may have erred – or been deliberately perverted.

Doctor of mercy – or murder?

Eastbourne doctor John Bodkin Adams specialised in treating wealthy old ladies, but some people suspected that he went on his rounds with a blank will form in one hand and a bottle of morphia in the other. At least twenty-five of his patients died mysteriously, leaving him large bequests, and in December 1956 Dr Adams was arrested for the murder of one of them. But an Old Bailey jury found him not guilty, and none of the other cases was ever brought to trial. Did he practice euthanasia – or murder?

On the night of 13 March 1956, in Eastbourne, Sussex, a retired Lloyd's underwriter, Jack Hullett, suffered a heart attack. His physician, Doctor John Bodkin Adams, injected him with a dose of morphine and a few hours later Jack Hullett died. Dr Adams was a friend of the family – indeed he had introduced Hullett, a widower, to his second wife, Gertrude Joyce Tomlinson, known as 'Bobbie'.

From the day of Jack Hullett's death, Bobbie was close to mental breakdown, and Adams supplied barbiturates to help her sleep. On 17 July, in a letter to Robert Hanscombe, an old family friend, she spoke of suicide. Suddenly, two days later, she was taken ill. For the few days after Thursday 19 July, Mrs Hullett was unconscious much of the time. Adams, who was in attendance, failed to get her to hospital and did not even call for a second opinion until Saturday 21 July.

Two days later, after falling into a coma, Bobbie Hullett died without regaining consciousness. She had survived her husband by only five months. Adams certified the cause of death as cerebral haemorrhage but Dr Francis Camps, the Home Office pathologist, did not agree. Six days after the death of Bobbie Hullett he reported his suspicion that she had died of barbiturate poisoning and not from a haemorrhage.

Adams, who lived in Kent Lodge, a large house in the centre of town, was one of Eastbourne's wealthiest and most fashionable doctors. Born in Northern Ireland, he was a staunch Methodist, a non smoker and near-teetotaller whose only vice appeared to be an addiction to chocolate. His practice in Eastbourne had flourished for almost 30 years, but even before the death of Bobbie Hullett, gossip had begun about the number of legacies he had been left in the wills of his former patients, mostly rich old women. The rumours finally attracted the attention of a friend of both the Hulletts and Dr Adams – Richard Walker, Chief Constable of Eastbourne.

Walker had inquiries made and it was quickly established that before she fell into her final coma – and only two days before her death – Mrs Hullett had given Adams a cheque for £1000. He had immediately driven to his bank and asked for special clearance. Within hours the amount was credited to his account. After Bobbie's death, it emerged that she had also bequeathed her Rolls-Royce to him.

Full enquiry

Chief Constable Walker now decided to initiate a major investigation by calling in Scotland Yard for the first time in the history of Eastbourne's police force. Detective Superintendent Herbert Hannam and his assistant, Detective Sergeant Charlie Hewitt, arrived from Scotland Yard. Hannam's investigation began shortly after Bobbie Hullett's death, in July 1956. He nominated a number of detectives from the Yard to work for him nationwide and six detectives in Eastbourne were taken off all other duties to work by his side.

Hannam and his team of detectives examined

wills and interviewed relatives, nurses, hotel staff and domestic employees. They discovered that, over a period of some years, Adams had enjoyed bequests totalling £45,000. He had been left two Rolls-Royces and a great deal of silver, jewellery and antiques. During his career he had been a beneficiary in at least 132 wills and had acted as an executor in a number of other cases.

While the murder investigation was under way, evidence of other crimes accumulated. In the last days of one woman's life, Adams had forged 32 cheques drawn on her account, amounting to £18,000. Having persuaded two other women to leave their house and move into a flat, Adams sold the house and kept the money for three years. He returned it only when he was served with a writ. And when another of his patients died, in 1953, Adams forced his way into her house and asked to see the will. When it appeared that he was not a beneficiary, Adams is alleged to have said: 'Well, I deserve something for looking after her.' Immediately he rummaged through the house and made off with a new typewriter and several pieces of bric-à-brac.

The inquest into the death of Bobbie Hullett was held in August 1956 at Eastbourne Magistrates Court. Hannam, who was present at the inquest, continued his investigations for a total of six weeks and provided detailed reports for the Director of Public Prosecutions, Sir Theobald Mathew.

The earliest of these cases concerned a widow, Mrs Emily Louise Mortimer, who had died in 1946. Dr Adams gave the cause of death as cerebral thrombosis. Later he received a £5000 bequest.

Gertrude 'Bobbie' Hullett, whose death from barbiturate poisoning in July 1956 aroused the suspicions of her friends and led to the police investigation

Kent Lodge, the large Victorian house from which Dr Adams ran his practice. He was particularly successful in attracting wealthy private patients among Eastbourne's elderly residents

Mrs Edith Alice Morrell was the widow of Alfred Morrell, a wealthy Liverpool food importer. She retired to Eastbourne and Adams became her doctor; in March 1949, she drafted a new will leaving the entire residue of her estate to Adams.

In the spring of 1949, Mrs Morrell went to Cheshire to visit her son. There she suffered a heart attack and was admitted to a private room in the Cheshire Hospital. Some weeks later she travelled back by car to a nursing home in Grassington Road, Eastbourne.

Dr Adams decided to continue prescribing drugs to control Mrs Morrell's irritability and her pain. From the summer of 1949 onwards she was given regular doses of both heroin and morphine. Adams arranged for her to be moved to the Esperance Nursing Home, to which he sent many of his patients. But she was uncomfortable there and later moved to the Cumberland Hotel, into a suite in which she stayed every year when the staff at Marden Ash, her 10-bedroom mansion, were on holiday. Early in 1950 Mrs Morrell returned home to Marden Ash, where a team of day and night nurses cared for her.

Soon Mrs Morrell depended on Adams' visits. On 8 March 1950, he hurried from Marden Ash to see her solicitor, Mr Hubert Sogno. Adams told Mr Sogno that Mrs Morrell had forgotten her promise to leave him her Rolls-Royce and a box of jewellery. Would he draw up a codicil in accordance with her wishes? The solicitor was doubtful about Adams' request and suggested that he should pretend to accept the jewellery box to please the old lady but then hand it back to a nurse in another room. When Adams protested that Mrs Morrell seriously wanted him to

Mrs Julia Bradnum died in May 1952. When her body was exhumed, it showed that, whatever the cause of death, it was not cerebral haemorrhage as Adams had declared

enjoy the gifts, Mr Sogno suggested they wait for her son Arthur Morrell to visit the following week before drafting a new codicil. When Adams tried to insist, the solicitor told him that it was quite impossible, and he left.

In a codicil dated July 1950, Mrs Morrell left Adams her home and chattels if her son should die before her. Her last will, dated 24 August 1950, provided for Adams to receive an oak chest containing silver after her death. But only three weeks later she sent for Mr Sogno and made a final codicil cutting Adams entirely out of her will.

On 13 November 1950 Mrs Morrell died and Adams certified the cause of death as cerebral thrombosis. He sent Mrs Morrell's executors a bill for his services totalling £1750. They paid it, and although Adams had been cut out of the will, Arthur Morrell gave him the Rolls-Royce, the oak chest containing silver and an Elizabethan cupboard.

Hannam wondered whether Adams had abandoned his hopes of a bequest and had counted on the executors settling his bill. If he had deliberately killed Mrs Morrell out of avarice then evidence about the drugs she had been given would be crucial. Mrs Morrell's nurses had been keeping detailed records of her progress and treatment since June 1949. These records showed that Adams had been prescribing narcotics and other drugs in larger and larger quantities. Near the end the doses had become massive.

Mrs Annabella Kilgour, a widow, lived in Staveley Road, Eastbourne. She had been ill for several weeks, and was being looked after by Miss Osgood, a state registered nurse. On 27 December 1950 Adams visited Mrs Kilgour, and Nurse Osgood reported that she seemed restless. Adams replied that he would give Mrs Kilgour an injection to help her get a good night's sleep. The nurse was astounded as she watched the doctor give an injection that she regarded as being greatly in excess of the normal dose, particularly in view of Mrs Kilgour's age. 'This will keep her quiet,' Adams said. Mrs Kilgour at once fell into a coma and died the next morning.

When Adams arrived Nurse Osgood told him: 'Mrs Kilgour is dead. You realise, doctor, that you have killed her?' The nurse told the Scotland Yard detectives: 'I have never seen a man look so frightened in my life.' Adams gave the cause of death as cerebral haemorrhage. In her will Mrs Kilgour had left him cash and an antique clock.

Adams started to visit Mrs Harriet Maud Hughes in her flat in King Edward's Parade, Eastbourne, during the summer of 1951. In July Mrs Hughes added a codicil to her will to the effect that she should be cremated. A month later, in August, she added another codicil that provided for a bequest of £1000 each to two close acquaintances of Adams, Mr and Mrs Thurston.

Irene Swaine, Mrs Hughes' domestic help, was certain that by this time her employer was completely under the doctor's influence. Mrs Hughes had mentioned changing her will again, and went with Dr Adams to her bank in Eastbourne's exclusive Meads district. The doctor asked the bank manager to make him the executor of her will, explaining that it was Mrs Hughes' express wish.

Some of Adams' medical equipment – medical bag with portable sterilising tray, bone saw, optometer and lenses, swabs, large syringe and gynaecological forceps

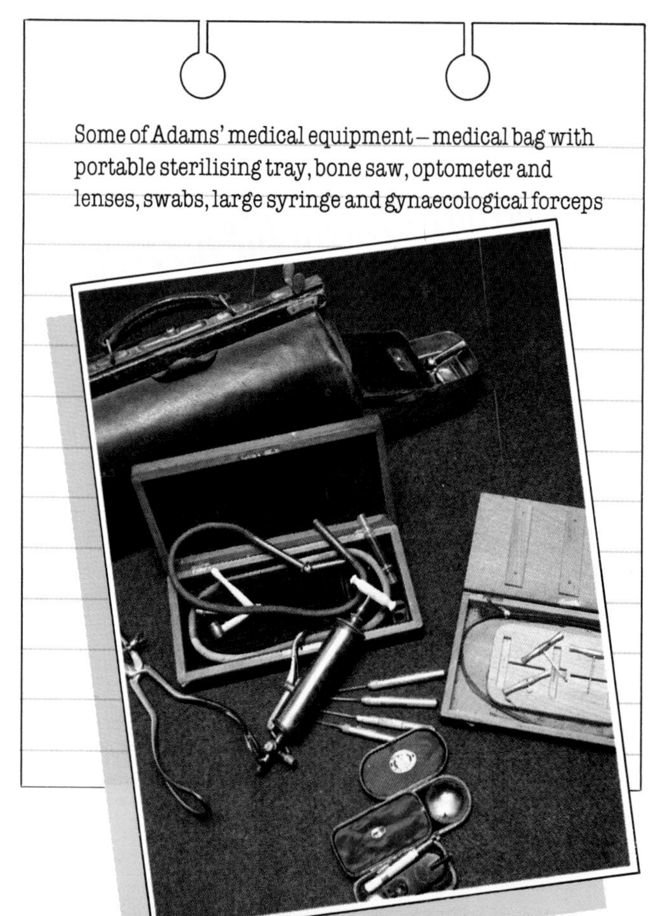

The guest house in Eastbourne where Hilda and Clara Neil-Miller lived. There were only thirteen months between their deaths – and most of their estate was left to Adams

When Mrs Hughes returned home, after the doctor had left, she told Mrs Swaine: 'You should have seen the bank manager's face – he was most surprised at my choice.'

Mrs Swaine described the final chapter of Mrs Hughes' life: 'I always thought there was something funny about her death in 1951. It was too sudden. There were times towards the end when she did not seem to be herself or in her right mind. She had been taking sleeping tablets. I assume they were prescribed by Dr Adams. There were many bottles of medicine in the room.' Mrs Hughes died, aged 66, on 29 November 1951 and Adams entered the cause of death as cerebral thrombosis. Scotland Yard concluded that afterwards Adams received ninety per cent of the two Thurston bequests, giving his friends the Thurstons 10 per cent for the use of their name in Mrs Hughes' will.

Mrs Julia Bradnum, a strong, healthy woman of 82, lived in a three-bedroomed house on the outskirts of Eastbourne. In the spring of 1952 Adams told Mrs Bradnum that her will was not legally valid and brought her a draft of a new one. Mrs Bradnum agreed to make a new will and asked a close friend, Mrs Mary Hine, if she would witness it.

On the evening of 26 May 1952 Mrs Bradnum was well and in good spirits. Mary Hine and some other friends had arranged to go on a coach trip the next day. When they arrived at Mrs Bradnum's house, she was not about, although she normally rose early. They decided to let her sleep a little more. Finally, she awoke and complained of pains in her stomach. Mary Hine went to a friend's house and telephoned Dr Adams. He came, examined Mrs Bradnum, and told Mrs Hine she was dead. On the death certificate he gave the cause of death as cerebral haemorrhage. It turned out that Dr Adams was the sole executor of Mrs Bradnum's will.

After Bobbie Hullett's death four years later, a niece of Mrs Bradnum, Mrs Lily Love, wrote to the chief constable suggesting that her aunt's death was also suspicious. During the investigation that followed, the Yard exhumed Mrs Bradnum's body. Unfortunately, it had decomposed too much to provide any conclusive evidence of murder, but it showed clearly that she had not died of cerebral haemorrhage as Adams had stated.

Hilda and Clara Neil-Miller came to Eastbourne from Scotland in 1940, after the death of their brother. Save for a widowed sister-in-law in Bournemouth, the Neil-Millers had no family. Their modest income was derived from investments inherited from their father and a life-time loan of capital from their sister-in-law.

Bequests

Only 13 months separated their deaths. Hilda died on 15 January 1953, and bequeathed her entire estate to her sister Clara. Clara died on 22 February the following year, leaving most of her estate to her doctor, John Bodkin Adams.

Mrs Welch, a resident at the guest-house where the sisters lived, spoke of the last occasion on which Adams visited Clara: 'Dr Adams was called to Miss Clara Neil-Miller one night in February 1954. She was suffering from either a cold or influenza. He remained in her bedroom for 45 minutes before leaving. I later became worried as I heard nothing. I opened the door and was horrified at what I saw. This was a bitterly cold winter's night. The bedclothes had been pulled back and thrown over the bedrail at the base, and her nightdress had been folded back across her body up to her neck. All the windows had been flung open. A cold gush of wind was sweeping through the bedroom. That is how the doctor had left her.' Clara Neil-Miller died the following day.

Clara's bequest to Adams, Hannam established, amounted to almost £5000. He also discovered that, in the weeks preceding her death, Clara had made out cheques payable to Adams for £300 and £500. The reasons for the payments were unclear. They were presumably not for medical treatment as, apart from her cold, Clara had not been ill.

Mrs Elizabeth Sharp, the Neil-Millers' landlady and friend, was interviewed by Hannam and Hewitt.

Mr Edward Clark (left) and Mr Geoffrey Lawrence QC, counsel for the defence, arrive at Eastbourne Magistrates Court for the Adams hearing. Lawrence and Clark also represented Adams at the Old Bailey trial two months later. Lawrence – whose bold decision not to call his client as a witness meant that counsel for the prosecution were denied the opportunity to cross-examine him – secured an acquittal

Both believed that the evidence of Mrs Sharp would prove vital. 'Mrs Sharp was the key to the whole case. She had been involved with many of the victims. She was ideally placed, running this sort of rest-home for the elderly, and she knew much about their personal and financial backgrounds.' Twice, the Yard detectives interviewed Mrs Sharp. Hannam and Hewitt were convinced that one more visit would be enough to persuade her to tell them what she knew.

But there was not to be a third visit. The detectives were called to London for a meeting with the Attorney-General, Sir Reginald Manningham-Buller, and the Director of Public Prosecutions, Sir Theobald Mathew. Back in Eastbourne, matters moved quickly. Mrs Sharp died, and in the same week her body was cremated. Hewitt was suspicious.

Home Office pathologist Dr Francis Camps was granted an exhumation order to examine the body of Clara Neil-Miller. Doctor Camps found Clara's lungs congested. She had died, not of a coronary thrombosis as Adams had stated on her death certificate, but of pneumonia.

James Priestly Downs was a widower, a wealthy, retired bank manager. When he fractured his ankle, during the spring of 1955, Adams had him taken to a local nursing home. After a fortnight of Adams' treatment he was in a coma. Canon F. Hilton Jackson, a close friend of Downs, visited him in April 1955. The canon later said: 'I was completely surprised. He was lying in bed, his mouth wide open, his eyes glazed, and he hardly seemed to be breathing. I am certain he didn't recognise me.'

Some months earlier, Downs had burnt his will in a fit of temper. While under Adams' care, he had a new will drafted. After nine unsuccessful attempts to sign it, while apparently drugged, he was helped by Adams to mark it with an 'X'. Only a month after his accident, James Downs died. Under the terms of the new will, Adams received £1000.

The evidence in Hannam's reports to the Director of Public Prosecutions was damning, but all of it was circumstantial. Would it be enough to convict Adams? Hannam and Hewitt believed that they could successfully bring a manslaughter charge, but though they were convinced he had killed many times, they were doubtful whether he could be convicted of murder.

Police interviews

Apart from the charge of murder or manslaughter, there was also evidence that Adams had forged National Health Service prescriptions and made false declarations on a number of death certificates. But it was decided to pursue the capital charge if at all possible. Hannam interviewed Adams four times. The third interview, on 26 November, was held at Eastbourne police station. Hannam referred to the death of Mrs Morrell and Adams replied: 'Easing the passing of a dying person is not all that wicked. She wanted to die – that cannot be murder. It is impossible to accuse a doctor.'

By now, the Attorney-General had made up his mind on the Adams case, and on 19 December 1956 Herbert Hannam called at Kent Lodge, and arrested Adams. The doctor looked stunned. He said: 'Murder? I do not think you could prove it was murder – she was dying in any event.' As Adams put his overcoat on, his receptionist caught hold of his hand. Her tears began to flow and Adams said to her quietly: 'I will see you in heaven.'

After his arrest, Adams spent three months on remand in Eastbourne, Lewes and Brixton. The preliminary hearing took place before Eastbourne magistrates in January, and on the twenty-fourth they decided to commit the doctor for trial at the Old Bailey. Finally, in March 1957, Dr John Bodkin Adams stood before Mr Justice Devlin in the Number One Court of the Old Bailey, and in an accent still strong with Ulster overtones he pleaded not guilty to the murder of Mrs Morrell. The evidence of Mrs Morrell's nurses was crucial to the prosecution case, but the Attorney-General made little of it. The nurses themselves were confused about the routines they had followed six years before

Above: the prosecution case was first heard during the committal proceedings at Eastbourne Magistrates Court in January 1957. Among those involved in the prosecution were (from left) John Leck (legal assistant to the Director of Public Prosecutions), Detective Superintendent Hannam, D. I. Pugh, Dr C.H. Corby (pathologist) and the counsel – Mr Melford Stevenson QC, Mr Malcolm Morris and Mr Bryan Prior
Right: Eastbourne magistrate Lionel Turner, before whom, on 31 January 1957, Adams was committed for trial at the Old Bailey
Below right: Dr A. Sommerville, the coroner for East Sussex, gave evidence at the Eastbourne hearing about Adams' behaviour during the last days of Bobbie Hullett's life. Adams had telephoned him the day before Bobbie's death to arrange a 'private' post-mortem. Dr Sommerville was shocked when he was told that the patient was still alive but that Adams *expected* her to die and was uncertain what to give as the cause of death. Coroners do not normally arrange 'private' post-mortems and doctors do not usually alert them until after there has been a suspicious death

in administering the patient's drugs, but the details of her dosages were read from their notebooks. Geoffrey Lawrence QC, counsel for the defence, brilliantly exploited their confusion.

The wrangle lasted 17 days – at that time it was the longest murder trial in British history. Adams was acquitted on 10 April 1957.

By now police believed that Adams had killed a total of 25 or more of his patients. The Director of Public Prosecutions never brought any of these other cases to trial.

Adams was struck off the Medical Register, but four years later was reinstated. He began practising again and no fresh allegations were ever made against him. He lived quietly in Eastbourne until his death on 4 July 1983, leaving an estate valued at £402,970.

Adams had a devoted band of friends, and his patients trusted him. But in the opinion of many people, Dr John Bodkin Adams died an unconvicted mass murderer.

Who kidnapped Lindbergh's baby?

A German immigrant, Bruno Hauptmann, was executed for murdering Charles Lindbergh jnr, the American aviator's baby son, in March 1932. His trial was a charade and the evidence indicates that he was innocent after all

On 21 May 1927 Charles Lindbergh achieved the first solo Atlantic crossing in a single engined aircraft, taking 33½ hours. He became world famous. Only five years later, his 20-month-old son, Charles Lindbergh jnr, precipitated the father into a darker fame. The baby was kidnapped, and then allegedly found dead. The case caused a world-wide sensation.

The publicity-shy Colonel Charles Lindbergh and his wife Anne had built themselves a weekend retreat in Hopewell, New Jersey. They usually spent weekdays with Anne's mother, Mrs Morrow, at her Englewood home but on Tuesday 1 March 1932 the weather had been wet and windy for several days and baby Charles had caught a cold. Anne, deciding to extend their stay at Hopewell even longer, summoned the baby's nurse, Betty Gow, from the Englewood house.

By 8pm the two women had settled the baby down for the night. Shortly after 9pm Charles Lindbergh heard a snapping sound, as if of breaking wood, outside the house, but thought no more of it. At 10pm Betty Gow, making her final check in the darkened nursery, found an empty cot.

Beneath the window at the south-east corner stood a suitcase. This and the floor below were smudged with yellow clay; Lindbergh noted that it matched the soil outside. Prominent on a radiator grating between window and suitcase was an envelope. Lindbergh left it unopened. 'Touch nothing!' he told the horrified women.

The period of shocked inactivity was short-lived. The Hopewell police were called and went immediately to the area below the nursery window. There they found the primary clues: two holes in the ground; a blurred impression about 12 inches (30 centimetres) long, suggesting the print of a foot encased in sacking; a small footprint (which turned out to have been made by Anne Lindbergh earlier); and a three-quarter-inch (19-millimetre) chisel. At a distance of between 60 and 75 feet (18 and 23 metres), they discovered the ladder that became the

kingpin of the case. Crudely built, it lay in three sections, the top one 10 feet (3 metres) from the bottom two, which were held together by a dowelling pin; one of the rungs and a lower piece of the side rail were split.

The envelope on the radiator grating was opened to reveal a note, which read:

Dear Sir,

Have 50000$ ready 25000 in 20$ bills 15000$ in 10$ and 10000$ in 5$ bills. After 2-4 days we will inform you were to deliver the mony. We warn you for making anything public or for notifying the Pol [word blurred] The child is in gut care Indications for all letters are singnature and 3 holes.

The 'singnature' was two interlocking blue circles, creating an ellipse within which was a solid red oval, the whole pattern crossed with three square holes.

Ransom demand

Two days later, the Lindberghs published a personal appeal, offering immunity to the baby's kidnappers: 'Our only interest is in his immediate and safe return.' Their efforts were rewarded, for on 6 March a letter arrived, promising to pay attention to the baby's health but warning that, because of the publicity, he would now have to be held 'for a longer time as we expected'. The ransom was raised to $70,000. Ill-spelt and bearing the vital signature, the letter appeared genuine.

At this point Dr John Francis Condon, known as 'Jafsie', entered the plot. He was a retired schoolmaster and part-time teacher who had spent his life conventionally enough in the service of education but, at 72, had apparently become quite eccentric. Condon was as self-contradictory concerning his

Above: Charles Lindbergh and his wife Anne, photographed at a New York airfield in 1929
Below: The *Spirit of St Louis*, photographed over London.
Opposite: Charles Lindbergh jnr celebrates his first birthday

reasons for involving himself in the drama as he was later about other aspects of his evidence. He claimed that he wanted to 'put down crime in my own country'. He lived in the Bronx district of New York from choice and it was to the small-time, parochial Bronx *Home News* that he sent his offer of $1000 (his life savings) and the promise not to inform, in return for the baby's safe delivery. This offer appeared in the issue of 8 March. Two days later, Condon received a pencilled letter that read: 'If you are willing to act as go-between in Lindberg cace pleace follow strictly instruction. Handel incloced letter personaly to Mr. Lindbergh. . . .' Enclosed was a smaller envelope.

The note inside gave instructions to advertise in the New York *American*: 'MONEY IS REDY'. The announcement went in on 11 March, over the name 'Jafsie'. The following evening a telephone call led Condon to a rendezvous near Woodlawn Cemetery, where he met a man who called himself 'John' and claimed to be a Scandinavian and go-between for a gang that had planned the kidnapping for a year. They were holding Charles Lindbergh jnr on a boat, six hours away, and 'John' promised to send the baby's sleeping-suit as proof that he was acting for the gang.

On 16 March a child's woollen sleeping-suit duly arrived, with a demand for $70,000 ransom. Lindbergh identified the sleeping-suit and, with difficulty, raised the money. On 2 April a further note was delivered to Lindbergh. It read: 'The boy is on boad [boat] Nelly . . . you will find the boad . . . on Elizabeth Island.'

Early on the morning of 3 April Lindbergh and Condon set off in a Sikorsky Amphibian, for Vineyard Sound, on the coast of Massachusetts. All that day and the next they scoured the waters. Coastguard cutters joined in the search but there was no 'boad Nelly'.

Meanwhile, the police began to investigate Violet

Dr J.F. Condon – 'Jafsie' – a retired schoolteacher who volunteered to act as go-between with the kidnappers

Sharpe, a 28-year-old English girl who worked as a maid for Elizabeth Morrow, Lindbergh's mother-in-law. Popular among the staff, Violet was encouraging a relationship with Septimus Banks, the Morrows' middle-aged butler. Police questioning revealed that Violet had taken Anne Lindbergh's telephone call to Betty Gow on the morning of the kidnapping; she therefore knew of the changed plans. Violet's initial alibi for the evening of the kidnapping was slight: a cinema date with a man whose name she had forgotten. Inspector Walsh,

Below: Charles Lindbergh arrives at Walter Swayze's funeral parlour in Trenton, New Jersey, to identify the body. 'I am perfectly satisfied it is my child,' he said

who was in charge of the questioning, bullied her into remembering that she had spent the evening in a New York State grill with someone called Ernie and another couple. Walsh traced an Ernest Brinkert, a small-time crook and former manager of a taxi company, whose cards had been found in Violet's room. By that time Violet had gone into hospital for minor surgery, beyond Walsh's reach.

The action had again ground to a halt; now in hope, now in despair, Anne waited for the next development. It came all too suddenly. The New Jersey police, having supposedly combed every inch of the hills round Hopewell, had left to search new ground, so the road from Princeton was deserted when a truck driver, William Allen, discovered the corpse of a child in the woods.

The woodland grave was quickly surrounded by police and detectives. A comparison of what was left of the infant's face with a photograph reinforced their fears but, for absolute confirmation, blue shreds of cloth were removed and held against remnants from Betty Gow's workbox. They appeared to match; there seemed little doubt that this was the end of the search. The county physician then performed an autopsy; the cause of death was given as 'a fractured skull caused by external violence', at least two months before.

Identification

On 13 May Lindbergh and Dr Van Ingen, the New York physician who had cared for the baby, saw the corpse. Van Ingen made a detailed examination, paying particular attention to the skull size, teeth and distinctively overlapping toes; a sample of hair had been analysed and compared with a piece kept by Mrs Morrow. But it was left to Lindbergh to make the final identification. 'I am perfectly satisfied that it is my child,' he said.

Violet Sharpe, out of hospital but now morose and withdrawn, was recalled for questioning. Nervously, she identified Brinkert from a photograph and, astoundingly, admitted to his having rung her at Englewood one and a half hours after she took Anne's telephone call. Then she disintegrated into hysterical sobs. What happened next belongs in the realm of melodrama. From somewhere, Violet took a bottle of potassium cyanide, poured crystals and water into a measuring glass and drained the mixture. By the time the doctor arrived, she was dead.

Shortly after Violet's death, Ernest Brinkert telephoned the police and was cleared of any knowledge of the girl. The *real* Ernest, surnamed Miller, also appeared with convincing proof of both his knowledge of Violet and his innocence of the crime.

The police now turned to the only means of tracing the kidnappers left: the ransom bills. Clients of major banks were provided with the numbers of listed gold certificates deliberately included in the payment, and so began a two-year paper chase headed by the New York City Police.

At around this time, the police also became much influenced by the ideas of a young and impressively qualified psychiatrist, Dudley Schoenfeld, who postulated a theory of a kidnapper whose subconscious motive was to act out delusions of power. This was how the 'lone kidnapper' theory grew up. Whether from desperation or naive enthusiasm, the police unquestioningly adopted Schoenfeld's criminal portrait. An 'identity kit' was published describing a tallish, thin-faced man with high cheekbones, pointed chin and contemptuous expression, wearing no overcoat and speaking with a German accent. From that time the police noted only ransom money passed by a man fitting this description.

On the morning of Saturday 15 September 1934, the manager of a petrol station was handed a $10 gold certificate for petrol. He accepted the obsolete currency with some reluctance but the customer, with a slight smile and a German accent, reassured him: 'They're all right. Anyone will take them.' 'You don't see many of them any more,' said the manager. 'No,' replied the customer. 'I have only about a hundred left.'

The manager, still uneasy, took the car's registration number as it drove away: 4U-13-41,NY. The note was verified as one on the Lindbergh list. The licence number was checked with the State Motor Vehicle Bureau and was found to have been issued to a Bruno Richard Hauptmann, 1279 East 222nd Street, in the Bronx.

Bruno Richard Hauptmann in the summer of 1934 with his own baby son. In September he was arrested for extorting money from Lindbergh following the kidnap

The Lindbergh trial at Hunterdon County Court in 1935. Prosecution witnesses included Betty Gow, the baby's nurse (top) and Mrs Anne Lindbergh (above)

When Hauptmann was arrested, his first explanation for possessing the notes – that he had hoarded against inflation and this was his last note – manifestly contradicted both his comment to the petrol station manager and his later story. His house was searched by detectives but they found nothing that they could consider incriminating and Hauptmann was unceremoniously bundled off to the old, ramshackle Greenwich Police Station and subjected to further questioning.

The investigation had deteriorated into a murder hunt. Dr Schoenfeld had recommended quiet and restrained questioning for his 'psychological type'. There was nothing either quiet or restrained about the inquisition to which Hauptmann was subjected almost continuously during the next two days. But Hauptmann replied in the calm, barely responsive manner that he was to maintain throughout his trial. He provided alibis for every date that interested the police.

On East 222nd Street, the police had followed their trail out to the garage. Here they struck gold. Behind Hauptmann's work-bench one of the detectives discovered two boarded-up compartments; together, they contained Lindbergh ransom bills to the amount of $13,760. Anna, Hauptmann's wife and the mother of his year-old son, watched in mute horror. She had never seen the money before; she had no explanation. Hauptmann had: his German friend and trading partner, Isidor Fisch, dying of tuberculosis, had decided to return to Leipzig on 6 December 1933. Among the personal effects he had left with his associate had been a shoebox tied with string, which Hauptmann had put on a shelf in a closet and forgotten until, just at the end of August 1934, rain had leaked into the closet and soaked the box. Investigating, he had found the certificates. By this time, Fisch was dead and since he had owed Hauptmann nearly $5000 the latter had no compunction about using some of the money. No, he had had no idea they were ransom bills. Why had he hidden them in the garage and lied? He claimed to have been afraid of conviction as a gold-hoarder.

He was disbelieved, charged with kidnapping and murder, and on 2 January 1935 'the trial of the century' began in Flemington, New Jersey.

New Jersey State Attorney General David T. Wilentz acted for the prosecution: a stylish, ambitiously clever young lawyer, Wilentz was noted for his rending sarcasm and rapier-like wit. Cynical and politically motivated, he cared little for truth, justice, Hauptmann or even Lindbergh in a case that was, to him, merely a stepping-stone in his career. He was out for a kill.

Edward J. Reilly acted for the defence. Reilly's urbane rhetoric did not fully conceal the blustering toughness that had earned him the nickname 'The Bull of Brooklyn'. His record of almost 2000 acquittals, mostly in murder cases, had recommended him to the *New York Evening Journal* as a sponsored counsel, in exchange for Hauptmann's exclusive story. Whatever the reasons for Reilly's almost total failure to organise the case efficiently, the choice for Hauptmann was disastrous. In Lloyd Fisher, Reilly's able young deputy, Hauptmann had, perhaps, the only lawyer who demonstrated a real concern for his fate. With two junior counsels, Fisher finally took over the case – too late.

Justice Thomas Whitaker Trenchard was, at 71, a judge of the old school, benevolent in attitude but punctilious, with a solid reputation for irreversible decisions.

The prosecution's case rested on the 'lone kidnapper' theory. Hauptmann was to be identified as 'John' of the cemetery through the ransom bills found in his garage and the sudden affluence in his life-style after the date of Condon's handing over the money. But this was not enough. By means of the ladder, the ransom notes and the presence of a *corpus delicti* (or tangible evidence of murder) he was to be placed at the scene of a capital crime. 'We demand the penalty for murder in the first degree,' intoned Wilentz.

Millard Whited, a Sourland Mountain lumberman, swore to having seen Hauptmann in the vicinity just before the kidnapping and to having received no payment for his testimony. Defence witnesses described him as a known liar. He later admitted being paid by the police.

Then came the farcical interlude of Amandus Hochmuth, an octogenarian, who claimed to have seen a car containing a ladder and a red-faced man whom he identified as Hauptmann running into a ditch near the Lindbergh estate on the day of the kidnapping. Yet later research discovered that Hochmuth had already been reported as nearly blind from cataracts.

About the most credible and unimpeachable eyewitness of the case was the defence's William Bolmer, a Princeton University graduate and garage-owner, who saw a man and a woman with a telescoped ladder in a Ford car near Hopewell on the morning of 1 March. He positively identified the ladder and as positively refused to identify Hauptmann as the man. His testimony was ignored.

Wilentz had called out, it seemed, every state detective and, one after another, the defence witnesses went down. 'Where are they getting these witnesses?' cried Hauptmann. 'They are hurting me!' The defence was helpless.

After 11 hours and 14 minutes, spent by Hauptmann pacing his cell and listening to the howling mob outside, the jury returned to give their verdict: 'We find the defendant, Bruno Richard Hauptmann, guilty of murder in the first degree.' As the judge delivered his death sentence, an impatient reporter shouted the words out to a screaming crowd. 'A cry for blood,' whispered Fisher.

Bruno Richard Hauptmann in his cell at Flemington, New Jersey, on 14 February 1935 – the day after his sentencing for the murder of the Lindbergh baby. Hauptmann had spent the previous night in a semi-conscious state, weeping bitterly, but soon regained the composure and air of cold indifference he had assumed during his trial. Protesting his innocence to the press, Hauptmann declared that he would go to the electric chair 'like a man' if his appeal failed. In private he said: 'If someone does not die for the death of the child then always the police will be monkeys. So I am the one who is picked out to die'

The news was greeted with general rejoicing. National honour had been vindicated, a sacrificial offering had been made to assuage the public's thirst for vengeance. Of the American press only the *New York Times* pointed out that the kidnapping was still unsolved. Ford Maddox Ford, its English correspondent, wrote: 'The affair cannot but have . . . the aspect of the most famous and fortunate man in the world versus a miserable shred of human jetsam.'

As though galvanised into action by their loss of the case, the defence moved swiftly. Anna Hauptmann went on a fund-raising tour among the German-American communities and the period from mid-February to October 1935 saw two stays of execution, appeals to the New Jersey Court of Errors and the US Supreme Court of Appeals and a petition for a writ of habeas corpus. All were refused. The grounds of biased and prejudicial proceedings and several constitutional points of law were disallowed and no new evidence was admitted.

On 16 October 1935 an incident occurred that – had there been more money, time and public concern – might have been instrumental in saving Hauptmann's life. Harold Hoffman, the 39-year-old governor of New Jersey, already uneasy about the case, granted a request from Hauptmann for interview and decided to re-examine the evidence.

Petition for pardon

In the course of this some thought-provoking material was unearthed, but the search was neither easy not conclusive. Hoffman had no money for a systematic enquiry and requests from the investigating officer to the FBI and N.Y. City police for more agents and detectives were refused. A final petition to the New Jersey Board of Pardons had been rejected and the date of execution set for 17 January. Hoffman granted a further month's reprieve but, as he later wrote:

> I, too, was to feel some of the futility of the search, to sense that indefinable, mysterious force threatening to destroy anyone who dared to question that the Lindbergh crime had been solved and that full and complete justice had been meted out to all participants.

Their time had run out. Wilentz, his patience exhausted, insisted that the law must take its course and on 3 April 1936, after a final, desperate postponement of two days, Hoffman had to admit that he had no further power to grant reprieve. Hauptmann, in his last statement, repeated, 'I protest my innocence. . . .' At 8.44pm Bruno Richard Hauptmann went to his death in the electric chair. The crowd this time was hushed. 'My brother is dead,' said Hauptmann's sister. 'They cannot torture him more.'

The case that shamed America

In April 1920, two men were killed while delivering wages to a shoe factory. Two Italian anarchists – Nicola Sacco and Bartolomeo Vanzetti – were executed for the crime, but they may have been innocent victims of political prejudice

On 23 August 1977 the new Governor of the Commonwealth of Massachusetts, His Excellency Michael S. Dukakis, issued a proclamation, effectively absolving two working men, Italian immigrants, whom the Commonwealth had executed on a charge of murder exactly 50 years before. It came a little late; even the consciences it might have salved were long since dead. And yet Governor Dukakis was making some kind of amends for his predecessor by five decades, Governor Fuller, and a measure of justice was being offered to Nicola Sacco and Bartolomeo Vanzetti, who had died in Charlestown Prison, Boston, in the first minutes of 23 August 1927.

In the afternoon of 15 April 1920 two men were murdered in the small Massachusetts town of South Braintree, a place mainly devoted to the manufacture of shoes. A paymaster, Frederick A. Parmenter, accompanied by a security guard, Alessandro Berardelli, was carrying the workers' weekly wages, a sum of $15,776.51, from the Railroad Avenue offices of the Slater and Morrill shoe factory to the plant itself, a short distance away on Pearl Street. They never arrived. In full view of a number of bystanders, two men attacked the paymaster and guard, shot them both, putting two bullets into Parmenter and four into Berardelli, seized the pay-boxes, and escaped in a Buick that drew up to secure their getaway. A third member of the gang emerged from hiding and also entered the car. For some weeks, no arrests were made.

At this time, the American establishment was in the grip of a terror of communism, of radicalism, of anarchism, a time when to be foreign, or left-wing, or pacifist, as were many recent Italian immigrants in the New England states, was to be considered a revolutionary conspirator. It was this atmosphere that conditioned the arrests, the trial, the seven years of waiting and the executions.

Arrests made

The police at Bridgewater, Massachusetts made the arrests on 5 May while following up a crime committed in December 1919, virtually identical to the South Braintree affair, except that, although shots were fired by both sides, no one was hurt and the money was saved. The Bridgewater police chief, Michael Stewart, had a line on the affair, or thought he had. He investigated the local Italians, and found two who aroused his suspicions. One of them, Mike Boda, owned a Buick similar to that used in the hold-up, and Boda lived with one Coacci, a radical under sentence of deportation. After the second robbery occurred, Stewart visited their house and found Coacci ready to leave, his bags packed. Boda's car was at a nearby garage awaiting repairs. Stewart arranged to be notified when anyone came to collect it. On 4 May four Italians did so. When the garage owner pointed out that the car's licence had expired, the men left. Two of them boarded a streetcar. The police intercepted it and arrested the men. Each had a gun, and one of them a pocketful of shells. One man also carried radical writings. His name was Bartolomeo Vanzetti, a fish peddler from Plymouth, Massachusetts. His companion, a shoeworker from Stoughton, Massachusetts, was called Nicola Sacco.

Sacco and Vanzetti had emigrated from Italy some years before the war. Sacco, 29 at the time of his arrest, came from a family of prosperous winegrowers in the south; Vanzetti, three years older, had left a father who owned a substantial farm in Villafalletto in the north-west. After arriving in the United States, Sacco worked in shoe factories and became prominent in working-class protest. He also joined an anarchist circle, as did Vanzetti. Yet he was trusted at his factory, served as occasional night-watchman and, for that reason, he claimed, carried a gun, as his employer was to verify. Vanzetti had gone through a variety of manual jobs until he took a leading part in a strike at a cordage factory in Plymouth and was sacked. Deciding he would no longer work for the rich, he began to sell fish.

Webster Thayer, who tried Sacco and Vanzetti, was famous neither for discretion nor for good judgement

Identification by witnesses

After their arrest, the two men panicked, and lied about their guns and ammunition. They were put before witnesses of the two crimes, some of whom identified them, some of whom did not. Some of these witnesses said they were not the men, and were never disclosed to the defence. The accused were never put in line-ups, but as part of the identification procedure were made to crouch in the act of shooting. Consequently, some witnesses genuinely thought they were the robbers. Eventually it was decided to charge Vanzetti alone with the Bridgewater crime (Sacco had been at work all day), and both men with the South Braintree killings.

The other Italians disappeared from the case. Coacci was arrested, proved he had been at work on 15 April, and was deported. Boda was not arrested, and at once sailed for Italy.

Vanzetti went on trial for the Bridgewater attempt at Plymouth. The trial began on 20 June with Judge Webster Thayer, aged 63, a local man from Worcester, presiding.

Vanzetti produced 16 witnesses to testify that he had been peddling eels all day on Christmas Eve, eels being traditionally eaten by Italians on that day. These witnesses covered the day from 7am. The crime had taken place soon after 7.30am. The witnesses were all Italians, and were therefore disbelieved. Vanzetti's anarchist opinions were shamelessly introduced. Vanzetti was found guilty and sentenced to fifteen years' imprisonment.

Eleven months later, on 31 May 1921, the trial of Sacco and Vanzetti for the South Braintree killings began. It was held at Dedham, with Judge Thayer presiding again. Essentially, this trial was a much longer and more detailed re-run of its predecessor.

District attorney Frederick Gunn Katzmann. He was known as a proficient although verbose prosecutor not above using bully-boy tactics. His lengthy and ironic cross-examination of Sacco on his political beliefs was to prove damaging indeed

Identification was proving equally unsatisfactory. Vanzetti's account of a day selling fish was again supported, and again disbelieved. Sacco had a more elaborate alibi. He claimed that he had been to Boston on the day of the murders, had visited the Italian consulate to obtain a passport, intending to return to Italy, had lunched with some fellow radicals, and returned later that day. A clerk at the consulate remembered him, for he had brought a photograph much larger than the required size. It

SACCO FLAYS CAPITALISTS IN FIERY SPEECH IN COURT

Holds Courtroom Spellbound by Address---Went to Mexico to Escape War Service, He States---Proud of Having Been a Slacker

The cap episode, which was to prove a valuable weapon to the prosecution, cartooned in Boston newspapers

was easy for the district attorney, Frederick Katzmann, to shake this. Obviously Sacco had gone to Boston on some other day, and taken that photograph to ensure that he would be remembered. And the radicals were his pals, after all.

Under cross examination by Katzmann, Sacco admitted that he had fled to Mexico during the Great War to avoid conscription. More damaging still was the fact that both men had lied about the guns and why they had procured them. They had acquired them, said the defence, for self-protection, because they were terrified by the deportations, and by the death of their friend, Salsedo, a leader of their anarchistic group, in police custody. This explanation for carrying guns could not, in that time, sound convincing. And worse was to come.

The prosecution succeeded in planting in the jury's minds the idea that the gun found on Vanzetti was that of Berardelli, the slain security guard, picked up by Vanzetti after the murder (and still in Vanzetti's pocket three weeks later when he was on his way to collect the murder car). Ballistics experts were produced to prove that the bullet that had actually killed Berardelli had come from Sacco's gun. When the state police expert, Captain Proctor, took the stand, Katzmann knew, from his discussions with him, that Proctor would not make a definite identification. He therefore asked Proctor whether he had any opinion as to whether the bullet was fired by Sacco's gun, and Proctor replied, obligingly: 'My opinion is that it is consistent with being fired by that pistol.' This verbal legerdemain weighed on Proctor's conscience. Two years later he signed an affidavit stating that he had only meant that the bullet *could* have come from Sacco's gun.

Sacco's cap

And then there was the business of Sacco's cap. A cap was found in the street after the killings, and witnesses identified it as Sacco's. A tear in the lining was particularly damning, for that tear was made, it was claimed, by Sacco's habit of daily hanging the cap from a nail at his place of work. Only after the trial was it admitted that the chief of police at South Braintree had made that tear in the lining, cutting the cap open in the hope of establishing some mark of identification. The prosecution had little more to offer than that, but it was enough. On 14 July the jury retired. After some five hours they returned verdicts of guilty of murder in the first degree. Not until 29 April 1927, almost six years on, did Webster Thayer pass sentence of death.

In the meantime, Thayer did a fair amount of talking, as he had done during the trial. He was also kept busy denying motions for a new trial, which the defence put forward at regular intervals. There were eight such motions, all refused by the very judge who had presided over the trial. In May 1926 the Supreme Judicial Court, which is the Massachusetts Court of Appeal, confirmed the convictions, finding that there had been no legal defect in the trial.

An extraordinary development had occurred in November 1925. In the next cell to Sacco in Dedham jail was a young Portuguese, Celestino Madeiros, under sentence of death for robbery and murder. In a note smuggled to Sacco and passed by him to his lawyers, Madeiros confessed to committing the South Braintree crime.

He said that he had worked with the Morelli Gang, professional Italian criminals. Though evidence showed that such a gang existed, it rested mainly on Madeiros, who was unstable, an epileptic, and a man with nothing to lose, who might well have expected to profit if he could have got some high-powered lawyers to take an interest in his case. In the end Madeiros was executed in Charlestown Prison on the same night as Sacco and Vanzetti.

In the years between the Dedham trial and the execution, the world came to learn of Sacco and Vanzetti. From the earliest days of the case there had been a Sacco and Vanzetti Defence Committee

Above right: Abbott Lawrence Lowell, president of Harvard (above) and head of the advisory committee appointed by Governor Fuller on 1 June 1927. On 27 July the committee reported its findings, and on 3 August Fuller decided to refuse clemency

run by Italian anarchists and a few liberal allies. They had raised funds, hired lawyers, and tried to keep the case in the public eye. When Judge Thayer denied the Madeiros motion, at last the case moved on to a wider stage. Respectable Bostonians began to have their doubts, and a leading article appeared in the *Boston Herald* urging a new trial. The article gained something – a Pulitzer Prize.

Slowly, something was stirring. There were the beginnings of a sense of shame, shame that was to become outrage. One particular revelation must have convinced many doubters. When the defence vainly argued the Madeiros motion for a new trial, they were also armed with depositions from two agents of the Department of Justice, Fred Weyand and Lawrence Letherman. These two men testified that the department had never believed Sacco and Vanzetti guilty, but urgently desired that two such dangerous anarchists should be deported. It had accordingly handed over a mass of evidence to Katzmann. As the affidavits said: 'Every one of us believed they ought to be deported. They were anarchists, they did not believe in organized government or private property.'

Celestino Madeiros who, while in prison with Sacco, passed him a note confessing to the crime

On 5 April 1927 the Supreme Judicial Court confirmed Thayer's last denials, and four days later the judge pronounced the death sentences.

Protest now reached a volume that could not be denied a hearing. Governments attempted to intercede, with Soviet Russia and fascist Italy in strange accord. Scientist Albert Einstein protested, and writer Thomas Mann, and violinist Fritz Kreisler. Another victim of injustice, Alfred Dreyfus, offered help. Spurred by this support, joined now by liberals and communists alike, the defence committee laboured on through that last summer, and the governor of Massachusetts, an automobile tycoon named Alvin T. Fuller, at last yielded a little to the rising pressure. Fuller postponed the executions, which had been set for the week beginning 10 July, and appointed an advisory committee of three men to reconsider the entire case. They were Abbott Lawrence Lowell, a member of the great Boston dynasty of Lowell, and president of Harvard; Samuel W. Stratton, president of the Massachusetts Institute of Technology; and a retired judge of the Probate Court named Robert Grant.

Right: Governor Alvin T. Fuller, one of the richest men in Massachusetts, was elected to the State House (below) in 1924. He set the date for the execution, but barely 36 minutes before the appointed hour, he announced a 12-day postponement

Right: thousands of people lined the streets of Boston in the critical hours before the execution
Below right: Nicola Sacco (right) and Bartolomeo Vanzetti – self-made martyrs or victims of justice?

The committee met from 11 to 21 July. It interviewed Thayer, Katzmann, jurymen and witnesses, but it did not allow lawyers to cross-examine the other side's witnesses. It was a sad farce, but it had moments that are intensely revealing. For example, when a Mr Crocker told how Thayer had come unbidden to his table at the University Club and raved about anarchists, Grant superciliously asked: 'Do I understand that you are repeating what was said to you at a social club by a fellow member of that club?' Hopes for the defence rose, however, over the matter of Sacco's Boston alibi. Two Italians, both journalists, Professor Felice Guadagni and Albert Bosco, had said that they had met Sacco that lunch hour at a restaurant in Boston's North Square, and that they knew the date because they were going on to a dinner in honour of James T. Williams, editor of the Boston *Transcript*, a dinner held on 15 April. Now Lowell produced a paper describing just such a dinner on 13 May and accused the two Italians of fraud. Next day Bosco proved that there had been two dinners, the first on 15 April. Lowell apologised and accepted their honesty (an episode omitted from the transcript of the hearings).

Vanzetti's eels

The defence's other apparent success was in the matter of Vanzetti's eels on that long-ago Christmas Eve. The defence searched the account books of various fish wholesalers and found an American Express Company receipt for a barrel of eels shipped on 20 December 1919 to B. Vanzetti, Plymouth. The receipt was taken to Fuller's secretary, and vanished from the case.

And that was, in effect, the end. The Lowell Committee confirmed the verdicts. Fuller concurred. Execution was set for 10 August. The defence fought on and obtained yet more hearings, including, almost beyond belief, one in which Thayer himself presided and ruled that he had shown no prejudice. A bare 36 minutes before the hour, Fuller announced a postponement of 12 days. The defence sought frantically until the final hours for a Judge of the State or Federal Supreme Court who would grant a stay. None would. Michael Musmanno, a young Pittsburgh lawyer who had abandoned his practice for the fight, led this last battle, and with an hour to go was still pleading with Attorney General, Arthur Reading, for clemency. Reading refused. (Months later he was indicted and dismissed for accepting bribes.) By 12.30am on 23 August 1927 Nicola Sacco, Bartolomeo Vanzetti and Madeiros were all dead.

The order had been that they should go to the electric chair in the week beginning 23 August, and the Commonwealth of Massachusetts had at last been prompt to act. In fact, the Commonwealth was running scared. The world was up in arms, with angry crowds in London and the U.S.S.R., 100,000 demonstrators in Paris, and a general strike called in Buenos Aires. In Boston itself, a demonstration of 100,000 workers was planned. Only 200 turned out. Those who invaded Boston were not the workers of America; they were anarchists and communists, artists and liberals, and informed New Englanders who had studied the case and were ashamed. Some

Above: Vanzetti's sister, Luiga, travelled to America at her brother's telegrammed request several weeks before the execution
Below: Vanzetti's Harrington & Richardson revolver (top) and Sacco's Colt automatic (bottom)

fervently believed the men were innocent; some did not know, but found the seven years of waiting to die an obscenity; some detested an uncaring establishment that knew nothing, and thought less, of the beliefs that inspired many good men in a sad world.

Most writers who have dealt with the case have taken Vanzetti's innocence for granted. Add to that his remarkable writing and an icon of a saint tends to replace the portrait of a living man. It is hard to believe that he could have harmed a living soul, but the indisputable fact is that on the night of his arrest he carried a gun and ammunition, the purpose of which was never explained satisfactorily.

Sacco was very different. He had a wife, Rosina, who supported him all through the seven years, a daughter, Ines, born after the arrest, and a son, Dante. Active, tough, pugnacious, extroverted, Sacco could stand bravely up to a savage cross-examination. He would not have robbed and killed for himself. He was seemingly happy and, by the standards of that day, well-paid. But he might have killed in the hope of building a different world, and he too went armed.

That Vanzetti did not commit the Bridgewater crime is certain. The evidence against him was worthless and the strength of his alibi irrefutable. And there is more. Some forty years later, Francis Russell, author of *Tragedy in Dedham* (1962), a scrupulously fair and enormously detailed study of the case, tracked down a vital witness, Beltrando Brini. Brini had been 13 at the time, and Vanzetti had lodged with his family in Plymouth. When Russell approached him Brini was in his fifties, and a schoolmaster. But on that Christmas Eve he had been with Vanzetti on his round, from early morning, before the crime, right through. Russell asked Brini whether he had told the truth. Brini had spoken confidently in court, so confidently that Katzmann had claimed that he had been coached to recite a fabricated tale. In the last days before the execution, too, Brini had been to Fuller to repeat his story, and to demand that he should be tried for perjury if Fuller disbelieved him. Now Brini told Russell, quite simply, that it had all been true. His manner convinced Russell, but the Bridgewater crime stays unsolved.

Differing views

The killings at Braintree raise more complex issues. Some writers differ from the general verdict of innocence. Robert Montgomery in *The Murder and the Myth* (1960) argues that both men were guilty, while Russell concludes that while Vanzetti was innocent, Sacco was probably guilty. The case for Sacco's (or indeed Vanzetti's) guilt rests on three main factors. The first is, of course, the guns and ammunition. Each man had bought his gun under a false name, and Vanzetti had no permit. Vanzetti said he was armed because he was afraid of being robbed; Sacco that he planned a hunting expedition (not one of his known recreations) and then that he needed the gun for his occasional stints as night-watchman (which was true). More likely an explanation, considering the atmosphere created by Salsedo's death, is that they were eager to get rid of their weapons and may well have been on their way to do so. But this line was barely hinted at in the

Radical lawyer Fred Moore (top) with Eugene Debs, leader of the American Socialist party

trial. And, in any case, they did have those guns.

The second suggestion of guilt comes from the aforementioned tests on Sacco's gun. It must be mentioned that a test in 1961 was carried out with a modern comparison microscope, and provided conclusive evidence that one bullet did come from Sacco's gun. But Vanzetti's gun had gone from one Italian to another, and it is hardly proven that, even if the gun and bullets were what they purported to be, it was Sacco's hand that had fired them.

Third came disturbing statements from surprising sources. One of the most passionate defenders of Sacco and Vanzetti was the novelist Upton Sinclair, whose book *Boston, August 22nd* (1928) weaves a fictional framework around an almost documentary account of the case. For Sinclair in 1928 the men were martyred heroes. But later Sinclair visited Sacco's family, and wrote in 1953: 'I felt certain that there was some dark secret there. Nobody would be frank with me, and everybody was suspicious. . . .' Fred Moore, a radical lawyer from California, had defended the two men at the Dedham trial, and worked on the case until 1924, but surprisingly was told to desist by Italian anarchist members of the Defence Committee. In particular there was the revelation of the old anarchist Carlo Tresca, doyen of the Italian group to which Sacco and Vanzetti belonged. In an interview with *New Yorker* magazine, Tresca said: 'Sacco was guilty, but Vanzetti was not.' That, in substance, is the case for the prosecution, and it is worth noting that the most telling parts came out long after the trial.

Two last points seem to tilt the balance the other way. The first is that in spite of a thorough investigation of anarchist organisations in the United States and in Italy, no trace of the stolen money was ever found. No one supposes that Sacco and Vanzetti were common criminals. If they did kill, they killed to get money for their cause, and that cause cannot be shown to have profited. The second does not apply if both men were guilty. But if Sacco was guilty and Vanzetti not, could Nicola Sacco, a man whose whole creed was based on love for his fellows, have dragged Vanzetti down with him, when it was in his power to save him? Could it also be possible that, in all those years of unswerving protestation of innocence, Vanzetti was telling the truth of himself and lying about his friend?

In the end there is only one certainty. Whatever they did or did not do, Sacco and Vanzetti's trial was so tainted by racial and political prejudice that it shamed the Commonwealth that conducted it. The proclamation of Governor Dukakis on 23 August 1977 was not a posthumous pardon for, as his advisers in their report to him stated: 'The granting of a pardon is often thought to reaffirm guilt, if not legally then at least in the eye of public opinion.' The report dwelt on the grounds for continuing doubt, on the prejudice and hostility of the judge, on the unsatisfactory identification, on the false testimony with regard to Sacco's cap, on the Morelli theory, on the ballistics evidence, and it concluded that the correct course was to remove, by proclamation: 'Any stigma and disgrace from Sacco and Vanzetti, from their families and descendants, and, as a result, from the Commonwealth of Massachusetts.'

The funeral procession was the largest Boston had ever seen, but it was not the most peaceful. Mounted police charged the crowds that had plagued them for weeks

Murder in Provence

When a well-known English scientist and his family were found murdered at their holiday campsite in southern France, no motive could be established, but suspicion soon fell on a particular local family

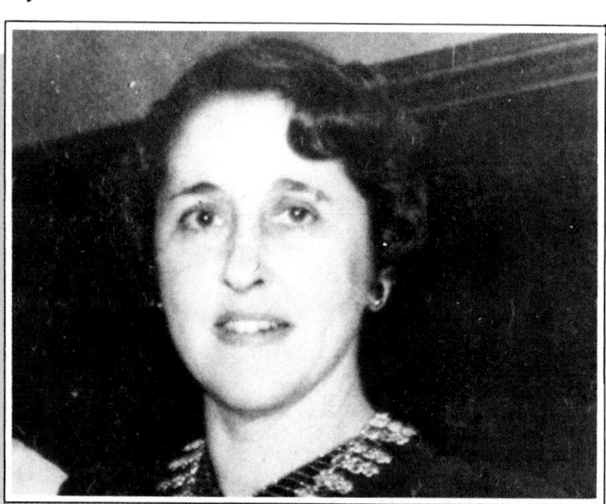

On the evening of 4 August 1952 Sir Jack Drummond, a well-known English nutritionist, his wife Ann and their 10-year-old daughter Elizabeth were motoring through France on a camping holiday. They were travelling between Digne and Villefranche on the Route National 96 and stopped at a lay-by for the night. The site overlooked a farm called La Grand' Terre and Sir Jack thought that he and his family might be able to get some provisions early in the morning before they set off again.

La Grand'Terre was the property of the Dominici family. Gaston Dominici, the 75-year-old patriarch of the family, had relinquished the responsibility of farming the land to his nine children and now spent most of his time wandering over the hills with his goats. Water was scarce in this area during the summer and the local farmers had devised a system whereby they took it in turns to water their crops. The previous day it had been the turn of the Dominicis and the fields were watered by Gustave Dominici who, although not Gaston's eldest son, had taken over the running of the farm. Gustave had been over-anxious to give the land a good soaking and this had resulted in a heavy landslide onto the Marseilles-Digne railway line that skirted the farm. It had taken Gustave nearly a whole day to clear the track of mud and he had then gone to the nearest village to report the incident to the railway foreman, Faustin Roure. Roure had assured Gustave that he would inspect the area the following morning. Little did he realise the scene he would face.

At around 5.45 on the morning of 5 August factory worker Jean-Marie Olivier was riding home on his motorcycle when Gustave Dominici ran out into the road. Gustave was shouting and seemed to be in great distress; he told Olivier that there was a body on the bank of the river and he thought that there was murder involved. Olivier left immediately to inform the gendarmes in Oraison.

Faustin Roure arrived to survey the damage caused by the landslide at about 7am. By the railway track he met Clovis Dominici, Gaston's eldest son, with a railwayman named Marcel Boyer; they had found the bodies of a man, a woman and a small girl, near to a car.

It was about 7.15am before the first policeman arrived at the scene of the crime. Police Sergeant Louis Romanet and a gendarme called Bouchier were approaching the scene when they were met by Aimé Perrin, whose brother was married to a Dominici daughter. The family had apparently grown anxious at the length of time it was taking the police to arrive and had despatched a search party to see if they were coming. Once they reached the spot, Romanet began by examining the car. The green Hillman Estate had a GB plate and the registration number NNK 686. It was parked on the side of the road on a gravel patch underneath a mulberry tree. The inside of the car was in total disarray, and the policeman noticed a shred of flesh that had been caught in the rear bumper. Together with Bouchier, Romanet made a complete inventory of the articles lying around the car. There was a camp-bed with some rugs draped over it, two seats, a child's hat, some money and a notebook with English writing in it. Bouchier and Romanet then began examining the bodies of the victims.

The first body that they saw was that of a woman. She was partly covered by a rug, which concealed the upper half of her body. The woman was in her forties, brown-haired and stockily built. She was wearing a red flowery dress and her arms and legs were bare. Under one arm there was a large bullet wound; rigor mortis had already set in – so she had been dead for some hours. The second body was that of a man, lying under a camp-bed on the other side of the road. He was about sixty and had thinning fair hair, a small moustache and a gaping bullet wound in his chest. Romanet carefully recorded the positions of the two bodies – a detail that was to prove very important in the ensuing investigations. The man was lying with his head towards La Brillanne in the direction of Marseilles; his body was hunched up and a trail of blood could be followed from a water sprinkler on the other side of the road where he had obviously tried to escape from his assailant. The woman was lying to the left of the car and at a right angle to it.

It was only after having taken down these details that Romanet became aware of the presence of Gustave Dominici. 'What a night,' said Gustave, 'we were very frightened.' The full significance of this remark took time to hit the policemen. Why should Gustave have been frightened? Had he seen something of the nocturnal happenings? Was he somehow involved in the incident? Romanet was shocked when Gustave informed him that there was yet another body – on the bank of the river.

As Romanet went down the stony path he noticed various objects strewn along the way and wondered if robbery had been the motive of the crime. He then came across the body of a young girl about 10 years old, who was lying on her back, her arms and legs spreadeagled in the form of a cross. She had sustained the most appalling injuries to her head, which had been smashed by some kind of blunt instrument. She, too, had been dead for some time.

Among the objects Romanet found in his search of the area were another notebook bearing the name Jack Cecil Drummond, several cartridge cases and one live bullet, all American carbine ammunition.

Above: La Grand'Terre farm in southern France. In the summer of 1952, this was the scene of the brutal murder of Sir Jack Drummond (above left), his wife Ann (left) and their 10-year-old daughter Elizabeth (right)

Gustave was asked for a preliminary statement, but said only that he had seen the English family at about 8.30 the previous evening, and then again at 11.30 when they had driven into the farm courtyard. He had heard several shots at about 1am but had not got up to investigate, assuming them to come from poachers' guns.

At 8.30am Police Doctor Dragon arrived and was busy examining the bodies when he noticed an old man strolling towards him, wearing dark velvet trousers, a striped shirt, and an old broad-brimmed hat. This was Gaston Dominici, who told him that he had just heard of the tragedy after taking his goats up to the hills. But Gaston seemed unperturbed by the murders, leaning against the mulberry tree and smoking a pipe.

The local police then sent for Superintendent Edmond Sébeille, a young officer who had a good record of success. He had led 14 murder enquiries and had solved every one of them. He arrived at midday, having spent the intervening hours trying to find experienced officers to assist him, by which time important clues had been destroyed by the number of sightseers who had trampled the area. But he was able to confirm that the cartridges had been fired from an American carbine, and discovered a chip of wood from the butt under the dead child's head, suggesting that she had been battered with it. Sébeille was puzzled by an odd statement from Gustave Dominici to the effect that the farmer may have left his fingerprints on the car door when helping a policeman to open it: the policeman later denied such an incident. Finally, the gun itself was found under the carcass of a sheep in the river.

It was indeed a carbine, from the Rock-Ola factory in Chicago. It was in an extremely poor condition, parts of it being held together by means of an aluminium ring more commonly used to fix identity

Far left: on 12 November 1953 the police gathered at the farm to carry out a reconstruction of the crime. All the witnesses were called to re-enact their parts in the proceedings (left)

tags on to bicycles. The fact that the gun was in such bad condition convinced Sébeille that the murderer was a native of the area – if a person had come into the area with the specific aim of murdering someone, he would have been expected to have at least carried a reasonable firearm. Sébeille was also convinced that now they had the murder weapon, the murderer would soon be caught. A gun like that was fairly easy to identify, and he felt sure that someone would soon recognise it – as Sébeille said, 'the gun will speak'.

A number of curious things had led Sébeille to conclude that one of the Dominicis was guilty. Gaston's behaviour had been extremely suspicious. He had been walking up the path with Sébeille after having searched the area where the little girl had fallen, and as they approached the mulberry tree, Gaston had pointed to it with his stick and, obviously without thinking, said, 'There, that's where the woman fell. She didn't suffer.' Then, having noticed the policeman's surprise, he carried on, apparently unbothered, with the words: 'I say that, but I'm only supposing.' Another incident for which no reasonable explanation had been given took place when Officer Girolami, another member of the investigation team, found a newly washed pair of trousers, still dripping, on a washing line at Grand'Terre. Both Gaston and Gustave denied either owning or washing them.

The first solid indication the police had that the Dominici family were not telling the whole truth came when one of the police officers staged a watch on the farm throughout the night. Yvette had told the police in her statement that they had heard the shots at about one in the morning as she was feeding the baby, and that although the lights had been on the family had been too scared to look out of the window to see what was happening. But during the watch, no lights were seen. Surely the baby had not changed its feeding habits?

Left: the scene of the murder is unchanged today – the mulberry tree still stands and travellers still camp by the roadside

It soon became obvious to the police that at some stage between the discovery of the bodies and the arrival of the authorities the Dominici family had conferred and agreed on their story. It looked as if they had all given alibis for each other, making it very difficult for the police to get at the truth.

Gustave lied

Meanwhile Superintendent Sébeille remained convinced that the gun would eventually lead him to the murderer. All the Dominici family denied knowledge of it, though Clovis appeared strangely startled when it was shown to him.

Gustave was having difficulty supporting his original statement. First, the police had discovered from a statement taken from Jean-Marie Olivier that Gustave had hailed him from *behind* the car; although Gustave still maintained that at this stage he had only just discovered the body of the child and had immediately run into the road some distance from the car to find someone to alert the police. Eventually Gustave admitted that he had been lying. He had discovered the body and had run towards the road, allowing the first vehicle he had seen to pass as it bore a Swiss number plate and probably had a foreign driver. He then started to walk towards the car when he saw Olivier coming along the road on his motorcycle. He was adamant he had hailed Olivier before he had reached the car.

Gradually the police were beginning to piece together the evidence for the investigation. It seemed to Sébeille that whichever direction he turned he was confronted with another lie from a member of the Dominici family. One of the most vital discrepancies in Gustave's story had come to light while the police were questioning a man by the name of Paul Maillet. Maillet had been the leader of the local Resistance group and had fallen under suspicion of the Drummond murders when the police had discovered some guns that he had kept hidden in his kitchen since the war. The police had promised to make things very difficult for him if he did not cooperate. Maillet said that he had gone to the farm to see if Yvette could sell him any potatoes. He had noticed that Gustave was looking very tired and drawn, and when Yvette went to check her stock Maillet asked Gustave if he was feeling all right. It was then, Maillet said, Gustave had told him that he had heard screams on the night of the murder and when he discovered Elizabeth the following morning the child had not been dead; in fact, it was the movement of her arm that had drawn his attention to her in the first place. He said that he had then heard a rattling sound coming from the child's throat and had gone over to her. There had been no further movement so he had gone back to the road and alerted the passing motorcyclist.

For the first few hours Gustave denied that the child had been alive when he first saw her, but when he was confronted with Maillet he eventually admitted that it was true. The foundations of his story were beginning to crumble. Gustave was formally charged with, and convicted of, not helping a person in peril of death. During his two months in prison he admitted nothing else and was released in December.

Crime reconstructed

More than a year after the murders had been committed Sébeille decided that the time had come to stage a reconstruction at the scene.

The date was set for 12 November 1953, a day that dawned cold and grey. Barriers were erected each side of the area and all traffic unconnected with the case was diverted away from the area. The Drummonds' motor car was driven to the spot and parked where the family had camped. The articles that had been scattered along the path and around the car were present and the camp-beds were placed where they had been found by the police. The police even went to the extent of wrapping an officer in the rug to take the place of Lady Drummond's body. All the witnesses had been called, including one Jean Ricard who had not been questioned since the morning of the murders. Along with Ricard there were Sergeant Romanet and Gendarme Bouchier, Faustin Roure and Jean-Marie Olivier. Roure was the first to be accompanied to the scene; he followed the course that he had taken the morning of the crime and commented on the position of the body. It was, he said, in exactly the same position as he had seen Lady Drummond – parallel to the car and covered by the rug.

Next it was the turn of Jean Ricard, who on the morning of 5 August had been walking along the road to catch his bus. He had noticed the disarray surrounding the car, had gone for a closer look and had also seen the body lying parallel to the car. The two policemen, however, were equally sure that when they first saw the body it had been lying at right angles to the car. Lady Drummond's body had obviously been moved between the time of its supposed discovery at 7am and the time of the arrival of the police at 7.30am.

During this time the police had gone to fetch Clovis Dominici who had been working at the railway station in Lurs. If the Dominici story was to be believed, Clovis had first seen the body at 7am in the morning and Sébeille now asked him if the body was lying at the correct angle. Clovis was looking very anxious by this stage, as though he was not quite sure of what to say for the best. Eventually he told the police officer that the body had been lying at right angles to the car when he had first seen it – thereby contradicting the other witnesses. When Clovis was confronted with the other witnesses he became unsure of his story and conceded that he may well have been mistaken – the body could well have been parallel to the vehicle.

Gustave Dominici was then brought from Grand' Terre to the scene of the crime. Jean-Marie Olivier was asked to ride around the bend in the road as he had on the morning of 5 August and Gustave was told to show the police exactly where he had stopped Olivier. Gustave walked some distance from the car and when Olivier came around the bend began waving his arms to attract his attention. Olivier showed a gesture of annoyance and skidded to a halt, claiming that Gustave had been nowhere near the place where he had stood on the morning of the crime. Olivier walked back towards the car and stopped just in front of the Hillman's bonnet. It was here, he said, that Gustave had waved him down. When Sébeille gave Gustave the rug and told him to place it where he had first seen it, Gustave lost his temper and refused point blank to do so. Sébeille threw the rug at him and informed him that he had no choice in the matter; he would remain at the murder spot all day if necessary. Eventually Gustave agreed and positioned the rug by the ditch

After Gaston confessed to the Drummond murders, it was decided to hold a further reconstruction of the crime. In this photograph (below) he is seen holding his walking stick in one hand and the murder rifle in the other; a police officer takes the part of young Elizabeth Drummond. Minutes later 75-year-old Gaston astounded the police by taking off at a run and attempting a suicide leap from the railway bridge (right). This action left the police in no doubt of his guilt

where he claimed to have discovered the body – at right angles to the car. As far as Sébeille was concerned this was the evidence he needed to convince him that it had been Gustave who had moved the body on that morning. It was already obvious that Gustave had lied about his position in relation to the car when he had stopped Olivier. Whatever Gustave had heard, seen or done that night, the time had come for him to be subjected to some serious questioning. He was accompanied to the farm to get a jacket and his family's reaction to his being taken in for questioning was one of apparent panic. Gaston lost all sense of calm, cursing everyone. Yvette and Gustave's mother sobbed in the kitchen, and when it was announced that Clovis was also to be questioned there was further hysteria.

Eventually, Gustave admitted that he had moved the woman's body, 'to see if she was breathing', and then told his version of the events that took place that August night. He told Sébeille that he had heard the shots at one in the morning. He was unable to go back to sleep afterwards and had gone downstairs when he heard his father getting ready to take the goats to the mountain. He had asked Gaston whether he had heard the shots and Gaston replied that it was he who had fired them. Gustave said that he had asked his father what he had been doing. Gaston replied that he had gone out to do some poaching, had got into an argument with the man and had ended up shooting the entire family. Sébeille was stunned; this was not what he had expected at all. He took Gustave straight down to the magistrate's office where the still sobbing man made his formal confession. It took Gustave a while to sign the written account of the admission and after he had the magistrate started questioning him about some points on which he thought Gustave was rather vague. He asked if Gustave had known about the gun but Gustave still maintained that he was ignorant of its existence. The magistrate also found it hard to believe that Gustave had spent two months in prison to protect his father. When he asked Gustave if his father had thanked him, he shouted that the old man was ungrateful and he added that Clovis was also covering up for his father.

Broke down

When Clovis was brought before the police, he too broke down and admitted that his father had told him that he had murdered the campers but, unlike Gustave, he said that he had known of the existence of the gun, which he had seen in a shed on the farm some years earlier.

On Friday 13 November the police went to Grand' Terre to arrest Gaston, who remained adamant about his innocence and appeared distraught when Sébeille told him that both his sons had accused him of the murders. Both Gaston's sons were presented to him during the day and both of them repeated their accusations to his face – Clovis with a sad confidence, and Gustave with a great deal of hesitation and

A picture of composure, Gaston is led into the courtroom at the start of his trial. By this time, the old man had retracted his confession, denying all knowledge of the crime

stammering. The questioning went on until the following day.

A young policeman called Victor Guérino was appointed to guard Gustave. He had been chatting with Gaston for a while when he noticed that the old man was crying. Guérino asked him what was wrong and could not believe his ears when the old man replied that he was crying because his sons had told the truth. It was he who was the murderer. Gaston said that he had been shocked and scared by Sir Jack and had begun to shoot indiscriminately, killing the entire family.

Guérino knew that he must get this information to his superiors as soon as possible before the old man composed himself and denied the story. Gaston refused to tell Sébeille his story but he would, he said, tell the magistrate what had happened. The magistrate was sent for and Gaston repeated his confession to him, developing the story. He had hidden behind the mulberry tree and watched Lady Drummond undress. Sir Jack had spotted him and it was this that caused the argument. Eventually Gaston agreed to tell his story to Sébeille and further embellished the tale. Gaston had gone out with the sole intention of watching Lady Drummond; he had got as far as touching her before he was spotted. Gaston appeared to be quite at ease with his story and was not really worried by the prospect of going to prison. He asked for and was assured receipt of some wine, some tobacco and a rather large amount of money from the farm. He spent a comfortable night in the Palais de Justice and was apparently unperturbed when he was informed the following morning that there was to be a further reconstruction of the crime, following which the magistrate would decide whether or not to charge him.

There were still a few points of fact to clarify; but the first priority was to establish exactly where the murder weapon had been hidden on the farm since the war. Gaston led them to a shed near the forge on the farm and took them inside, pointing out the shelves where he had originally kept the gun. This complied with the evidence given by Clovis and also Gustave – who had once again changed his story and admitted that he had seen the gun before in the shed where the farm implements were stored. Gaston then led the police to the scene of the murders, to re-enact them. The police took the part of the victims with Dominici telling each of them what to do. When it came to the killing of the child one officer took off at a run towards the river with Gaston following at a sedate walking pace. When he was ordered to run as he had on the night of the crime, the old man took off at such speed that for a moment the officers did not realise what was happening. Rather than running over the railway bridge Gaston was running towards the edge of the bridge with the obvious intention of hurling himself onto the track below. He was caught just in time and for the police any doubts that he was guilty were dispelled. They were further convinced by the way Gaston used the gun that he was apparently unaware, as the murderer had been, that the gun was in fact a semi-automatic and that he had wasted a cartridge every time he had reloaded.

Gaston was therefore charged with the murder of the Drummonds and taken to the prison in Digne.

Gaston's trial

Gaston Dominici talked to his lawyers, and by the time the case came to court he had taken a leaf from his son Gustave's book and changed his story. He had, he said, gone to bed early on the night in question, had risen at 4am to take his goats to the mountain and was unaware of any crime until his return home at 8am.

Meanwhile Gustave had succumbed to family pressure and had also retracted the statement in which he had accused his father of the murders. Clovis was the only member of the family to stick to his original story, even though this course of action caused him to be ousted from the safety of the Dominici family's protective circle.

The date of Gaston's trial before the Basses-Alpes Assizes at Digne was set for the 17 November 1954, over two years after the crime had been committed. The trial lasted for 11 days and ended when Gaston was sentenced to death.

As soon as Gaston had been taken to Les Baumettes Prison an appeal was made by his defence lawyers. They claimed that Gaston had revealed some important evidence from his cell. An order was made for Gaston to be questioned in the prison and members of the Paris Sûreté went to Digne to carry out further investigations. Gaston's lawyers insisted that the evidence disclosed by their client was crucial and demanded a confrontation between Gaston and Gustave as soon as possible. The meeting of the two men was arranged, and took place on 8 March 1955.

Gaston claimed that a few days after the murders he had overheard a conversation between Gustave and Yvette, in which the word jewellery was mentioned and the death of the child referred to. Gustave denied that such a conversation had ever taken place, and to any other questions he simply replied: 'I know nothing, and my father is innocent.' He offered no explanation as to why his father should have made a new statement and apparently none was asked for. No official record was made of this confrontation between Gaston and Gustave: yet another blunder by the police. They had already erred in the matter of the shred of flesh that was found on the car bumper, and thought to have been torn from Sir Jack's hand in his efforts to escape his murderer; this was assumed to have been lost between the scene of the crime and the police laboratories until Sébeille admitted in his memoirs that he had actually kept the flesh as a memento of the case. The police had also assumed that the murderer had wasted one cartridge in two because he was not aware of how to use the gun, but subsequent investigations have shown there was in fact some obstruction in the weapon preventing the other bullet being fired. This was not discovered at the time simply because the gun was never examined by a firearms expert.

The police may have been convinced that they had tried and convicted the right man but the public certainly was not. In 1960 a television station interviewed Gaston in his prison cell; the old man once more pleaded his innocence and one very important viewer was convinced by what he saw. President Charles de Gaulle issued a statement of clemency soon after the programme, offering no explanation of his motions but using his prerogative of silence.

Gaston thus ended his days a free man, not at Grand'Terre, but living comfortably in an old peoples' home nearby. Gustave and Yvette sold the farm to a hotelier but the business failed and the 'rooms vacant' sign now hangs creaking in the wind. The mulberry tree still stands on the roadside by the gravel patch; it is thicker and more gnarled today than it was then but it still offers shelter to the odd passer-by. The scene has not changed, and neither have the opinions of the local people; they still believe that the true murderer of the Drummonds escaped. But the surviving Dominicis continue to maintain a stubborn silence.

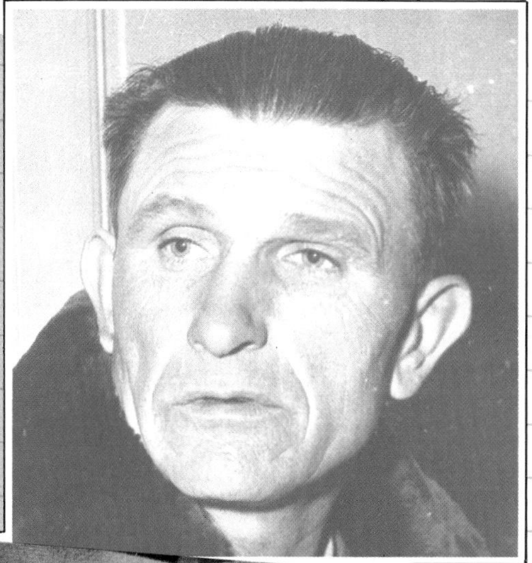

Top: a picture of Gustave Dominici taken in 1967 after his divorce from Yvette
Above: Gaston Dominici on his release in 1960
Right: the grave of the Drummond family in the cemetery at Forcalquier: 'They were lovely and pleasant in their lives and in their death they were not divided'

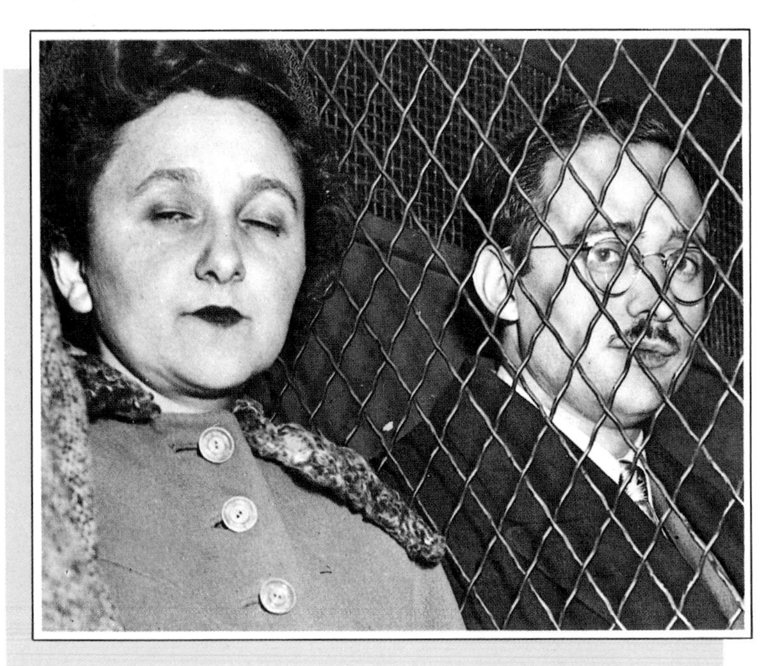

Spies or Scapegoats?

On March 29 1951, Julius and Ethel Rosenberg were found guilty of having conspired to betray American atomic secrets to the Soviet Union during the Second World War. In 1953, protesting their innocence, they died in the electric chair at Sing Sing Prison, the first Americans ever to be executed for espionage in peacetime. Doubt and controversy still surround the case and the mystery has never been completely resolved

In the autumn of 1949, President Harry S. Truman announced to a stunned America that the Soviet Union had just exploded its first atom bomb. The Soviets' test explosion marked the end of the American nuclear monopoly and the start of the Age of Armageddon in international political affairs. It also signalled, however, a new era in American domestic politics, an era characterised by anti-communist hysteria and demagoguery.

The witch-hunt reached its climax on 19 June 1953 with the executions of Julius and Ethel Rosenberg for their alleged role in a communist spy ring. But, despite the certainty of the prosecution, the press, and the American people, the Rosenberg case remains one of the most perplexing and controversial in the 200-year history of American jurisprudence. Many of those who have investigated the case believe that the Rosenbergs' guilt was never satisfactorily demonstrated at their trial, and that even the 'spy ring' itself may have been an FBI fabrication. Could the Rosenbergs have been framed? And why would anyone want to frame them?

The fundamental scientific knowledge needed to make an atom bomb had been published long ago and was freely available to physicists in every country of the world; the remaining problems that Soviet scientists faced had been technical ones. Given the knowledge that the problems *could* be solved – which the American annihilations of Hiroshima and Nagasaki in 1945 had demonstrated to everyone – there was no doubt that a nation with the resources of the Soviet Union *would* eventually solve them. But although it was obvious to many of America's nuclear scientists that the Soviets would soon acquire the bomb, it was not so obvious to ordinary Americans.

Republican politicians, who were frustrated by Truman's surprise victory in the 1948 presidential elections, began to make political capital out of the president's announcement: Senator Karl Mundt condemned 'the prevailing laxity in safeguarding this country against communist espionage', and Congressman Richard Nixon complained of 'the Truman administration's failure to act against red spies in the United States'. Writing in the New York *Journal American*, Nixon protested that Americans were entitled to know 'the facts about the espionage ring which was responsible for turning over information on the atom bomb to agents of the Russian government'. Did such an espionage ring exist?

A few days after the Truman announcement FBI boss J. Edgar Hoover ordered his top aides to find the thieves who had stolen the secret of the atom bomb. With that, a politically motivated invention became an unarguable reality in the minds of America's vast federal police apparatus.

The chain of events that eventually led to the execution of Julius and Ethel Rosenberg began in London on 2 February 1950, with the arrest for espionage of the British nuclear scientist Klaus Fuchs. Fuchs, who was then 38 and head of theoretical physics at Britain's Harwell atomic energy base, had been working on the wartime programme – the Manhattan Project – to develop the atom bomb at Los Alamos, New Mexico. He undoubtedly had access to sensitive information. Following a lead provided by the CIA, MI5 investigated Fuchs. Five months later he was arrested and after a week he confessed to passing classified information to the Soviets. While working in America he had dealt with 'one Soviet agent only' – a man he knew by the code name 'Raymond'.

This revelation at once triggered an intense nationwide manhunt across the United States involving all 52 FBI field offices and the resources of every police department in the country. Bureau agents swarmed into Los Alamos and began combing frantically through every piece of paper in its files, and thousands of known or suspected communist sympathisers were re-evaluated in the light of a possible Fuchs connection. 'Raymond' had to be found whatever the cost. Yet, for all its scope and urgency, the search should have proved utterly futile. Fuchs had provided no biographical data whatsoever about his American contact, and his description was so vague that, as Hoover acknowledged, it could have fitted 'millions of people'. The publicity attending the search would have been bound to alert Fuchs' accomplice to the danger and either driven him underground or sent him fleeing abroad, but the FBI produced a miracle.

Richard Nixon sat on the senate committee formed to examine censure charges against Senator Joseph McCarthy (above) – yet, in the late Forties, Nixon himself had tried to make capital out of anti-communism

On 15 May 1950 they interrogated a 39-year-old chemist named Harry Gold. For the first week of the interrogation Gold maintained that he knew nothing whatsoever about Klaus Fuchs. And it seemed to be true. During the same week, FBI agents in London showed Fuchs pictures of Harry Gold on three separate occasions. Fuchs was supposed to have passed information to his contact at seven different meetings – four in New York, one in Cambridge, Massachusetts, and two in Santa Fe, New Mexico – just five years before. Yet Fuchs failed to identify Gold.

Then, on 22 May, Gold suddenly agreed to confess that he was, after all, Fuchs' American contact, 'Raymond'. Just one hour later, a cable from London announced triumphantly that Fuchs had at last identified Gold. A coincidence? Or the result of an FBI strategy that required Fuchs to identify no one until somebody was found who would confess?

Harry Gold's confession covered not just Fuchs, but a whole rogues' gallery of traitors for whom he had acted as a courier over a period of some years. Hoover could not have hoped for a better witness.

Gold had been indicted on 9 June for conspiring to commit espionage, but his trial was postponed while the investigation continued. In July he pleaded guilty to a charge of conspiring to get information

Left: a United States atomic test at Bikini Atoll in the Pacific in 1946. Three years later, the Soviet Union exploded its first atomic bomb – a feat made possible, many Americans believed, by a spy ring passing research data to the Soviets

concerning atomic energy for the Soviet Union. The prosecutor, Gerald Gleeson, suggested that the government might not wish to present any evidence against Gold but Judge McGranery said that he would insist on enough evidence to convince him that Gold had indeed committed the crimes with which he was now charged.

On 15 June 1950 Alfred Dean Slack, a chemical engineer, was arrested on charges of having delivered samples of 'a powerful new high explosive' to Harry Gold in 1944. SYRACUSE CHEMIST SEIZED IN SPY RING, blared the *New York Times* headline, and NEW ARREST LINKED TO FUCHS. In the excitement, it was overlooked that the explosive involved, RDX, was a pre-First World War discovery, that it had nothing whatsoever to do with atomic research, and that the charges brought against Slack made no mention of Klaus Fuchs.

The juggernaut was rolling now. On the next day, 16 June 1950, acting on further information from Harry Gold, FBI agents arrested 28-year-old machinist David Greenglass at his New York home and charged him with having betrayed Los Alamos atomic secrets to the Soviets in 1945.

Greenglass, like Fuchs, had worked at Los Alamos during the critical years 1944 to 1946. His position had been a lowly one – he had been employed in the machine shop, turning out experimental parts of the atom bomb detonation system to designs provided by senior scientists. Known to be an ex-member of the Young Communist League, he was promptly goaled.

Greenglass confession

Although no one knows for certain what discussions Greenglass had with the government during this period, it is almost certain that he arrived at an agreement involving a light sentence for himself and full immunity from prosecution for his wife Ruth – who was also implicated – in exchange for his co-operation in any future proceedings.

David Greenglass' confession was made public on 16 July 1950. Who had recruited him as a Soviet espionage agent? The request had been transmitted to him by his wife in the winter of 1944. And who had made the suggestion to her? 'Well, you've got me anyway,' Greenglass is reported to have said, 'I might as well admit it. It was my brother-in-law, Julius Rosenberg.'

On 17 July 1950 Rosenberg was arrested, followed on 11 August by his wife Ethel. Six days later the two Rosenbergs and Anatoli Yakovlev, a former Soviet vice consul, were indicted for conspiring to betray atomic secrets to the Soviet Union – although the indictment of Yakovlev was purely a formality as he had already left the country. The arrests continued. Morton Sobell, one of Julius Rosenberg's old classmates at New York's City College, was arrested

Top: the arrest of Julius Rosenberg on 17 July 1950. His wife Ethel (above) was arrested three weeks later

at the Mexican border in Laredo, Texas, on 18 August. Sobell later claimed that he had been kidnapped by the Mexican security services at the request of the FBI while on a trip. But the FBI version was that Sobell was attempting to flee as a result of the other arrests.

A new indictment was voted against Yakovlev and the Rosenbergs on 10 October with Sobell and David Greenglass added to the list of defendants. Greenglass appeared at a hearing a week later and pleaded guilty, but he remained unsentenced. The final indictment of the Rosenbergs and Morton Sobell was issued at the end of January. Harry Gold and Ruth Greenglass were named as co-conspirators but not as defendants, so that they could give testimony against the Rosenbergs without being subject to legal action.

On 6 March 1951, seven months after their arrest, Julius and Ethel Rosenberg's trial opened at the Federal Courthouse, Foley Square, New York City, with Judge Irving Kaufman presiding. Representing the United States was Chief Prosecutor Irving Saypol, who was renowned for his toughness in the courtroom when questioning suspected traitors. He was assisted by Myles Lane, James Kilsheimer, and by the man who later became Senator Joseph McCarthy's chief aide in the notorious hearings at Fort Monmouth Army Base, Roy Cohn. Representing the Rosenbergs was defence attorney Emmanuel Bloch, a family friend who had almost no previous experience in criminal proceedings. The jury was made up of eleven men and one woman, all of whom had already read a great deal about the Rosenbergs in the press and must have formed at least a tentative opinion about the case. The charge was conspiracy to commit espionage in wartime. The Rosenbergs pleaded innocent.

In all, 23 witnesses appeared for the prosecution. Of these, only four were of central importance – David and Ruth Greenglass, Harry Gold, and self-confessed communist Max Elitcher, another of Julius Rosenberg's old classmates and a lifelong friend of Morton Sobell. The other 19 witnesses were all called to confirm small details of the prosecution's case, or to clear up obscure technical and scientific points. Thus, all the prosecution's major witnesses were implicated in the same crime that the defendants were accused of. And while in normal cases the exclusive reliance by the prosecution upon accomplice witnesses would be viewed as highly dubious, if not frankly unacceptable, in this particular case it seemed to have just the opposite effect.

The first witness for the prosecution was Max Elitcher, who had worked during the war as an electrical engineer with the Navy Department. He described various meetings and phone calls involving either Julius Rosenberg or Sobell in which he was 'told' about espionage activities and asked either to contribute classified information or to aid in recruiting other agents at the installation where he worked. None of Elitcher's testimony in this regard could be independently corroborated since no outsiders were ever present during the discussions. Elitcher also described driving with Sobell one summer night in 1948 to a street near Rosenberg's home. Sobell had said that he had to deliver some information that was 'too valuable to be destroyed and yet too dangerous to be kept around'. When they arrived, Sobell left the car carrying a 35mm film canister, disappeared briefly, and then returned without it.

Cross-examination revealed that Elitcher had no idea what the canister might have contained. He had not witnessed the delivery and thus he had no idea of its final destination. And later he admitted that it was fear of prosecution for having lied in 1947 on a Loyalty Oath that had impelled him to tell his story to the FBI when they had first questioned him after Julius Rosenberg's arrest.

Electronics engineer Morton Sobell (left), the Rosenbergs' co-defendant. He was sentenced to 30 years in prison

The next witness was David Greenglass, husband of Ethel Rosenberg's sister Ruth, and the government's much heralded 'iron link' in its case against the atom spies. Under Roy Cohn's questioning, Greenglass described how Julius Rosenberg had initially recruited him for Soviet espionage work. In November 1944, while he was stationed at Los Alamos and Ruth was still living in New York, Julius had approached Ruth, confided to her that David was working on the atom bomb, and suggested that David could 'help his friends' by supplying classified information. Ethel Rosenberg, who had also been present, informed Ruth that Julius 'was giving information to the Soviet Union'.

Ruth relayed the Rosenbergs' suggestion to David and eventually he complied. At first, he supplied some general information through Ruth. Then, while on leave in New York in December 1944, he gave Julius a 'lens-mould' sketch, the names of some top project scientists, and a list of possible communist sympathisers at Los Alamos. Ethel Rosenberg typed up this information from his notes. Before David returned to Los Alamos, they had worked out a plan whereby more information could be passed to a courier Rosenberg would send out to New Mexico. Julius cut the side of a 'Jell-O' packet into two pieces, gave him one piece to keep, and said the courier would identify himself by presenting the other. Some months later, on the morning of Sunday 3 June 1945, Harry Gold had appeared at David and Ruth's new apartment in Albuquerque and asked for Greenglass, saying: 'Julius sent me.' Greenglass walked to his wife's purse and took out his piece of the Jell-O box. Gold produced another piece and when they checked them the two halves fitted. Greenglass gave Harry Gold two more lens-mould

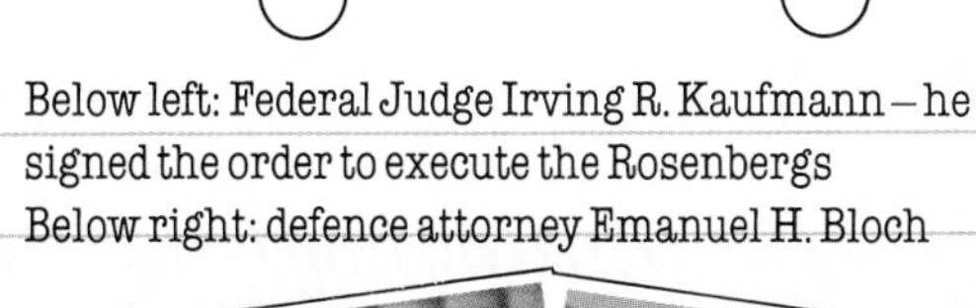

Below left: Federal Judge Irving R. Kaufmann – he signed the order to execute the Rosenbergs
Below right: defence attorney Emanuel H. Bloch

sketches and some further data in exchange for the sum of $500 in cash.

Then, in February 1950, Julius had come to Greenglass with the news that Harry Gold would soon be apprehended in connection with Klaus Fuchs' arrest, and urged that he should prepare to flee the country. The warning was repeated again in April and, during the following month, Rosenberg provided money totalling some $6000 and details of an escape route that would take Greenglass and his family via Mexico and Switzerland to the safety of communist Czechoslovakia.

Ruth Greenglass corroborated her husband's evidence. Cross-examination did nothing to shake the certainty of her manner, and it was evident that the jury believed everything she said.

The Greenglasses had provided the only *direct* evidence that the Rosenbergs had obtained information about the atom bomb. But David and Ruth were self-confessed spies with clear motives for implicating the Rosenbergs and moreover – it emerged later – there was a feud over business matters between the two families.

The story of the escape money raises baffling questions that have never been asked before. Why would the Soviets have had the least interest in spending such a large sum on the escape of someone as insignificant as David Greenglass? The money could hardly have been Rosenberg's own. He was a poor man with a bankrupt business, and if he did have $6000 to spend, why would he have given it to Greenglass instead of using it to flee the country himself? Yet the money did exist. It ended up in the bank account of the Greenglasses' defence attorney O. John Rogge – and there are signed receipts to prove it. Where did the money come from? The Greenglasses were as poor as the Rosenbergs, and no bank would have lent such a sum without collateral.

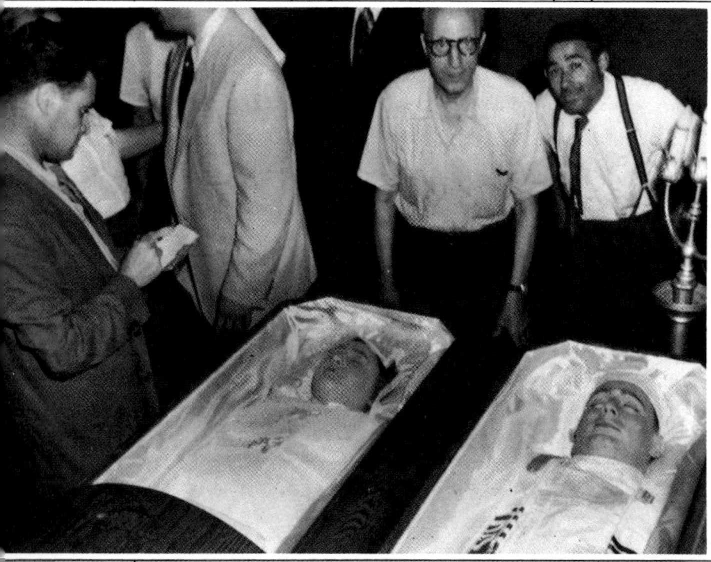

The bodies of the two 'atom spies' lie in the parlour of a Brooklyn undertaker after their electrocution

No direct link was ever established between the Rosenbergs and Anatoli Yakovlev; the only connection was provided by the testimony of Harry Gold, the last major witness for the prosecution. Unfortunately, Gold was not the most reliable of witnesses, and in fact had never met the Rosenbergs.

Gold confirmed that he was the courier sent to collect information from David Greenglass. He recounted every step he had taken, beginning with his arrival in Albuquerque from Santa Fe, where he had collected information from Klaus Fuchs. The following morning, 3 June 1945, Gold had visited the Greenglasses, identifying himself by means of his half of the Jell-O box and the code-words: 'I come from Julius'. After collecting the information – which consisted of 'three or four handwritten pages plus a couple of sketches' – Gold had returned immediately to New York and handed over both Fuchs' and Greenglass' material to his Soviet spymaster, Anatoli Yakovlev.

Gold admitted collecting information from Greenglass and passing it to the Soviets, but what had this to do with the Rosenbergs? The code-words 'I come from Julius' – or in the Greenglasses' version 'Julius sent me' – provided some sort of connection between Gold and the Rosenbergs. But if Julius *had* been a spy, would Soviet couriers have used his real name as a code-word?

Fabricated story

Since Gold always worked through Yakovlev and had never contacted Julius Rosenberg, it followed that his half of the Jell-O packet must have come from Yakovlev. But Yakovlev could only have obtained it from Julius Rosenberg – Greenglass had already testified that Rosenberg himself had cut the Jell-O box in half.

The Jell-O box story is therefore the only remaining evidence – discounting hearsay – of the Rosenbergs' connection with the Soviets. However, it depends entirely on the testimony of Gold and the Greenglasses, and there are independent grounds for suspecting that Gold's journey to New Mexico was a complete fabrication.

Emmanuel Bloch opened the case for the defence by calling Julius Rosenberg. Rosenberg denied every piece of evidence the prosecution had presented. Saypol, cross-examining, asked Rosenberg if he had been a member of the Communist Party. Rosenberg pleaded the Fifth Amendment, refusing to answer on the grounds that to do so might tend to incriminate him.

New York, 20 June 1975 – the Rosenbergs' sons, Michael (left) and Robert, protest against the FBI's refusal to release transcripts of their parents' trial

When Ethel Rosenberg took the stand, she corroborated her husband's testimony, and gave evidence about the animosity between the Rosenbergs and the Greenglasses that had resulted from the collapse of the machine shop business owned by Julius Rosenberg and David Greenglass.

The case for the defence amounted to little more than a simple denial; against the word of the prosecution witnesses and that of the United States government, it was hardly a defence at all.

In his summation to the jury, Chief Prosecutor Irving Saypol stated categorically that 'these conspirators stole the most important secrets ever known to mankind and delivered them to the Soviet Union. No defendants ever stood before the bar of American justice less deserving of sympathy.' Before the jury retired, Prosecutor Saypol and Judge Kaufman met them privately and told them that only a fraction of the case against the Rosenbergs had been presented in court – the government had much more evidence that could not be made public for security reasons. It is easy to imagine the effect of that announcement upon the jury's deliberations.

The verdict had been all but certain from the outset. After nine hours, the jury arrived at a unanimous decision: they found the two Rosenbergs, and their co-defendant Morton Sobell, guilty as charged.

A week later, on 5 April 1951, the court reconvened to hear Judge Kaufman's sentence. The defendants had been tried under the Espionage Act of 1917, which normally carried a maximum penalty of 20 years' imprisonment. Violations in time of war were punishable by a maximum of 30 years' imprisonment or death, but the provision for the death sentence had never been used. The alleged offences were supposed to have been committed during the war but, at the time, the Soviet Union had been an ally. In his final speech, defence attorney Bloch pointed this out and added that the Rosenbergs continued to maintain their innocence.

Before delivering sentence on the Rosenbergs, Judge Kaufman said: 'I consider your crime worse than murder. I believe your conduct in putting into the hands of the Russians the A-bomb . . . has already caused the communist aggression in Korea with the resultant casualties exceeding 50,000, and who knows but that millions more of innocent people may pay the price of your treason.' The Rosenbergs sat in silence, their faces rigid with fear. Then they heard the sentence of death.

The execution was originally set for 21 May 1951. The Supreme Court was asked on four separate occasions to review the case, but it refused each time. Committees to save the Rosenbergs were formed. Petitions were signed. Pleas for clemency were sent to Truman and, later, to Eisenhower. New lawyers searched frantically for fresh evidence, but uselessly – America was bent on revenge.

The last act

The execution had been postponed to 9 March 1953 in order to await the outcome of appeals. By the time that date approached, letters and telegrams to the White House calling for clemency had reached a total of three million. Among them were direct pleas from the former head of the Manhattan Project at Los Alamos, Dr Harold Urey, Albert Einstein, Pablo Picasso, James Wolfe, chief justice of the Utah Supreme Court, and Pope Pius XI. But it was to no avail. On the morning of 19 June 1953, a specially convened sitting of the Supreme Court overruled the final stay of execution by a vote of six to three. Execution was scheduled for 8pm that evening.

As the hour drew near, over 5000 people gathered in New York's Union Square to protest. Simultaneously, in capitals around the world, hundreds of thousands took to the streets to show their anger. At 8.06pm Julius Rosenberg died in the electric chair. Ten minutes later, after two unsuccessful attempts to electrocute her, Ethel Rosenberg followed. Both of the Rosenbergs died still protesting their innocence.

But their story did not end there. The debate over their guilt or innocence continues today, over 30 years later. Those who believe in the Rosenbergs' guilt say that they deserved to die for their crimes. Others see them as martyred scapegoats framed by a vindictive government. The final question, though, is not whether Julius and Ethel Rosenberg were guilty or innocent but whether they were fairly tried. And the verdict on that question appears to be that they were not.

Was Hanratty innocent?

The brutal attack in an A6 motorway lay-by in August 1961 that left a man dead and a woman paralysed shocked the country. The police were under pressure to catch the gunman, and a small-time London crook, James Hanratty, was quickly arrested, tried and hanged. He had always protested his innocence, and very soon after the execution someone else began making elaborate and consistent confessions to the murder

The knock on the car window was sharp, insistent. Valerie Storie and Michael Gregsten were startled. They had driven into a cornfield, to be alone together after a brief separation while Gregsten had been on holiday with his wife and children. It was the balmy summer evening of the 22 August 1961. As so often before, they had called in at the Old Station Inn, Taplow, for a drink, and gone from there to the cornfield at Dorney Reach. They had driven quite a distance into the cornfield so that no one would disturb them. The knock on the car door was not only annoying: it was strange and menacing.

Gregsten wound down the window. At once, a black revolver was thrust through it. The man, who was standing outside in a neat, dark suit, spoke in a cockney accent: 'This is a hold-up,' he said. 'I am a desperate man. I have been on the run for four months. If you do as I tell you, you will be all right.'

He climbed into the back of the car and started to bark out orders. First, he told Gregsten to drive further into the field. Then, after waiting two hours, until it was completely dark, he ordered him to drive out of the field, and they embarked on a weird and terrifying journey, around the west and north-western suburbs of London, then out again northwards on the A6 road. The man told them he was on the run, and that he had 'done the lot' (a prison expression). Several times, at crucial moments, he said: 'Be quiet, will you, I am finking'; he was unable to pronounce 'th'. He was particularly curious about the couple's sexual relationship.

The gunman began looking for somewhere off the road where he could have 'a kip'. Soon after the village of Clophill, the car climbed Deadman's Hill. Gregsten was ordered to turn off the road into a picnickers' lay-by. He obeyed. The gunman asked Gregsten to pass over a bag that was in the front. In a quick movement, meant perhaps as an attack, Gregsten turned round with the bag. The man fired his gun twice and Gregsten was shot through the head, dying instantly.

He forced the now hysterical Valerie Storie into the back of the car, and raped her. Then he made her help him drag the dead, blood-soaked Gregsten out

Research scientist Michael Gregston – murdered in cold blood on the evening of 22 August 1961

of the driver's seat and into the road. Sitting beside the body of her lover, Valerie Storie pleaded with the gunman to go. He seemed undecided. Suddenly, he turned and fired a series of bullets at her. She felt her senses go and keeled over. He then reloaded and fired again as she lay perfectly still, holding her breath. The man prodded her with his foot, got into the car and drove off with a grinding of gears towards Luton in Bedfordshire.

Valerie Storie lay there, unable to move, feebly waving her petticoat for perhaps as long as three hours. She was found at 6.45am, and rushed to Bedford Hospital where, even before she was operated on, she made a statement to police officers. Soon afterwards, the police issued a description of the man they wanted to interview. The wanted man, said the *Evening News*, was about 30, 5½ ft [1.68 m], medium-built, with dark hair, pale face, deep-set brown eyes, dressed in a dark brown suit and with a cockney voice – Valerie stuck to this description.

Valerie Storie – she worked with Gregston and had been his lover for several months. After the attack Valerie lay in the road, unable to move, for hours, until she was found by a farm labourer on his way to work

Murder weapon

Few murder stories have electrified the British public as the A6 murder did in the days that followed. The coverage in the newspapers and on television was prodigious. By the evening of 23 August, the missing car was found, parked behind Redbridge underground station in east London.

On the evening of 24 August came the most valuable of all clues: the murder weapon. A London Transport cleaner found a fully loaded .38 revolver, with five boxes of ammunition, underneath the upstairs back seat of a 36A bus.

By now, the case had been taken over by one of Scotland Yard's most senior detectives, Detective Chief Superintendent Acott. He appealed to landlords and landladies for information about 'odd' tenants. One response to this appeal came from the manager of the Alexandra Court Hotel, Finsbury Park. Some of his regular guests had complained about a man who had booked in to the hotel on the day after the murder, and had behaved extremely oddly ever since. He had locked himself in his room for five days, and was constantly walking about at night and talking to himself. Police from Highbury duly came and took the offending guest – who was booked in as a Mr Frederick Durrant – to the police station for questioning.

The man said at once that his name was not 'Durrant' but Peter Louis Alphon. He told them he had been to see his mother in Streatham on the evening of 22 August, and had spent the night at the Vienna Hotel, Maida Vale. A call to the Vienna established that a 'Mr Durrant' had booked in for the night of 22 August, and had paid for his room. The police concluded that Alphon was above suspicion, and consequently released him from custody.

There were many sightings and interviews of this kind over the next few days. Then, on 31 August, William Ewer was sitting in his umbrella shop in Swiss Cottage with his bereaved sister-in-law Janet Gregsten, when suddenly, according to a story he later told journalists, she clutched his arm and pointed to a man going into a cleaner's shop across the arcade. She was, she said, sure that the man fitted the description of her husband's killer. To humour her, Ewer dashed into the cleaner's, but could not find the man, who had called himself J. Ryan. But the next day he saw him again, entering a flower shop, and contacted the police. The police inquiries showed that Ewer's 'suspect' had arranged to have flowers sent to a Mrs Mary Hanratty at an address in north London.

On 31 August, the day of Janet Gregsten's 'sighting' of Ryan, Valerie Storie was moved from Bedford Hospital to Guy's in London. As she was moved, the police issued what was called a 'new description' of the murderer, stemming from a 'change' in her evidence. The man they wanted now had 'large icy-blue, saucer-like eyes'. No one has been able – or prepared – to explain why she changed her evidence.

It was not until 11 September, nearly three weeks after the murder, that the police got the vital clue that was to lead them to both their main suspects. On that day, in the very same Vienna Hotel, the proprietor turned over a chair in a basement room and two cartridge cases fell onto the floor. The police were contacted, and the cases were soon identified as having come from the murder weapon.

When the manager of the hotel, William Nudds,

was first asked about the people who stayed in the hotel at the time of the murder, Detective Chief Superintendent Acott was not aware that he had a criminal record. Nudds' first statement deals with the only two guests in the hotel who had not been ruled out by Acott's inquiries. The first was James Ryan, the man spotted by Janet Gregsten. On 21 August, the night before the murder, Ryan had stayed in the large basement room in which the cases were later found. Nudds' statement said that Ryan had been shown to his room on the night of 21 August, and had had breakfast on the morning of 22 August. Ryan had asked how to get to Queensway, and Nudds had told him to get on a 36 bus. This was, of course, extremely damaging to Ryan, since the gun had been found under the back seat of a 36A bus.

The second man dealt with in Nudds' first statement was 'Frederick Durrant' – who had already been questioned by Highbury police on 27 August, and had admitted his real name was Peter Alphon. 'Durrant', said Nudds, had stayed in an upstairs room, number 6, on the night of the murder (22/23 August), had been shown to his room late at night, and had stayed in the room, without breakfast, until about noon on 23 August. This, of course, absolved Alphon because he could not have been the A6 murderer if he was being shown to a room in Maida Vale, late on the evening of 22 August.

On 21 September, Nudds was hauled out of his house and taken once again to Scotland Yard, where he made a further statement.

This statement, which was substantially supported by the hotel documents, firmly contradicted Nudds' first statement. It implicated 'Durrant' (Alphon) from beginning to end. It showed that he had been in the room in which the cartridge cases were found, had been out certainly after midnight, had lied about the time he came in, and had behaved extremely oddly throughout. The alibi that Alphon had provided to Highbury police had been smashed. On the other hand, Ryan, who had been implicated originally, was now hardly worth bothering about. He had been in the hotel the night before the murder, anyway. There was nothing suspicious about his behaviour. The gratuitous reference to the 36 bus in the first statement had been dropped in the second statement.

It seemed that Alphon was Acott's man. On 22 September – the day after Nudds' second statement – Acott summoned Alphon's mother to the Yard where she was unable to verify the alibi her son had given to Highbury police: that he had spent the early evening of 22 August with her.

The hunt for the murder suspect did not last long. Shortly before midnight that night, Peter Alphon strolled voluntarily into Scotland Yard. He was interrogated for much of the night by Acott. The following day, 23 September, he stood in a number of identity parades. No one picked him out, but Acott remained enthusiastic and the *Evening News* reported that Alphon was going to Ampthill that evening – presumably to be charged with the murder.

Identity parade

But there was one all-important identification parade to go through first. On the morning of Sunday 24 September, Alphon lined up with nine other men in front of Valerie Storie's hospital bed. She failed to identify Alphon, so police suspicion began to fall on Ryan again.

On 25 September, the day after the identification parade, Nudds was hauled into Scotland Yard for yet another gruelling interview, this time lasting seven hours. By the end of the day, he had signed a *third* statement, which concluded that his first statement had been right after all, and that the second had been concocted from start to finish because he wanted to help the police. All the information about 'Durrant' being out until late at night was, he said, untrue. 'Durrant', as per the first statement, was *in* all night, from quite early on. Moreover, the remark

about Ryan asking for the 36 bus, deleted from the second statement, could now be reinstated. Ryan was now suspect number one. Who was this man?

After the curious 'sighting' by Janet Gregsten and William Ewer, the police had quickly discovered that 'Ryan' was the alias of James Hanratty, who was a small-time thief.

At once, the police let it be known on the underworld and newspaper grapevines that Hanratty was now the man they were looking for. On several occasions Hanratty, who was wanted for a number of robberies in north London, telephoned newspapers and also Acott to say that he had nothing whatever to do with the A6 murder, but was reluctant to give himself up as he was wanted for the robberies.

All this, plus the fact that Hanratty was vague as to where he had been at the time of the murder, naturally fuelled Acott's suspicions. A nation-wide police hunt was launched. On 11 October, Hanratty was found in a Blackpool café and taken to a police station. After a long, inconclusive interview, throughout which Hanratty insisted that he had nothing to do with the murder, he was taken to Bedford by the police.

On the morning of Saturday 14 October, another identity parade lined up in front of Valerie Storie's bed. She asked each man to say the sentence that had stuck in her mind from that awful August night: 'Be quiet, will you, I am thinking.' Each one spoke the words. Finally, she called out Hanratty's number. That evening, at Bedford, James Hanratty was formally charged with the A6 murder.

The trial started on 22 January 1962, and lasted for 21 full days, at that time the longest murder trial

Below: the cornfield at Dorney Reach where the couple were approached by the gunman. They drove to this desolate spot after an evening in The Old Station Inn (right) at Taplow
Above right: on the morning of 23 August, the murder car was driven from Dorney Reach, around the north-western suburbs of London, and then out again northwards on the A6 road

Witnesses for the prosecution: Roy Langdale (top), a hardened criminal and prison 'grass'; and Charles 'Dixie' France (above), Hanratty's former friend and 'fence'

in British history. The great thrust of the case against Hanratty depended on identification, and in particular the identification that had been made in court by Valerie Storie.

Yet Valerie Storie had made another equally certain and confident identification three weeks earlier, and there were further problems with her identification. According to her own evidence, she was forced by the gunman to keep her eyes firmly fixed on the road in front, and caught only a three-second glimpse of the killer as he turned to kiss her. Then there was the curious way the identity parade was conducted. Valerie Storie herself admitted that Hanratty's well-publicised ginger hair stood out. On top of that, he was almost certainly the only man on the parade with a cockney accent.

The strongest other piece of evidence against Hanratty came from his former friend Charles 'Dixie' France. France, a small-time 'fence' (a receiver of stolen goods), who lived near Swiss Cottage, told the court that Hanratty had once told him that underneath the back seat of a bus was a good place to hide things. Hanratty did not deny telling France this, nor did he deny the coincidence that the murder gun was found under the back seat of a bus.

It also told against Hanratty that the cartridge cases were found in the Vienna Hotel, in the very room in which he stayed the night before the murder was committed.

Finally, the case against Hanratty was bolstered by a familiar figure in big British criminal trials: the prison grass. Roy Langdale was already a hardened criminal at 24. He agreed to appear as a witness against James Hanratty and, in return, was let off on probation in a fraud case. His evidence, however, was not strong. He insisted that he, and he alone, walked with Hanratty in the exercise yard. Hanratty, however, could only just remember him as a Brixton inmate. Two other prisoners in Brixton at the time told the court that they had habitually exercised with Hanratty, that Hanratty had consistently proclaimed his innocence, and that he had had little contact with Langdale.

All the evidence against Hanratty, apart from the identifications, was circumstantial. There was no direct forensic evidence to link him with the killing.

On 17 February, the jury retired. They returned six hours later to ask the meaning of the words 'reasonable doubt' and then retired again. Four hours later they returned with a unanimous verdict of guilty. Hanratty's appeal was dismissed on 12 March. Despite a petition of 90,000 names collected by the Hanratty family, the Home Secretary, R. A. Butler, refused to commute the sentence or to recommend a royal pardon, and Hanratty was hanged at Bedford Prison early on the morning of 4 April 1962.

The case against him had never seemed strong. Many observers of the case felt that what damaged Hanratty most was precisely the area of the case that, after his death, seemed powerfully to argue his innocence: his alibi.

When James Hanratty heard, through the underworld grapevine, that he was wanted for the A6 murder, he rang Detective Chief Superintendent Acott on 5 October 1961 to deny it. Acott asked him where he had been the previous 22 and 23 August, and Hanratty replied that he had been with 'three

Valerie Storie arriving at the trial. Was it possible that she could be mistaken as to her attacker's identity?

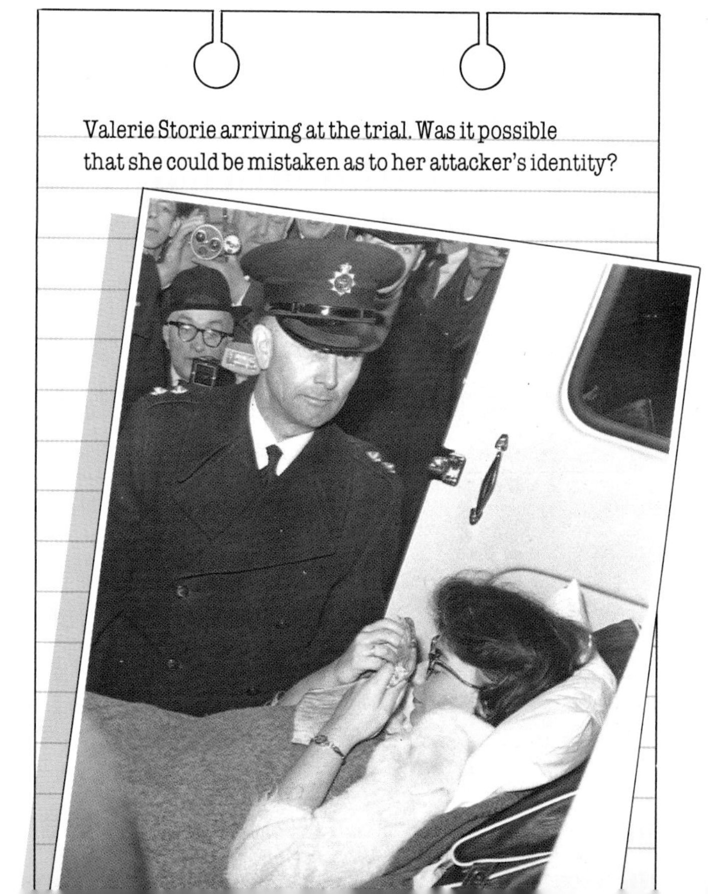

friends' in Liverpool. When Acott pressed him for details of these 'three friends', Hanratty would not supply any. Instead he stole a car and drove to Liverpool, and thence to Blackpool, where he was caught and arrested.

In his interviews after his arrest, he continued to say that he was in Liverpool at the time of the murder. He claimed that he had caught a train from Euston in the late morning, had left his luggage in the left luggage office at Lime Street station with an attendant 'with a withered or turned hand', and wandered down Scotland Road looking for a 'fence' or a thief who lived, he thought, in Carlton or Tarleton Road. Shortly before 5pm, he had gone into a sweet shop in Scotland Road and asked the way to Carlton and Tarleton Roads. He was given directions by an elderly lady, who 'had a young girl with her'. He had returned to the city centre and at about 6pm he approached a man outside a billiard hall near Lime Street station, offering to sell him a gold watch.

Mrs Olive Dinwoodie (centre) – she gave powerful evidence in support of part of Hanratty's claim that he was in Liverpool at the time of the murder

Mrs Dinwoodie

In support of this part of the alibi, there was powerful evidence. There *was* a man with a damaged hand at Lime Street station, who agreed that he had taken a case on that particular day from a young man looking like Hanratty.

Mrs Olive Dinwoodie, one of the most important witnesses in the case, said that on 21 and 22 August (Monday and Tuesday) she had served in a friend's sweetshop – Cowley's in Scotland Road. She recalled a man, whom she identified from photographs as Hanratty, calling into her sweetshop late one afternoon and asking the way to Carlton or Tarleton. On that day Mrs Dunwoodie had had her young granddaughter with her in the shop.

Prodigious efforts by the police had established Hanratty's movements for almost every minute of 21 August – even the prosecution's own inquiries placed Hanratty firmly in London all day Monday. If Mrs Dinwoodie recognised Hanratty correctly, then Tuesday was the only day he could possibly have been in the sweet shop.

Up to that part of the evening, then, Hanratty's alibi story seemed to hold up. But after that it fell to pieces. He stuck rigidly to his inadequate story that he had spent the night in Liverpool with three men, and all police attempts to verify the alibi failed. The trial started, therefore, with Hanratty having a good alibi up to about six in the evening, but having only a poor one thereafter.

The situation became infinitely worse when, after the first week of the trial, Hanratty told his astonished counsel that he wanted to change his story. He had not, after all, spent the night of 22 to 23 August in Liverpool. He had spent it in Rhyl. His lawyer, Michael Sherrard, was appalled. Again and again he warned his client of the dangers of changing his alibi so late in the proceedings. If this new story were false, he warned, Hanratty's entire credibility on every issue would be at stake. But the young man, by this time thoroughly frightened, insisted that he must tell the truth in the witness box.

What was this 'truth', which he now spilled out to his anxious lawyer? He had, he said, given up all hope of finding Carlton or Tarleton Road and, acting on impulse, had decided to travel to Rhyl. He had been there before, earlier in the summer, and had met 'John', a man who worked at the fairground and who had suggested he might know how to get rid of stolen goods. With his gold watch and other stolen goods burning a hole in his pocket, he had hopped on a bus opposite Lime Street station and gone to Rhyl, arriving there as it was growing dark. He had asked vaguely for 'John', but very soon he needed to look for somewhere to spend the night. He had knocked at a few boarding houses and had eventually been put up in one that was near the station. He described the boarding house very distinctly, and included the unlikely fact that there was a green bath in the attic.

Hanratty's solicitors at once instructed an inquiry agent, who quickly found 'John'. His real name was Terry Evans. Evans confirmed at once that he had met Hanratty earlier in the summer and, indeed, had put him up for a night in his house. Warned of Hanratty's plight, Evans then joined in visiting the guest-houses near Rhyl station, asking if they had a green bath in their attic.

At 'Ingledene', in Kinmel Street, which backs on to the station, they were rewarded. Yes, there was a green bath in the attic, and the guest-house and the landlady, Mrs Grace Jones, almost exactly fitted Hanratty's description. Moreover, she confirmed at once that a young man had come to her house the previous summer and had been put up for two nights. She thought it was in the week 19 to 26 August, and she agreed that the young man looked very much like the picture of Hanratty that was shown to her. Without further delay, she was whisked down to Bedford.

Unfortunately, she could produce no documentary evidence of her story, and the prosecution shredded her tale and reduced her almost to tears. No one, except Mrs Jones, came to court to say that Hanratty had been to Rhyl on 22 or 23 August, and her testimony had been torn to tatters. Hanratty's determination to tell 'the truth' had had the terrible result of which Sherrard had warned. He had not proved his new alibi, and he was tarred with all the ignominy of having changed his original alibi.

Before his execution, however, more Rhyl people came forward with evidence that seemed to substantiate his story. In the following six years, no less than eight substantial witnesses (many of them supported by friends and family) made powerful statements to back Hanratty's alibi.

Charlie Jones, a newspaper seller, said that in late August 1961 he was selling papers at Rhyl bus station, when a young man in his mid twenties got off a bus and asked him where he could find 'John', a fairground worker with a taxi. Jones had directed him into town.

Christopher Larman said he left Rhyl on 23 August, and on the previous night was doing a round of public houses to say goodbye to friends, when a young man approached him. He was carrying a suitcase and his hair looked rather strange. He asked where he could get lodgings for the night, and Larman sent him towards Kinmel Street. Larman identified Hanratty from his picture in the papers after he was convicted, and made a statement to his lawyers – a statement that was destined never to reach the Court of Appeal.

Mrs Margaret Walker, perhaps the strongest of all the witnesses, said that in the late evening of 22 August 1961 a young man with a London accent, wearing a dark suit, came to her house and asked her for lodgings for the night. She refused. Mrs Walker was absolutely certain of the date.

Mrs Ivy Vincent and Mrs Betty Davies, who also lived in South Kinmel Street, both said that a young man, whom they described exactly as had Mrs Walker (and exactly as Hanratty looked), came looking for lodgings during late August.

Trevor Dutton said he came into Rhyl on the morning of 23 August to put some money in a bank. The date was stamped into his bank-book, which he has kept. A young man with a London accent approached him and tried to sell him a gold watch. He described Hanratty's jacket.

Right: the guest-house run by Grace Jones (below right) where Hanratty said he stayed on the night of the murder. He had visited Rhyl to find fairground worker Terry Evans (below left), known to him as 'John'

Two separate police inquiries in 1967 and 1968 were set up to investigate all this evidence. The findings were never published, but the Home Secretary of the time, Roy Jenkins, refused to reopen the case. Nor was the extraordinary new information confirming Hanratty's alibi the only evidence after his death that he may have been wrongly convicted. Almost as soon as sentence was passed, another man started to confess to the A6 murder. He was none other than the original police suspect in the case: Peter Alphon.

One of the most fascinated observers in the public gallery during the long A6 trial was Jean Justice, a man with an abiding interest in criminal law. The case was only halfway through when Justice became convinced of Hanratty's innocence and intrigued by the curious role of Peter Alphon.

He met Alphon a few days after the conviction. The two men got on well. Slowly, Alphon began to confide in Justice. First, he drew a strange diagram that appeared to suggest that he had committed the A6 murder. Then he confessed to Justice, though always obliquely. When he discovered that Justice was alerting the police to this he was furious.

Confessions continue

Until Hanratty's execution in April, Alphon went on acting very strangely. He telephoned Charles France, Hanratty's former friend and a crucial witness in the A6 trial, uttering all sorts of terrible threats, including: 'If Hanratty dies, you die!' This threat was never tested, for on 16 March a fortnight before Hanratty's execution, France took an overdose of drugs and killed himself.

The confessions, usually by telephone, continued long after the execution. During 1963 and 1964, their form grew clearer. Alphon claimed that he had been hired to separate Michael Gregsten and Valerie Storie. He said he was paid £5000 to do it. The murder, he claimed, had not been planned, and had been partly an accident. He also claimed that there had been a plot to frame Hanratty. The gun, he said, had been planted under the back seat of the bus by Charles France, and France had also put the cartridge cases in the Vienna Hotel. Jean Justice drew up a dossier of these confessions and supplied it to Fenner Brockway, then MP for Eton and Slough. Brockway initiated a debate in the House of Commons on 2 August 1963 but the Home Secretary, Henry Brooke, refused to hold a public inquiry.

All Jean Justice's attempts to get some publicity for the curious behaviour of Peter Alphon came to nothing, but the issue gradually forced its way into the public's attention during 1965, with the publication of a book by Lord Russell of Liverpool, and during 1966 with further articles, and another debate, this time in the House of Lords.

Peter Alphon – the original suspect in the case, he confessed to the A6 murder at a world press conference in May 1967, five years after Hanratty's execution

In May 1967, Peter Alphon went to Paris and held a world press conference, where he confessed, in detail, to the A6 murder. Occasionally he would deny his confession, usually to some specially selected newspaper that he loathed. But he would always repeat it again to journalists or (in a specific and very detailed letter in 1969) to the Home Secretary. Since 1971, however, none of the people he had rung up regularly during the Sixties have heard from him.

It is, of course, extremely difficult to assess whether these confessions were genuine. The important details always remained the same, yet most commentators have dismissed Alphon as a 'crank' who 'flipped' after his brief experience as a suspect for the murder in 1961. Many people think he must have got some perverse pleasure from the notoriety that surrounded his confessions. All this may well be so. Nevertheless, the author finds it very curious that there are so many external facts that link Alphon with the A6 killer, and so very few, if any, that rule him out:

1) Alphon looks strikingly like the Identikit picture of the killer drawn up by Valerie Storie. His eyes, which are deep-set and hazel, are similar to those described by Valerie Storie immediately after she was raped and shot.

2) When excited, Alphon lapses into a cockney accent, and pronounces 'th' as 'f' like the murderer.
3) Alphon spent much of his childhood in the area of Slough and Taplow and knows it well, as the murderer had appeared to, whereas Hanratty claimed not to have done.
4) Alphon was the first suspect for the murder. He was hunted by the police, which proved that he had lied to them about where he was on that night.
5) For four or five days after the murder, Alphon behaved very strangely in his hotel room.
6) The motive Alphon ascribes to the A6 murder – the separation of the couple – seems far more credible in view of the chronology of the evening, than the 'lust' motive ascribed to Hanratty.
7) Alphon's driving – erratic and inexperienced – exactly fits that of the murderer, while Hanratty was a skilled driver and car thief.
8) Alphon was identified by a Richmond woman who was attacked by a man claiming that he was the A6 murderer.
9) According to the proprietress of the Old Station Inn, Taplow, Alphon was there on the night the murder had taken place.
10) Perhaps the most extraordinary evidence of all comes from Alphon's bank records, which he allowed journalist Paul Foot to examine. Alphon opened two accounts at Lloyds Bank in the Strand, almost immediately after he was released as a suspect for the A6 murder. From October 1961 to June 1962, £7569 was paid into these accounts, in units of between £100 and £800. The money was quickly spent and the accounts were closed. Almost all the payments were made in cash over the counter. Inquiries have shown that almost exactly £2500 was paid to Alphon in this period by newspapers who printed his story. Almost exactly £5000 is unaccounted for. Alphon is not a rich man, and in the time Jean Justice knew him he was always short of money. The coincidence of these big payments and what he said about his reward for doing the A6 murder is extraordinary.

It is remarkable that a 'crank', confessing from some love of notoriety, should so closely fit the bill of the murderer, even in the eyes of the investigating police at the time: so remarkable in fact, that it is difficult not to take his confessions seriously. After all, if Alphon *is* a crank, that hardly rules him out as the A6 murderer. Whoever committed the crime was, after all, certainly a crank, of the wildest and most violent variety.

About James Hanratty Paul Foot is more certain. His conclusion is that Hanratty most certainly did not commit the A6 murder, and that the hangman then did his duty on the public's behalf – in error.

Right: James Hanratty senior was convinced of his son's innocence and, right up to his death from cancer in 1978, was relentless in his campaign to clear Hanratty's name

2
Conspiracy and cover-up

When powerful people seek to suppress important information, either because it threatens their interests or exposes their evil or incompetence, the very structure of democracy is at risk.

Death of a plutonium worker

In rural Oklahoma on the evening of 13 November 1974, plutonium worker Karen Silkwood died when her car veered off the road and crashed. She was on her way to meet a *New York Times* reporter to discuss safety issues at the plant where she was a laboratory analyst. Silkwood had been openly concerned about health risks at the plant, and only days before, she had been contaminated with plutonium and was worried about the effects. How had this happened? Was her crash an accident?

At 7pm on Wednesday 13 November 1974 Karen Silkwood left a union meeting at the Hub Cafe in Crescent, Oklahoma. She was going to the Holiday Inn in Oklahoma City – 30 miles (48 kilometres) away – for a rendezvous with a *New York Times* reporter to talk about safety at the Kerr-McGee plutonium plant where she worked as a laboratory analyst. It was a cold, dry night with a light wind blowing. Karen got into her white 1973 Honda Civic and drove along Highway 74 south towards Oklahoma City, across the Cimarron River and past the plant.

The road was virtually straight, passing through flat farmland. About 7 miles (11 kilometres) from the Hub Café, her car veered across the road and on to the grass verge on the left hand side. After travelling 80 yards (70 metres), it crashed into a concrete culvert running under the highway, hitting the wall at about 45 miles (70 kilometres) per hour. The car ended up on its left side. Truck driver James Mullins spotted the white Honda at about 7.30pm and stopped to investigate. He noticed some papers strewn on the ground by the car. In the driver's seat was a young woman, the blood on her face partly dried. He saw that she was dead.

The exact reasons for Karen Silkwood's fatal car crash remain a mystery. But she is seen by many as a martyr for the anti-nuclear-power cause. However, the hazards of the nuclear industry had been the last thing on Silkwood's mind when she had joined Kerr-McGee in 1972. Indeed, she was excited at the prospect of taking up employment in the expanding field of nuclear power.

She was employed as a laboratory analyst at Kerr-McGee's plutonium plant on the Cimarron River in Oklahoma. The company manufactured fuel rods,

containing plutonium pellets, to be used in fast-breeder reactors. Silkwood performed quality-control tests on the plutonium pellets and checked the fuel rods for flaws.

It seems that the dangers of handling plutonium were not at that time fully realised and the risk of contamination at the plant was high. It has been said that teenagers were employed as cheap labour at the plant; training and information about health and safety were minimal; and workers were frequently found to be contaminated, or 'hot', having then to undergo brutal and painful 'scrubdown' treatment using harsh detergents.

Initially Silkwood was not particularly active in the union – the Oil, Chemical and Atomic Workers Union (OCAW) – which she joined soon after she started work at the plant. She had taken part in a small and ineffectual strike several months after she joined the company; the union was demanding higher wages, better training and improved health and safety programmes. But Karen later began to grow concerned about safety at the plant. In 1973 an accident with plutonium-contaminated waste caused seven workers to inhale 400 times the weekly limit of insoluble plutonium permitted by the Atomic Energy Commission (AEC).

On another occasion Silkwood herself was found to be contaminated. On 31 July 1974 she had been working a shift in the laboratory, checking plutonium pellets. After she had left, health physics technicians checked the air-sample filters for the three shifts that day and discovered that the filters used before and after Silkwood's shift were clean, while those used during it were highly contaminated. Puzzlingly, radiation tests showed that on her shift only Silkwood herself was contaminated.

Karen Silkwood's 1973 Honda Civic after the fatal crash. The reasons for the crash are still not clear: the road was virtually straight, and the surface was dry – and Karen was an experienced driver; yet her car veered off the road and over a concrete culvert, crashing into a wall

Complaints to AEC

A week later Silkwood was elected to the union bargaining committee; her concern was health and safety. The OCAW had fought hard for the health and safety of oil and chemical workers and now it decided to lodge complaints with the AEC about conditions at the plutonium plant. The AEC had been set up by Congress in 1946 with the dual role of stimulating uranium production and at the same time regulating the development of atomic energy. The union officials at the Cimarron plant were told to make studies and document incidents ready for a meeting with the AEC. Karen Silkwood took her role very seriously and began making notes on contamination incidents, asking questions of health technicians and interviewing workers.

However, Silkwood's union activities were unpopular with the company and fellow workers alike. The latter were afraid that her health and safety findings could lead to the plant shutting down. Union membership by August 1974 was at an all-time low and the company began a drive to decertify the OCAW as a representative body for the workers. A vote on the issue was to be taken on 16 October.

The three-person union committee – Silkwood, Jack Tice and Jerry Brewer – left for Washington on 26 September. There they met top union officials, including Tony Mazzocchi and his assistant Steve Wodka, and presented a catalogue of complaints to the AEC. The delegation accused Kerr-McGee of failing to keep levels of exposure to plutonium to a safe level, failing to monitor worker exposure and failing to educate and train workers adequately. It cited 39 cases to illustrate the allegations. The AEC decided to investigate.

In a move to convince workers at the plant that the union was necessary to protect their safety, the OCAW invited two experts to a union meeting to talk about the dangers of plutonium and the health risks involved. The week before the vote of 16 October, two nuclear scientists – Dean Abrahamson and Donald Geesaman – told the workers that plutonium was one of the deadliest substances in the world and caused cancer, and that the AEC 'safe'

Meryl Streep as laboratory analyst Karen Silkwood in the 1983 film *Silkwood*

standards were inadequate. The workers voted against decertifying the union, and negotiations began on the pay and conditions contract that was agreed annually between the company and the work force. Meanwhile, Karen Silkwood was preoccupied with a secret mission.

After the meeting with the AEC, she had told Mazzocchi that she suspected quality-controllers at the plant of touching up photographs of fuel rods to cover up flaws. She claimed that faults showing up on negatives were being painted out. Scientists disagree on what the consequences of a defective fuel rod in a reactor might be, but some say leaking fuel rods could cause a serious explosion. Mazzocchi realised the union could have a trump card in its hand – but concrete evidence was needed before the story could be leaked to a national newspaper. Such publicity would give the union a strong bargaining position in the contract negotiations with Kerr-McGee. Silkwood was to provide evidence for a meeting with *New York Times* reporter David Burnham on 13 November.

The more she investigated, the more anxious she became. She told a friend, former Cimarron worker James Noel, that she believed that 40 pounds (18 kilograms) of plutonium – enough to make three atomic bombs – had gone missing from the plant. In fact, 24 pounds (10.8 kilograms) of this was in 'hold-up' – the amount held in pipes at the plant. But the rest was unaccounted for. Silkwood lost weight and slept badly, even though she was taking sleeping pills prescribed by her doctor. She had started taking the pills in May 1974; by November she was using them as a tranquilliser; perhaps by that time she was taking two pills a day.

On 31 October Silkwood had a minor road accident. She swerved off the road and down an embankment, she said, to avoid hitting a cow. The right side of her front bumper was dented and the right rear lights smashed, but no damage to the *left* side of her car was recorded.

Five days later Silkwood was again found to be contaminated. The right sleeve and shoulder of her overalls showed a contamination level forty times higher than the AEC safe limit. Her nasal smear showed a high level of contamination, too, yet the air in the laboratory did not. Karen was scrubbed down. Next day her right arm was contaminated and her nostrils showed an even higher level of contamination. The following day the levels were very high. Checks on Silkwood's home showed high contamination levels and a urine sample contained plutonium from a batch workers had not handled for months.

Further tests

Karen was terrified; she believed she had plutonium in her lungs and that she was going to get cancer and die. Kerr-McGee agreed to send Silkwood, her boyfriend Drew Stephens and flatmate Sherri Ellis for further examination at the AEC-owned Los Alamos Scientific Laboratory in New Mexico. After two days of tests, Stephens and Ellis were told their results were 'statistically insignificant'. Dr George Volez informed Silkwood that her lungs contained half the maximum permissible lung burden stipulated by the AEC.

Silkwood, Stephens and Ellis flew back to Oklahoma City on the evening of Tuesday 12 November. Karen was apparently in good spirits and ready for the important meeting with the *New York Times* reporter the following night.

Next day she attended a bargaining meeting between the union and management as part of the negotiations for a new contract. At 5.30pm she went to a union meeting at the Hub Café in the small town of Crescent, about 6 miles (9 kilometres) north of the Cimarron plant. The meeting ended at 7pm. Silkwood had made a brief report on the day's negotiations. Her colleague Jean Jung said Silkwood was clutching a large brown folder and a notebook. She set off on the familiar road she travelled to and from work nearly every day. Less than 2 miles (3 kilometres) past the Kerr-McGee plant, her car left the road and hit the concrete culvert, and Karen was killed in the crash.

Truck driver James Mullins discovered the car at around 7.30 and Oklahoma Highway Patrol officer Rick Fagen and the Guthrie Fire Department ambulance were on the scene by about 8pm. Silkwood was cut out of the Honda and taken to Logan

County Hospital, where she was pronounced dead on arrival. Fagen picked up some papers strewn around the car and tossed them into the front seat. In her purse – lying near the car – were two marijuana cigarettes, a pill and half a tablet. Tests later showed that the pill was a sleeping pill and the half-tablet was too small to analyse. The wreck was hauled out of the culvert by garage owner Ted Sebring and one of his employees, Harold Smith. The car knocked against the wall as it was being recovered. Sebring, Smith and Fagen later gave conflicting reports as to whether the Honda was damaged further during the recovery. Such evidence was crucial to the theory that Silkwood's car was forced off the highway – as it left unanswered the question of how dents were caused to the left rear end of the car. Fagen did not find any skid marks on the road surface. He filed an accident report the following day, concluding that Silkwood, under the influence of drugs and alcohol, had fallen asleep at the wheel.

To other people, this account of Silkwood's death was not satisfactory. The union decided to hire accident investigator Adolphus Pipkin, who examined the wreck – by now in Drew Stephens' possession.

The dent on the rear left side of Silkwood's car, allegedly caused during its recovery from the scene of the crash. Yet the report made by accident investigator Adolphus Pipkin, who examined the wreck, supported the theory that the vehicle was forced off the road, by something travelling behind it

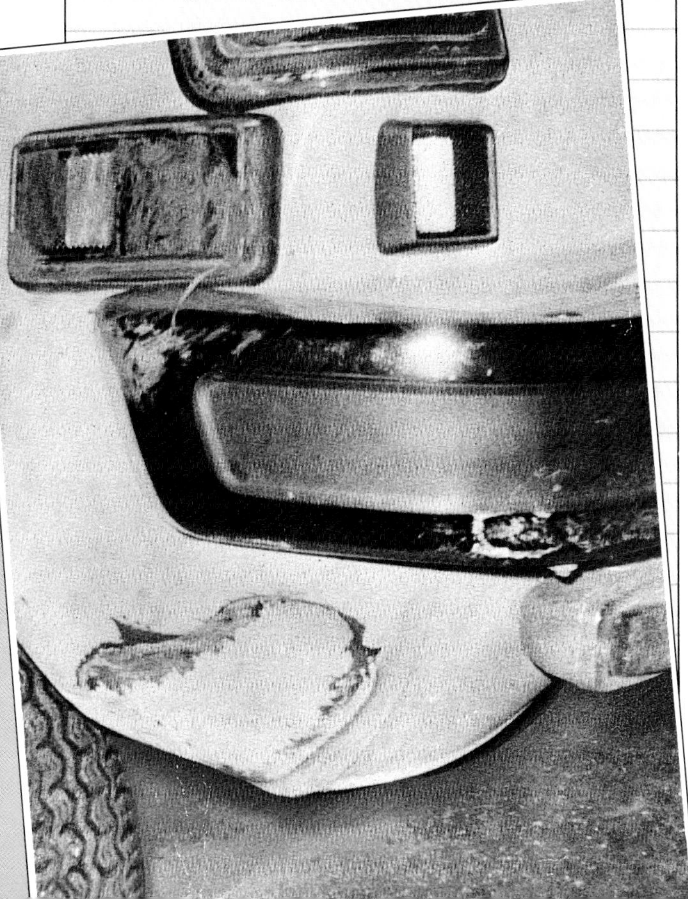

Pipkin's report, issued a month after Silkwood's death, noted that her car had gone off the left side of the road, whereas in other accidents where the driver had fallen asleep, the car had always drifted off to the right, because of the crown on the road surface. He also said the dents in the rear bumper of the Honda were made by something moving from the rear, rather than during removal, because of the direction of the scratches.

Pipkin had also remarked that the steering wheel of the Honda had been bent forward at the *sides*, indicating that the driver was awake and gripping the wheel with both hands at the time of the accident. If she had been asleep her body would have fallen against the wheel on impact and the pressure would have bent the wheel at the *top* and *bottom* instead. ABC television conducted tests with a car like Silkwood's on the stretch of road where the accident occurred. They concluded that if the driver had been asleep, the car would have come to a halt before hitting the concrete culvert. The autopsy on Silkwood concluded that her death was an accident and found methaqualone (sleeping pill) in her body. The union called in the FBI and asked the AEC to look into health and safety at the plutonium plant.

AEC report

The FBI investigation concluded five months later that Silkwood's death was accidental and closed the file. The AEC report dealt with three issues: Silkwood's contamination; the OCAW's allegations of falsification of quality-control records at Kerr-McGee; and complaints made by Silkwood, Tice and Brewer about health and safety at the plant. The AEC concluded that Silkwood had been contaminated outside the Cimarron plant and that she had eaten and inhaled plutonium. The plutonium that had contaminated Silkwood's flat had come from pellet lot 29 which had been delivered to Washington in August 1974, apart from a sample kept in a vault at the Kerr-McGee plant. Silkwood had not worked directly with lot 29 nor had she had access to the vault. It was never reported whether any of the sample had gone missing.

On the question of quality-control, the AEC reported that laboratory analyst Scott Dotter had admitted touching up negatives of fuel rods with a felt-tipped pen. He said this was only to cover up flaws in the negatives, not the rods. He had done this without the knowledge or approval of his superiors. An AEC analysis of the negatives supported Dotter's explanation; it reported that, 'None of the markings was used to obscure weld defects themselves.' The AEC report did not find serious cause for concern over safety conditions at the plant. Although it substantiated 20 of the 39 allegations put forward by Silkwood, Tice and Brewer, only three of these were

Danny Sheehan (above), chief counsel for the Silkwood estate during the court case against Kerr-McGee, and Sara Nelson (below), who co-founded the Supporters of Silkwood organisation to campaign for justice

found to be violations of the AEC rules, and these, the report said, did not threaten the health and safety of the workers.

After Silkwood's death the Kerr-McGee company took vigorous security steps. It closed the plant for two weeks in December as AEC inspectors carried out their investigations. Kerr-McGee closed the Cimarron plant for good in January 1976 claiming that it had not been as profitable as the company had wished. The decision came shortly after the Nuclear Regulatory Commission (NRC) had recommended certain improvements be made there.

When the Justice Department dropped the Silkwood case, the National Organisation of Women (NOW) took it up. Its aim was to lobby congress to investigate the contamination and death of Silkwood. A sub-group, the Supporters of Silkwood (SOS), was formed and, a year after Silkwood's death, they took a 7000-named petition to congressmen Senator Lee Metcalf and Senator Abraham Ribicoff, who agreed to hold an investigation. In charge of the case would be Win Turner, chief counsel to the Government Operations Subcommittee, John Dingell, the chairman of the House Subcommittee on Energy and Power and congressional investigator Peter Stockton. They gained some access to FBI files on Silkwood but gave up by 1977 because of red tape.

Civil suit

The SOS then brought in civil rights lawyer Danny Sheehan and filed a civil suit against Kerr-McGee. There were three charges: 1) negligence by Kerr-McGee in the handling of plutonium that contaminated Silkwood; 2) conspiracy by 23 members of the Kerr-McGee Corporation to deprive Silkwood of her civil rights: for instance, trying to prevent Silkwood and others improving conditions at the plant; punishing Silkwood, Tice and Brewer for complaining to the AEC about conditions at the plant; and allowing surveillance and harassment of Silkwood and others; and 3) violation of Silkwood's civil rights as members of the FBI joined the conspiracy.

Sheehan engaged the help of private investigator Bill Taylor, who claimed to have learnt from an FBI 'mole' that a lot of evidence about the Silkwood case was being covered up and revealed that Silkwood had been under heavy surveillance for some time before her death; he also claimed there were transcripts of taped conversations in the Silkwood file.

Three different judges presided over the court proceedings. The first one – Judge Luther Eubanks – resigned from the case after Sheehan filed an application to have him removed because of remarks he had made in court that threw doubt on his impartiality. The second – Judge Luther Bohanon – was replaced by Judge Frank Theis after Bohanon's connection with Robert Kerr, the founder of the Kerr-McGee Corporation, was discovered: Kerr had apparently helped secure Bohanon's judgeship.

In September 1978 Judge Theis dropped the conspiracy charges against Kerr-McGee and the FBI defendants. Even if, he argued, Sheehan had been able to prove the conspiracy and cover-up, there was no civil law under which the Silkwood estate could sue for damages. He also said that the Civil Rights

Act of 1871 – on which Sheehan had based much of his case – applied only to blacks and other minorities. The Silkwood team now concentrated on the negligence charge. The SOS collected $452,000, through loans, benefits and contributions, to cover the cost of the investigations and trial, and brought in experts to testify about the dangers of plutonium. Under the Oklahoma law of 'strict liability', the owner of a dangerous substance is liable for injury caused by it.

In order to win the case, the Silkwood team had to prove that:
1) Plutonium is 'ultrahazardous'
2) Silkwood had been contaminated with plutonium owned by Kerr-McGee
3) Silkwood did not contaminate herself
4) Contamination had led to personal injury of Silkwood between 5 and 13 November
5) Kerr-McGee was wantonly negligent in protecting its workers.

Silkwood supporters putting up a memorial sign at the scene of the fatal accident after the court case brought against Kerr-McGee by the Supporters of Silkwood. They succeeded in proving Kerr-McGee's negligence, and an award of $10.5 million was made to the Silkwood estate. But for many the case is not yet closed – and the question of how Karen died remains unanswered

The claim was for $1.5 million compensation for Silkwood's physical injury and emotional pain and $10 million damages as punishment to Kerr-McGee. After expenses the money would go to Silkwood's three children. The trial – Oklahoma's longest – began in March 1979 and lasted 10 weeks. Nuclear physicist and medical doctor John Gofman explained the link between plutonium and cancer and attacked the AEC and NCR safe limits. He was alarmed that Kerr-McGee had failed to inform staff at the plant of the dangers involved in working with plutonium, at the lack of training and the inadequate security there. Former health physics technician Kenneth Plowman said there was one contamination after another, pellets were thrown around and bags of waste hidden when the AEC inspectors visited the plant. Former Kerr-McGee worker Ron Hammock testified that faulty welds were ground down with sandpaper to make them look acceptable.

The Silkwood team won the case and the trial set certain precedents: Judge Theis defined plutonium as 'ultrahazardous' and defined injury in radiation cases ('injury' could be to cells, bone or tissue and might not be immediately visible or detectable). The Silkwood estate was awarded $10.5 million. Kerr-McGee appealed, but in 1984 the Supreme Court upheld the ruling. Silkwood partisans saw this as a victory, but questions still remained unanswered.

Bill Taylor

The circumstances of Karen Silkwood's fatal car crash have not yet been discovered and no witnesses have come forward. There is still the question of whether Silkwood was under surveillance by the FBI, how her contamination occurred, and whether plutonium had gone missing from the plant as she had claimed. The Silkwood estate is still fighting to bring the conspiracy charges to court.

Bill Taylor for one was not satisfied that the case was closed. He has had no concrete evidence to go on, only theories and hunches. Taylor has continued his search to uncover fresh clues, often returning to the scene of Silkwood's death. One important lead strengthened his belief. He claimed that his source at the FBI had leaked information about the top secret Silkwood file. In it, he alleged, was an account of Silkwood's car crash. If such information were ever to come to light in detail, the investigation into the Silkwood case would have a fresh start and the truth about the tragic affair might eventually be revealed. But for now the events surrounding the death of plutonium worker Karen Silkwood remain a mystery.

Tragedy at Chappaquiddick Island

On a warm midsummer night in July 1969, a car plunged from a bridge on Chappaquiddick Island, off the coast of Massachusetts. Next morning, the body of 28-year-old Mary Jo Kopechne was found in the submerged vehicle and Senator Edward Kennedy – the last presidential hope of the famous American family – informed the police that he had actually been driving the car at the time of the accident. Later, it was established that Mary Jo had been alive – and conscious – for a time after immersion in the pond. Why had Kennedy delayed telling the police for so long? Could the young woman have been saved? His television broadcast to the nation in which he tried to give a satisfactory explanation of the night's events was met with disbelief and cynicism, and many people still believe that an intricate and widespread cover-up operation had taken place

As dawn broke on Saturday 19 July 1969 two early morning fishermen – Robert Samuel and Joseph Capparella – crossed on the small, two-car ferry *On Time* from Edgartown to Chappaquiddick Island, drove east along Chappaquiddick Main Street and turned the car off onto the dirt track that led down across Dyke Bridge to the Atlantic Ocean. Dyke Bridge straddles Poucha Pond and is about three quarters of a mile (1.2 kilometres) from Main Street. After an hour's fruitless casting, the fishermen made their way back from the beach towards Poucha Pond and the bridge. Samuel slowed down to a crawl to see if there was any sign of fish. Something shiny glinted out of the water on the south side of the bridge, about 30 feet (10 metres) out. Samuel stopped the car and got out for a better look. The outline of an upturned car could just be made out under the water.

The Edgartown Chief of Police, Dominick Arena, went immediately to the scene and attempted to dive down to investigate the vehicle. He was 6 foot 4 inches (1.93 metres) tall and a strong swimmer, but the current in Poucha Pond defeated him. He pulled himself up onto the undercarriage of the car, just below the surface, where he sat waiting for the diver he had summoned.

At 8.45am the fire chief, two firemen and a scuba diver, John Farrar, arrived on the scene. Arena asked one of his men to find out, from the submerged car's licence number, the name of the owner. Within minutes Arena was told that the car was registered to Edward M. Kennedy. Farrar saw that the car had rolled over completely. Diving down into the swirling water, he saw a flash of white through the rear window. Two sandalled feet came into view. Farrar quickly stuck his head in a shattered rear window. He knew people had sometimes survived as long as five hours in submerged cars. But when he touched the thigh of the young woman he realised that rigor mortis had set in and that she had been dead for hours. It was apparent, however, that she had been alive – and conscious – for a time after immersion in the pond. Her body was fixed in a sitting position, her arms outstretched, and her fingers gripped the edge of the seat; she appeared to have been craning her neck to get the last bit of air in the car. Her blue eyes were open and her lips were parted slightly. Farrar brought her body up out of the water.

Police Chief Arena later said that when he first saw the body he thought to himself: 'She looks like a child's doll. She's dressed for a party. Neat and nice. Buttons all buttoned, everything in place, like a child going to a party.' The blonde girl was demure-looking and petite in her black slacks and white blouse. He wondered if she was a Kennedy and if this incident meant another tragic death for the family.

The police chief called for the medical examiner, the undertaker and the vehicle recovery service. Farrar dived again and reappeared with a gold chain and a handbag. The chain had fallen from the girl's waist as he was bringing her to the surface. The purse contained two keys to rooms at the Katama Shores Motor Inn, 2 miles (3 kilometres) outside Edgartown, a little money, some personal items and a US Senate pass in the name of Rosemary Keough. She was one of six girls who had checked into, but not slept at, the motel the previous night.

Death by drowning

Dr Donald Mills soon arrived on the scene with the undertakers. Dr Mills, a modest, unassuming man, who had practised in Edgartown for 35 years, noticed white foam and a speck of blood around the nose and mouth of the dead girl – a sign of death by drowning. He could see no obvious injuries or broken bones. He pulled down her slacks and discovered the young woman was wearing nothing underneath them. He pushed against the wall of her stomach and decided that she probably was not pregnant. He tipped her body over to examine her back and water gushed out of her mouth. 'Death by drowning,' he said. 'Not a question about it. They didn't need me for this one. Well, I'm finished. You can put her in the hearse.'

Arena could not work out why the accident had not been reported. Just before the doctor and undertaker had arrived on the scene he had received some odd news from Jonathan Ahlbum, the driver of the tow truck summoned to lift Kennedy's Oldsmobile from Poucha Pond. Ahlbum told Arena that on the way to the bridge he had seen Kennedy standing in

Edgartown Police Chief Dominick Arena – he tried to reach the submerged vehicle, but was defeated by the current

John Farrar, who recovered the body of Mary Jo Kopechne from the bottom of Poucha Pond

the ferry house, which was on the Chappaquiddick side of the creek.

Arena telephoned headquarters shortly afterwards and was told that Kennedy was at the Edgartown Police Station and wanted to talk to him.

Kennedy and his two friends, his cousin Joe Gargan and attorney Paul Markham, had made themselves at home in Arena's office by the time Arena arrived. The senator appeared a little depressed, but clear-eyed and composed. Arena said he was sorry about the accident. Then he tried to conceal his surprise when Kennedy told him: 'Yes, I know about it. I was the driver.'

Arena examined the contents of the handbag brought up by scuba diver Farrar, and said: 'Well, do you happen to know where Rosemary Keough comes from? I think we'd better notify her next of kin.' Kennedy paused, then he said: 'Well, it wasn't Rosemary Keough. It was Mary Jo Kopechne. I've already notified her parents.'

Kennedy agreed to write out a statement. Meanwhile Arena returned to the scene where rescuers were still looking for bodies. His deputy Christopher 'Huck' Look was watching the car being hauled out of the pond. Was it the one he had seen the night before, the one that had driven off at speed to avoid him? His suspicions were confirmed and he told Arena what he had seen in the early hours of 19 July.

At about 12.45am on the Chappaquiddick road, Look said he had seen a black sedan turn into Dyke Road – the dirt road that led to Dyke Bridge. There appeared to have been a man and woman in the front, and someone – or some object – in the rear. The car stopped and, thinking they had lost their way, Deputy Look had stopped his car and got out. He had approached the car but when he was about 30 feet (10 metres) away it had roared down the dirt road in a cloud of dust.

Above: curious spectators flock to the scene of the fatal accident at Dyke Bridge to watch the recovery of Kennedy's car from the water
Inset: when the Oldsmobile was hauled from the pond, the doors were found to be locked and the windows smashed

When Arena returned to his office, Kennedy was pacing the floor and Paul Markham was at a desk writing in longhand. Arena asked how the statement was going. Kennedy did not answer, but Markham said: 'It's coming along.' A few minutes later, Markham handed the paper to Arena, saying it should be typed. Arena sat at his desk, put paper in the typewriter and typed the short statement Markham had written for Kennedy. The following is a complete transcription:

On July 18, 1969, at approximately 11.15 on Chappaquiddick Island, Martha's Vineyard, I was driving my car on Main Street on my way to get the ferry back to Edgartown.

I was unfamiliar with the road and turned onto Dyke Road instead of bearing left on Main Street. After proceeding for approximately a half mile [0.8 kilometres] on Dyke Road I descended a hill and came upon a narrow bridge. The car went off the side of the bridge. There was one passenger with me, Miss Kopechne, a former secretary of my brother Robert Kennedy. The car turned over and sank into the water and landed with the roof resting on the bottom. I attempted to open the door and window of the car but have no recollection of how I got out of the car. I came to the surface then repeatedly dove down to the car in an attempt to see if the passenger was still in the car. I was unsuccessful in the attempt. I was exhausted and in a state of shock. I recall walking back to where my friends were eating. There was a car parked in front of the cottage and I climbed into the back seat. I then asked for someone to bring me back to Edgartown. I remember walking around for a period of time and then going back to my hotel room. When I fully realized what had happened this morning, I immediately contacted the police.

Ten hours had elapsed since the accident. Kennedy's statement amounted to a confession that he had left the scene of a fatal accident – a serious matter. As far as Kennedy was concerned the first part of this mess had been tidied up.

Surprisingly, there was no autopsy carried out on Mary Jo's body, either then or later. On Saturday afternoon she was flown home to Pennsylvania, and on the following Tuesday Kennedy himself flew out to the funeral. On Friday, at a court hearing at Martha's Vineyard Kennedy was given a two-month suspended jail term and a year's driving ban for leaving the scene of the accident.

By pleading guilty to a minor charge, Kennedy had avoided a public examination, under oath, of the circumstances surrounding the girl's death. That night he went on television to appeal to the nation. The broadcast, made from the family home at Hyannis Port, Massachusetts, was carried by all the major American networks and beamed around the world. The 37-year-old senator appeared tense but in control as he delivered the following broadcast:

'My fellow citizens, I have requested this opportunity to talk to the people of Massachusetts about the tragedy which happened last Friday evening. . . .

'On Chappaquiddick Island, off Martha's Vineyard, I attended on Friday evening, July 18, a cook-out I had encouraged and helped sponsor for the devoted group of Kennedy campaign secretaries. When I left the party, around 11.15pm, I was accompanied by one of those girls, Miss Mary Jo Kopechne. Mary Jo was one of the most devoted members of the staff of Senator Robert Kennedy. For this reason, and because she was such a gentle, kind and idealistic person, all of us tried to help her feel that she had a home with the Kennedy family.

'There is no truth, no truth whatsoever, to the widely-circulated suspicions of immoral conduct that have been levelled at my behaviour and hers regarding that evening. There has never been a private relationship between us of any kind. I know of nothing in Mary Jo's conduct on that or any other occasion – the same is true of the other girls at that party – that would lend any substance to such ugly speculation about their character. Nor was I driving under the influence of liquor.

'Little over one mile [1.5 kilometres] away, the car I was driving on an unlit road went off a narrow bridge which had no guard-rails and was built on a left angle to the road. The car overturned in a deep pond and immediately filled with water. I remember thinking as the cold water rushed in around my head that I was for certain drowning. Then water entered my lungs and I actually felt the sensation of drowning. But somehow I struggled to the surface alive. I made immediate and repeated efforts to save Mary Jo by diving into the strong and murky current but succeeded only in increasing my state of utter exhaustion and alarm.

'My conduct and conversations during the next several hours to the extent that I can remember them make no sense to me at all. Although my doctors informed me that I suffered a cerebral concussion as well as shock, I do not seek to escape responsibility for my actions by placing the blame either on the physical, emotional trauma brought on by the accident or on anyone else. I regard as indefensible the fact that I did not report the accident to the police immediately.

'Instead of looking directly for a telephone number after lying exhausted in the grass for an undetermined time, I walked back to the cottage where the party was being held and requested the help of two friends, my cousin Joseph Gargan and Paul Markham, and directed them to return immediately to the scene with me – this was some time after midnight – in order to undertake a new effort to dive down and locate Miss Kopechne. Their strenuous efforts, undertaken at some risks to their own lives, also proved futile.

Edward Kennedy puts his case to the nation on prime-time television a week after the tragedy at Chappaquiddick. Some Americans were almost hysterical in their support of the senator; others rejected his account as a cover-up

Awful curse

'All kinds of scrambled thoughts – all of them confused, some of them irrational, many of them which I cannot recall and some which I would not have seriously entertained under normal circumstances – went through my mind during this period.

'They were reflected in the various inexplicable, inconsistent and inconclusive things I said and did, including such questions as whether the girl might still be alive somewhere out of that immediate area, whether some awful curse did actually hang over all the Kennedys, whether there was some justifiable reason for me to doubt what had happened and to delay my report, whether somehow the awful weight of this incredible incident might in some way pass from my shoulders. I was overcome, I'm frank to say, by a jumble of emotions – grief, fear, doubt, exhaustion, panic, confusion and shock.

'Instructing Gargan and Markham not to alarm Mary Jo's friends that night, I had them take me to the ferry crossing. The ferry having shut down for the night, I suddenly jumped into the water and impulsively swam across, nearly drowning once again in the effort, and returned to my hotel about 2am and collapsed in my room.

'I remember going out at one point and saying something to the room clerk.

'In the morning, with my mind somewhat more lucid, I made an effort to call a family legal advisor, Burke Marshall, from a public telephone on the Chappaquiddick side of the ferry and belatedly reported the accident to the Martha's Vineyard police.

'Today, as I mentioned, I felt morally obligated to plead guilty to the charge of leaving the scene of the accident. No words on my part can possibly express the terrible pain and suffering I feel over this tragic incident. This last week has been an agonising one for me and the members of my family, and the grief we feel over the loss of a wonderful friend will remain with us for the rest of our lives.

'These events, the publicity, innuendo and whispers which have surrounded them and my admission of guilt this morning raise the question in my mind of whether my standing among the people of my state has been so impaired that I should resign my seat in the United States Senate. . . . For me this will be a difficult decision to make.

'It has been seven years since my first election to the Senate. You and I share many memories – some of them have been glorious, some have been very sad. The opportunity to work with you and serve Massachusetts has made my life worthwhile.

'And so I ask you tonight, people of Massachusetts, to think this through with me. In facing this decision, I seek your advice and opinion. In making it, I seek your prayers. For this is a decision that I will have finally to make on my own.

Four of the party girls arrive at Martha's Vineyard for the inquest. From left to right: Susan Tannenbaum, Nancy Lyons, Esther Newburgh and Rosemary Keough

'It has been written a man does what he must in spite of personal consequences, in spite of obstacles and dangers and pressures, and that is the basis of all human morality. Whatever may be the sacrifices he faces, if he follows his conscience – the loss of his friends, his fortune, his contentment, even the esteem of his fellow men – each man must decide for himself the course he will follow. The stories of past courage cannot supply courage itself. For this, each man must look into his own soul.

'I pray that I can have the courage to make the right decision. Whatever is decided and whatever the future holds for me, I hope that I shall be able to put this most recent tragedy behind me and make some further contribution to our state and mankind, whether it be in public or private life. Thank you and goodnight.'

The reaction in America to the broadcast ranged from cold, cynical rejection of it as a cover-up to almost hysterical support. Somewhere in the middle was the majority – people genuinely puzzled by the tragedy and by Edward Kennedy's explanation of how the tragedy happened.

Kennedy's statement was designed to dispel rumours about the party and his relationship with Mary Jo. It suggested a kindly, paternalistic relationship between the senator and Miss Kopechne – he helping her to get over the death, in 1968, of Robert Kennedy. The next ordeal was the inquest on Mary Jo, from which press and public were excluded.

'Criminal conduct'

Kennedy and his friends stuck to his original story. Judge James Boyle had problems with Kennedy's statement. In his findings he noted: 'I infer a reasonable and probable explanation of the totality of the facts is that Kennedy and Kopechne did *not* intend to return to Edgartown at that time; that Kennedy did not intend to drive to the ferryslip and his turn on Dyke Road was intentional.'

The judge concluded that, if Kennedy knew of the Dyke Bridge hazard – as he must have done, having driven on the road on previous occasions – 'his operation of the vehicle constituted criminal conduct'.

The inquest transcript was not released until three months later – at the end of April 1970. Kennedy had provided and paid for lawyers for the five party girls and for three of his male friends.

But in March 1970 Leslie Leland, foreman of the Duke's County Grand Jury on Martha's Vineyard, had formally asked the district attorney to convene the jury. He declared: 'I just feel we have certain duties and responsibilities as jury members to fulfil. A great deal of time has passed since the girl died and it is time the public found out what happened.'

The jury had opened in special session under Democratic Party stalwart Judge Wilfred Paquet, a

Paul Markham (left) and Joe Gargan, who apparently helped Kennedy in his attempts to rescue Mary Jo

Kennedy supporter. He had lectured the jurors for an hour and a half about the limitations of their responsibilities. To the astonishment of the jurors they were not provided with a transcript from the inquest. They could consider only information given to them by the district attorney, or facts of which they had personal knowledge. The district attorney had provided practically no information, and the jurors had only their suspicions of a cover-up. Had they seen the transcript, which was not released until the following month, they would have read Judge Boyle's verdict on Kennedy's 'criminal conduct'. Hampered by such restrictions, the jury disbanded. When the inquest testimony was released, Kennedy put out a statement rejecting Judge Boyle's critical report and concluding: 'For myself, I plan no further statement on this tragic matter.'

It was apparent that Kennedy's account of the tragedy at Chappaquiddick was inadequate for many people and raised numerous doubts and questions. The discrepancies and mysteries led to various theories and speculation about what actually *did* happen. The most obvious oddity in Kennedy's story is that he drove down Dyke Road *by mistake*. Twice that day he had driven on Dyke Road to go to the beach for a swim. It is a 90-degree turn off a metalled road onto the rough, bumpy dirt-track that is known as Dyke Road.

Kennedy said his speed on Dyke Road was 20 miles (30 kilometres) per hour. But an expert on automobile accidents commissioned by the *Reader's Digest*, using a computer and government-approved techniques, decided that Kennedy was driving at around 34 miles (53 kilometres) per hour.

This expert, Raymond R. McHenry, also concluded that by approaching the bridge at 34 miles (55 kilometres) per hour – and it could have been faster, McHenry estimated – Kennedy invited disaster. Why was he driving so fast?

How did Kennedy escape from the submerged car? In his statement, his memory of the events immediately after the car left the road is very vague. When the Oldsmobile was recovered from the pond, the doors were found to be locked and three of the windows were either open or smashed in. Given that the vehicle had ended up on its roof, the force of the water pouring in through the window would have been extremely strong. If Kennedy – a large-framed man, 6 foot 2 inches (1.88 metres) tall – could manage to get out of the car, why was it impossible for Mary Jo – slender and 5 foot 2 inches (1.57 metres) tall – to do the same?

Air pocket

Could Kennedy, along with Markham and Gargan, have succeeded in rescuing Miss Kopechne? Water safety experts concluded, after an analysis of the water current, that it would *not* have posed an 'insurmountable obstacle to a poised and experienced swimmer determined to rescue someone'.

Could Mary Jo have been saved? Diver John Farrar, who brought up her body, said he thought she had been breathing from an air pocket. Gene Frieh, the undertaker, later disagreed with Dr Mills, who said she had drowned. Frieh found the body held 'very little moisture' and told reporters that death 'was due to suffocation rather than drowning'. Farrar gave another reason why he thought Mary Jo had not drowned: the body he brought up was too buoyant to be full of water. If help had been summoned immediately, it is likely that Mary Jo could have been saved.

How – and why – Kennedy had actually made it back to Edgartown was equally puzzling. The 500-foot (150-metre) channel had strong currents and – expert swimmers stressed – a person would have to be in a very fit state to cross it successfully. The validity of Kennedy's statement relies to a great extent on the claim that he was exhausted and confused as a result of the accident, and he had apparently just been involved in strenuous attempts to rescue Mary Jo. No one saw him arrive back at the Shiretown Inn in wet clothes.

Kennedy's excuse for his otherwise inexplicable behaviour was that the accident had left him in a state of shock and confusion. Dr Robert Watt – Kennedy's family doctor – who examined the senator on his return to Hyannis Port, said that Kennedy was suffering from 'a possible concussion and an acute cervical strain'. The morning after the accident, however, Kennedy showed no signs of exhaustion, confusion or neck strain. He was seen wearing a prescribed neck brace on only one occasion – at the funeral of Mary Jo Kopechne on 22 July.

All the people involved in the Chappaquiddick incident have kept quiet about the events of 18 July. It has never been satisfactorily explained just what sort of a party took place that evening or how much drink was consumed. No thorough examination of Mary Jo Kopechne's body was carried out. Had she had sexual intercourse prior to the accident? Was she perhaps pregnant? Did she die by drowning or by asphyxiation? Were there, as some reports have suggested, bloodstains on her blouse? The process of removing her body from the scene of the accident was swiftly carried out, as was her burial several days later; attempts to exhume the corpse and perform an autopsy were stalled and, eventually, quashed. The fact that the inquest was held behind closed doors succeeded in further concealing the truth.

Various odd rumours and theories have been put forward in an attempt to reveal the truth about Chappaquiddick. Some have speculated that a third person was in the car with Kennedy and Mary Jo. Another strange report about the night was that the senator's nephew, Bobby Kennedy's son Joe, had been seen wandering through the streets of Edgartown, soaking wet, at about 3am. Joe, who was in his late teens, had been participating in the regatta that weekend. Was Kennedy covering up for someone? One of the strongest theories is that Kennedy was not even in the car and knew nothing of the accident until the next day. But Deputy Look had reported having seen two or three people in the car.

Senator Edward Kennedy at the Democratic convention in August 1980. Kennedy failed to seize the Democratic nomination from Jimmy Carter. His involvement in the Chappaquiddick affair, and the inconsistencies in his account of what happened, wrecked Kennedy's reputation and had a detrimental effect on his political career

Political career

In his book *The Bridge At Chappaquiddick*, Jack Olsen expounds another theory. Kennedy might have been driving towards the beach intentionally with Mary Jo. When Look approached the car at the junction, Kennedy might have feared a scandal that would have damaged his political career (his wife Joan was at home, three months pregnant at the time). After the car sped off, Kennedy might have stopped further down the road and got out, telling Mary Jo to drive on alone for a short distance in case the officer followed them. Kennedy might then have decided to return to the motel, assuming that Mary Jo would turn up next day. Both these theories beg one big question, however. Why would Kennedy say he had been in the car at the time of the accident? Surely any scandal that arose over the matter would be less of a blow to his future political career than being directly implicated in an accident that involved a dead girl?

The most recent comment that Kennedy has made about the Chappaquiddick affair was during a television interview in 1979 when he was asked: 'Do you think, senator, that anybody will ever believe your explanation?' His response amounted to garbled nonsense, which was almost incoherent.

Will the press and television bring up the Chappaquiddick affair again if Edward Kennedy seeks the nation's highest office? America's principal newspaper, the *New York Times*, has commented: 'There ought to be no hesitation to rake over this puzzling affair. If Mr Kennedy used his enormous influence to protect himself and his career by leading a cover-up of misconduct – there would hang over him not just a cloud of tragedy but also one of corruption, of the Watergate kind. And as we know from Watergate, there is no graver question for a president than whether he can be trusted to respect the law.' As Kennedy himself commented with regard to President Richard Nixon's cover-up of Watergate: 'If this country stands for anything, it stands for the principle that no man is above the law.'

The setting for the party on 18 July was the tiny Lawrence cottage situated in the centre of Chappaquiddick Island, on a quiet lane with the Chappaquiddick fire station as its near neighbour. It was owned by a New York lawyer and rented out at weekends. It had a combined living room and kitchen, two bedrooms, each with twin beds, a bathroom and no telephone. Senator Edward Kennedy's cousin, Joe Gargan, had made the arrangements to rent the cottage for a couple of days that weekend, and a cook-out party was planned for the Friday night for the reunion of various former secretaries and aides of Robert Kennedy during his 1968 presidential campaign.

There were 12 people at the gathering. Besides Kennedy, there were four married men under 40 – Joe Gargan, attorney Paul Markham, lawyer Charles Tretter and Raymond La Rosa (apparently an experienced scuba diver) – and 60-year-old chauffeur John Crimmins. The six unmarried women – all under 30 – were Mary Jo Kopechne, Susan Tannenbaum, Maryellen Lyons, Ann 'Nancy' Lyons, Rosemary Keough and Esther Newburgh.

The party had started at round 8.30pm. Two cars were available at the cottage – Kennedy's black Oldsmobile 88 and a rented white Valiant. Vodka, rum, scotch and beer were available, steaks were barbecued and Rosemary Keough and Charles Tretter drove back to Edgartown in the Oldsmobile to pick up a portable radio to liven up the party. Foster and Dodie Silva, who lived just down the road from the party cottage, later said they had heard 'raucous singing', chanting, cheering and yelling coming from the cottage until about 1am.

Reports of Kennedy's departure and return are sparse and vague. Only one of the partygoers has since talked about the party to newsmen; Esther Newburgh has described the get-together as a 'strictly for fun affair' but was emphatic that there had been very little drinking during the evening. None of the guests admitted to having had more than three drinks each.

Kennedy and Mary Jo Kopechne's absence was noticed some time after 11.15pm, according to the guests, who assumed that the pair had returned to Edgartown. Some of the guests had been aware that Gargan and Markham had left the party for a time and later returned. Nothing had been said of the accident or rescue attempts. Several people went for a late-night stroll. When they realised the last scheduled ferry had gone, the ten remaining guests spent the night at the cottage – most of them bedding down in a primitive fashion, with blankets, on the floor.

The following morning, the girls were driven back to Edgartown, and all the guests had left Martha's Vineyard by the time the questioning about the accident began. The cottage had been cleared up; the landlady found only a few Coke bottles when she arrived at the cottage on the Saturday morning. The keeper of the town dump reported seeing three unopened bottles of gin discarded there that morning, however, suggesting that someone had been desperate to cover up evidence of alcohol.

Rumours of drunken orgies abounded but no concrete evidence emerged to substantiate any of them. The veil of silence has remained carefully intact so that the full truth about the party at the secluded cottage – which may have thrown some light on the accident itself – has not yet been revealed.

The living room of the tiny cottage. After the departure of Edward Kennedy and Mary Jo Kopechne, the remaining partygoers stayed the night here, although most of them were booked into hotels on Martha's Vineyard

The cottage that was rented for the reunion party on 18 July 1969. Just what sort of a gathering took place here no one – apart from the 12 guests – really knows

Assassination at Manila airport

Benigno Aquino, affectionately known as 'Ninoy', charismatic leader of the political opposition in the Philippines, flew into Manila airport at midday on 21 August 1983. Within minutes of stepping off his aircraft he was lying dead on the ground with a bullet through his head. Beside him on the tarmac lay the body of a second man. This, claimed the government of Ferdinand Marcos, was Rolando Galman, who had penetrated the massive security arrangements and gunned Aquino down. The authorities maintained that Galman was a hit-man working for the communists, but at the commission of enquiry some very different stories about him emerged and many people suspected the Marcos government itself of the crime. Less than three years later, Ferdinand Marcos was deposed and Aquino's widow Corazon became the country's new leader

As China Airlines (CAL) Flight 811 began its descent to the international airport at Manila, capital of the Philippines, a round-faced, bespectacled passenger disappeared into the lavatory. When he came out, he was wearing a lightweight bullet-proof vest beneath the jacket of his white safari suit. 'Of course, if they hit me in the head, I'm a goner anyway,' he joked to his companions. Just before the aircraft landed, he bowed his head briefly in prayer, then sat back, calm and composed.

It was approximately 1pm on 21 August 1983, and Benigno 'Ninoy' Aquino was coming home from three years of self-imposed political exile in the United States to lead the growing opposition to the government of President Ferdinand Marcos. Aquino was anything but a welcome guest to Marcos, who had once kept him in prison for more than five years. The Philippines government had refused to issue him with a passport to re-enter his own country; more seriously, it had warned that his safety could not be guaranteed if he did come back.

Aquino was travelling under an assumed name yet, at the stopover in Taipeh before the final leg of his trip, he had received alarming news when he had telephoned his wife Corazon in the United States. His face white with shock, Aquino had told one of his party: 'They're going to get me at the airport, then kill the guy who did it.'

Aquino's arrival in Manila was expected with rapture by his many supporters. The capital was festooned with yellow ribbons, symbol of his party, and some 20,000 excited Filipinos had gathered at the airport to welcome him, among them the politician's 75-year-old mother. And the government had prepared its own greeting – a massive security operation at the airport designed to seal off the entire passenger arrival area and the tarmac in the vicinity of Aquino's aeroplane. Even so, on the short flight from Taipeh, Aquino's aides made no secret of their concern for his safety. He was uncharacteristically subdued, but still defiant: 'I can't allow myself to be petrified by the fear of assassination and spend my life in the corner.'

The aides were proved correct in all their fears. Less than one minute after leaving the aircraft, Benigno Aquino lay on the tarmac, blood gushing from a massive wound at the back of his skull. A few feet away from him lay the body of another man, dressed in blue trousers and a white shirt. There was pandemonium around the aeroplane as heavily-armed Filipino troops and security men screamed into their walkie-talkies, mingling with airline officials and the shocked passengers from Flight 811.

A number of foreign journalists and television crews had been travelling with Aquino and, although security men tried to prevent them sending out their dramatic stories, their accounts were soon making headline news around the world. All were broadly agreed on the sequence of events after the aircraft had parked at gate 8. First onto the air bridge 'tube' after it was connected were three or four uniformed soldiers who approached Aquino and began to lead him along the tube towards the main door. As they left, other guards in plain clothes stopped journalists from following, and finally closed the main door at the end of the tube.

The last time any of the journalists saw Aquino alive, he was being escorted by at least five uniformed men onto the platform of the steps that led down the tube service door to the tarmac below. A few seconds later, a single shot rang out then, after a brief pause, two or three more. Inside the aircraft people rushed to the windows to find out what was going on, and saw Aquino face down in his own blood. There was no sign of the uniformed troops who had been with him in the tube just a few seconds earlier but, as the journalists watched in horror, several members of the airport security unit, Aviation Security Command (Avsecom), fired at the body of the second man. One, in particular, placed his automatic rifle on the man's body and coldly pumped bullet after bullet into his stomach. Other Avsecom men fired shots in the air, forcing the watching journalists in the aeroplane to duck as Aquino's body was rushed away in an Avsecom van.

Official briefings

It was five hours before the Filipino authorities allowed the story that already horrified the world to be reported within the country, and a whole rumour-filled day before President Marcos publicly presented the official version of events at Manila airport. Looking frail and ill, Marcos asserted that he had 'almost begged' Aquino not to return. His killer, Marcos said, had clearly been a professional, firing a single shot from a .357 Magnum – one of the most powerful handguns in the world – into Aquino's head from a range of 18 inches (46 centimetres). Aquino's security men were not armed, the president insisted, but they had tried to shield him with their own bodies.

Official briefings later provided the press with more information. The alleged assassin was 5 feet 6 inches (1.67 metres) tall, weighed about 12½ stone (79.4 kilograms), and was between 30 and 35 years old. The only clue to his identity was the word 'Rolly' embroidered on the waistband of his underpants and an 'R' engraved inside his gold wedding ring. Yet even without a name to go on, the Marcos regime had no hesitation in attributing the killing to a communist plot, deliberately designed to blacken the Philippines government with its allies abroad, above all in the United States – President Reagan was due to visit Marcos in a few months' time. According to officials, Aquino's killer had disguised himself in the uniform of an airport maintenance worker in order to penetrate the intensive security. When Aquino had arrived on the tarmac from the service steps, the man had rushed out from his hiding-place beneath the CAL aircraft, shoved past the escort and fired the fatal shot. Avsecom troops had then shot him dead.

Two days after Aquino's death, as his widow Corazon and their children arrived in Manila for his funeral, President Marcos announced the formation of an official commission under the Chief Justice of the Supreme Court to undertake 'a free, unlimited and exhaustive' investigation into the murder. It was swiftly repudiated by the Aquino family, the

Aquino's mother, who was waiting at the airport, grieves at the news of her son's death

Aquino's funeral procession. From this time protests against Marcos became more violent

opposition party and the strong Catholic Church, all of whom accused the government of choosing 'Marcos mouthpieces' to carry out a cover-up. The president subsequently made a somewhat extraordinary offer of a £30,000 reward for information leading to 'the arrest of the killer or killers' – and this was also ridiculed. Had not Marcos himself already assured the nation that the assassin was the man in the blue trousers, in the pay of the communists, whom the troops had shot?

There was, in addition, mounting disbelief that the security authorities still could not identify the alleged killer, despite having his fingerprints and other physical leads. Surely, opposition leaders insisted, a professional hitman would already be known to the police? 'Anyone out there know Rolly?' asked one newspaper headline sarcastically. And other equally uncomfortable questions were being raised about the Marcos version of events. As the opposition leader, Salvador Laurel, pointed out, how could a lone assassin have penetrated the tight security cordon of some 2000 troops without inside assistance? How could he have known exactly where to lie in wait for Aquino, who came down the service steps instead of disembarking normally? Who were the soldiers with Aquino just before he died, and where were they now? Why was the alleged killer riddled with bullets instead of being captured for questioning?

As pressure on the authorities mounted, a name for the dead man in the blue trousers was finally released, nine days after the assassination. He was Rolando Galman, officially described as 'a notorious killer and gun for hire'. Government sources reported that Galman was known to have links with left-wing subversive groups. But, according to his family, he had been taken from his home by armed men four days *before* the death of Aquino. And two days *after* the assassination, more armed men had picked up Galman's common-law wife Lina and held her for some days – the first of a number of mysterious summonses.

Another sensation followed. Philippines air force officers, it was established, had picked up Galman's mother and sister after the killing and held them incommunicado for four days before the corpse was publicly identified.

Early in September 1983, the government's commission of inquiry opened its hearings. It was boycotted by Aquino's family and the opposition party. One of the first witnesses was a government pathologist, Dr Benvenido Munoz. In sworn testimony, Dr Munoz asserted that the shot that killed Aquino came from a weapon pointed upwards at the back of his head. The bullet had then been deflected downwards to exit through his jaw. It was highly controversial evidence. Aquino's family had already

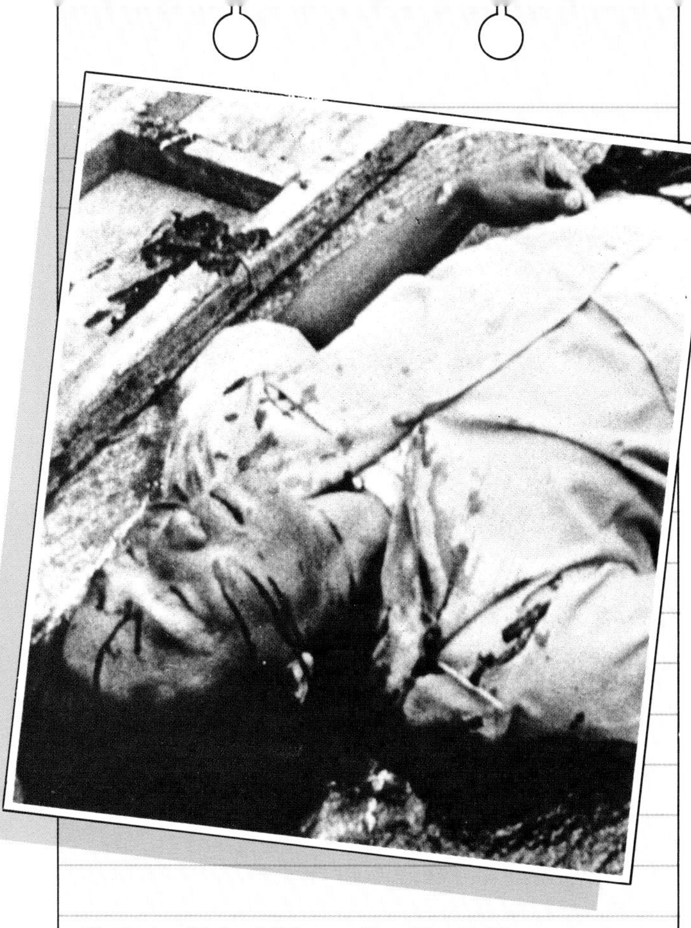

The body of Roland Galman, alleged by the Marcos government to be a killer hired by a left-wing group, and shot down by Avsecom guards

Below: one of the photographs that helped to pinpoint the movements of security guards and members of Aquino's escort just after the shooting. The man ringed, Captain Kavinta, could not explain why he was running *away* from the scene

announced that examination of his corpse (before it was laid in state for mourners to pay their respects) had established clearly that he was killed by a bullet in the skull just below his left ear, fired from behind and slightly above him, which had travelled on a sharp downward trajectory to exit just below the mouth. These findings were later confirmed.

The alleged assassin, Galman, was certainly no taller than Aquino. To fire such a shot when, as the government insisted, Aquino was already on the tarmac, Galman would have had to be holding the pistol aloft at the moment of pulling the trigger. Highly unlikely, the opposition claimed, pointing out that Dr Munoz's experience of forensic examination in gunshot cases was severely limited. As it happened, his findings were soon forgotten. On 10 October 1983, under severe pressure, all five Marcos-appointed board members resigned, on the very day they were due to hear testimony from the five soldiers who had been Aquino's escort.

New enquiry

President Marcos moved swiftly to conciliate the opposition. He announced the formation of a new commission of investigation, headed by a widely respected retired judge, Mrs Corazon Agrava, and invited critics to nominate four other acceptable members for the new board. The Agrava Commission began work in November and soon showed that it meant business.

The Marcos administration never budged from its original version that the assassination was a communist-inspired plot carried out by Rolando Galman. The regime's key testimony in the Agrava hearings came from General Fabian Ver, Chief of Staff of the armed forces and a man many Filipinos considered the most powerful in the land. In some fourteen hours of questioning, General Ver politely and urbanely took the commission through the military's story from the time in early 1983 when it became clear that Aquino was thinking seriously about returning to the Philippines.

According to Ver, reports of a plot to kill Aquino and blame the Marcos government had surfaced in July 1983. As a result, Ver initiated 'Project Four Flowers' to examine the rumours and foil the plot. When it was discovered that Aquino was on his way home, a subsequent project, 'Operation Plan Homecomer', was designed to protect him: it failed.

General Ver's assured performance did no noticeable damage to the government's case, but his subordinates who went before the commission were far less impressive. The picture that emerged from hours of testimony from officers and other ranks actively involved in 'Homecomer' was one of worried men clinging hard to stories that often started to break down under scrutiny.

But the most extraordinary military testimony came from what wags were quick to nickname 'the five wise monkeys' – the team of five men that had escorted Aquino from his aeroplane and down the service steps. 'Saw nothing, heard nothing, said nothing,' was the repeated theme of their evidence. The obvious incredulity of the Agrava board and the hostility of the public gallery could not budge them as, one after another, they insisted that despite being within a few feet – even a few inches – of Aquino they had nothing to contribute about the moment of his death.

Sergeant Claro Lat was actually holding Aquino's right arm when the fatal shot was fired. 'I heard a big bang,' he testified, then Aquino had gone limp and he could not hold him up. Lat fell on top of the dying man, then got up and ran for cover. Surely he must have seen something of the killing, the board asked. 'No, everything happened so fast that I failed to witness it.'

Private Rogelio Moreno was a few feet behind Aquino, ideally placed to see if an assassin had shot him from behind. 'Unfortunately,' Moreno testified, 'I was looking somewhere else at that moment.' All he saw was Aquino falling and a man in blue trousers with a gun in his hand. Paraffin tests on Moreno two days after the assassination found several specks of nitrate on both hands. Moreno claimed, however, that this was because he had been on the shooting range the day before Aquino's arrival in Manila.

Sergeant Filomeno Miranda testified that he was the last of the escort party descending the service stairs; he heard a shot, glanced up and saw Aquino and Sergeant Lat falling. Moreno had immediately taken cover nearby. In the face of the board members' obvious disbelief, Miranda insisted that he had seen nobody else on the tarmac – not his colleagues in the escort team, not Galman, not even the Avsecom troopers who were blazing away at the alleged killer's body.

Above: members of the second commission of enquiry headed by Mrs Agrava and nicknamed the 'Agravators'. The sessions were usually open to the public and attended daily by crowds of people who heckled unpopular witnesses

The most intense interest centred on the testimony, lasting eight hours, of Sergeant Arnulfo de Mesa, a baby-faced mountain of a man, at 24 the youngest of the escort. A skilled marksman and karate expert, de Mesa had been one step behind and above Aquino on the service stairs, with both hands on Aquino's left arm. De Mesa insisted that the escort group was already on the tarmac, heading for

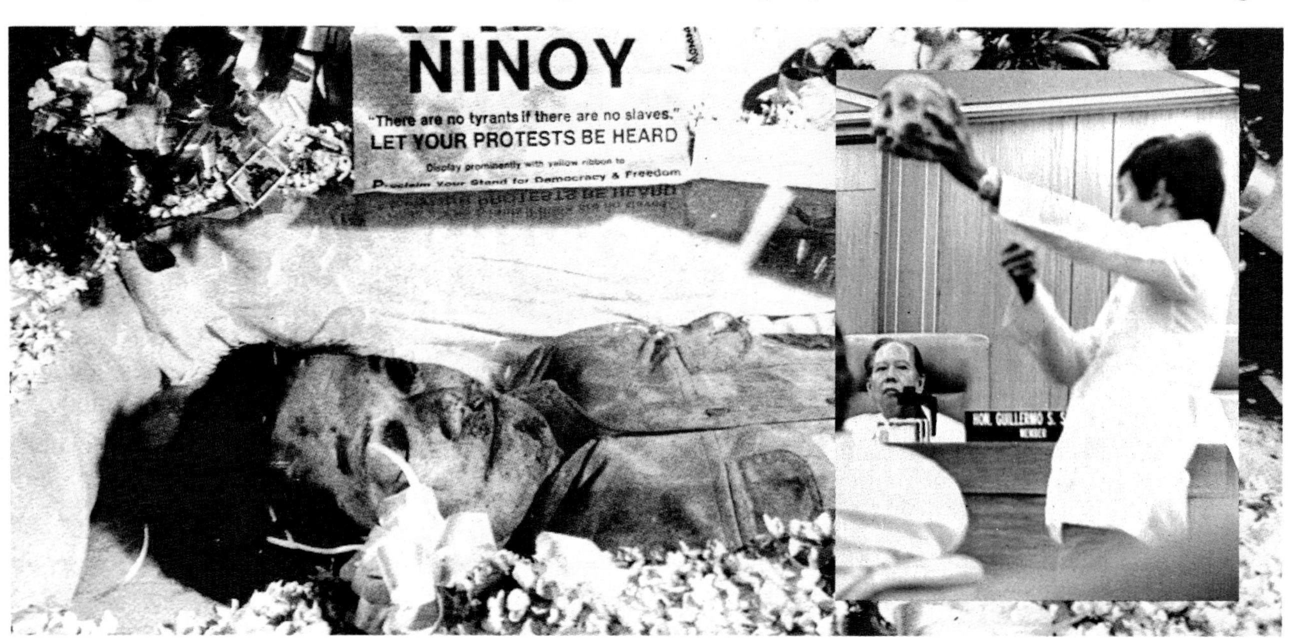

the waiting Avsecom troop carrier, when he suddenly felt a hand holding a gun nudge his right shoulder. There was a shot, de Mesa said, then he turned and felled the gunman with a karate chop, forcing him to drop the Magnum .357 pistol he was holding. De Mesa said he had picked up the gun and run for cover.

At the end of the escorts' evidence, a frustrated Mrs Agrava gave them a piece of her mind. 'Only two possibilities can be surmised from your testimonies,' she snapped. 'One is that Galman could not have been on the tarmac when Aquino was shot . . . because it is difficult to believe that none of you saw him shoot Aquino. The other possibility is that all of you are not telling the whole truth, you are trying to hide something from the board.'

An Avsecom officer, Captain Llewellyn Kavinta, was on tarmac security duty when Aquino's aircraft arrived at gate 8. Kavinta was shown a photograph, taken from inside the CAL aircraft, of a man sprinting across the tarmac, gun in hand. He agreed that the figure was himself. 'This was before the shooting, when we were already going to deploy, going to the staging area,' he asserted. But in one corner of the photograph two bodies were partially but clearly visible. Surely, then, it must have been taken *after* Aquino was shot? He agreed nervously that he must have been mistaken. So why had he been running *away* from the scene of the crime? Amid much barracking Kavinta said lamely, 'I can't remember.'

Aquino's security escort, 'the five wise monkeys' who claimed to have seen nothing of the killing

Taped clues

All the military witnesses who had been in the vicinity of Aquino just before and after he died were instructed to perform one final, macabre task before the commission allowed them to step down. They had to read aloud, often at different speeds and with varying inflections, passages from the transcript of a tape-recording made inside the CAL aeroplane by several journalists, including Sandra Burton, a *Time* magazine correspondent. Burton had been close behind Aquino as he left the aircraft and had kept her recorder running when the pushing and shoving began in the airbridge tube as security men obstructed the journalists. On her tape, and on others made by television crews, different male voices can be heard saying in Tagalog, the Filipino language, what sounds like: 'Here he comes . . . I'll do it . . . Them, let them do it . . . Go on! Shoot! Shoot!' Burton testified that, as she was being forced back into the aircraft, she recorded a single voice saying, 'I'll do it.' A shot is then heard on the tape, then voices wailing, 'What's happened?' Three more shots ring out, the confusion increases and a man shouts, 'He's dead, he's dead.' This is followed by a flurry of shots.

Played over and over again before the commission, the tapes never lost their dramatic impact on listeners. Lawyers for the armed forces accepted their authenticity, but challenged the validity of accepting the recordings as legal evidence on the ground that what was being said on them was not completely clear. A Japanese expert in 'voice printing' had prepared an analysis of the different voices they contained, but this was not admissible, the military's lawyers argued, because they had not been given the chance to question the expert on his qualifications and technique.

Some of the testimony most damaging to the government came from the civilian witnesses who appeared before the commission. A lawyer, José Espinosa, exposed the government's lies in claiming that it took a long time to identify the dead man in the blue trousers as Rolando Galman. Espinosa had once acted for Galman, and his evidence made it clear that – far from being an anonymous corpse – he was known to the security authorities long before the assassination, and may even have had close contacts with senior officials involved in 'Homecomer'.

According to Espinosa, Rolando Galman had been arrested early in 1982, charged with robbery, car theft and possession of an unlicensed gun. But, instead of facing an ordinary criminal court as an offender with a previous record, Galman was sent to a military detention centre, Camp Olivas, under a special order introduced by President Marcos under martial law for use mainly against political offenders. Espinosa had got to know Galman towards

Left: the body of 'Ninoy' lies in state, showing clearly the hole where the bullet exited through the chin
Inset: Government pathologist Dr Munoz shows the first commission of enquiry the path of the bullet, with the aid of a demonstration skull

Above: President Marcos (right) and General Ver. Ver was described by Aquino before his death as the man he had most cause to fear in the Philippines

the end of 1982, and in January 1983 Galman's wife Lina had retained him to work for her husband's release from detention.

Espinosa revealed that he had asked a high-ranking air force intelligence officer, Colonel Arturo Custodio, for advice on securing Galman's release: on one occasion, he told the commission, Colonel Custodio had accompanied him to Camp Olivas for a meeting with his client. Late in February 1983 Galman was released because the Philippines Defence Ministry had said there was no case pending against him. 'He wasn't released because of my efforts,' Espinosa testified, but he had advised Galman to stay out of trouble and avoid associating with 'shadowy characters'.

A day or two after the assassination, Espinosa had asked Colonel Custodio what he knew about the killing. Custodio, he believed, was close to Avsecom. According to Espinosa, the colonel had replied with something like, 'They're crazy, that guy was already dead when they dumped him on the tarmac.' At that point, Espinosa had no idea that 'that guy' was his former client Rolando Galman. Whom did he think Custodio meant? 'As far as I can recall,' replied Espinosa, 'I think what Colonel Custodio told me was that it may have been the military escort who shot the late senator.'

A few more days after the assassination, the newspapers had carried the first pictures of Aquino's alleged assassin, still officially unidentified. The commission wanted to know why Espinosa had not come forward then to provide identification of his former client. 'Because I believe that the military would be the first to know, because Rolando Galman was under their detention for almost a year. They should know that it was Galman who was there at the airport.' Had anybody from the government subsequently asked Espinosa about the Aquino killing and his late client? 'No, sir!' he replied with a chuckle, 'I think they found it hard to find me.'

Several airport workers on duty when Aquino arrived also significantly undermined the government's case. Fred Viesca, a cargo handler, testified that he was no more than 20 yards (18.3 metres) from the rear of the China Airlines aeroplane at gate 8 when he heard a single shot. He looked up to see a man in a white suit fall from the mid section of the service door steps. Viesca panicked and ran off, hearing more gunfire behind him, but he was adamant that Aquino had not yet reached the tarmac when he was killed, as the official version maintains.

A Philippines Airlines (PAL) ground engineer, Raymondo Balang, bravely came out of hiding to give the commission his story. He said that he had been on the tarmac near CAL 811 when it landed and had seen the man he later discovered to be Rolando Galman among the soldiers and security men gathered there. 'He was just standing there, smiling with them.' Balang testified, explaining to the commission that he had gone into hiding when he learned that military intelligence was looking for him. Balang's story was supported by an account on US television by Ruben Regelado, another PAL worker on duty at the time. He returned from hiding in Japan and said a third PAL employee had told him of seeing Aquino shot from the service stairs.

Dramatic testimony

Efren Ranas offered perhaps the most dramatic – and for the government, the most damaging – eyewitness testimony. A private security guard on tarmac duty about 15 yards (13.7 metres) away from the service steps to gate 8, he described how he had heard a single shot when Aquino was about four steps above the ground. After the shot, Aquino's head seemed to be hanging to one side, and it appeared that he was being supported bodily by two members of the escort. On reaching the tarmac, they let Aquino's body fall to the ground. Blood was clearly visible on the back of his white jacket.

The last category of evidence examined by the Agrava Commission concerned the possible timing of the final moments before the assassination. Analysis of the various tape-recordings and videotapes made available established that the shot that killed Aquino was fired 11 seconds after a US television crew, filming inside the CAL aircraft, lost sight of him when he was led into the airbridge tube. On the videotape made by a Japanese crew, the first shot is heard 9.2 seconds after Aquino and his escorts began to descend the nineteen service steps towards the tarmac below.

The official military view is that Aquino could have covered the distance between the top of the steps and the spot where his body fell to the tarmac in just 11 seconds 'at a fast pace'. The members of the Agrava Commission made several visits to gate 8 to re-enact the scene: they found that it took them between 13 and 15 seconds to descend the steps to the tarmac at a normal pace. The difference of a few seconds in these estimates in anything but trivial – according to Sandra Burton's tape-recording, the whole bloody business, from the first to the last shot, took barely 17 seconds.

The hearing dragged on until December 1985 and ended predictably: 25 military men and one civilian linked to the killing of Aquino were acquitted, and the Marcos government closed the case for good.

However, Aquino's death had an unexpected outcome. In the wake of the murder his widow, Corazon Aquino, became the focus for the opposition to the Marcos regime and, in a snap election held in February 1986, she ran against Marcos for the presidency. Despite overwhelming evidence of fraud, Marcos declared himself the winner. Outraged, the Filipino people deposed Marcos and forced him to flee to Hawaii.

Mrs Aquino duly took office. One of her first acts as president was to form the Presidential Commission on Human Rights, to be chaired by Jose Dickno, a former senator and political prisoner of the Marcos regime. Mr Dickno said that the commission would be investigating 800 summary executions, at least 600 missing persons, and at least 5000 cases of torture that had occurred in the Philippines since the early 1970s. But its first task would be to re-examine the evidence in the Aquino murder case.

'If we can prove there was collusion, and there's strong enough evidence already, that would be enough to declare a mis-trial, and begin the case all over again.'

Meanwhile, the machinations of Marcos were already working against the widow-president. Announcing the existence of underground hit squads working for Marcos, Vice-President Salvador Laurel said in March 1986: 'We are supposed to be eliminated. Without Cory Aquino and myself, it would be very easy for Marcos to make a comeback.'

Below: Mrs Corazon Aquino being sworn in as the new president of the Philippines after Marcos had fled to Hawaii, taking with him, it was widely rumoured, a large fortune in misappropriated funds

Who killed Norma Jean?

Marilyn Monroe was declared dead from barbiturate poisoning at her Los Angeles home on 4 August 1962, yet the autopsy revealed no trace of the 47 Nembutal capsules she was meant to have taken. Was her death an accident or suicide? Some people believe she was killed by top figures in the American establishment.

On Sunday 5 August 1962, the world reeled at the news that Marilyn Monroe was dead. Moreover, the evidence screamed, she had committed suicide. All the signs were there – the tell-tale medicine bottles, an apparently high level of barbiturates in her blood and, of course, the well-known saga of her emotional problems. Marilyn's divorces, her stormy love affairs, her appalling professional difficulties and, finally, her sacking from her last film *Something's Got to Give* had all been well-documented.

What more proof was necessary? A few weeks after the tragic news – after any lingering suspicions that there had been foul play were allayed by a coroner's rushed report – Hollywood, America and the world went back to business. For a while it seemed the circumstances of Marilyn Monroe's death, if not her legendary status, would be forgotten by all. But subsequent inquiries have shown that the evidence is inconclusive. The case remains open to this day.

Mainly, it has been the simple facts of the case that have prevented it from ever being satisfactorily closed. All the forensic medical detail relating to Marilyn's death by barbiturate poisoning suggests not suicide, but death by other causes. Equally important, there is little indication that in the last few weeks of her life Marilyn had been suffering the chronic depression or desperation characteristic of the suicidal. She was at times, however, in a near catatonic state, unable to sleep as usual and dependent on narcotics. She was trying to get over her sacking from 20th Century-Fox, an abortion and the last traumatic year and a half.

Her problems had come to a head 18 months previously. On 20 January 1961, two and a half months after filming had finished on her last completed film, *The Misfits*, Marilyn was divorced, amid some acrimony, from the playwright Arthur Miller. 'She was on a slide into the longest depression of her existence,' Norman Mailer would later write, in his biography *Marilyn*, on this period in her life. Physically and mentally exhausted, Marilyn was admitted to the Payne-Whitney Psychiatric Clinic in New York on the recommendation of her doctor and against her will. As soon as she could she appealed to Lee and Paula Strasberg, her drama coaches and mentors, who ignored her cry for help. She then contacted Joe DiMaggio, her second husband, from whom she had been divorced in 1956 but who had remained close to her, and he had her released into his care. There followed three weeks of rest in the Neurological Institute of Columbia-Presbyterian. She returned to Hollywood and began commuting from there to New York. In June 1961 she had a gall bladder operation but recovered well.

Early in 1962 Marilyn moved to 12305 Fifth Helena Drive in Brentwood, Los Angeles, a single-storey house with a garden and swimming pool she seldom used. Around this time rumours of her friendships with President Kennedy, and his brother, Attorney General Robert F. Kennedy, spread from Hollywood to Washington DC and back again. For a while, it seems, she was very close to the president. Their relationship can be traced to before Kennedy's big forty-fifth birthday celebrations held at New York's Madison Square Garden on 19 May. On that occasion many Americans had been shocked by Marilyn's sexy rendition of 'Happy Birthday, Mr President/Thanks for the Memory', delivered in person in front of 17,000 Democrats and broadcast coast-to-coast. She had interrupted filming on *Something's Got to Give*, the film she had begun work on in April, infuriating its director George Cukor, to be at the party. Indeed, in the first three weeks' filming, Marilyn turned up on just six days.

Of the Kennedys, it was Robert with whom Marilyn was to become most closely linked. Through parties at the home of Pat Lawford, Kennedy's sister, and her husband, film star Peter Lawford, who had effected the introduction, they met several times that summer and may have embarked on an affair. Marilyn even dropped hints that she might marry Kennedy (already married with seven children) to friends such as Robert Slatzer and the English journalist W. J. Weatherby, though she told her masseur Ralph Roberts (to whom she was very close), 'It's not true. I like him, but not physically.' Certainly Marilyn telephoned Kennedy incessantly, and often in some distress, at the White House, but her calls were usually intercepted by his secretary Angie Novello. Eventually her attempts to speak to him failed to get through at all.

When it thus became clear to Marilyn that Kennedy could not risk the scandal of being associated with her, she was angry. It is alleged by Robert Slatzer that she planned to hold a press conference to reveal how Kennedy had used her and lied to her and then left her alone and disappointed.

Marilyn Monroe, sacked for absenteeism, leaves the set of *Something's Got To Give.* Was her subsequent depression enough reason for her to have committed suicide?

'Last sitting'

After her inevitable sacking from *Something's Got to Give* in June, Marilyn spent her time seeing or telephoning friends, and regularly visiting her psychiatrist Dr Ralph Greenson. She also sat for photographers, most notably Bert Stern, who completed the famous nude 'last sitting', and purchased a whole new wardrobe from Jaks of Beverly Hills and Saks of New York. She seemed to be physically fit, having fully recovered from a virus infection.

Marilyn is said to have had two meetings planned for 6 August, the day after her death was officially announced. According to Slatzer, the press conference would go ahead if she did not hear from Robert Kennedy that weekend: at the very least, she threatened to reveal her supposed affairs with the Kennedys; she also planned to make public certain government secrets she had learned from these 'lovers', the effects of which revelations would have been 'like a bomb-shell'. Her other meeting was to have been with her lawyer, Mickey Rudin. Marilyn had planned to change her will and remove the main beneficiaries, Lee and Paula Strasberg. She felt that they had manipulated her into making out a will she did not want.

Marilyn's personal confrontation with Robert Kennedy would apparently have taken place on the evening of Saturday 4 August. She was to dine at the Lawfords' house. Ralph Roberts was to have been her escort, and Robert Kennedy had reputedly been invited too. During the day Marilyn spent time with Dr Greenson, her housekeeper Eunice Murray and Pat Newcomb. She was otherwise busy in the house or on the telephone. One of the last people she spoke to on the telephone was her stepson Joe DiMaggio Jr. She laughed and joked with him for some time. Half an hour afterwards, according to Murray, she retired to her room, never to be seen alive again. It was around 7.30pm.

It is from this point that the events of Marilyn Monroe's last night alive become confused by a welter of conflicting evidence. According to the official report, Lawford stated that he had called Marilyn around 8pm. He says he asked her, 'Hey, Charlie, what happened to you?' Marilyn replied that she was too tired to come by. Her voice sounded slurred, as if she had been drinking or was drugged. She apparently said to him, 'Say goodbye to Pat, and say goodbye to the President and say goodbye to yourself, because you're such a nice guy.'

Lawford apparently realised that Marilyn might be trying to commit suicide. He claims that he called his manager and asked him to call and check up on Marilyn. The manager was reluctant, warning Lawford that the possible scandal would be catastrophic: 'You're the brother-in-law of the President of the United States!' The manager promised that he would telephone her lawyer Mickey Rudin and tell him to come to Marilyn's aid, if indeed she needed any assistance.

According to journalist and biographer Anthony Scaduto, Marilyn tried to reach Ralph Roberts, who was out. His answering service took the call, and when Roberts checked in later to see if there had been any telephone messages, he was told that there had been only one call, 'from a woman who sounded fuzzy-voiced and troubled.'

And what of Attorney General Robert Kennedy? It is a matter of record that he was in California that day. He checked into the St Francis Hotel in San Francisco on Friday 3 August with his wife, Ethel, anda few of their children. He was scheduled to be on the Ernie Kovacs television show on the Sunday. He was to speak before the San Francisco Bar Association on Monday, then head north-west to inspect a number of reservoirs on behalf of the Department of the Interior.

A police photograph of Marilyn's nightstand – telling evidence of the star's chronic dependency on drugs

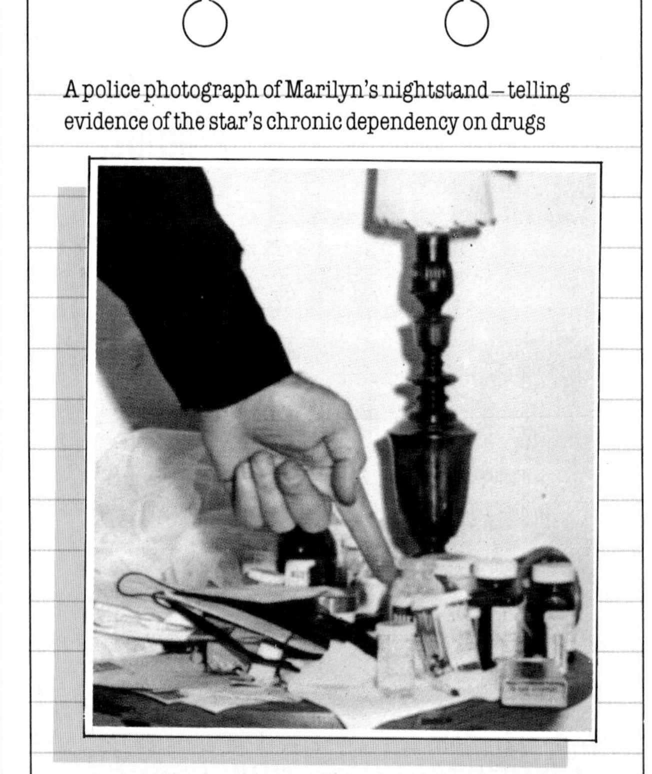

Above: despite her confident appearance, Marilyn was hopelessly insecure, and suffered several breakdowns

There is one theory that late on the Friday Kennedy secretly made his way 340 miles (550 kilometres) southwards and checked into the Beverly Hills Hotel in Los Angeles. He was, of course, supposed to have met up with Marilyn at the Lawfords' dinner party on Saturday evening. Did he speak with her in the few hours before she died? Did he visit her on that day? Some eyewitness accounts say that he did. FBI reports, however, say that Kennedy spent the weekend at the ranch of Mr and Mrs John Bates in Gilroy, California.

Marilyn's housekeeper Eunice Murray's testimony about her own whereabouts is unreliable, and it is difficult to be sure at what time she found Marilyn's body. Sergeant Jack Clemmons of the Los Angeles Police Department, who was the first policeman to arrive on the scene, reports that Mrs Murray first told him that she had woken about midnight; later she, or the official report, changed this time to around 3am. Whatever time she awoke, apparently worried about Marilyn, she had been puzzled by the sight of the telephone cord snaking across the hallway, from where the telephone usually sat in the small bedroom, and under the door to Marilyn's bedroom. This had suggested to her that something was amiss, as Marilyn hated to sleep with a telephone in her room. Mrs Murray says that she had then become 'alarmed' when she saw, from under Marilyn's door, a light on in the room. Later, in a subsequent interview, she changed this evidence. She had to, for it was not possible to see any light shining from under that door. Marilyn had recently had a new white carpet laid there and it was so thick that it had originally prevented the door from being shut. A worn spot attested to this.

However Mrs Murray was alerted, she was sufficiently worried to call Dr Greenson, who advised her first to knock and shout at Marilyn's door, then to go outside and look through the bedroom window. When she returned to the telephone extension she was calling from and described Marilyn lying still and naked on the bed, with no covers (although it was a cool night), Greenson said he would call immediately. He told Mrs Murray to telephone Dr Engelberg, Marilyn's doctor.

Greenson arrived minutes later, broke Marilyn's bedroom window, and entered the room. He unlocked the door and re-emerged in the hall, announcing, 'We've lost her.' Mrs Murray said that she then 'observed that rigor mortis had already set in . . . saw that the telephone was under her . . . she was lying on it.'

Conflicting accounts

According to several conflicting accounts, the two doctors each report having arrived after 3am. Each man claimed to have pronounced Marilyn dead, one at 3.35, the other at 3.50. Engelberg also stated that it was he who found her dead. Greenson said, in his police statement and also in a later interview with the columnist Maurice Zolotow, that when he found Marilyn she was lying on the bed with one hand on the receiver of the telephone and the index finger of her other hand in the dial. This would have been a difficult position for her to have achieved if, as Mrs Murray stated, Marilyn was actually lying *on top* of the telephone.

When Sergeant Clemmons arrived at the house at 4.40am he regarded the scene with considerable suspicion. Before calling the police Mrs Murray had apparently summoned her son-in-law, Norman Jeffries, to repair the window that had been broken by Dr Greenson. She had both the washing machine and spin-drier going and she was removing food from the refrigerator and disposing of most of it. Moreover, she was filling cartons with unidentified objects and carrying them off to the trunk of her car. Clemmons subsequently charged that the scene had definitely been arranged. It did not look like the scene of an overdose victim's death. He says that he suspected murder right from the start.

Clemmons was told on arrival that Marilyn had been dead for approximately three hours. It was apparent to him that she had been dead for much longer than this. Not only was rigor mortis already established in the corpse, but hypostasis, or post-mortem lividity, had set in. The presence of this condition, which produces a purple pallor as a result of blood settling to the lowest level, suggests that Marilyn must have been lying in the same posture for some time. Since she had been lying on her stomach, her back and bottom were ashen and the front of her body was livid. In Clemmons' estimation, Marilyn had been dead at least eight hours.

Clemmons has said that the doctors present had explained that Marilyn's death was the result of her swallowing the contents of a bottle of Nembutal. She died, therefore, of a barbiturate overdose. This, too, aroused his suspicions. There was no sign in Marilyn's bedroom of a glass, or any other vessel for liquid with which a bottle of capsules might be swallowed, nor was there any sign of Marilyn having suffered the convulsions or violent vomiting that inevitably accompany such an overdose. Clemmons was relieved that morning by a Sergeant Byron. This officer claims that, in assisting with the investigation, he counted 15 medicine bottles on Marilyn's nightstand. In the coroner's report, issued two weeks later, only eight bottles are mentioned.

The Chief Medical Examiner, or coroner, for Los Angeles County in 1962 was Dr Theodore Curphey.

Below: Marilyn was buried at Westwood Memorial Cemetery, west of Hollywood, on 8 August 1962
Bottom: Joe DiMaggio (left) arranged the funeral; with him are his son Joe jnr (right), one of the last people to speak to Marilyn, and Inez Nelson, Marilyn's former business manager, with her husband

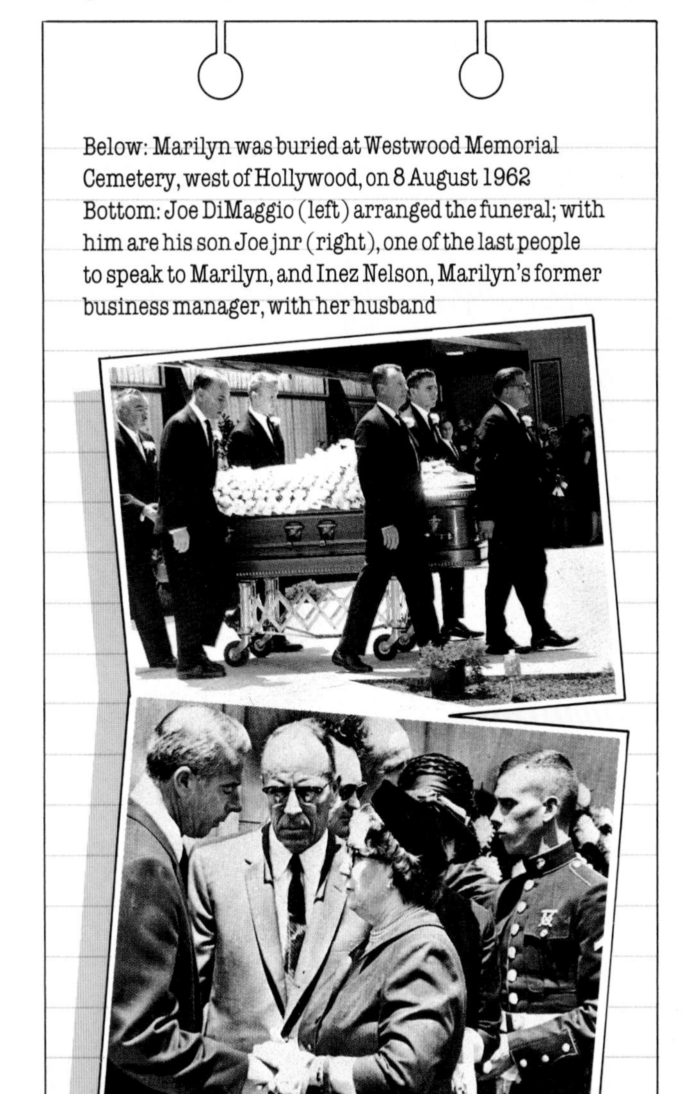

Dr Thomas Noguchi – he carried out the autopsy on Marilyn, but his report was full of inconsistencies and anomalies, shedding little light on the cause of death

His final verdict on the case was given in a press release that was issued less than two months from the day Marilyn died:

> On the basis of information obtained, it is our opinion that the case is 'probable suicide' ... beside her bed was an empty bottle that had contained fifty Nembutal tablets. The presumption is that Marilyn took 47 of them at one time.

This statement was misleading. It did not make clear that Marilyn's Nembutal prescription (which the official report itself lists) was for 25 capsules to a bottle. This was quite clearly stated in the pill-bottle inventory in the police report, which identifies the only Nembutal bottle found as 'Empty Container #20858, 8-3-62, Nembutal, 1½ gr., #25'. Forensic pathologists in the United States have insisted that 25 Nembutal capsules could not have raised the level of pentobarbitone (Nembutal) in her blood and liver to where it was. There would have had to have been a *second* bottle at hand for Marilyn to have taken 47 pills. What had since happened to it? Was it one of the seven bottles that had supposedly gone missing? And why did the highest medical authority in Los Angeles say in his carefully worded report that Marilyn died because she swallowed *tablets*? Nembutals are available only in capsule form.

Curphey did not trouble to organise the usual coroner's investigation or inquest into Marilyn's death. Instead, he assigned the case to the Suicide Prevention Team of Los Angeles, a body consisting of just two psychiatrists. Its appointment suggests that Curphey had prejudged the case as suicide. Its findings were along similar lines.

Had there been a thorough and believable autopsy report for the authorities to fall back upon, there would probably have been no outcry against the findings in later years. But this was not the case. What, then, was the actual evidence provided by the medical experts, and what does it say about the causes of Marilyn's death?

The part of Marilyn Monroe's autopsy called the 'toxicology report', signed by Dr Thomas Noguchi, who was then an assistant coroner (but subsequently achieved both fame and notoriety as the 'Coroner to the Stars'), was altered within a week of its first draft. The first version, dated 6 August, noted 4.5mg per cent barbiturates in Marilyn's blood. The second, a supplemental report dated 13 August, changed the 4.5 to 13mg per cent and also noted the presence of 8mg per cent of the potent drug chloral hydrate. There is another anomaly. In noting the examination of the kidneys, the autopsy report finds no drugs in any significant amount in these organs. But there ought to have been drugs there: it is impossible for these drugs to be ingested, digested and then absorbed into the blood without passing through the kidneys, where the filtered impurities would have been trapped and detected in the autopsy.

No Nembutal

When Dr Noguchi examined the contents of Marilyn's stomach, all he found were about 'two teaspoonfuls of a brown, mucoid fluid'. He did not analyse it. Neither the duodenum (the entrance to the small intestine) nor the small intestine itself was examined. Noguchi claims that the facilities to do so were not available at the time and that such tests could not be made. Nowhere did Dr Noguchi find any sign of gelatin from the 47 Nembutal capsules, nowhere were there any traces of the bright yellow dye the capsules are coloured with, a dye that would be certain to stain the digestive tract.

With no residue of the drugs in her kidneys, it follows that Marilyn could have been killed by only one, possibly two, agents: either she took several suppositories containing the drug, or she was injected with it. No suppositories were found in either Marilyn's colon or vagina. There was, however, one fresh bruise on the upper part of her left hip – a typical injection site.

This lack of evidence seriously undermines the official version of Marilyn's death – that it was caused by swallowing 47 Nembutal capsules. In 1974 Marilyn's old friend Robert Slatzer (who, in fact, claims to have been married to her briefly in 1952) hired private detective Milo Speriglio to re-investigate the case. That year, and again in 1975, they failed to re-awaken official interest, but they succeeded in 1982 in producing the testimony of the former deputy coroner of Los Angeles, Lionel

Grandison. It was Grandison who had signed Marilyn's death certificate in 1962. In 1982, by charging that he was coerced into this action, he was able to convince the Los Angeles Board of Supervisors that they should re-examine Marilyn's death.

In his 1982 testimony, Grandison argued that the entire original investigation (such as it was) had been grossly mismanaged. He said that he viewed the body, saw the original diagrams of it made by Dr Noguchi, and noted that there were *several* bruises. Dr Noguchi's report, he claimed, had later been altered to register only one bruise. Grandison also stated that several vital objects that had been entrusted to the coroner's safe had since disappeared. One was Marilyn's red diary, through which Grandison says he thumbed, 'looking for next of kin'. Instead of names and addresses of relatives, he claims to have found several references to President Kennedy and to his brother, Attorney General Robert Kennedy. There were also notes about Mafia mobsters as well as details of a plot against the Cuban leader Fidel Castro.

Another item Grandison said he saw was a possible suicide note. He recalled:

> There was a note that was basically illegible in that we could not determine who had signed it, but there definitely was a note there which might have possibly given the indication that Marilyn had committed suicide. Later that note disappeared.

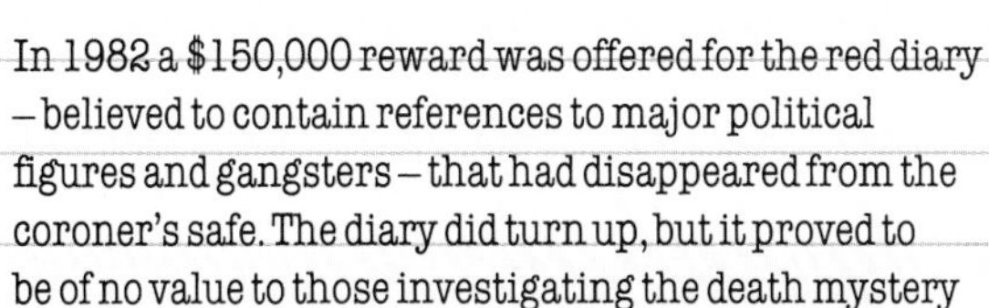

In 1982 a $150,000 reward was offered for the red diary – believed to contain references to major political figures and gangsters – that had disappeared from the coroner's safe. The diary did turn up, but it proved to be of no value to those investigating the death mystery

Marilyn's friend Robert Slatzer in the early Eighties outside the bedroom in which she died. He continues in his attempt to uncover the truth behind Marilyn's death

As well as the diary and the note, several more of Marilyn's personal effects, such as jewellery, had gone missing. In 1962 Grandison cautiously noted these irregularities. Twenty years later he spoke out about them and added that he had heard much speculation bandied about the coroner's office that Marilyn had been murdered, and claimed, too, that he heard the name of Robert Kennedy mentioned in that context. Grandison also said that there had been two separate autopsy reports and that the original had been replaced soon after he had seen it; moreover, he had witnessed three changes in the 'cause of death', from 'suicide' to 'possible suicide' to, finally, 'probable suicide', which is the official designation for accidental suicide. Interviewed by Slatzer, Grandison even suggested that there had been many acts of sexual intercourse with the dead body. Grandison's accusations border on the unbelievable at times.

Despite the fact that he knew all this Grandison had, in 1962, been asked to sign Marilyn Monroe's death certificate, a duty he was rarely required to carry out. He claims that when he protested to his boss, Dr Curphey, he was told he had no option but to sign the certificate.

Grandison's revelations, the doubtful medical evidence and the charges made by ex-policeman Clemmons combine to cast doubt on the official explanations of Marilyn's demise. With so much clashing information, what are we to believe happened on that fatal summer evening?

Over 20 years on, there are a host of hypotheses offered by those still seeking answers to the mystery

Marilyn with Joe diMaggio (right) and columnist Walter Winchell in about 1954. In 1956 a radio broadcast by Winchell alerted the FBI to the communist sympathies of playwright Arthur Miller, to whom Marilyn was married

During their investigation into the death, private detective Milo Speriglio and his client Robert Slatzer determined to find out to what extent the Federal Bureau of Investigation (FBI) was interested in the activities of the film star. Under the Freedom of Information Act, they were able to apply for the release of FBI files on the actress.

FBI representatives have stated that Marilyn was never regarded as a security risk, yet the documents given to Speriglio and Slatzer do not go very far towards corroborating that official claim. Only some pages were released; others were heavily censored. Several requests for specific documents were dismissed. 'None of the information being withheld is appropriate for discretionary release,' the FBI said in a letter to the two investigators in June 1980. All that was revealed was that the FBI had been interested in Marilyn mainly because she was the wife of playwright Arthur Miller (above), a suspected communist. In 1956 Miller had been subpoenaed before a subcommittee investigating 'unAmerican' activities.

In the United States, only the FBI may confiscate telephone records; since two men had, by all accounts, confiscated Marilyn's records from the local telephone exchange shortly after her death, there was reason to suspect FBI involvement. In material released to Speriglio and Slatzer, however, the FBI flatly denied that they possessed any such records (which they referred to as tapes).

of Marilyn Monroe's death. Inquirers such as Robert Slatzer, author of *The Life and Curious Death of Marilyn Monroe*; Milo Speriglio, the full-time private investigator employed by Slatzer and author of *Marilyn Monroe: Murder Cover-Up*; and the *New York Post* reporter George Carpozi, author of *Who Killed Marilyn Monroe?*, all published their conclusions around the time when Lionel Grandison was emerging with his story.

A key piece of Slatzer's evidence attempts to point the finger at Robert Kennedy. Slatzer has interviewed one of several elderly women who were playing cards in a house opposite Marilyn's on the day she died. She claims they saw Robert Kennedy and another man, who carried a satchel that looked like a doctor's bag, entering Marilyn's house.

In a subsequent interview with the neighbour's daughter, Slatzer was told how the woman in question passed the same story to a reporter, but the story never appeared in print. After that, she claimed two unidentified men called on her every other day and warned her to 'keep her mouth shut'.

There is a major mystery surrounding Marilyn Monroe's missing telephone records, which detailed every call she made during her last months. These could have proved or disproved the existence of Marilyn's relationship with the Kennedys, but they were mysteriously confiscated on the Monday morning following her death. (It is known, however, that her long-distance telephone bill from 27 May to 5 August amounted to $209, which does not suggest she made a great many calls to Washington DC or, indeed, anywhere else.) Two well-dressed men with

'Eastern accents' (probably from either New York or New England, both Kennedy strongholds) removed those records from the Brentwood branch office of the General Telephone Company. It has been alleged that the Chief of Police of Los Angeles, William H. Parker, was with them.

In the United States, the privacy of such records is protected by the 1934 Federal Communications Act; only the FBI has free access. If these two 'well-dressed' men were FBI agents, it may be that Parker accompanied them to sanction their activities. Later, though, the columnist Florabel Muir, who claimed to have seen Marilyn's telephone records, reported that they were in the possession of Chief of Police Parker.

Muir told Slatzer that Parker bragged to her that the records were 'my ticket to get Hoover's job when Robert Kennedy becomes president'. History has since revealed John and Robert Kennedy's failed attempts to get rid of J. Edgar Hoover, the FBI's chief since 1924. It was said that Hoover had something on every single elected official with anything to hide. Parker's protection of telephone records linking Kennedy and Marilyn Monroe would have put him in a very much stronger bargaining position with Kennedy in view of this fact.

According to Robert Slatzer, he telephoned Parker to see if the story about the records was true. He pretended to be a researcher working for Florabel Muir and asked Parker if he could look at the telephone records.

'Florabel's already seen them,' Parker barked in reply. 'Why has she got you calling me?' Then he hung up. It is believed that Parker jealously guarded Marilyn's telephone records even after Robert Kennedy was assassinated in Los Angeles in June 1968, and that shortly after his own death in July 1976, they disappeared from his office.

There is a possibility that at the time of her death, Marilyn Monroe's house was bugged. This suggestion is tied to the allegation that Robert Kennedy and Marilyn were having an affair. The 'bugging' hypothesis depends on events beginning in the Fifties, when the young attorney Robert Kennedy was at the height of his racket-busting career, investigating labour-union crime in particular. One of his chief targets was the large and highly corrupt

Below: Marilyn as the sleeping chanteuse Cherie in the 1956 film *Bus Stop*

Above: Jimmy Hoffa, president of the Teamsters' Union – did he bug Marilyn's home, even murder her, as part of his personal vendetta against her alleged lover Robert Kennedy?

Teamsters' Union. Its president from 1958 had been Jimmy Hoffa, who was at the centre of a racketeering empire involving management, union men and underworld figures. As Kennedy and Hoffa became more and more powerful, their feud grew fiercer.

When John Kennedy became President in 1961, and Robert Kennedy became Attorney General, life became very difficult for Hoffa. He was forced to take drastic action and he set out to defame Robert Kennedy and his brother. He enlisted the help of Bernard Spindel, one of the best wire-tapping men in the business, who had begun his career with Army Intelligence during the Second World War.

Hoffa sent Spindel to Los Angeles with orders to bug the homes of a number of Kennedy's friends. It is believed that he bugged Marilyn's house and Pat and Peter Lawford's beach home. If this is true, then someone could have had an audible record of Marilyn's last moments.

Robert Slatzer has put forward what he alleges to be information obtained from the Los Angeles County District Attorney's investigation in 1982 (efforts to obtain official statements from the Los Angeles authorities have so far failed). It seems that while searching for evidence of wire-tapping in Marilyn's old house, investigators discovered what could have been old telephone bugging lines. This information was not released officially, however; Slatzer claims to have gathered it from an interview with the current owners of the house at 12305 Fifth Helena Drive. He also claims to have interviewed a roof-repairing man sent for by the current owners who, while climbing about in the eaves, allegedly found wire-tapping equipment. The man told Slatzer that he filled half a small dustbin with wires, cable, microphone devices and transmitters. These could have proved invaluable.

Slatzer's private detective Milo Speriglio shocked the world in 1982 with further revelations about tapes that allegedly bear the sounds of Marilyn's last living moments. He claims that his secret informer on the case played sections to him over the telephone. At first, he says, a woman is heard being slapped around. There are small cries. Then there is a thud – like a body hitting the floor – followed by more cries, but these are muffled. Later a man's voice asks: 'What are we going to do with the body?' This and other undisclosed information led Speriglio to his claim that Marilyn's killers were a top politician and a film star. He does not name them.

There is also a theory about Marilyn's death that involves a frequently told story of the Mafia and a 'faked suicide' plot. Apparently, Robert Kennedy's attempts to withdraw gambling licences provoked revenge from a famous personality who was both a friend of Marilyn and had Mafia links. With his encouragement, Marilyn is supposed to have planned to fake a suicide by a pretended – or *actual* – overdose. If the latter were true, it would explain Marilyn's curious inquiry of her housekeeper Eunice Murray on 4 August about the availability of oxygen in the house. 'Is there any oxygen around?' Marilyn had asked. Oxygen is used to bring round victims of

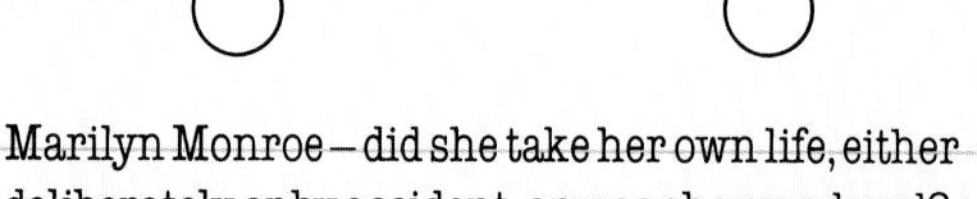

Marilyn Monroe – did she take her own life, either deliberately or by accident, or was she murdered?

The plaque on Marilyn Monroe's tomb at Westwood Memorial Cemetery, Hollywood; the roses arrive twice weekly from her devoted ex-husband Joe DiMaggio. More than 20 years on, and despite the efforts of a number of investigators, the circumstances of Marilyn's tragic death remain shrouded in mystery

barbiturate overdoses. Having taken her overdose, Marilyn would have telephoned Robert Kennedy at the Lawfords' home. She was supposed to say she was killing herself, at which Kennedy was to spring to the rescue – and a press scandal would ensue. But perhaps something went wrong, and Marilyn could not get through, or nobody arrived in time to save her life.

Investigators like Slatzer and Speriglio continue to chip away at what they believe was the cover-up of Marilyn Monroe's death, though that there was one has yet to be proved conclusively. There remain four possible causes of the death. She *may* have committed suicide, unable to continue her confused, sometimes harrowing existence; or, for similar reasons, she may have taken an accidental overdose with no grimmer intent than the shutting out of one miserable, lonely evening. She may have been murdered for political or personal gain, or she may have been accidentally killed by those visiting her armed, for various reasons, with hypodermic syringes and drugs.

British theory

British investigative journalist Anthony Summers produced what is probably the definitive account of Marilyn's own private world in his book *Goddess: The Secret Lives of Marilyn Monroe*, which was published in the autumn of 1985. Summers added little to the researches of Slatzer and Speraglio, but he did produce a convincing – if circumstantial – theory to account for at least some of the discrepancies concerning the events that occurred between 7.30pm on Saturday 4 August when the star had retired to her room, and 4.40am on the following day when Sergeant Clemmons arrived at the scene and examined the body.

According to Summers, *someone* – presumably aware of the last, hazy telephone call to Lawford – went round to the house on Fifth Helena Drive and found Marilyn unconscious but still alive. This agent then arranged for her to be whisked to hospital, but she died en route, and it was considered best to take the body back to the house and lay it out as it would have been if events had taken a natural course. If true, this would explain at least the discrepancies in accounts of the position of the telephone in relation to the body.

Following the publication of Summers' book speculation arose that the inquiry might be reopened. But in late November, the Los Angeles Coroner's office issued a statement to the effect that this was not to happen.

What must be considered is that, because of her status as a world-renowned film star and sex symbol, her death, even if it had been more conventional, would inevitably have provoked a whirlwind of inquiries, questions and rumours – and with these all the ensuing denials and 'cover-ups'. Accordingly, it is probably too late for there ever to be a balanced, unemotional investigation into Marilyn Monroe's death. The truth may never be known.

Murder in the Bahamas

In July 1943, Sir Harry Oakes, 'the richest baronet in the British Empire', was found burned and battered to death at his home in the Bahamas. The man tried for the crime was the victim's son-in-law, a member of one of France's most distinguished families. The investigation was very questionable and he was acquitted, but to this day no official attempt has ever been made to find the real murderer. Was Oakes in fact killed in a fight with a gambling syndicate? And did the Duke of Windsor, formerly King Edward VIII, who was then governor of the islands, have reasons for wanting the case closed?

At 7am on Thursday 8 July 1943, the Duke of Windsor, formerly Edward VIII of England, who was at that time governor of the British colony of the Bahamas, was awakened to be told that Sir Harry Oakes, the Bahamas' richest and perhaps best known resident after the duke himself, had been found dead on his bed at Westbourne, one of several homes he owned in Nassau. The 69-year-old baronet, who was a favourite of the duke, had been murdered. His head had been smashed with a sharp instrument, and his chest, legs and genitals had been burnt.

After hearing the news, the duke did nothing for two hours, and then made his first move: he attempted on the telephone to censor news of the murder and confine it to the Bahamas. He failed. Harold Christie, one of the leaders of the islands' society, who had discovered the body, had in panic telephoned a number of people, one of them a Nassau newspaperman who had immediately telegraphed news of the death to the major press agencies.

The duke then rang Christie, who was still at Westbourne. Shortly afterwards he made a call to Commissioner R. A. Erskine-Lindop, head of the Bahamian police. What was said between them remains a mystery, but Erskine-Lindop should have known that the duke had three obvious courses of action: he could leave the investigation to the Bahamas police force; he could seek assistance from the FBI, since the USA was only 90 miles (145 kilometres) away; or, most obviously, since the islands formed a Crown Colony, he could call in Scotland Yard. Instead, at 10.50am, nearly four hours after first hearing the news, he placed a call to Captain Edward Walter Melchen, chief of the Homicide Bureau of the Miami Police Department.

Melchen was a staid and unimaginative policeman, plump and bespectacled. He was apparently picked by the duke for no other reason than that he had served as a bodyguard to the Windsors when they had visited Miami. He was later to testify in court that he did not think the duke's request that he come immediately to Nassau was unusual – but unusual it certainly was. According to Captain Melchen, the duke told him, without naming the dead man, that a 'leading citizen of the Bahamas had apparently committed suicide', and asked if the police captain could fly over to confirm the details so that 'there would be no problems'. Melchen said that he would, and arrived at Nassau with Captain James Otto Barker, head of Miami's Bureau of Criminal Investigation, shortly before 2pm.

Their first sight of the body lying on the stained and scorched bed ruled out any possibility of suicide – a fact that the duke, who had heard all the details from Christie, must have known. Around the left ear were four triangular wounds, at least three of which had penetrated the skull, and the face was spattered with blood. The pyjama-clad corpse lay on its back and part of the cloth was burnt away, revealing the seared flesh underneath; 'wet' and 'dry' blisters were visible on the chest and abdomen. The circumstances showed that the killing could not have taken place while the body was in this position: a rivulet of blood ran from the left ear, across the cheek and nose, indicating that at some time after the attack Sir Harry must have lain on his right side; furthermore, the mattress *under* his body had been scorched. The mosquito netting that normally hung over the bed had been burnt away, and there were sooty marks on the ceiling of the bedroom, in the corridor outside, down the staircase and in the ground-floor hall. Most bizarre of all, the body was covered in feathers, which had apparently come from one of the pillows.

There was a plethora of bloody handprints, some smeared, some still wet, on two of the walls of Sir Harry's room. There were further bloody prints on a door leading to the balcony outside the room that Christie had used, which was separated from Oakes' room by one empty bedroom and a bathroom. To the dead man's right stood a flimsy Chinese folding screen, sooty but not obviously bloodstained. This was to play an important part in the ensuing drama.

The Duke and Duchess of Windsor in May 1943. The duke was governor of the Bahamas, and had a close friendship with Sir Harry Oakes. The first person to be told of Oakes' death, he was deeply involved in the investigation

Harry Oakes was born on 23 December 1874, the third child of a lawyer who was head of an old military and land-owning family in the village of Sangerville, Maine. At the age of 23, he set off to the Klondike in Alaska to seek his fortune as a gold prospector, and determined that if ever he discovered a promising vein he would hold on to his claim, even if it meant excavating it alone.

In the end Harry Oakes achieved all the goals he had set himself. He became a multi-millionaire – 'the richest baronet', as one newspaper put it, 'in the British Empire' – and he gained this status with very little outside help. In 1910 he staked claims on the shores of Kirkland Lake in Canada and, with just $2.65 in the pocket of his tattered trousers, he searched for and found what was to become known as the Lake Shore Mine. No one knows precisely how much it eventually produced, but by the Thirties, Oakes' fortune was thought to be in the region of at least £200 million.

The Bahamas stretch for more than 700 miles (1120 kilometres) off the east coast of Florida. New Providence Island is the most important; it was here, in the capital of Nassau, that Sir Harry Oakes met his death

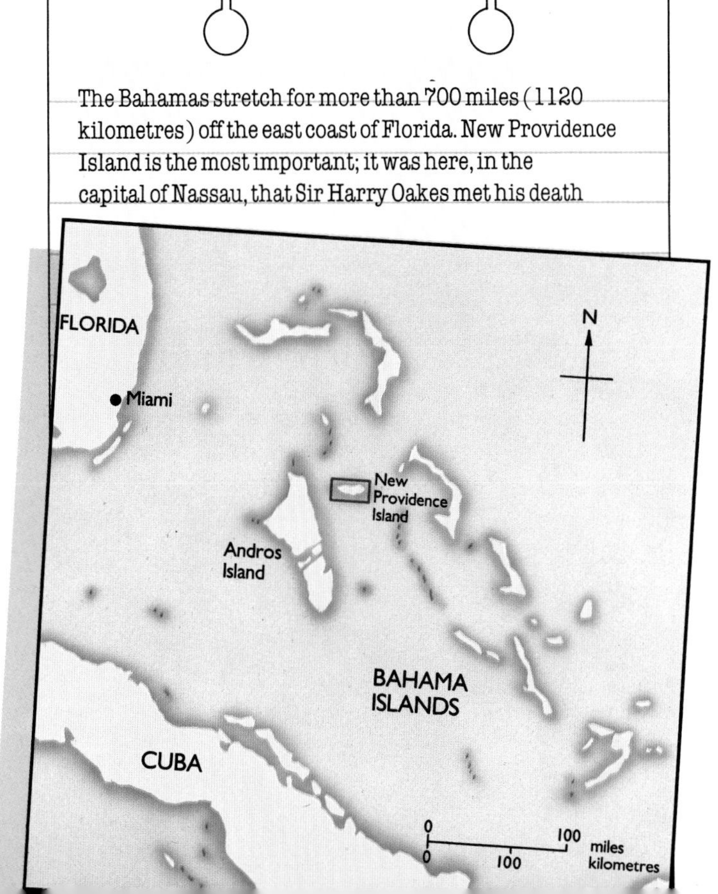

Favourite child

Oakes remained a bachelor until, at the age of 49, he met and fell in love with a blue-eyed 24-year-old. The gentle and well-educated Eunice MacIntyre was equally captivated by him, despite the difference in their ages. They married and had five children; the first, Nancy, born in May 1924, was to be Harry's favourite offspring.

Oakes, who had been living in Canada, fell out with the Canadian government over the taxation of his mines. In the mid Thirties he moved to the Bahamas, and made his base at a house called Westbourne, just outside the capital of Nassau on New

The wealthy Bahamian property developer Harold Christie. He had stayed the night at Oakes' house, and discovered the body himself on the morning of 8 July 1943

Providence Island. In due course, he became a British citizen.

After bestowing the sum of £90,000 on St George's Hospital in London, he was made a baronet in King George VI's birthday honours list in June 1938. George VI had assumed the throne in December 1936 after the abdication of his elder brother Edward VIII. As Duke of Windsor and governor of the Bahamas, the ex-king was to be deeply involved in the investigation of Oakes' death.

Harold Christie was the first person to be interviewed by Melchen and Barker. He was then 47 years old; his family had been resident in Nassau and its environs for 250 years. A member of the islands' Executive Council and a property developer, he was second in wealth only to Oakes himself.

With Christie's help the Miami detectives pieced together the dead man's movements since the previous afternoon. Sir Harry had called on Christie at his office shortly after lunch. Then, since he intended to go and see his wife in their house at Bar Harbor, Maine, he went to the office of the Colonial Secretary to gain the formal exit visa that was necessary in wartime. He telephoned the Duke of Windsor's secretary to confirm a golf date with the duke, and returned to pick up Christie for a game of tennis at the Westbourne house.

After the set, the two men held a small cocktail party for friends in the Westbourne mansion. By 11pm the guests had all left, except for Christie, who often slept at houses at which he had dined – it was a good way, he later explained, of escaping the constantly ringing telephone and the petitioners who pestered him. On this particular night he borrowed a pair of pyjamas from Oakes, chatted while Sir Harry undressed and ducked under his mosquito netting, and then went to his own room. There he read for a while and fell asleep at about 12.15am.

During the night, said Christie, he was awakened by the tropical storm that had blown up, but fell asleep again until just before 7am. When he awoke he looked at his watch and shambled onto the balcony that connected his room with Sir Harry's. He entered the darkened bedroom, then saw the charred remnants of the mosquito netting and realised that something was hideously wrong. He put a glass of water to his friend's lips, for the body was still warm. He then claimed to have dabbed the bloody face with a towel with which he later wiped his own bloodstained hands.

Realising that the baronet was dead, Christie ran

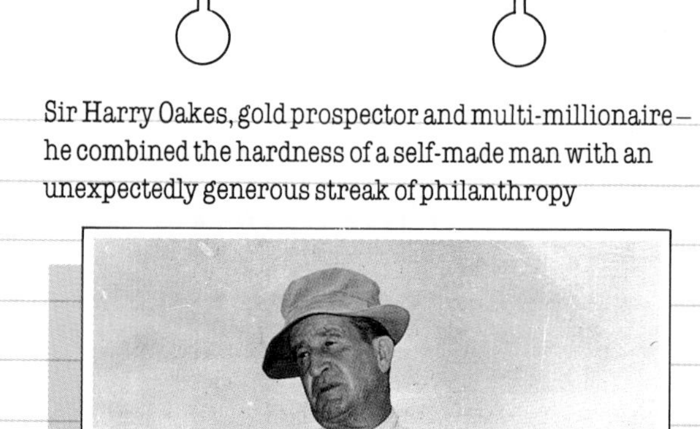

Sir Harry Oakes, gold prospector and multi-millionaire – he combined the hardness of a self-made man with an unexpectedly generous streak of philanthropy

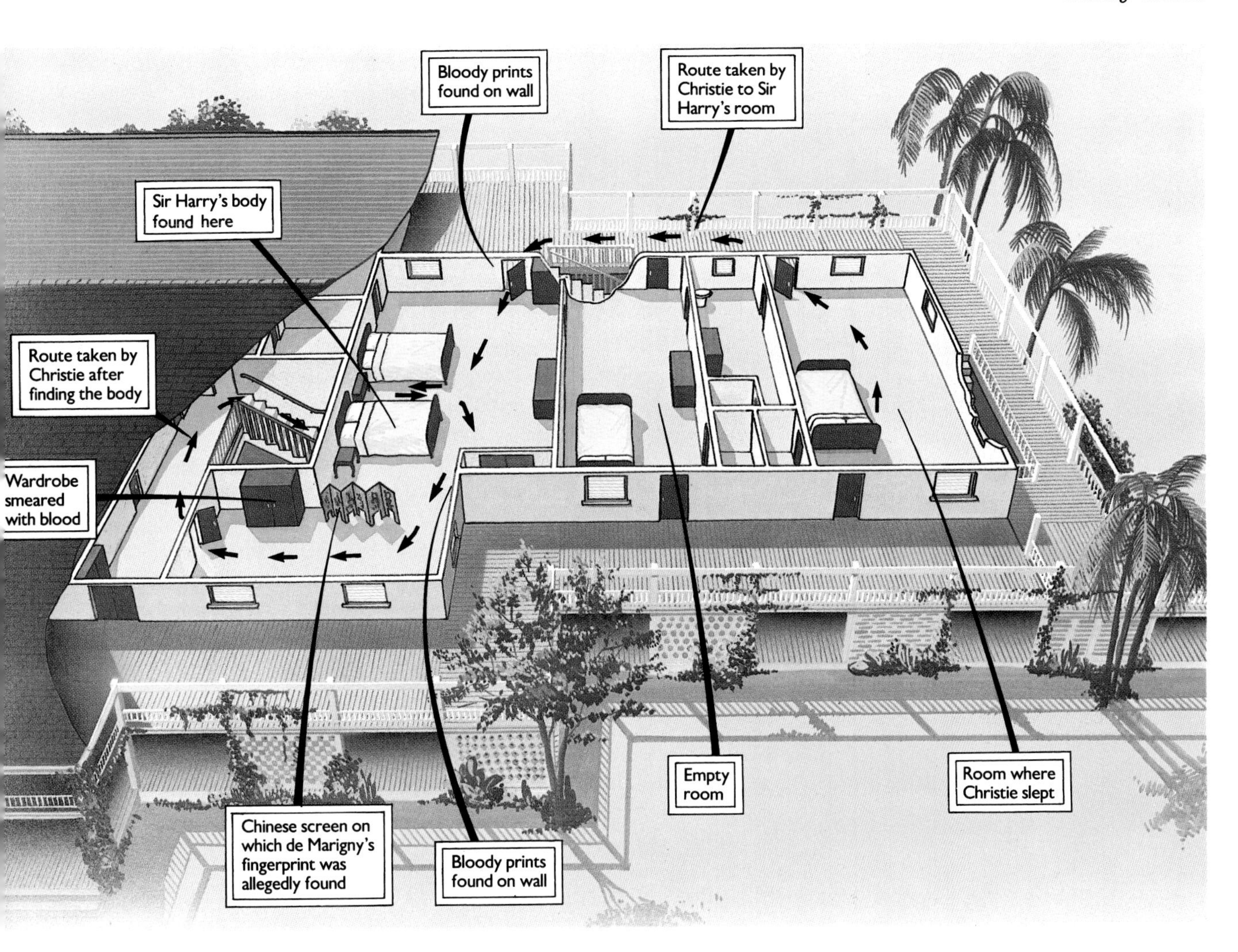

A second floor plan of Westbourne, showing the rooms used by Oakes and Christie, and Christie's routes before and after the discovery of the body. It is based on a sketch made by a Royal Air Force officer on 14 July 1943, for the trial of Alfred de Marigny

down the stairs, calling for servants and for Mrs Madeline Kelly, the wife of Sir Harry's business manager, who lived on the estate nearby. The bedroom and the corridor outside were, he claimed, 'smoky', but he remembered few exact details because he was in a 'funk of terror'. As Mrs Kelly arrived on the scene he began telephoning people – the police, his brother Frank, and various friends of Sir Harry. Perhaps significantly, it was only many years later that he admitted that the first person he had rung was the Duke of Windsor.

Inept investigation

The duke and Christie were rarely out of touch by telephone for the rest of that day and the following day. Captain Melchen routinely and unimaginatively interviewed everyone who visited Westbourne, while his colleague Captain Barker pottered about looking for clues. Barker's investigation must rank as one of the most careless and inept in forensic history. Barker, head of Miami's Police Fingerprint Division and supposedly an expert, had apparently forgotten to bring a fingerprint camera (a boxed instrument with built-in lights, used to take photographs of 'latent' prints on walls, windows, and so forth). There was a Royal Air Force camp in Nassau with its own well-equipped military police division which, of course, possessed a fingerprint camera, but Barker later claimed that he 'hadn't thought' of borrowing it. Instead, he dusted fingerprint powder onto wet, bloodstained prints – thus destroying them – while leaving dry prints until the following day, by which time, he hoped, the humidity following the storm would have lessened. Meanwhile, he allowed policemen and visitors to Westbourne to roam around the bedroom, destroying possible clues.

At 4pm on Friday, the day after the murder, the Duke of Windsor arrived at Westbourne and had a private chat with Captain Barker. Both the duke and Barker are now dead, so no one can know what took place; but within two hours of their talk a suspect was arrested.

He was Count Marie Alfred Fouquereaux de Marigny, an aristocratic Frenchman, brilliant amateur yachtsman, latterly a chicken-farmer – and son-in-law to Sir Harry by his marriage to the

Count Alfred de Marigny's friend and lodger, the Marquis Georges de Visdelou Guimbeau, with his girlfriend Betty Roberts, who were called as witnesses in the trial

baronet's favourite child, Nancy. Haughty and self-opinionated, he had a profound disdain for the Duke of Windsor.

The previous year the 32-year-old de Marigny had caused a sensation in the Bahamas by running off with the 18-year-old Nancy Oakes. Nancy, a petite, freckle-faced redhead, had been in love with the tall, debonair Frenchman for two years. The couple went to New York where they were married in the Bronx County Courthouse. Lady Oakes, staying at Bar Harbor, collapsed in a faint when she heard the news. Sir Harry reacted in typical fashion. 'So you're married,' he said to Nancy over the telephone. 'How much do you want?' 'Nothing,' she replied. To the baronet's astonishment she was telling the truth. Neither she nor her new husband ever asked the millionaire for a penny.

As father- and son-in-law Oakes and de Marigny had at first got on remarkably well. De Marigny was building up his buiness with the sort of unremitting hard work that Sir Harry admired. Oakes' biographer, Geoffrey Bocca, told how Sir Harry and de Marigny were having dinner together one evening when the baronet suddenly slapped his son-in-law on the back. 'Frenchie,' he said, 'you are a son of a bitch for marrying my daughter, but I like you. I don't give a damn about your past life. No man with any guts bothers about his or anybody else's past life. I don't. The only thing that matters to me is that you make Nancy happy.'

This friendly situation was not to last. On one occasion, de Marigny's off-handed disregard for the Duke of Windsor threw Sir Harry into a white-hot rage. Threatening to have de Marigny horse-whipped, he bellowed at the top of his voice, 'You've been doing this sort of thing for far too long around here, damn you! As far as I'm concerned, you are out, do you understand?' But in the paradoxical style typical of him, his anger evaporated as soon as it had come. 'Not a bad sort, de Marigny,' he commented to his terrified 15-year-old son, who had witnessed the scene. 'You've got to get to know these Frenchies.'

The acrimonious atmosphere that existed between Oakes and de Marigny was common knowledge in Nassau. But de Marigny's story was not, in the circumstances, one that a guilty man as worldly wise as the count would have been likely to give.

On the night of the murder, de Marigny's wife Nancy was away, staying with her mother at Bar Harbor. He had been out racing his yacht the previous afternoon, and had returned to his home in Victoria Avenue to dress for dinner. Later, at the Prince George Hotel, he had met his friend and lodger the Marquis de Visdelou, the Marquis' girlfriend Betty Roberts and some other friends, including Dorothy Clark and Jean Ainslie, the wives of a couple of Royal Canadian Air Force officers who were stationed locally. After some drinks, the entire group, 11 in all, set off for a noisy dinner party at de Marigny's house. By the time they got there the storm had begun; sheets of rain were falling on the patio where de Marigny had originally intended to seat his guests. Plates and cutlery were hastily

Nancy Oakes, aged 18, at about the time she eloped with and married Alfred de Marigny

moved indoors and dried, while the count lit candles and hurricane lamps to decorate the dinner tables.

Towards midnight, Mrs Clark and Mrs Ainslie drove with de Marigny through Nassau to the women's billet at Hubbard's Cottage, almost next door to Westbourne.

De Marigny recalled that Westbourne was dark as he passed it at about 12.30am. He dropped the two women off, turned the car around and drove past Westbourne again. All was still, quiet and dark.

Barker and Melchen asked de Marigny to bare his arms. Together with Erksine-Lindop, they peered through a magnifying glass at his arms, hands and beard and claimed that some of the hairs on them were singed. De Marigny explained that the singeing must have occurred when he lit the hurricane lamps for his dinner party. He then accompanied the police while they searched his house. They asked him to produce the shirt he had worn the night before, and in his usual haughty manner he told them that such matters were beyond him: he didn't know where the maid put his laundry. When Captain Barker examined the suit he had worn that night and announced, suspiciously, that it was newly pressed, the count reacted indignantly.

Powerful motorboat

De Marigny's story could neither be proved nor disproved. The two Miami officers noted his admission that he had passed Westbourne at what appeared to be a relevant time. Yet they paid little regard to two other accounts of that fateful night.

A caretaker at Lyford Cay, 17 miles (27 kilometres) away at the opposite end of New Providence Island from Nassau, came forward to report having seen a powerful motorboat pull in by the pier and several men, strangers to the island, disembark. They had entered a waiting car and driven off. Some time after midnight they had reappeared, climbed back aboard the boat, and sailed away.

The second story came from Superintendent Edward Sears, a traffic controller and one of the islands' most highly regarded policemen, who had known Harold Christie from childhood. He had been driving through Nassau at about midnight, when a station wagon passed him at a junction. The driver was in darkness, but Sears would stake his reputation on the passenger having been Christie.

Early on the morning after the murder, Barker decided that the air had dried enough for another attempt at dusting fingerprints. Among the bloodstains he found several handprints about 3 feet (1 metre) from the floor, close to Sir Harry's bed; these, he deduced, had been made by Sir Harry as he tried to get up after his attacker's first blow had landed. It was a specious piece of reasoning, for the blood was far too badly smeared to yield any clear prints. In any case, despite the obvious violence done to the body and the bed, there were no indications of an actual struggle; no furniture had been knocked over, for instance. The prints may equally well have belonged to the attacker, or even to Harold Christie, who had knelt beside the bed to attend his friend and admitted to having bloodied his hands in the process.

Downstairs, Captain Melchen had gathered all the witnesses together to question them. The Marquis de Visdelou, Betty Roberts, Jean Ainslie, Dorothy Clark and the other guests from de Marigny's party were all there. Mrs Ainslie and Mrs Clark testified that de Marigny had left them at Hubbard's Cottage at about 12.30am, and the marquis confirmed that the count had been in bed at 3am. Then de Marigny himself arrived and was questioned separately by Melchen.

It was 4pm on that Friday when the Duke of Windsor called at Westbourne and had his private talk

Harold Christie (left) with Sir Harry Oakes on a visit they made in 1941 to the spot in the Bahamas where Columbus is though to have landed on 12 October 1492

with Barker upstairs in Sir Harry's bedroom. As he came down again, de Marigny was standing with Melchen in the ground-floor room. The duke stared coldly at the man who had so often slighted him. It was at that moment, de Marigny told Geoffrey Bocca years later, that he first felt uneasy; 'something turned' in the pit of his stomach, he said, 'a feeling of being trapped, a feeling of fear.'

At 6pm de Marigny was formally charged with the murder of Sir Harold Oakes, his father-in-law. As he was being arrested, the autopsy on Sir Harry's body was being completed at Nassau mortuary. It was performed by Dr Lawrence Wylie Fitzmaurice, acting chief medical officer of the Bahamas, and watched by Dr Hugh Arnley Quackenbush, Sir Harry's doctor. Both were highly competent medical men, but neither had anything but the most rudimentary knowledge of forensic pathology.

Quackenbush examined the body soon after its discovery, and concluded that Sir Harry had died between about 3am and 5.30am. Some of the 'wet' blisters on the body were, he claimed erroneously, caused before Sir Harry's death.

Sir Harry's corpse was then moved to the Nassau hospital morgue, where it was examined a second time by Dr Fitzmaurice. The head wounds were responsible for the baronet's death. They had been caused by a blunt instrument, triangular in section, that had penetrated about 1 inch (2.5 centimetres) into the skull and brain tissue. There was 'contra-coup' bruising of the brain opposite the site of the wounds; this occurs when a heavy blow has caused the brain to 'bounce' off the interior of the skull. All the wounds had been caused by a forward and downward thrust; in other words, the blows could not have been administered while Sir Harry was lying on his back on the bed. In any case, the burns on his back, and the flow of blood from the ear wounds *over* the cheek and bridge of the nose, apparently against the force of gravity, showed that he had been placed in position on the bed after the attack.

On the fourth day of the trial Nancy, Countess de Marigny, talks to Raymond Schindler, the private investigator she hired to prove her husband's innocence

Dr Fitzmaurice estimated the time of death at between 1.30 and 3.30am – much earlier than the time suggested by Dr Quackenbush. The discrepancy between the times given by the two doctors did little for de Marigny's peace of mind; it simply meant – in view of the testimony of the two women he had taken home – that he could have been at Westbourne at the time of the killing.

No murder weapon had been found, but the detectives vaguely speculated that the wounds might have been caused by one of several spiked railings that were missing from the fence around Westbourne. What the detectives needed was proof that de Marigny had been in the dead man's bedroom. And suddenly, spectacularly, they seemed to have it.

Marigny's fingerprints

On 15 July 1943 Sir Harry's body was put in a coffin and flown from Nassau to Bar Harbor, Maine, where it was to be buried at Dover Foxcroft Cemetery. After the funeral service about a dozen people went back to the Oakes local home, including the detectives Melchen and Barker. Lady Oakes lay down on her day-bed and her funeral guests gathered around her. Suddenly Captain Barker began a remarkable performance. Pacing the room and making dramatic gestures to illustrate his points, he told the assembled guests how he believed that de Marigny had committed the murder. Barker claimed that de Marigny had taken a railing from the Westbourne fence, climbed into Sir Harry's bedroom and struck the older man down. Sir Harry had clawed at the walls, smearing them with his own blood and had fallen unconscious. The count had then sprayed the bed with an insecticide gun (kept in the bedroom to deal with mosquitos), set fire to the bedding, placed the body on the burning bed and set fire to Sir Harry's pyjamas. Barker finished with a startling statement: he had found several of de Marigny's fingerprints in the murdered man's bedroom. 'You have?' exclaimed his chief, Melchen, in obvious amazement. Later he was to admit that this was the first he had heard of the 'damning' evidence.

For Nancy de Marigny, it was the final straw. Already distrustful of the two Miami detectives and certain that her husband could never have committed the crime, she stormed out of the house and booked a ticket for New York. There, through her

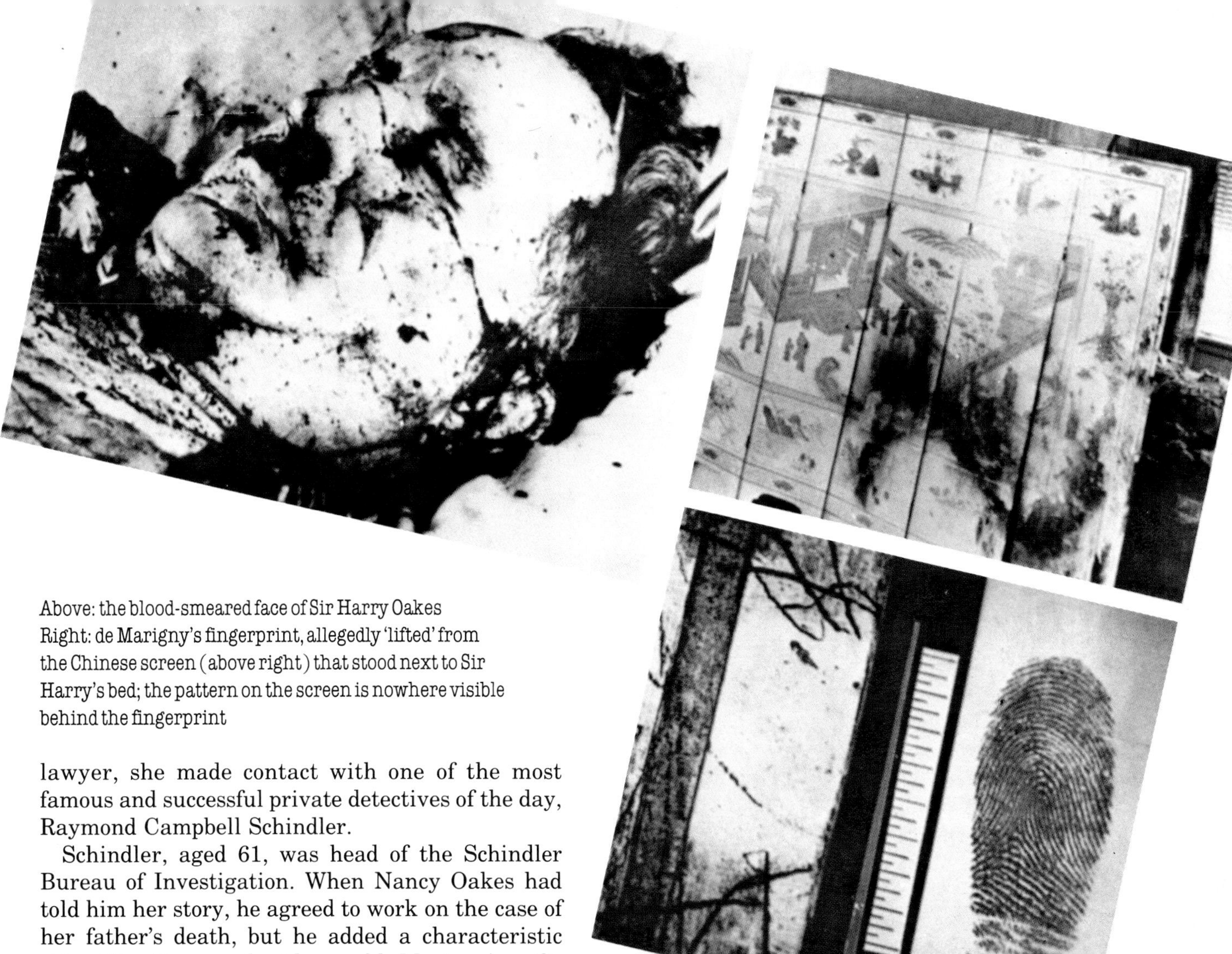

Above: the blood-smeared face of Sir Harry Oakes
Right: de Marigny's fingerprint, allegedly 'lifted' from the Chinese screen (above right) that stood next to Sir Harry's bed; the pattern on the screen is nowhere visible behind the fingerprint

lawyer, she made contact with one of the most famous and successful private detectives of the day, Raymond Campbell Schindler.

Schindler, aged 61, was head of the Schindler Bureau of Investigation. When Nancy Oakes had told him her story, he agreed to work on the case of her father's death, but he added a characteristic rider: if he discovered evidence of de Marigny's guilt, he would hand it over to the authorities. Nancy acquiesced in this demand.

Schindler arrived in Nassau with a team of secretaries and myriads of pressmen about 10 days after the killing. He immediately found himself at odds with the Bahamian police.

After some difficulty, Schindler gained access to Westbourne with the help of Geoffrey Higgs, the barrister who had been assigned to de Marigny's defence. He was appalled by the lax nature of the investigation, particularly when he found uniformed policemen scrubbing the walls outside Sir Harry's bedroom. 'Those are handprints!' he protested. 'Stop it! We'll never get them back!' The constables scrubbed on. Schindler calmed down and asked them to wait until he had telephoned their superiors. 'Why are you so determined to wash off these prints?' he asked. 'Because, sir,' came the stubborn reply, 'these prints are not those of Count de Marigny; therefore, they'll only confuse the evidence.'

Probing further, Schindler discovered that the 'several' prints described by Barker as having been made by de Marigny in fact amounted to one: a print of the little finger of the count's left hand which, the Miami detective claimed, had been 'lifted' from the Chinese screen in Sir Harry's bedroom. At this point Schindler contacted Maurice B. O'Neil, superintendent of the Bureau of Investigation of the New Orleans Police Department, past president of the International Association of Identification and one of the world's experts in the study of fingerprints.

It became evident to Schindler that the two Florida investigators had been guilty of complicity in an investigation of disastrous ineptitude. Apart from Barker's dubious handling of the fingerprint evidence, no effort had been made to find the alleged murder weapon, the spiked railing.

The story of the mystery boat at Lyford Cay had also been virtually ignored. The report by Superintendent Sears of seeing Christie driving in Nassau at the time of the murder was dismissed out of hand, despite Superintendent Sears' rank and his standing in the Bahamian police.

In October 1943 Count de Marigny was brought to trial before Sir Oscar Bedford Daly, Chief Justice of the Bahamas, in the islands' Supreme Court. Much of the evidence was merely circumstantial; the brunt of the argument came when Barker's fingerprint evidence was presented. Maurice O'Neil tore it, and Barker's reputation, to shreds.

To begin with, fingerprints are generally 'lifted' – usually by dusting them and applying sticky tape – only if the object on which they are found is immovable. The flimsy Chinese screen on which de Marigny's print was supposedly found was not only easily movable, but was actually being used as an exhibit in the courtroom.

Second, it is standard practice to photograph a print *in situ* before lifting it. Barker admitted he had not done this because, he said, he had 'forgotten' his fingerprint camera and had not troubled to borrow one for the purpose.

Third, O'Neil testified that a pattern of small circles, readily discernible on the screen at the alleged position of the fingerprint, was nowhere to be seen on the background of the lifted print. In addition, no trace of a fingerprint was to be found at the place on the screen, outlined in pencil by Barker, where it was said to have been found.

Fourth, and most damning, Geoffrey Higgs, counsel for the defence, asked O'Neil whether the print could in fact have been lifted from the cellophane wrapper of a packet of cigarettes that had been offered to de Marigny during his interview with Melchen the day after the murder; or whether it could have come from the decanter of water he was given; or from the glass into which he poured the water to drink. To all these questions O'Neil answered, 'Yes'.

Sir Oscar Daly spent five and a half hours in a scrupulous summing up, but it was all too obvious that he was convinced by O'Neil's evidence. He was, however, restrained in his choice of words: 'Barker made statements incredible for an expert. One would think an expert would be more careful,' he said. The jury agreed. They found de Marigny not guilty by nine votes to three. Eric Hallinan, the islands' attorney general and the man responsible for de Marigny's prosecution, was asked after the trial what would now be done to find the real murderer. 'Nothing, as far as I am concerned,' he said. 'The case is completely closed. Call it a day.'

There, for over 40 years, the matter has officially rested. Reliable criminologists do not now doubt that de Marigny was 'framed'. So who *did* kill the cantankerous Harry Oakes?

Harold Christie had been on the scene and had admitted finding the body and smearing the wall with his bloodstained hands. But of all the principals, Christie had the least motive for murdering the baronet, who not only was his friend but had boosted his business on the islands enormously. Besides, Christie, by nature a nervous man, made no attempt to run away or to invent an adequate story.

For some years after the killing it was rumoured that the act had been perpetrated by black dissidents – there had been serious riots in Nassau shortly before the murder – and that the burning and 'feathering' of the body had been part of a voodoo ritual. But the practice of voodoo has never been prominent in the Bahamas, the murder bore no relation to voodoo practice, and Sir Harry was liked and respected by the poorer black Bahamians.

Meyer Lansky, one of the mobsters who, according to biographer Marshall Houts, murdered Sir Harry

Gambling theory

The likeliest theory advanced so far was one put forward by Marshall Houts in 1972 in a book published in the United States under the title *King's X* – a phrase used in American children's games for 'king's excuse', a claim for exemption from being caught or 'tagged'. Houts, a former judge, law professor and wartime FBI agent, claimed to have gained his information from unnamed 'informers'. The story they gave him was briefly this.

On the afternoon of Wednesday 7 July, the day before the murder, a large power boat carrying five men drew into Nassau harbour from Miami, Florida. Three of the men had worked on prohibition-defying rum-running trips organised in part by Harold Christie; all of them now worked for 'Organised Crime', the association set up by Charlie 'Lucky' Luciano, Benjamin 'Bugsy' Siegel and the 'mob's' financial wizard, Meyer Lansky. When prohibition had been ended prostitution, narcotics and gambling seemed to be the new 'rackets'. Neither Luciano nor Lansky was eager to be connected with the first two.

Siegel had already begun to negotiate to buy up a small Nevada shanty town named Las Vegas. By his efforts it was to be one of the foremost gambling

Benjamin 'Bugsy' Siegel – it was his gang that, Marshall Houts alleges, killed Oakes because he was impeding their attempts to build a gambling empire in Nassau. Siegel was eliminated in 1947 on the orders of the Syndicate directors, including his old associate 'Lucky' Luciano

capitals of the world, and Nassau, with all its rich residents and richer potential, seemed another ideal site for a gambling kingdom. According to Houts' informants, Lansky had approached his old associate Harold Christie and, through him, the Duke of Windsor, as part of his plan to gain a toe-hold on the island paradise.

Christie was probably enthusiastic: he had seen no wrong in breaking the prohibition rules, and on the mainland gambling was sanctioned in many areas. The duke had himself been an habitué of the casinos of Monte Carlo and should have posed no problem. But Sir Harry Oakes was an entirely different prospect. Like many 'hard' men, he was in many ways highly moral. He would have no truck with the idea of planeloads of gamblers descending on 'his' world. Christie reported this to Lansky, and Lansky in turn put pressure on Christie and the duke: if the deal did not come off, Christie's mother and the duchess would suffer.

On the night when Lansky's 'boys' arrived in their boat at Nassau harbour, Christie dined with Oakes and his friends and then persuaded Sir Harry to come with him to meet Lansky's associates, perhaps to negotiate. Oakes, unknown to Christie, took his automatic with him. Aboard the mobsters' boat, his notorious temper flared, and he pulled the gun. One of the crew hit him with a four-pronged winch handle – causing the curious holes in his head – and he fell unconscious. The mob bundled the body into the back of a station wagon and one of them drove with the terrified Christie through the streets of Nassau to Westbourne. During the trip Christie was spotted in the passenger seat of the vehicle by Superintendent Sears.

Once at Westbourne, the gangster told Christie to go to bed and stay there until his normal time of rising. Then he sprayed the body with the inflammable insecticide kept in the room, set fire to the bed, and placed the body on it – presumably tearing the pillow and releasing feathers in the process. The intention was to conceal the assault on Oakes, but the job was bungled. Lansky, Houts' informants said, had the men responsible 'stringently disciplined' for the unauthorised murder. And the following morning Christie and the duke had the job of finding a 'culprit'.

The day the president died

When John Kennedy was shot in Dallas in 1963, his killer, Lee Harvey Oswald, was said to have acted alone. But there is considerable evidence to the contrary

At 11.40am on Friday 22 November 1963, President John Fitzgerald Kennedy of the United States and his wife Jacqueline landed at the airport of Love Field, Dallas, Texas. Within an hour, the 46-year-old president was to be killed by a bullet – one of the several that were fired on that fateful day.

As Kennedy was preparing to leave Washington earlier that morning, he had made the prophetic remark: 'If anybody really wanted to shoot the president it is not a very difficult job – all one has to do is to get on a high building some day with a telescopic rifle and there is nothing anyone can do to defend against such an attempt.' He did not know that this day had already dawned.

Soon after 11.50am the motorcade set off from the airport with Kennedy in the rear seat of the presidential limousine with his wife Jackie on his left.

The Governor of Texas, John Connally, and his wife sat in front of them in the open-topped car. The crowd was so enthusiastic that Mrs Connally leaned back to say delightedly to the president, 'Mr Kennedy, you can't say Dallas doesn't love you!'

The car passed the seven-storey Texas School Book Depository at about 12.30pm, travelling at about 11 miles per hour (18 kilometres per hour). As it went down Elm Street, three shots were fired into it from a range of about 80 yards (75 metres). The exact number and direction of the shots have given rise to bitter controversy that still rages.

What is certain is that there were at least three shots, and possibly more. The first hit Kennedy at the top of his back and exited through his neck, but was not fatal. He raised his hands and clutched his neck and said, 'My God, I'm hit!' A few seconds later, Governor Connally was wounded in the back by a bullet that travelled down his arm, smashed his wrist and finally lodged in his thigh. The third bullet was the fatal one. It hit Kennedy in the head and exploded his brain and skull.

The shots all seem to have been fired from the direction of the Texas School Book Depository, and the only bullet that was recovered matched the type used with a rifle found on the sixth floor, along with three spent cartridges. The rifle, an Italian Mannlicher-Carcano, had been bought from a Chicago mail-order firm by Lee Harvey Oswald, using the alias 'A. Hidell', on 20 March 1963.

Oswald had abandoned his rifle and gone down to a lunch room on the second floor. Police, who had seen a rifle barrel poking from the sixth-floor window, raced to the warehouse and saw Oswald standing nonchalantly by a drinks-vending machine. Oswald was asked if he worked in the building and, when other workers said that he did, the police continued their search without holding him for questioning.

He made his way to his flat at Oak Cliff, where he changed and picked up a .38 revolver. About 1.15pm he was challenged in the street by Patrolman J. D. Tippit; Oswald shot the officer dead, but was seen seeking refuge in a cinema and arrested. Palmprints on the assassination rifle led police to charge him with the killing of both Tippit and Kennedy.

John and Jackie Kennedy set off across the tarmac of Love Field airport, Dallas, on 22 November 1963

While there can be no reasonable doubt that rifle shots, including the fatal bullet, were fired from the window on the sixth floor of the book warehouse, many witnesses were positive that other shots had come from a sloping area of Dealey Plaza, to the right and front of the president's car, that became known as the 'grassy knoll'.

At least three witnesses, one a police officer, claimed to have been warned away from the area by a man carrying what appeared to be secret service credentials. But inquiries showed that no secret service agent had ever been stationed there.

Was this 'agent' a second rifleman? Other witnesses, including a railway worker called Lee Bowers, described seeing two men by the boundary fence shortly before the assassination, one of whom could have been the 'agent'. Others said that they had seen a man running away from that area towards a railway siding after the shooting and driving off in a black car, into which he had hurriedly thrown something.

Among other witnesses who claimed to have heard a shot coming from the grassy knoll behind them was Abraham Zapruder, a Dallas clothing manufacturer. The ciné film he took of the assassination on his home movie camera has become the most famous amateur film footage of all time. It provided

Frames from the film shot by Abraham Zapruder as he watched the presidential motorcade. The film provided crucial evidence about the exact time of the shots that killed Kennedy

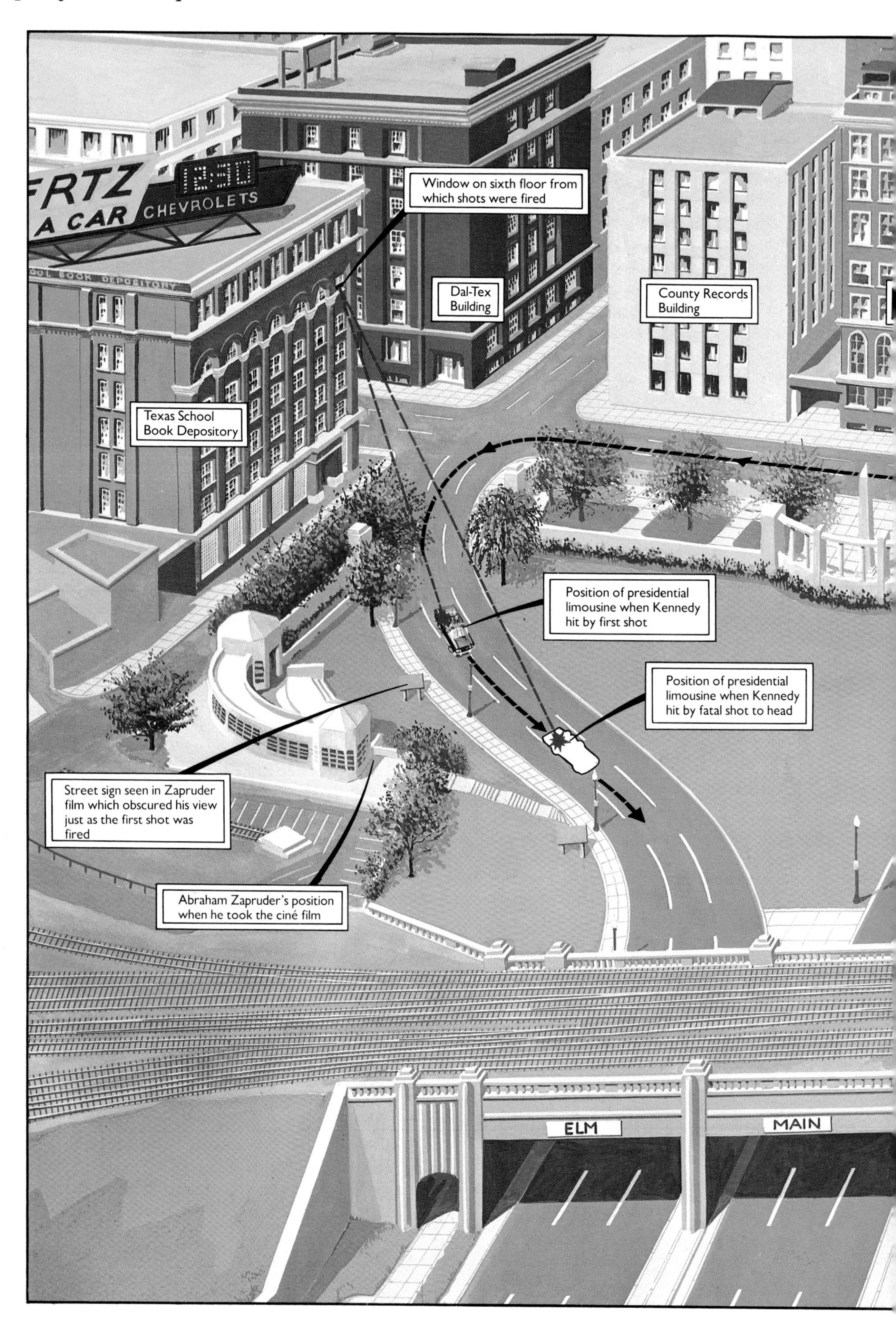

FRTZ
A CAR
12:30
CHEVROLETS
Window on sixth floor from which shots were fired
Dal-Tex Building
County Records Building
Texas School Book Depository
Position of presidential limousine when Kennedy hit by first shot
Position of presidential limousine when Kennedy hit by fatal shot to head
Street sign seen in Zapruder film which obscured his view just as the first shot was fired
Abraham Zapruder's position when he took the ciné film
ELM
MAIN

crucial evidence about the exact time of the shots and the interval between them.

The evidence of Zapruder's film can also be interpreted as supporting the theory that a gunman on the knoll fired the fatal shot, perhaps using an explosive bullet. The film shows a section of the president's skull flying off backwards as though he had been hit from the front. His body also jerked backwards when, according to the laws of motion, it should have lurched forwards under the impact of a high-velocity bullet from behind. It has been suggested that Kennedy jerked backwards as a result of a muscular spasm caused when his brain was struck and because the limousine had accelerated very suddenly after the first shot. This spasm and the acceleration could also account for the fact that bone and brain matter were found in the street well behind the calculated position of the car at impact.

If there were two riflemen, then there must have been some sort of conspiracy, even if the second gunman were no more than an accomplice of Oswald. The commission under Chief Justice Earl Warren that was set up at once by the new president, Lyndon Johnson, to investigate the assassination, had a specific brief from him 'to exorcise the demon of conspiracy', because the international implications of a conspiracy against the president of the United States were so horrendous. The commission questioned an enormous number of witnesses and exhaustively analysed the medical evidence of the autopsy. But none of the 'second gunman' evidence was recorded in the Warren Commission's report.

If there was a gunman on the knoll, he could have fired and missed, and then not fired again when he saw that the president had been hit. The number of shots fired is still in doubt in the minds of some of those who have studied the assassination. Several witnesses thought that they heard four shots. A congressional committee, later known as the House Assassinations Committee, conducted its own inquiry much later, reporting in the summer of 1979. Acoustics experts, who had examined a sound-recording of the event, gave evidence that four shots had indeed been fired. And the House Assassinations Committee had the benefit of new and dramatic evidence: a second recording, made unintentionally on a police patrolman's radio equipment, that had lain ignored for 16 years.

Even if the Warren Commission was justified at the time in ruling out the presence of a gunman anywhere other than in the book warehouse, there remains evidence for the existence of *two* snipers.

Shortly after the shooting, when police were searching for the gunman, a man was detained for questioning in the nearby Dal-Tex office block after a sharp-eyed liftman reported that he seemed to

Left: the scene at Dealy Plaza

An enlargement of a photograph of the corner of the book warehouse. Inside the open window on the top floor, the cartons arranged by the gunman are clearly visible

have been behaving suspiciously. The man gave his name as Jim Braden and assured police that he had been in the building to look for a telephone and that he was in Dallas not to see the motorcade but because he was in the oil business. When they heard on their radios that Oswald had been arrested at about 1.50pm, the police released Braden. Later it was discovered that he had given a false name and was, in fact, a known criminal called Eugene Brading, who had links with the Mafia. Yet he was never reinvestigated.

The essential question about the president's assassination is: was he killed by a single fanatic who was operating entirely on his own, or was his murder the result of a conspiracy? How many people were involved in the shooting is central to that question. And the answer to that may be found in an analysis of the number of shots that were fired in the very brief time in which the assassination was accomplished.

The conclusion of the Warren Commission was that there was only one rifleman, who was positioned in a sixth-floor window of the Texas School Book Depository. Three spent cartridges were found in the 'sniper's nest' of cardboard cartons that the rifleman had set up behind the window and that he had precipitately abandoned after the shooting. Microballistic analysis of the bullet fragments recovered after the shooting indicated that they had all come from the Mannlicher-Carcano rifle found hidden among the book cartons. So it seemed to the police that three shots had been fired and that they had all come from the window.

But some witnesses among the hundreds of people watching the motorcade, in and near Dealey Plaza, testified to hearing four shots.

Ballistic tests showed that the Mannlicher-Carcano rifle, which undoubtedly belonged to Oswald, had fired some shots, but it was not possible to establish how many. The timing of the shots is crucial, and the only firm evidence about it rests on the amateur ciné film shot from the grassy knoll by Abraham Zapruder. His film was running at 18.3 frames per second. Between frames number 205 and 225 – probably in frame 210, in which the view of the limousine in the lens was obscured by a street sign – the president was hit by what is believed to have been the first shot, and reacted by raising his hands to his throat. From the speed of the car, the position of the street sign, and the speed of Zapruder's film, it can be seen that the car was about 60 yards (55 metres) from the warehouse and that the first, non-fatal, bullet came from the sixth-floor window.

Fatal shot

Frame 313 of Zapruder's film shows, in horrifying detail, the exact moment when Kennedy was shot in the head. According to the frame speed, the limousine was then approximately 85 yards (80 metres) from the warehouse. As the line of sight from the sixth-floor window to the limousine was blocked by an oak tree until the car reached the position it was in at frame 210, it follows that 103 frames must have elapsed between the moment when Oswald had a clear view and the impact of the fatal shot. With the camera running at 18.3 frames per second, that allows only 5.6 seconds to cover the whole of the shooting. And between the first bullet that hit Kennedy in the throat and the bullet that struck his head, it seems to have been generally agreed that there was a third shot. The Warren Commission assumed that this intermediate shot had missed. If there was a fourth shot it, too, presumably missed.

The commission paid great attention to the question of whether or not it was physically possible for a single rifleman to fire three aimed shots, two of them accurate, in a mere 5.6 seconds. Sharpshooters tested the Mannlicher-Carcano on targets representing the upper part of a body and a head, set at the appropriate distance. The targets were stationary and the marksmen had unlimited time to aim their first shots, yet none approached the performance allegedly put up by Lee Harvey Oswald. Furthermore, Oswald had not been a particularly good shot while in the Marines – indeed, his lack of shooting prowess had always been something of a joke among his comrades.

Tests showed that the fastest rate at which this particular rifle could be reloaded and fired was 2.3 seconds, not counting the time needed for accurate aiming at a moving target. It is true that the telescopic sight fitted to the rifle magnified the target four times. But the sight was defective – it made the weapon fire slightly above and to the right of target. Some experts, however, have concluded that given Oswald's position and the direction of the target this defect could actually have been to his advantage.

The Warren Commission's own findings do raise doubts about the claim that one rifleman could have fired the three shots. And if four shots were fired, as some witnesses insist, it was certainly impossible for one man to have dispatched them in the time assumed by the commission. There would have to have been a second gunman with a second rifle – and that immediately raises the nightmare of a conspiracy.

There is a strange conflict surrounding the commission's belief that the bullet that injured Connally first struck the president in the back of the neck. Kennedy's clothing was not examined in relation to his wounds during the autopsy. The FBI's search of the clothing indicated that there was a small hole in the back of Kennedy's jacket, about 6 inches (15 centimetres) below the top of the collar and 2 inches (5 centimetres) to the right of the middle seam. This coincided with a similar hole in his shirt, and there were traces of copper surrounding both holes, indicating that they had been caused by a bullet with a copper alloy coating, such as those fired from Oswald's rifle. But it is hard to see how this bullet could have entered the back of the president's neck, unless his shirt and collar had ridden right up to his ears. Further, the FBI report claims that the autopsy had shown that the bullet had penetrated to a distance of less than a finger-length, suggesting that it remained lodged in the victim's back. No evidence was offered in the report as to what happened to that bullet, which was not tracked through the victim's body to its source, as it should have been. And there is further evidence from a secret service agent, Roy Kellerman, who was present at the autopsy, that examination had also revealed a *shoulder* wound.

There seems to be no doubt that a bullet did exit from the front of Kennedy's neck, but if it was the one that entered his back it must have been travelling upwards. So it could not have entered Connally unless it had richocheted off the car – and that would have damaged it. These facts cast serious doubt on the conclusion that the same bullet struck and wounded both the President and Connally.

Lee Harvey Oswald after his arrest. Although his prints were 'lifted' from the rifle found in the warehouse, Oswald denied killing Kennedy and Patrolman Tippit

Two shots

Governor Connally did not believe that he was struck by the same bullet that first hit the president. He told the commission that he had heard a bang, which he believed to be the sound of a rifle being fired, and had then had time to turn first to his right and then begin to look to his left before slumping forwards with his chest wound. The film taken by Abraham Zapruder, together with snapshots taken by other spectators, tend to support Connally's recollection that the interval between his hearing the first shot and being struck himself was approximately one second.

In 1972 Dr Cyril Wecht, president of the American Academy of Forensic Science, was permitted to examine the autopsy evidence. He was able to show to his own and others' satisfaction that Connally and Kennedy must have been hit by different bullets. If that is so, then either one of the three bullets fired from behind did not miss, as the commission believed, or there were indeed four bullets. The House Assassinations Committee eventually concluded that four shots had almost certainly been fired; that one had come from the grassy knoll; and that Kennedy was probably killed as a result of a conspiracy between at least two gunmen.

More than 20 years after the assassination only

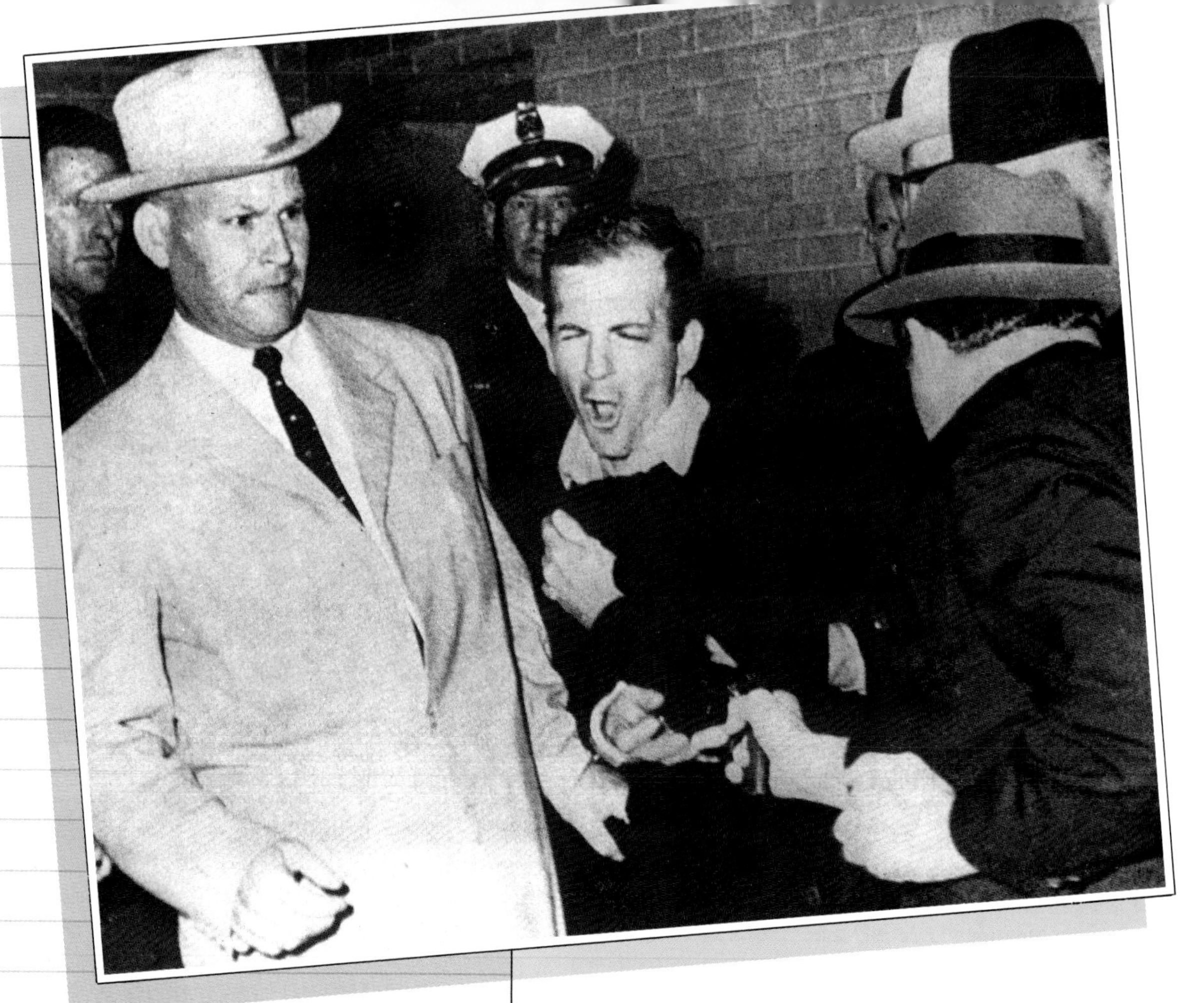

As Oswald is led from his police cell to be transferred to the county jail on Sunday 24 November, Jack Ruby steps forward from the crowd of pressmen and shoots him in the belly at close range

one thing is absolutely certain about the event – he died from brain damage caused by a bullet. Everything else – even the identity of the assassin – remains in doubt.

The motive of the assassin, who called himself Lee Harvey Oswald but used other aliases, has never been established because before he could be properly interrogated he was himself murdered in circumstances that look like a deliberate silencing operation. The assassin's killer, underworld gangster Jack Ruby, lived for four years after he shot Oswald but he, too, was never deeply interrogated.

Was the assassin a lone misfit who killed to draw attention to himself, to revenge himself on society or for some other totally private purpose? Or was he acting on behalf of some conspiracy and, if so, what was the organisation that had set up the murder and trained him for it? Was Ruby another private-motive killer, avenging the death of his president, or was he, too, part of a conspiracy that required the death of the assassin? Were vital facts about the assassination covered up by Washington officials for political or private purposes? Finally, was the assassin really an American called Lee Harvey Oswald or was he an impostor – a professional killer, possibly of foreign origin?

Lee Harvey Oswald was born in New Orleans on 18 October 1939, two months after his father had died. His hard-pressed mother placed her two other sons in a home where Lee joined them when he was three. Two years later, his mother married again and Lee rejoined her in a suburb of Fort Worth, near Dallas, Texas. But that comfortable existence ended when the new marriage collapsed in divorce. Lee and his mother moved to New York, where the boy played truant from school, though tests showed him to be intelligent. While still in his early teens he became interested in Marxism and the Communist Party. Shortly after his seventeenth birthday he joined the Marines, stating that he wished to be trained as a radar operator. In the early autumn of 1957 he was posted to a US air base in Japan. There, Oswald's work involved the flights of U2 spy aircraft which, flying above anti-aircraft missile range, took photographs over Soviet territory.

When he learned that he was being transferred to the Philippines, Oswald – who had acquired an automatic .22 calibre pistol against all Marine rules – grazed his left arm with a bullet. It was assumed by the authorities that he had wounded himself deliberately to avoid being moved. He was punished by being deprived of promotion to the rank of corporal, which may well have embittered him against authority. After further disciplinary problems, Oswald decided to defect to the Soviet Union, but he said nothing to his colleagues about his decision until he returned to the United States with his unit in November 1958. In preparation for his flight to the Soviet Union, he took a Marine Corps course and an examination in Russian in which he performed only modestly. He made no effort to hide his growing sympathy with Soviet communism.

In September 1959, he secured a discharge on the grounds that his mother needed his support, then applied for a passport, telling friends that he was going to Finland to attend a university there. As soon as he arrived in Helsinki he applied for a tourist visa to the Soviet Union and arrived there on 15 October. What really happened to Oswald in the Soviet Union remains something of a mystery because there is not much more than his word for any of it. After consulting Soviet officials, he visited the United States embassy in Moscow and announced that he had come to hand in his passport and renounce his American citizenship.

Oswald stayed in the Soviet Union for two and a half years. It is known that he spent most of the time in Minsk and that he married a Russian girl, Marina Prusakova, on 30 April 1961. For reasons that will be considered later, he decided to return, with his wife, to the United States. His passport was returned to him and the couple, with their baby daughter, arrived in America on 13 June 1962. They went to live at Fort Worth. After failing to find work as a Russian translator, Oswald went through a succession of jobs, the last one in the Texas School Book Depository in Dallas, where he started work on 16 October 1963. By this time the couple had had a second child, but Oswald was living separately from Marina in lodgings in Dallas. Marina was staying with the children at a friend's house in the nearby town of Irving.

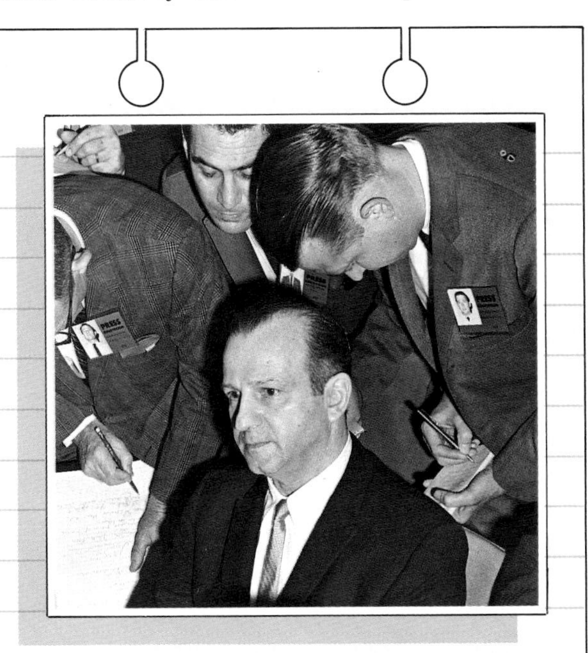

Jack Ruby, bar-owner and former mobster, holds a press conference during his trial in January 1964. Given a life sentence, he died in prison from cancer in 1967

The day after the shooting of Kennedy, Oswald was visited by his wife, his mother and his brother Robert, who all identified him. Then, soon after 11am on Sunday 24 November, Oswald was taken from his cell in police headquarters to be transferred to the county jail. He was led out, handcuffed, under the escort of several detectives, with television cameras trained on him and reporters firing questions. A short, powerfully built man stepped out and fired a .38 bullet into Oswald's belly. Oswald died in hospital without regaining consciousness. His assailant was former mobster Jack Ruby.

Mafia theory

Ruby had managed to get into the police building only a couple of minutes before Oswald emerged. Unless he had had remarkable luck, it would seem that he had been told the exact time to be there. He told the police that he had acted entirely on his own initiative, because he was in emotional turmoil over Kennedy's death and wanted to save Mrs Kennedy from the ordeal of having to appear as a witness at the assassin's trial. But this explanation hardly conformed to what was already known about his criminal character.

The Warren Commission concluded that Oswald had acted alone out of private motives. But many people who have studied the case believe that the commission was deprived of essential evidence and that Oswald was working for an agency that wanted Kennedy eliminated from the political scene. There are various theories currently circulating regarding the nature of this agency.

The Mafia theory suggests that Kennedy was killed at the instigation of mobsters who were threatened by the efforts being made by the Kennedy administration to eradicate organised crime. And the Mafia had an additional reason for being angry with Kennedy. He had failed to oust the communist leader Fidel Castro from Cuba, where the Mafia had run the gambling and crime extremely profitably during the previous regime.

There does seem to be evidence that the Mafia was involved with the assassination, though exactly to what extent remains unclear. But there are no known direct links between the Mafia and Lee Harvey Oswald that could explain how Oswald might have been set up by the mobsters to commit the crime for them and take the blame. On balance, therefore, the straightforward theory that the Mafia planned and carried out the assassination can probably be discounted.

The CIA theory supposes that certain right-wing

members of the CIA were opposed to Kennedy's general policy of liberalism, especially towards blacks, and hired Oswald to kill him and then hired Ruby to silence Oswald. While the CIA was deeply involved in other ways, there is no evidence that they hired and trained Oswald. The theory depends for its credibility on the belief that Oswald was a covert right-winger who went to the Soviet Union as a CIA agent. But the assassin's behaviour while he lived in the Soviet Union lends no credence whatever to this suggestion.

The Cuban theory is a much stronger possibility. At the time of the assassination, relations between President Kennedy and Castro, the pro-Soviet leader of Cuba, could hardly have been worse. Because of the threat to American interests, it was the CIA's duty to hatch plans for containing or removing the problem posed by Castro. There were two possible solutions – the assassination of Castro by a hired killer or his removal by a Cuban uprising, initiated and supported by an invasion of the island by anti-communist Cuban émigrés, most of whom were sheltering in the United States.

The CIA set about hiring a Mafia man to organise the assassination of Castro. Claiming that they represented a group of businessmen who wanted to see Cuba liberated, they approached Italian-born John Rosselli, who had once worked for the Chicago gangster Al Capone. Realising who was really behind the proposition, Rosselli secured the support of a criminal who was believed to be the leader of the American Mafia, Salvatore 'Sam' Giancana, who was keen to restore his organisation to its former position in Cuba. He undertook to recruit émigré Cubans and dissidents in Cuba itself to kill Castro, and other Cuban leaders who might replace him. The CIA technical department was to supply the means to achieve this.

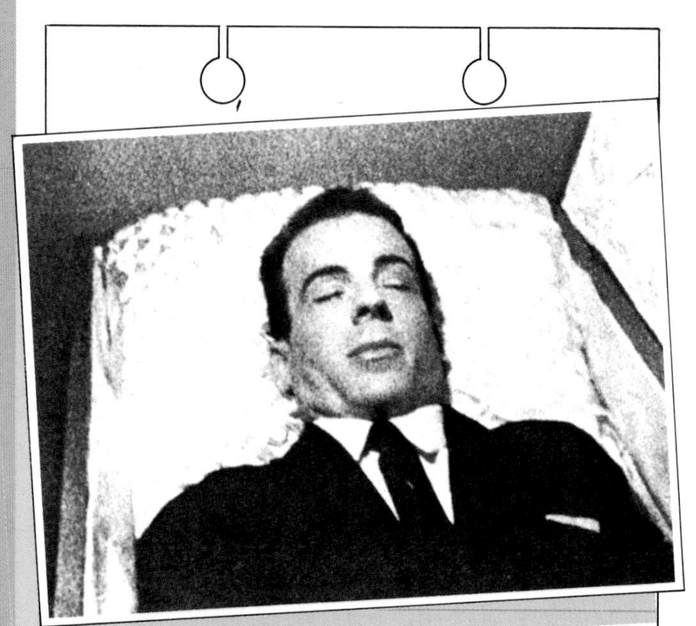

Lee Harvey Oswald, a final photograph for the CIA files. His shooting has become as much part of the Dallas mystery as the death of the president itself

But plans to kill Castro came to nothing, and the CIA decided to concentrate on its second plan – to assist an army of Cuban refugees to invade the island. The exercise ended in ignominious failure when the invasion force surrendered in Cuba's Bay of Pigs. The CIA was blamed for the disaster and its chief, Allen Dulles, was forced to resign.

Immediately afterwards the Kennedy brothers ordered the CIA to organise a more determined and highly secret operation to overthrow Castro and his regime; it was given the code-name Operation 'Mongoose'. Hundreds of CIA officers and contract agents were assigned to the task, which was to culminate in a triumphal march into Havana in October 1962. With so many people involved and the White House constantly pressing for 'boom and bang' on the island, there can be little doubt that news of 'Mongoose' leaked to the Soviet secret police, the KGB, and thence to Castro. The Soviets began building rocket-launching sites in Cuba and the world came to the very brink of nuclear war.

'Red alert'

The CIA learned of the threat and confirmed the existence of the missile sites by aerial reconnaissance. On 22 October 1962 Kennedy broadcast to the world his intention that the United States Navy would blockade Cuba and turn back any Soviet warships involved in the missile build-up. When the United States, Britain and NATO went onto 'red alert' the Soviets backed down and agreed not to install the missiles if the United States would give a guarantee that Cuba would not be invaded. The guarantee was given, but the Kennedy brothers continued to press the CIA to topple the Castro regime, and for a few months the CIA persisted with its Mafia connection through Rosselli.

In February 1963 the CIA terminated its abortive contract with Rosselli and the Mafia and began negotiations with someone who had more reliable access to Castro and other Cuban ministers. This was Rolando Cubella, himself a Cuban minister and a close friend of Castro. He volunteered his services as assassin, claiming to be disillusioned with Castro's regime and resigned to his leader's liquidation as the only way to end it. The CIA warmed to his approach because Cubella was known to have personally assassinated an intelligence official of the previous Cuban regime. Cubella was hired and given the code-name 'Amlash'.

Towards the end of October 1963 Cubella insisted on an assurance that the United States government

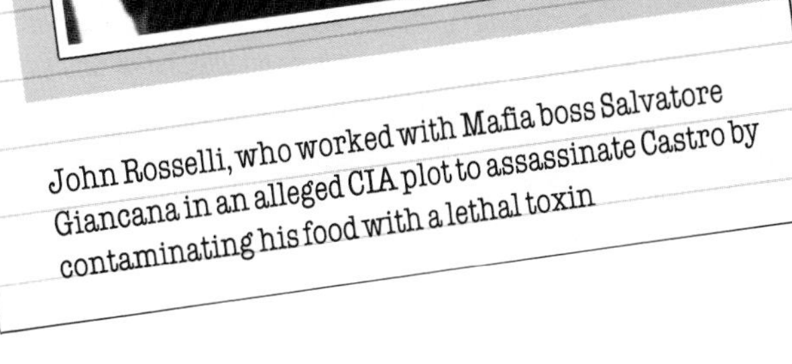

John Rosselli, who worked with Mafia boss Salvatore Giancana in an alleged CIA plot to assassinate Castro by contaminating his food with a lethal toxin

Fidel Castro of Cuba, who publicly warned US leaders that if they continued to threaten his life they ran the risk of being assassinated themselves. Did he hire Oswald to kill Kennedy?

would support him as Castro's successor. A promise that this condition would be met was given by a CIA officer who said that he represented Robert Kennedy. On the very day that President John Kennedy was killed, a CIA agent met Cubella in Paris and gave him a specially designed ballpoint pen that could inject its user with a lethal poison in so insidious a way that the victim would not know what had happened.

But Cubella's attempt to assassinate Castro was never made because Oswald got to Kennedy first. Furthermore, it is now considered likely that Cubella was an *agent provocateur* who told Castro of everything that was happening.

If the plot to kill Kennedy was organised by the Cubans, what support is there for the belief that Oswald was hired by them or was otherwise serving their purposes? The evidence that he was is very strong. After he returned from the Soviet Union in June 1962 Oswald soon became outspoken against American foreign policy, especially with reference to Cuba and the Castro regime, and became interested in the 'Fair Play for Cuba Committee', a left-wing organisation that urged official recognition of the Castro government. To demonstrate that he was more than just a loudmouth, he decided to kill the man who was then Castro's most outspoken opponent in the Dallas area – a retired army general called Edwin Walker.

It was apparently for this purpose that he bought the rifle with the telescopic sight. Before leaving the apartment where he was then living with his wife, he left a note in Russian telling her what to do if he was arrested. Then, on the evening of 10 April 1963, he took position outside General Walker's home and fired at him through the window of his study. Walker, who was uninjured, reported the attempt on his life to the police and a hunt was staged for the gunman, but with no success. Until he was caught after the Kennedy assassination, Oswald was not suspected of the earlier crime.

The link between Cuba and the Soviet Union was of course very strong, and the KGB was firmly installed in Havana. So while Oswald's connection could have been with Cuba alone, it could also have extended to the KGB. The fourth 'conspiracy' theory is that Oswald had direct links with the KGB. This is the strongest theory because of his residence in the

Soviet Union, his strong pro-Soviet sympathies and his Russian-born wife.

Oswald's arrival in Moscow as a defector from the much vaunted Marines was given prominence in the Soviet newspapers, and he was treated as something of a celebrity. His wages as a metal-worker were supplemented by a substantial allowance that doubled his income. This extra money was ostensibly paid by the Red Cross, but in reality came from state funds. From Minsk he wrote a letter to an American friend – intercepted by the CIA because it came from the Soviet Union – saying that he would kill anyone who opposed the Soviet Union. In spite of this, by July 1961 he had decided to return to his homeland. As it was the policy of the American government to encourage defectors from the United States to return home – if only because it undid the propaganda value to the Soviets – he was given back the passport that he had handed in so contemptuously less than two years before.

It was certainly odd that the Soviet authorities not only allowed Oswald to leave, but to take his Russian born wife and child with him. And it was later discovered that on at least one occasion Oswald had visited the Russian embassy in Mexico after his return home. However, no one at the Pentagon would blame Kennedy's death on Russia (it could have been an act of war) and there is evidence that FBI head Hoover covered up crucial facts.

There was an equal degree of panic in the CIA when the president was assassinated, but for a different reason. Officials there were fearful that the inevitable inquiry might uncover their plans for assassinating Castro and particularly their arrangements with Cubella and the Mafia mobsters, all of which had been as unproductive as the Bay of Pigs fiasco when American forces, which included a number of disaffected Cuban émigrés, failed in their attempt to invade Cuba and depose Castro. There, too, embarrassing documents were destroyed.

The possibility that the Kremlin had been involved in the Dallas tragedy was intensified in January 1964 when a KGB officer, Yuri Nosenko, defected to the CIA. He claimed to have proof that the Soviets had not been involved in the assassination in any way and laughed at the idea that the KGB would have used a person as unstable and as unreliable as Oswald. The CIA agreed that the choice of Oswald would have been odd because he was linked too obviously with the Soviet Union. But nevertheless the KGB might have selected him for that very reason – since it was so unlikely, it might not be believed. There is little, if any, doubt now that Nosenko was a false defector – a plant sent by the KGB to deceive the Americans on a number of issues. There was so much doubt about Nosenko's testimony that he was not permitted to give evidence before the Warren Commission. Yet Hoover still used all his influence to induce the government to accept Nosenko's claims as the truth because they supported his assertion that Oswald was a 'lone nut'.

This photograph of Oswald holding his rifle was considered strong evidence of his guilt. But critics allege that the photograph may have been faked

In the end, the long report of the Warren Commission did everything that Hoover, the FBI, the CIA and the State Department desired. It concluded that both Oswald and Ruby had acted alone and that there was no evidence of domestic or international conspiracy. But there were many who were deeply dissatisfied with the report, and in 1974 the House Assassinations Committee reversed this verdict.

One possibility – which may be remote but should not be entirely ignored, as it was by the Warren Commission – is that the killer was not in fact Lee Harvey Oswald the Marine who had defected, but an impostor, selected and trained in the Soviet Union. This theory has been forcefully presented in a book, *The Oswald File*, by Michael Eddowes, published in 1977. It is lent credence by the fact that official documents, made available under the United States Freedom of Information Act, show that as far back as 1960 the FBI suspected that the man who returned from the Soviet Union might be an impostor using Oswald's birth certificate. There is a memorandum from J. Edgar Hoover himself to this effect.

Politicians show no inclination to re-open the case, on the grounds that re-examination of the evidence could yield no political advantages and might do great harm. With the political, intelligence and security 'establishments' so stubbornly opposed to any re-opening of the case, it remains extremely doubtful whether any of it will ever be resolved.

3
Spies and secrets

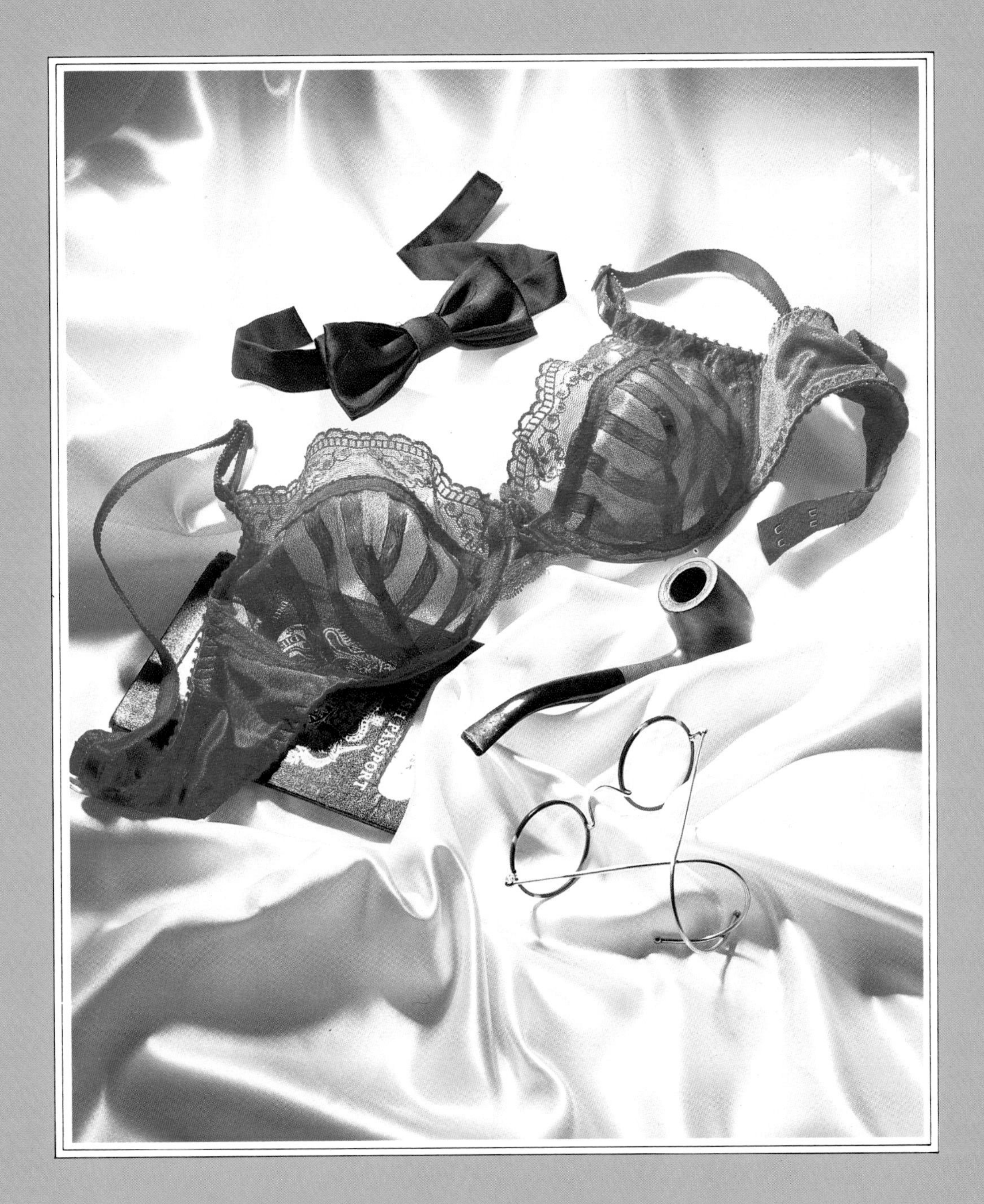

Since the Bolshevik Revolution in 1917, the intelligence game - between East and West has been played increasingly ruthlessly and secretly. Occasionally, however, the dark world of espionage is exposed in a blaze of publicity.

Who was the fifth man?

Exposed as spies – Philby, Burgess, Maclean, Blunt. Is there one more?

On Monday 28 May 1951, the head of the American Department at the Foreign Office was expected to attend a meeting with an officer of MI5, the British Security Service. But that morning he failed to turn up for work. His wife telephoned his office to say that a friend of his had come for dinner on the Friday evening, and that after the meal the two men had driven off together. They had not been seen since.

The explanation for what had happened did not become public knowledge until many months later. Donald Maclean and Guy Burgess, two of the most notorious British spies of the century, had defected to the Soviet Union.

The meeting Maclean had been asked to attend had been planned by the highest officers in MI5, who were going to confront him with evidence that he was a traitor.

One man who would have been there, and aware that Maclean was being investigated, was Harold 'Kim' Philby, chief Washington representative of MI6, the British Secret Intelligence Service. And Philby was a friend of Burgess.

Following the disappearance of the two men, Philby wrote a letter to the chief of MI6 in London, expressing his surprise. This letter, which in tone was uncharacteristic of Philby, confirmed the authorities' suspicions about him, too, and MI6 contacted MI5. They, it turned out, already had a large file on Philby which contained an entry noting an officer's suspicions that he was once a member of the Communist Party. Philby was recalled to London for questioning.

Despite intensive interrogation, his questioners were unable to prove his guilt, though they became convinced that he was indeed a spy. In September 1951, MI6 asked for his resignation, which he gave.

He returned to his earlier career of journalism and continued to live in England until 1955, when he was publicly accused by an MP of being the 'Third Man' who had helped Burgess and Maclean to escape. Harold Macmillan, then Foreign Secretary, officially cleared him, and MI6 arranged for him to go to the Middle East as a journalist. He settled in Beirut, from where he sent information to MI6 as well as copy to the *Observer* and *The Economist*.

Six years later, at the end of 1961, Anatoli Golitsin, a high-ranking officer in the KGB, arrived in the West and announced that he wished to defect. He was granted asylum in the USA, and brought with him a mass of secret information. He had worked in departments of the KGB that had given him access to intelligence operations abroad and, having a remarkable memory, had been able to recall many details about them. Early the following year he was interviewed by MI5. He described what the KGB called the 'Ring of Five' – five spies who had all been recruited at Cambridge before the war and who had reached official positions that gave them access to some of the most secret information about British security, foreign policy and intelligence.

What was unusual about the Ring of Five was that each member knew that the others were Soviet agents, because they had helped to recruit one another. The method customarily used by the KGB is to run spies separately so that their identities are unknown to each other – a safeguard in case one of them is caught.

Golitsin had never known the names of the Five, but he had seen and remembered the code-names of three of them – 'Stanley', 'Hicks' and 'Johnson'. 'Hicks' he was able to identify definitely: Guy Burgess, who had defected to Russia ten years earlier. He then provided the first hard evidence to implicate Kim Philby. He knew that 'Stanley' had been involved in important wartime operations in the Middle East. Philby fitted the description perfectly. Armed with further evidence, Nicholas Elliott of MI6, who knew Philby well, volunteered to go to Beirut and confront him.

Third Man

Two weeks after that confrontation, on the evening of Wednesday 23 January 1963, without a word of warning or explanation to his family, Philby disappeared. Back in London, the authorities could hardly have been surprised. They may even have been relieved. Six months later Philby was reported to be living in Moscow. He was then named officially as the Third Man.

Then, in 1979, following the publication of a book by Andrew Boyle, *The Climate of Treason*, the British public was shocked by the formal exposure in Parliament of the eminent art historian Sir Anthony Blunt as the 'Fourth Man'. Worse still, it was revealed that he had fully confessed his treachery to MI5 in 1964 in return for complete immunity from prosecution or exposure. For fourteen years this self-confessed traitor had continued in his position as Surveyor and later Adviser of the Queen's Pictures – a job that meant he was actually a member of the royal household.

If Blunt was indeed the Fourth Man, did he lead his interrogators to the Fifth?

Kim Philby had been immortalised in the public mind as the Third Man. But he was in fact the first member of the Ring of Five to be recruited. He entered Trinity College on a scholarship in 1929, having been a King's Scholar at Westminster School. At 21 he was already interested in radical politics, and numbered among his close companions former coal-miners and other workers who had reached Cambridge late in life on scholarships.

When the Labour Party was virtually annihilated in the general election of 1931, a group of Marxists formed the first communist cell at Cambridge. It became the centre of a major recruiting drive by the Communist Party of Great Britain, then only 11 years old. Philby never seems to have been a card-carrying member of the party, but he was associated with the cell, as was yet another undergraduate, called Guy Burgess.

Burgess, a little older than Philby, entered Trinity College from Eton at the age of nineteen, having already established a reputation as an aggressive homosexual. Highly intelligent, he soon became a Cambridge 'character' of notable wit and outrageous habits. He joined the Apostles, an exclusive Cambridge club – almost a secret society. At that stage it was a centre both of homosexuality and of communist belief.

The man who was instrumental in persuading

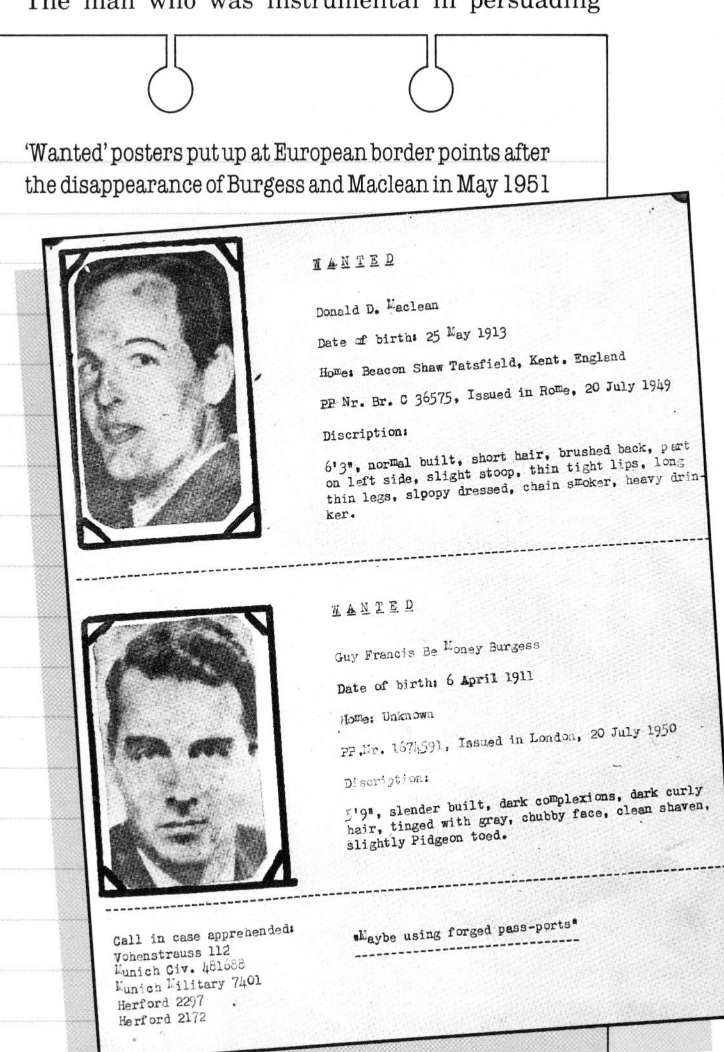

WANTED

Donald D. Maclean

Date of birth: 25 May 1913

Home: Beacon Shaw Tatsfield, Kent. England

PP Nr. Br. C 36575, Issued in Rome, 20 July 1949

Discription:

6'3", normal built, short hair, brushed back, part on left side, slight stoop, thin tight lips, long thin legs, slpopy dressed, chain smoker, heavy drinker.

WANTED

Guy Francis De Money Burgess

Date of birth: 6 April 1911

Home: Unknown

PP.Nr. 1674591, Issued in London, 20 July 1950

Discription:

5'9", slender built, dark complexions, dark curly hair, tinged with gray, chubby face, clean shaven, slightly Pidgeon toed.

Call in case apprehended:
Vohenstrauss 112
Munich Civ. 481688
Munich Military 7401
Herford 2297
Herford 2172

"Maybe using forged pass-ports"

'Wanted' posters put up at European border points after the disappearance of Burgess and Maclean in May 1951

Above: the ornate bay windows on the first floor of 10 New Bond Street belong to the flat that was Guy Burgess' London home from about 1948 until his defection in May 1951

Burgess to join the Apostles, and became a close friend, was Anthony Blunt, a brilliant young don who had graduated from Trinity in 1930 with a double first in modern languages. He had remained at Cambridge to do post-graduate work on his real love, the history of art. In 1932 he was elected a Fellow of his college and taken onto the permanent teaching staff.

Burgess was also friendly with a young undergraduate from Trinity Hall – Donald Maclean, who had been at Gresham's School in Norfolk, where his closest friend was James Klugmann. Klugmann was to become a life-long and openly dedicated member of the Communist Party and there seems little doubt that both young men were already ripe for recruitment to the communist cause when they arrived at Cambridge in 1931.

Philby graduated in 1933 with a second-class degree in economics. With £50 given to him by his father, he went to Germany, Austria and Hungary where he saw the rise of fascism at first hand. He returned to London in the spring of 1934 with an Austrian wife, Lizi. It is the considered view of MI5 that he was recruited to the service of the Comintern while in Vienna, and that his wife probably knew about it. Back in London, Philby became a member of the extreme right-wing Anglo-German Fellowship to mislead people as to his real beliefs. He secured a job as a journalist and set up a news agency with one of his wife's friends who was himself a Soviet agent throughout the war.

Philby's controller, 'Theo', was almost certainly Theodore Maly, a tall, handsome Hungarian who had been converted to atheism and communism by his experiences as a chaplain in the First World War. By now a Soviet citizen and KGB officer, he went to Britain to exploit pro-Soviet feeling among students. Philby recruited Burgess as one of his agents.

Controller 'Otto'

Like Philby, Burgess visited Cambridge often. Early in 1935, after discussions with his controller, it was decided that he should recruit Blunt. Burgess involved Blunt in a discussion of the latest turns of the international situation and then said, 'Anthony, we must *do* something to counter the horrors of Nazism. We just cannot sit here and talk about it. The government is pacifying Hitler, so Marxism is the only solution. I am already committed to work secretly for peace. Are you prepared to help me?' Blunt said that he would, but he had no idea, at that stage, what the work would ultimately entail. Burgess then introduced Blunt to the controller 'Otto', a middle European ('Theo' had by this time been transferred to Paris). His immediate job, he was told, was to recruit other agents at Cambridge.

Early in 1935, Blunt and Burgess acted to recruit Maclean, who had already been listed by the Soviets as likely to have a top-flight Whitehall career.

Maclean was recruited in something of a hurry because he was expected to gain a good degree and then to compete for entry into the Diplomatic Service, a move that had the enthusiastic support of 'Otto'. Maclean duly succeeded and was appointed to the Foreign Office in October 1935.

Until the outbreak of war, the other three men had to be content with jobs that provided only limited access to information of interest to the Soviet Union. Burgess began passing intelligence to his controller when he joined the BBC in 1936. In 1936 Philby went to Spain to cover the civil war as a freelance reporter, and a year later succeeded in establishing himself as the official correspondent for *The Times* with General Franco's Nationalist army. After the outbreak of the Second World War Philby managed first to enter the War Office and then, in September 1941, to penetrate the counter-intelligence section of MI6. Blunt joined MI5 in 1940 after a few months in France as part of the Army Intelligence Corps. By the time the war was under way, then, the four 'moles' had established themselves in highly sensitive positions.

We now know the identities of four of Golitsin's Ring; is it possible, from the evidence available, to work out who was, or is, the Fifth Man?

One man who must be considered as a candidate for the Fifth Man who spied for the Soviet Union has already been named. James Klugmann, the school-friend of Donald Maclean, joined the Communist Party openly in 1933. He was recruited during the war to the Special Operations Executive in Cairo, where he worked in the Balkans Division and was able to influence policy concerning Yugoslavia.

The time of Klugmann's original recruitment to the Soviet cause and the work he did for it during the war could qualify him for the title of the Fifth Man. But there is one factor that eliminates him in the view of MI5. He was always, even in Cairo, an open and committed communist, whereas the other known members of the Cambridge Ring had been required to work in a strictly conspiratorial manner.

Another extremely damaging spy recruited at Cambridge was John Cairncross, a scholarship boy from a poor home in Glasgow, who was so zealous in the communist cause that he was talent-spotted by Blunt, one of his tutors. Blunt gave his name to Klugmann, who in turn introduced him to 'Otto' in Regent's Park. 'Otto' ordered Cairncross to reject his open communism and take steps to get himself into a position in Whitehall.

Cairncross left the Communist Party in 1936. Although he would have preferred to pursue an academic career he competed for entry to the Foreign Office, and passed top of his list. He started off in the German department, where Maclean was also located, and began to give information to 'Otto'. Cairncross, therefore, was probably the second Soviet spy to infiltrate a secret department.

Below: Trinity College, where Blunt, Philby and Burgess were recruited. Maclean went to neighbouring Trinity Hall

John Cairncross, who fled to Rome following interrogation by MI5 in 1952. The authorities had evidence against him, but decided not to prosecute

In 1938, again at the suggestion of 'Otto', he applied for and got a transfer to the Treasury. Then, in 1942, because of his fluency in German, Cairncross was able to get onto the staff of the most secret establishment in Britain, the Government Code and Cypher School at Bletchley Park in Buckinghamshire. After the war, Sir Winston Churchill praised the staff at Bletchley, calling them 'the geese who laid the golden eggs and never cackled'. Cairncross, for one, had been cackling all the time; he even received a special commendation from Moscow for the information he had given his controller. After the war he returned to the Treasury where, though he did not rise to any eminence, he had access to policy documents and assessments, which he continued to hand over to the KGB.

One of the first moves made by MI5 after Burgess' disappearance was to search his flat in New Bond Street. Among documents found there was a bundle of handwritten notes about affairs in the Treasury. They included pen-portraits of various officials; these were obviously written by a talent-scout because they provided information about character weaknesses that the KGB might be able to exploit. A sharp-eyed secretary in MI5 recognised the handwriting as Cairncross's, and he was confronted.

Cairncross was allowed to resign quietly; he subsequently moved abroad and eventually obtained a post with the United Nations Food and Agriculture Organisation in Rome.

In 1952 MI5 had accepted the convenient view that Cairncross, although recruited as some sort of Soviet agent, had been small fry and that once out of contact with secrets he could safely be ignored. Fourteen years later, when Blunt confessed that he had been involved in his recruitment, MI5 was to uncover a very different story. An MI5 officer travelled to Rome to interrogate Cairncross. In general, extradition treaties do not allow for the return of

Anthony Blunt was exposed to the public as the Fourth Man only in 1979, even though he had confessed to being a traitor 14 years before

fugitives who have contravened the Official Secrets Acts. Cairncross, therefore, made a complete and full confession.

Cairncross' admission that he had been recruited by Klugmann was the first hard evidence of the latter's treachery – so, in return for a visit to Britain without fear of prosecution, Cairncross agreed to confront Klugmann. He threatened to expose Klugmann unless he, too, confessed to MI5, but Klugmann simply refused to see anybody from MI5 and the attempt came to nothing. Though MI5 realised that it had been grossly mistaken over Cairncross, it received some consolation when he named two former Cambridge associates who had also been recruited. One was still a civil servant; the other had also been in Whitehall but had retired to become a company director. Both declined to be interviewed although MI5 is confident that both were of assistance to Soviet intelligence. However, neither seems to qualify as the Fifth Man.

What of Cairncross' qualifications? The MI5 view is that he was not the Fifth Man, although it is true that he was recruited in the right place at the right time. According to Golitsin the Ring of Five were all friends. Blunt, Burgess, Maclean and, to some extent, Philby were snobs. It was no doubt because Blunt rather despised Cairncross that he revealed his recruitment to MI5, while doing all he could to guard his friends. In early 1986 Cairncross was still living and working in Rome. Although he had discussed his past – the allegations of treachery and his possible identity as the Fifth Man – with Italian and foreign journalists, he always maintained that he never knew Maclean and Philby were spies: a claim that, though unlikely, is just possible in view of the practice of keeping agents in ignorance of each other.

There are two remaining contenders for the title of Fifth Man. The first is an Englishman who has publicly confessed to having spied for the USSR – Leonard Long, known to his friends as Leo.

Long went up to Cambridge in 1935. From a working-class background, he seems to have had left-wing tendencies even before going to university. At Cambridge, he quickly became involved in the communist cell. An outstanding student of modern languages, he became a member of the Apostles, perhaps through the sponsorship of Blunt, who was his supervisor in French. Blunt also recruited him to the Comintern, but it is not known whether Long was introduced to a Soviet controller. In the event, it was Blunt himself who received Long's information and served as his controller during the war. Nor is it known whether he ever served as a courier or talent-scout, but his zeal for the cause was noticed by Michael Whitney Straight, who had been recruited by Blunt but later exposed him to MI5. When Straight was questioned in 1964, he mentioned Long as likely to have been recruited by Blunt.

After the war, in 1946, Blunt tried to get Long transferred to MI5 after he himself had returned to the art world. But Long secured an important intelligence post in Germany, where he worked until

Michael Whitney Straight – his confession in 1963 led to the interrogation and confession of Anthony Blunt

1952. He has said publicly that he did no further work for the Soviets after that date.

From 1952 onwards Long worked in London as an executive of Columbia Pictures. He too was exposed to MI5 by Straight in 1964 and confessed but, like Blunt, was not prosecuted. His case was hushed up and he was not publicly exposed until 1980, after Blunt himself had been revealed as a traitor and stripped of his knighthood. Long, now retired and probably still living in London, remains a strong contender as the Fifth Man, although he does not seem to have been a major Soviet agent in his own right as the other four were.

The final contender strongly suspected by MI5 of being the Fifth Man is also still alive, aged seventy-eight in early 1986. He is Alistair Watson, who has persistently denied ever having been a spy. He knew Blunt and was an Apostle at Cambridge. When Blunt confessed and was questioned, he was careful to avoid any direct mention of Watson, who was investigated by MI5 only because Blunt had remarked, 'If you are looking for people whom Burgess might have recruited, pay attention to those he praised lavishly, because he always tried to recruit them.' When Straight was questioned later by MI5 he described Watson as a communist and proponent of Marxism at Cambridge. Blunt then specifically denied that Watson had been recruited to Soviet intelligence. Inquiries showed that Watson had openly rejected his communist beliefs and, as an outstanding theoretical physicist, had joined the Admiralty research organisation in 1939. He worked there on highly secret projects and eventually headed a group who were doing work on the detection of submarines.

False statement

Watson's telephone was tapped, microphones were concealed in his home and he was followed. All that was established was that he was still a committed communist. This in itself indicated that he had made a false statement on his positive vetting form by failing to declare any such connection, and in 1967 the authorities used that as a reason for removing him from secret work.

Over six weeks of intermittent questioning Watson resolutely denied spying, but he admitted that he had met 'Otto' and that he had concealed his beliefs in order to get a job in a government defence establishment. Furthermore, he recognised three men from a spread of photographs of Soviet bloc intelligence officers working in London who were known to MI5. One of them had supervised the defection of Maclean and Burgess; another had controlled the MI6 spy George Blake; and the third had controlled the Admiralty spy John Vassall. Why had he met these particular men, the MI5 officers

Alistair Watson in 1979, after being questioned about his alleged role as a Soviet spy during the war

wondered, unless he were in some way involved in espionage activities?

Since his retirement, Watson has been interviewed by reporters and has admitted that MI5 had good reason to suspect him, although he maintains his innocence. Indeed, he has accused MI5 of pressing him so hard that he became confused. Those who do not accept his statements regard him as the best fit for the Fifth Man, particularly since Golitsin claimed that one of the Ring was a scientist.

The mystery of the Fifth Man's identity remains. There were, in addition to the five, many highly placed helpers or 'half-spies' who were as useful to the KGB as the full-blown spies themselves. They would provide cover for the spies' activities, assist them by acting as couriers and go-betweens ('cut-outs') and provide accommodation addresses. The list of those known by the security authorities to have been involved in this way is a long one. It includes several knights and others who have achieved high honours while continuing their clandestine lives.

These people cannot be successfully prosecuted because the only witnesses who could testify to their guilt (the security officers who investigated them) cannot appear in court without 'blowing their cover' – something that MI5 and MI6 are extremely reluctant to approve, unless the officers in question have already had their cover blown, or are near to retirement. Even if a court demands the presence of a particular witness, by issuing a subpoena, English law allows the Crown to override the demand. This right, enshrined in the institution of Crown privilege, means that the security services can simply refuse to let their officers appear in court, in order to guard against publicity. Furthermore, suspects cannot even be safely named while they are still alive because of the libel laws.

The framing of Stephen Ward

On 22 July 1963 Dr Stephen Ward was brought to trial at the Old Bailey, charged with living on the immoral earnings of prostitutes. Four days later he was dead from an overdose of the barbiturate Nembutal. Ward's activities – innocent or not – contributed to the disgrace of a cabinet minister, and the scandal rocked the nation, yet many people thought he was the tragic victim of a vengeful establishment

In the early Sixties the 'teenage revolution' was underway in Britain. There was a revolution, too, in the moral climate – the Second World War had stimulated a loosening of the social fabric. London was the Mecca of Britain, and it was there that the new morality could most obviously be observed. Property racketeers flourished because flats were in short supply and prostitution was rife. There were also the 'good time' girls who were promiscuous in the new way, but they were not common prostitutes and survived financially by 'hostessing' in night clubs or 'modelling'.

Every day the gossip columns of the popular press reported in mouth-watering detail the goings on at London parties where the young sons and daughters of long-established, moneyed families mingled with fashion designers, hairdressers, musicians and the ubiquitous 'models'.

It is small wonder that osteopath Stephen Ward, who had clawed his way up rapidly from provincial obscurity to a positively intimate relationship with the rich and newsworthy, should have been attracted to this milieu. Nor is it surprising that Christine Keeler should have been drawn into it. In 1958 the seventeen-year-old Christine began sharing Ward's Marylebone flat. While they were searching for more spacious accommodation they contacted Peter Rachman, a Polish property crook. Rachman persuaded Keeler to become his mistress and she lived with him for six months in 1959. After leaving Rachman, Keeler met sixteen-year-old Mandy Rice-Davies at Murray's Cabaret club, where they worked. They were both absent from work on New Year's Eve 1960, were sacked, and went to live for a while in a flat in Comeragh Road, Barons Court, before they again split up – Keeler to live with a Persian, Rice-Davies to live with Rachman.

Ward's osteopathic practice was now at its most active, but he was also taking great interest in drawing. He drew several members of the royal family and government ministers for the series of portraits he was preparing for the *Illustrated London News*. His social life became inextricably mixed with his professional one. During this period, Ward struck up an intimate friendship with Captain Eugene Ivanov, a Soviet naval attaché. The security services were, properly, concerned about the association and paid Ward a visit on 8 June 1961. Nevertheless, on 8 July he invited Ivanov to a party at his weekend cottage on the Cliveden Estate in Berkshire. Christine Keeler was now sharing Ward's new flat in Wimpole Mews and she, too, joined the party.

There was another sort of party, a much more formal one, at Cliveden itself that weekend. Lord

Astor was entertaining more than twenty illustrious guests, including Her Majesty's Secretary of State for War, John Profumo, and his wife, former film star Valerie Hobson. Some of the guests, 'complete with tiaras and cigars', went for a stroll through the grounds after dinner.

Ward's party were using the estate swimming pool and in their horseplay Keeler had ended up naked. Some of the Cliveden guests, including Profumo, chanced upon this scene. The next evening both parties again met at the pool, and Profumo asked Keeler for her telephone number. That same evening, Ivanov had sexual intercourse with Keeler.

The following Wednesday, Stephen Ward had a second visit from MI5, and on this occasion he was warned to be careful. Ward, inveterate name-dropper that he was, said that he knew Profumo.

Missile crisis

The Secretary for War had followed up his first encounter with Christine Keeler with alacrity. He called to see her at Ward's flat and had sexual intercourse with her there on several occasions.

Meanwhile, Ivanov was also seeing Keeler. He met her often at Ward's flat, but any sexual relationship they had was fleeting. On one or two occasions he narrowly missed meeting Profumo as one arrived and the other left, and this was a source of considerable amusement to Ivanov and Keeler. One evening, when Ivanov, Ward and Keeler were together, Ward lightly suggested to her: 'Why don't you ask Jack when the Germans are going to get the bomb?' The Soviets had already secretly taken the decision to site nuclear missiles in Cuba, and any information about the date on which it was proposed to deploy similar weapons in Germany could have been of great political significance.

MI5 were showing intense interest in Ivanov's movements. They had had confirmation from a Soviet defector that Ivanov was engaged in espionage, and on 9 August Profumo was tactfully warned about the acquaintance. No one, however, told Macmillan, and no one, apparently, made any direct connection with the name Christine Keeler.

But Profumo took the warning seriously and immediately sent Keeler a farewell letter. The affair was apparently unknown to MI5, and might well have remained so had it not been for Ward's incurable prattling, coupled with his continuing desire to become a man of importance. But Ward's brief encounter with MI5 had gone to his head: he told a friend that he 'often advised the Foreign Office on security matters'. He kept up his relationship with Ivanov, partly in the hope of visiting Moscow, but mainly to feed his delusion that he had influence in the British corridors of power.

In the following year came the Cuban missile crisis: on the evening of Monday 22 October 1962, President Kennedy announced to the world that Soviet missiles had been installed in Cuba. In London Ivanov intimated to a number of his contacts that he had authority to negotiate a solution to the crisis through unofficial channels, and on Wednesday he approached Stephen Ward. Ward, of course, was carried away by Ivanov's apparent confidence in his contacts. He telephoned the Foreign Office immediately, without success. Frustrated, he contacted one of his patients, a back-bench MP, Sir Godfrey Nicholson, who agreed to see Ivanov the same evening, and the next day passed on the proposal to a Deputy Under-Secretary at the Foreign Office. Meanwhile, Ward was establishing other contacts. He found another Conservative back-bencher, William Shepherd, lunching in the Kenya Coffee House in Marylebone High Street; he dropped a few famous names, mentioned Cliveden and Profumo, and suggested that Shepherd should meet Ivanov. Shepherd instigated some inquiries into Ward's background, and even went so far as to interview Percival Murray, the girls' former employer. He reported his findings to an acquaintance in MI5.

Mandy Rice-Davies – she worked at Murray's Cabaret Club with Keeler, through whom she met Ward

It was now that Colonel George Wigg, the labour MP who subsequently became Lord Wigg, was drawn, almost unwittingly and most mysteriously, into the affair. He was a keen opposition spokesman on defence affairs, and had already crossed swords with Profumo over the Vassall spy case. On 11 November Wigg went for lunch to the home of his political agent. As far as he was aware, no one except his wife knew where he was, but in the early afternoon he received a telephone call. The voice was muffled: it could have been male or female. But what it said was: 'Forget about Vassall; you want to look at Profumo.'

What happened next could not conceivably have had anything to do with Profumo. Keeler had once more left Ward's protection, and was staying with a West Indian, Johnny Edgecombe, in Boston Manor Road, Brentford. Edgecombe was involved in a fight with 'Lucky' Gordon, another West Indian, who had been terrorising her. Eight weeks later, she was in Ward's flat in Wimpole Mews, talking with Mandy Rice-Davies, who was also living there after having left Peter Rachman. Edgecombe arrived in a minicab in a highly agitated state and began ringing the doorbell insistently. When the two girls refused him access he fired seven shots into the door and window and fled in the cab.

First reports of the shooting made the last editions of the evening papers, and Edgecombe's arrest was announced in the daily papers the next morning, although the matter was given only slight attention: 'Miss Keeler, twenty, a freelance actress, was visiting Miss Marilyn Davies, eighteen, an actress, at Dr Ward's home. . . .' But Keeler was panicking.

A week later John Lewis, former MP for West Bolton, happened to meet Keeler and one of her friends, Paul Mann, a one-time racing driver. She was in an edgy mood: she was worried about what might come out in the trial of Edgecombe, who had that day appeared in court for a preliminary hearing. She talked about her affairs with Profumo and Ivanov, not realising that Lewis had little liking for Ward. Hearing Ward's name in the breathless tale, Lewis was immediately suspicious. He managed to impress upon Keeler that she should contact a solicitor as soon as possible – if her story was to be believed, she even possessed a very damaging letter. Lewis himself approached George Wigg.

Meanwhile Paul Mann and another friend had convinced Keeler that her story was worth money. It was sold to the *Sunday Pictorial* for £1000 – £200 in advance and £800 on publication – and a photocopy of Profumo's letter of 9 August 1961 was lodged in

Christine Keeler (left) and two of the men who shared her favours: John Profumo (below right), in 1961 Secretary of State for War in Harold Macmillan's Conservative government; and Captain Eugene Ivanov (above right), the Soviet naval attaché, pictured with his wife

the newspaper's safe, but the story was never to be published. On the same day the *Sunday Pictorial* moved Christine ('to be safe') from her flat at 63 Great Cumberland Place to an apartment in Park West, Edgware Road. By now, Stephen Ward was no longer in Wimpole Mews. He had found it impossible to keep up the rent, and have moved with Mandy Rice-Davies to Bryanston Mews, empty since Rachman's death the previous October.

The first the police heard of Keeler's story was on 26 January 1963, when Detective Sergeant Burrows, of Marylebone, interviewed her in connection with Edgecombe's forthcoming trial. She made the following statement:

> She said that Dr Ward was a procurer of women for gentlemen in high places and was sexually perverted; that he had a country cottage at Cliveden to which some of these women were taken to meet important men – the cottage was on the estate of Lord Astor; that he had introduced her to Mr John Profumo and that she had had an association with him; that Mr Profumo had written a number of letters to her on War Office notepaper and that she was still in possession of one of these letters which was being considered for publication in the *Sunday Pictorial* to whom she had sold her life story for £1000. She also said that on one occasion when she was going to meet Mr Profumo, Ward had asked her to discover from him the date on which certain atomic secrets were to be handed to West Germany by the Americans, and that this was at the time of the Cuban crisis. She also said that she had been introduced by Ward to the naval attaché of the Soviet Embassy and had met him on a number of occasions.

Johnny Edgecombe (left) and Aloysius 'Lucky' Gordon (right) being escorted from Wandsworth Prison to Lord Denning's inquiry into the affair

On 5 February Ward himself saw the Marylebone police and gave them a statement: 'Dr Ward said that if this matter, including the association between Mr Profumo and Miss Keeler, became public, it might very well "bring down the Government".' Ward also said that he was a close friend of the naval attaché of the Soviet embassy and that he had mentioned the matter to a member of MI5.

Special Branch was alerted, and the commander saw MI5. On his return he drew up a minute:

> The facts were already known to MI5 in broad outline. Their principal interest is, of course, the Soviet diplomat [who suddenly and without warning left Britain on 28 January 1963, two days after Keeler was first interviewed by the police] whose identity is known to them and in whose activities they are taking an interest. Officially *they are not concerned with the Profumo aspect* [author's italics] but they do know that Profumo is aware of the position and that such action as is possible is being taken by his solicitors with the newspaper. They believe it to be true that Profumo has told the Prime Minister of the matter but they do not know that for certain. I think it is wise for us to stay out of this business and MI5 agree.

Legal advice

Once more Profumo seemed to be safe, but he had his solicitors fully briefed. All parties took legal advice at this point. Christine Keeler suggested that she be paid a sum of £5000 in compensation if she did not publish her *Sunday Pictorial* article. Profumo's solicitor decided that matters were becoming serious: he consulted Mark Littman QC and then, with Littman and Profumo, called on the Attorney-General, Sir John Hobson. Profumo informed the Attorney-General that he had considered the matter very carefully and that he was prepared to prosecute.

The following day, Keeler's solicitor telephoned Ward's solicitor, and in the course of the conversation he remarked, 'She would like to have five'; Ward's solicitor replied, 'Oh, I am sure that will be all right. I will let you know.' On 6 February Ward wrote to Lord Astor asking for a £500 loan – which was sent in a gracious manner. Of this money, £50 only was paid to Keeler. The rest was, apparently, refused by her, and allegedly went to pay Ward's various debts. On 8 February, since these delicate negotiations appeared to have broken down, she signed the proofs of her article for the *Sunday Pictorial* and went into hiding.

Meanwhile, Profumo had not been idle. Mark Chapman-Walker, General Manager of the *News of the World*, had telephoned the prime minister's parliamentary private secretary, and told him of the rumours about Profumo and Keeler. Chapman-Walker first informed the head of MI5, and then interviewed Profumo. Once more Profumo denied any impropriety, and the following day, 4 February, he repeated his denial to the Conservative chief whip. The prime minister was told of Profumo's denial – and then somebody, it seems, suggested issuing a 'D Notice' to Fleet Street, requesting that no news involving Ivanov should be published as a matter of national security.

Ward, also, was busy. He telephoned the assistant editor of the *Sunday Pictorial* and, mustering all his charm, persuaded the newspaper that Keeler's story was at least partially untrue and offered his own story in exchange. On 17 March, six weeks later, this story appeared in the *Pictorial*, two days after the end of the trial of Johnny Edgecombe.

Desperately worried about what she might be asked in the trial of Edgecombe, Keeler set out with Paul Mann and a girlfriend in a car for Spain.

The trial of Edgecombe opened on 14 March, and Keeler's absence made the front pages of the newspapers. The following day, when Edgecombe was found guilty of possessing an illegal firearm, some newspapers found typically unsubtle ways of airing what they knew of the Profumo and Keeler affair, but only by suggestion and not by telling the facts.

Wigg realised that his moment had come for airing the entire affair in Parliament. After 11pm on Thursday 21 March 1963, in a debate on press freedom, he said:

> The press . . . has shown itself willing to wound but afraid to strike. . . . That being the case, I rightly use the Privilege of the House of Commons . . . to ask the Home Secretary . . . to go to the Dispatch Box. He knows that the rumour to which I refer relates to Miss Christine Keeler and Miss Davies and a shooting by a West Indian – and, on behalf of the government, categorically deny the truth of these rumours.

Other speakers, too, took up the theme without naming Profumo, and it was not until after 1.30am that a meeting could be held in the room of the chief whip. Profumo was there, dragged from his bed and groggy with the effects of a sleeping pill, as was his solicitor and various members of the government. They spent two hours drafting a statement for Profumo to make in the House of Commons.

At 11.08am the following day, he made his personal statement to the House, acknowledging his acquaintance with Ward, Keeler and Ivanov but firmly denying any sexual relationship with Keeler. He said that he had last seen Keeler in December 1961, and added: 'I shall not hesitate to issue writs for libel and slander if scandalous allegations are made or repeated outside the House.'

The rage in Fleet Street – a rage that could not be expressed – at this barefaced lie was immense. Every newspaper redoubled its efforts to find the 'missing model'. And then, learning a little of what was happening in Britain, Keeler appeared at the office of the British consul in Madrid, was tracked down by two *Daily Express* reporters and gave them an exclusive interview for a payment of £1400. But still no newspaper would challenge Profumo's threat of an action for libel, and all that Christine's confessions, as they appeared in the *Daily Express* of 26 March, consisted of were such innocuous revelations as: 'I have met Mr Profumo on several occasions. He was most courteous and gentlemanly.'

Profumo, despite all the innuendo that Fleet Street might muster, could still have got away with it, had it not been for Ward's incurable urge to talk. On the evening of 22 March he appeared on ITN News, and spoke indignantly of the 'dreadful position' that Profumo was in because of the 'baseless

Below: the Edwardian cottage on the Clivedon estate (bottom) where Ward held his famous weekend parties

rumours and insinuations'; and yet on 26 March he met Wigg at the House of Commons and all his self-importance came to the fore: he talked of Ivanov, the Cuban crisis and MI5. This was the first real evidence anyone had possessed that Profumo and Ivanov had been anything more than the most distant of acquaintances; and the first time that Wigg had heard of Ward's activities as an 'intermediary' with the Soviets. For nearly two years the country had been treated to a succession of espionage cases, and the suggestion that the Secretary for War had shared a girl's favours with a Soviet diplomat was political dynamite.

Keeler flew to London on 28 March, to be met by a large police escort and a mob of journalists. On 1 April she appeared at the Old Bailey to answer for her absence from Edgecombe's trial, and forfeited her surety of £40.

Then somebody with a desire to cause trouble began to communicate anonymously with the CID, suggesting that Stephen Ward was living on immoral earnings, and that he was being protected by friends in high places. The police, who had done their best to pursue the affair at the beginning of February, and who had found their efforts blocked by Special Branch and MI5, apparently decided that, this time, they were not going to be seen to be avoiding their duty. They began to take statements from Keeler and from other girls. On 11 April Mandy Rice-Davies was arrested on a charge – which later even the judge acknowledged had been designed to keep her in the country – of using a forged driving licence. She spent two weeks in Holloway on remand before being fined forty guineas.

Christine Keeler surrounded by newspaper cuttings in 1963. When the *News of the World* published her 'confessions' it sold an extra quarter million copies

Then Lucky Gordon was arrested for allegedly attacking Keeler, who was now living in Devonshire Street with her friend Paula Hamilton-Marshall. On 3 May he was committed for trial.

Ward was aware of the interest the police were taking in him, and he became seriously worried. Knowing that Profumo had lied, and believing that he was being prosecuted for his knowledge, he attempted to get the police inquiry stopped by appealing to the government. On 7 May he made an appointment with Macmillan's parliamentary private secretary and a member of MI5. At the meeting Ward told them:

> I made a considerable sacrifice for Mr Profumo . . . He wrote Miss Keeler a series of letters. . . . I don't know whether there is anything you can do . . . there is a great deal of potentially extremely explosive material in what I've told you.

And still Ward could not keep quiet. On 19 May he wrote to the home secretary:

John and Valerie Profumo make their way through reporters and cameramen on their arrival at their London home. After Profumo's resignation, the couple had retreated to Warwickshire to stay with friends

> It has come to my notice that the Marylebone police are questioning my patients and friends in a line, however tactful, which is extremely damaging to me both professionally and socially. This inquiry has been going on day after day for weeks. The instruction to do this must have come from the Home Office. Over the past few weeks I have done what I could to shield Mr Profumo from his indiscretion, about which I complained to the Security Service at the time. When he made a statement in Parliament I backed it up although I knew it to be untrue. . . . I intend to take the blame no longer. . . . May I ask that the person who has lodged the false information against me should be prosecuted.

He issued a copy of this letter to the press – but nobody published it – he wrote to his MP, as well as to to Harold Wilson.

Profumo resigns

The Profumos left for a short holiday in Venice on 31 May; the prime minister set out for northern Scotland. Both were no doubt aware that the trial of Lucky Gordon would begin on 5 June. On 3 June the Profumos returned unexpectedly from Italy, where John Profumo had confessed to his wife. He informed Macmillan's parliamentary private secretary and tendered his immediate resignation. Two days later, Keeler gave evidence in Gordon's trial at the Old Bailey. In the course of a chaotic hearing, Gordon announced that he was withdrawing instructions from counsel, and established the right to question the witness himself. He told the court: 'This is more or less a put-up case by Dr Stephen Ward, who is known as a crank. I want to show that what took place that night is a put-up thing.' He asked for a number of additional witnesses to be called, including two men called Fenton and Comarchio (who were with Keeler the night she was attacked by Lucky Gordon but were being shielded by her). The police said that they were unable to find these two, although it was later revealed that at the time Comarchio was being held on remand. On 6 June Gordon was sentenced to three years' imprisonment for assault. He immediately announced that he would appeal.

That night Ward appeared on the ITN current affairs programme, *This Week*. Asked point-blank if he had been running a call-girl ring, he replied confidently, 'Certainly not.' But two days later, on Saturday 8 June, Ward was arrested and charged under the Sexual Offences Act.

Now the press truly took their revenge, not on Ward or Keeler, but upon the establishment that had gagged them all those months. All the Sunday papers were highly critical of the way in which Macmillan had handled the affair; and the *News of the World* published the first part of Keeler's 'confessions', scooping up in the process an extra quarter of a million in sales.

A debate in the Commons was set down for 17 June, with a vote of no confidence. The government came close to falling: next morning the headlines read: 'PREMIER LIKELY TO RESIGN SOON' and 'MAC: THE END'. But somehow Macmillan rallied his forces, and it was announced that an inquiry into the whole affair was to be conducted by Lord Denning, a leading judge.

At Ward's committal proceedings, three weeks before the trial, the charges had been elaborated: living on the immoral earnings of three prostitutes – Mandy Rice-Davies, Christine Keeler and Margaret Richardson, otherwise known as Ronna Ricardo; inciting Christine Keeler to procure a girl under the age of 21 to have unlawful intercourse with a third person; and himself procuring a girl for the same unlawful purpose.

In evidence, Keeler had denied that she was a prostitute, but had admitted taking some money from Profumo and other men as a gift for her mother. Rice-Davies had said that she had been kept by Peter Rachman, but had also slept with (among others) the film star Douglas Fairbanks Jr and Lord Astor. Margaret Richardson had described a number of occasions on which she had been paid to have intercourse with 'clients' – she had used Ward's flat in Bryanston Mews West.

The trial of Stephen Ward opened at the Old Bailey on 22 July 1963. The police produced a new

Prime Minister Harold Macmillan, who wrote on 5 June 1963 in answer to Profumo's letter of resignation: 'This is a great tragedy for you. Nevertheless I am sure you will understand that in the circumstances I have no alternative but to advise the Queen to accept your resignation'

Christine Keeler (right) and Mandy Rice-Davies on the first day of Stephen Ward's trial. Ward was found guilty of living on the girls' immoral earnings

witness, Vickie Barrett, a real prostitute, who had turned out to have Ward's telephone number in her diary. She said she had done business with a number of men at Ward's flat and that Ward had promised to bank money for her, although she had never seen a single penny of it.

Where were Ward's prominent friends and acquaintances? None seemed prepared to appear in his support. The trial lasted eight days, and in his summing up, the judge, Mr Justice Marshall quoted: 'If a man knowingly assists a prostitute with the direct object of enabling her to carry on her trade, and knowingly lives wholly *or in part* on the earnings of prostitutes, which he assists, he is in our view guilty of the offences under the 1956 Act.'

The jury retired, and Ward talked with Tom Mangold of the *Daily Express*, saying: 'This is a political revenge trial; someone had to be sacrificed and that was me.' That evening he took an overdose of the barbiturate Nembutal.

While Ward lay in a coma in St Stephen's Hospital, Fulham, the trial jury came to its verdict. Ward was found guilty on two counts only: of living on the immoral earnings of Keeler and Rice-Davies. But the judge never delivered sentence, for on 3 August Stephen Ward died.

He was a vain man, a silly man, a snob – but a 'thoroughly filthy fellow', as he was called at his trial? He liked girls, quite possibly he would rather have been one. He loved the look of their bodies, and the clothes they wore, and their unpredictable emotions. He shared their sexuality vicariously: if he couldn't satisfy them himself, then he was prepared to find them a man who could – and if, at the same time, he did a favour for a rich and famous friend, that made things even better. Keeler and Rice-Davies were promiscuous, but they were not prostitutes, even if the jury thought them so, and the small sums they occasionally paid him as 'rent' were nothing compared to what he spent on them. After the trial, a distinguished High Court judge said privately that, had the papers for the Ward case come to him he would never have let it to go to jury.

So why was the case brought? The public saw it as revenge for Profumo's fall. Several aspects of the Ward case remain unsolved:

Questions unanswered

- Profumo's 'farewell' letter to Keeler is dated 9 August 1961. Why then did he later say that he had last seen her in December 1961? If he had visited her between September and December of that year, would not MI5 have protested?
- Where did Paul Mann get the money to take Keeler to Spain? Christine was able to contribute only some £20 of the money she had received from Ward's loan from Lord Astor. Mann told Lord Denning: 'I had my own means, untraceable resources,' but he refused to give further details.
- Whose was the telephone number found in Vickie Barrett's diary, which the police identified as Ward's? The original charge on his arrest named 17 Wimpole Mews as the premises at which he had lived 'wholly or in part on the earnings of prostitution'; and his telephone number there was Welbeck 6933. The Welbeck and Paddington exchanges were housed in the same building in Marylebone Road, and the boundary between the two areas ran down Montague Street and through Montague Square. Bryanston Mews lay to the west of this line, and Paddington 8625 was probably the telephone number of the late Rachman's flat. No records have survived to establish this, and the number is now that for premises in Church Street, half a mile away.
- Who paid some £5000 for the royal portraits from the exhibition of Ward's drawings that was showing during the trial? According to Frederick Read, who put on the show, the money was in the form of a bank draft, but he believed that it came from Roy Thomson, the proprietor of *The Times*, and that the drawings were given to Lord Snowdon. *The Times* has long been regarded as the mouthpiece of the security services, and it is perhaps not surprising that the man who handed over the money, who is described by Read as 'chameleon-like', should be suspected of coming from MI5. A few months later Thomson was elevated to the peerage.
- Why was Lord Astor not called as a witness by either defence or prosecution?
- In his book written and published shortly after the end of the trial, *The Profumo Affair: Aspects of Conservatism*, Wayland Young (Lord Kennet) asks some further questions, none of which has ever been satisfactorily answered:

  Why did Vickie Barrett break down when Ward died, confess to a journalist that she too had been lying, and then retract her confession? On whose instructions and with what right had Mandy Rice-

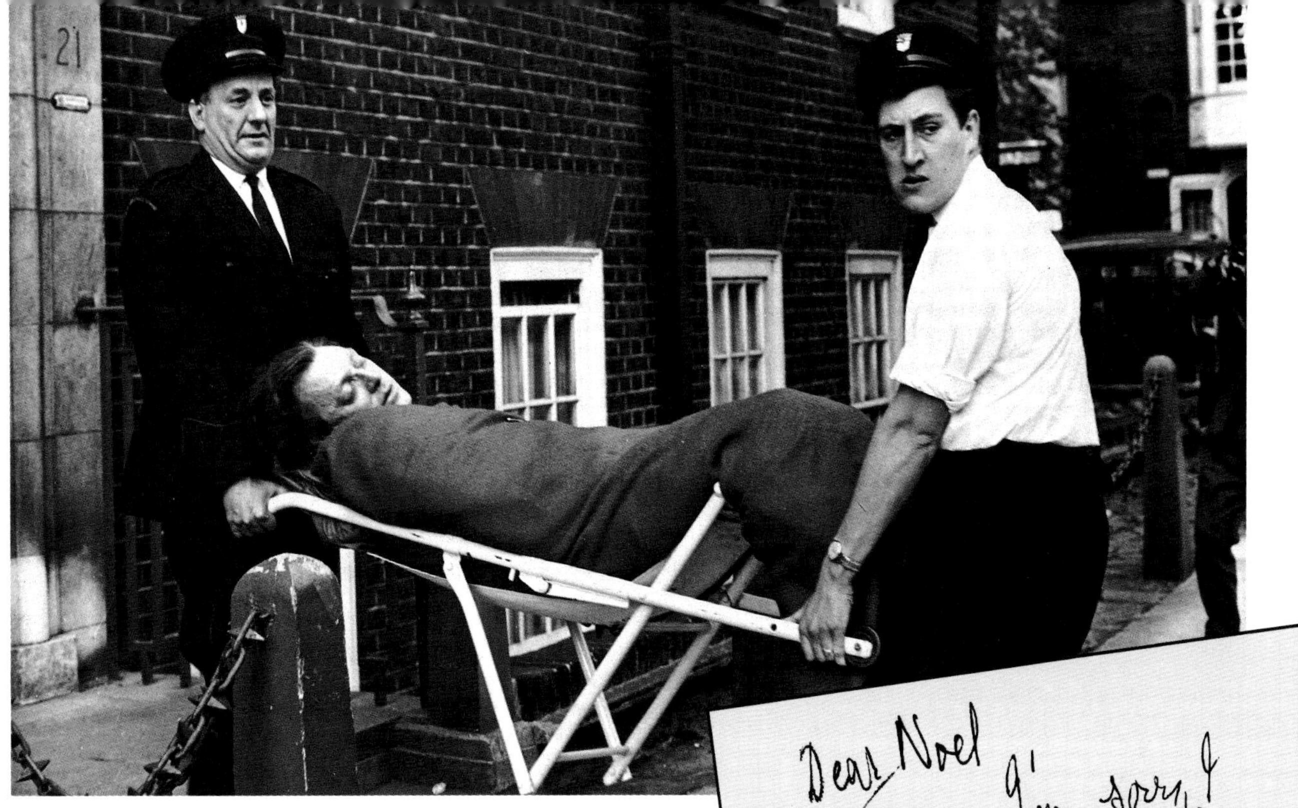

Above: on 31 July a comatose Ward was taken from the Chelsea home of his loyal friend Noel Howard-Jones, where he had spent the period of his trial on bail. He had taken an overdose of the barbiturate Nembutal and lay in a coma for fours days; he never regained consciousness. During the trial the prosecution presented Ward as a 'thoroughly filthy fellow', 'a wicked, wicked creature', and 'a depraved old man'
Right: the suicide note Stephen Ward left for Howard-Jones. It continued: 'after Marshall's summing up I've given up all hope . . . I'm sorry to disappoint the vultures'

Dear Noel
I'm sorry I
had to do this here!!
It's really more than I
can stand – the horror
day after day at the court
and in the streets. – It's not
only fear – its a wish not
to let them get me. I'd
rather get myself. –

Davies been forcibly kept in the country to give evidence against Stephen Ward? And, a question which seems to sum up the others, why did the police find it necessary to interview 140 people before they moved against Stephen Ward? How many people do they usually think it worth interviewing in order to prepare charges of poncing? Is it something like 140? Or is it more like four or five, as commonsense would suggest? If they carried out an almost unparalleled operation to get Ward, why did they do so? Who took the decision? How much did it cost? And what made Ward's offences worth it?

•Why were both Wayland Young and Ludovic Kennedy, engaged in preparing books about the Ward trial, refused access to the official transcript of the proceedings, a decision that was upheld by the Court of Criminal Appeal?

•What was on the ten-hour tape interview with Keeler that was called for in evidence in Lucky Gordon's appeal against his conviction, that was instrumental in getting his conviction quashed, and that subsequently led to Keeler being found guilty of perjury? Gordon's appeal was heard during the Ward trial, but does not seem to have influenced the proceeding at the Old Bailey in any way.

•Who broke into the Astors' home in Upper Grosvenor Street on 20 March 1963, rifled the mail (most of it replies to an advertisement for a new housemaid) and took just one letter? And who, the same day, broke into and vandalised Ward's cottage on the Cliveden Estate?

•And who made the anonymous telephone call to George Wigg on 11 November 1962 that drew his attention so strongly to the new scandal?

Stephen Ward and his friends had paid dearly for upsetting the Conservative government and its individual members. It is apparent that an unknown hand was active in steering the course of events to a damaging conclusion. Will we ever know who was the person responsible for taking those decisions and making those moves?

'Buster' Crabb's last dive

Against the strict orders of prime minister Anthony Eden, British Naval Intelligence sent a frogman to spy on the Russian cruiser *Ordzhonikidze*, at anchor in Portsmouth Harbour in April 1956 with Soviet leaders Krushchev and Bulganin aboard. But no information was ever gathered by the British, since the spy, Commander Lionel 'Buster' Crabb, never returned from his dive. The government was gravely embarrassed when the affair was revealed, and a mystery remained. What became of Crabb? Did he drown or was he caught by the Soviets and executed, or even recruited into their espionage service?

Of all the mysteries that have captured the newspaper headlines none has caused such embarrassment to the government of the day as the disappearance of the naval frogman Commander Lionel Kenneth Philip Crabb, OBE, GM, RNVR, in the waters of Portsmouth Harbour, Hampshire, on 19 April 1956. Crabb was carrying out an act of espionage that was so common as to be almost routine, but on that particular day the circumstances were so peculiar that the enterprise was fraught with the gravest political consequences should it go wrong – as it did, with catastrophic results in its wake.

The joint leaders of the Soviet Union, Nikolai Bulganin and Nikita Khrushchev, were visiting Britain on a goodwill mission by which the British government, under the premiership of Sir Anthony Eden, set great store for the improvement of East-West relations and the thawing of the Cold War. They had chosen to arrive by sea in the cruiser *Ordzhonikidze*, with a destroyer escort, and the ships lay moored at Portsmouth Harbour while the Soviet leaders and their entourage travelled to London by train. The proposed spying operation looked simple enough.

In the previous year British Naval Intelligence, which was then under Admiralty control, had made full use of a visit by the *Ordzhonikidze*'s sister ship, *Sverdlov*, to examine the new technology being incorporated in the new generation of Soviet warships. Tests had been made by Navy submarines and RAF reconnaissance aircraft. The most meticulous

examination was made by Crabb, who was selected for the task because he was easily the most experienced operator available. He was also a freelance, having been retired from the navy a few months previously, and if anything went wrong he could be disowned – the usual fate of a freelance spy.

Crabb's main task was to examine the submerged hull to see if the ship was fitted with a device codenamed 'Agouti'. This device reduced the effect of 'cavitation', which is responsible for much of the noise made by a ship's screws and increases the chance of long-range detection by sonar. Because of the depth and turbidity of the water Crabb had to make his assessments by feel, but he had become experienced at doing that through his work in removing limpet mines placed by enemy frogmen on the hulls of British ships during the course of the Second World War.

The *Sverdlov* operation was regarded as routine because whenever a British warship visited Leningrad the harbour swarmed with frogmen blatantly performing the same jobs. Full authority had therefore been given for the project and the Admiralty hoped that the same attitude would be taken with the *Ordzhonikidze*. Before the latter arrived, however, intelligence operations of any kind against her were expressly forbidden by Eden because, with the Soviet leaders aboard, it was a highly sensitive political situation. Unfortunately for Crabb – and for others – the order, which was interpreted by the Admiralty as coming from a 'wet' prime minister, was widely disobeyed.

As the Admiralty particularly did not want official involvement Crabb was an obvious choice and he accepted with alacrity, being short of work. It was appreciated that, at 46, he was rather old for the task and was not really fit, being overly addicted to cigarettes and alcohol, but he had proved his effectiveness only a few months previously with the *Sverdlov* mission.

The endeavour was foolhardy for a particular reason: extreme security precautions had been taken by the Soviets themselves to protect their leaders wherever they might be, and the penalty for any failure would be especially severe. The whole Soviet operation was under the personal control of the chief of the KGB himself, Ivan Serov. The British security authorities knew that he was staying aboard the ship and this should have alerted them to the fact that the crew would be specially watchful for any local security problem.

Below: Commander Buster Crabb entertains a party of students on the Isle of Mull in 1950. Crabb had tried his hand at various jobs after the war, but he had taken the first opportunity to return to diving; one of his first missions was to explore wrecks of Spanish ships sunk off the Isle of Mull in 1588. The navy had then asked him to test new diving equipment and, in 1956, finally conspired with MI6 to send him on his tragic mission, made near South Railway Jetty at Portsmouth Harbour (below left)

Colonel-General Serov (left) in London in March 1956 to discuss security for the Soviet leaders' April visit

On the afternoon of 17 April Crabb travelled by train to Portsmouth with his fiancée Mrs Patricia Rose, who went purely to keep him company. On the way he told her what he intended to do and said that the Admiralty was employing him, although it was doing so indirectly so that it would not seem to be involved if problems ensued.

Crabb left Pat Rose at Portsmouth station and she returned to London while he went into the town to meet an MI6 'minder' who had been detailed to assist him. The two then booked in at the Sally Port Hotel in Old Portsmouth High Street. Crabb signed his own name in the register; the minder called himself 'Bernard Smith'.

On the following morning, 18 April, the two men went to the dockyard to make a reconnaissance. Crabb decided to make his foray at about 7am on the following day.

On the morning of the dive, the 'minder', who in reality was a local MI6 officer called Teddy Davies, suffered a minor heart attack but insisted on carrying on with the operation. They must have had passes to enter the enclosed area, especially in view of the presence of the Soviet ships, so more people must have become aware of the arrival of Crabb, who was well known by sight as a 'character', and they must have divined his purpose.

After changing into his diving suit Crabb swam towards the warship 300 yards (275 metres) away, and was never seen again by his colleagues.

At 7.30am, according to a later Soviet statement, Crabb was seen by Soviet sailors swimming at the surface near one of the *Ordzhonikidze*'s destroyers.

When Crabb failed to return from the dive 'Smith' took his clothes and unused parts of his equipment and returned to the Sally Port Hotel, where he paid the joint bill and removed Crabb's possessions that were still there.

The Admiralty and MI6 decided to seek the help of MI5 in an attempt to cover up the disaster. Confident that such a cover-up would succeed, the Admiralty sat tight. Unfortunately, on 19 April, James Thomas, the First Lord of the Admiralty, was dining with some of the Soviet visitors and was asked: 'What was that frogman doing off our bows this morning?' The following morning inquiries were put in train and ministers were shocked and angered when they were told, grudgingly, what had happened. Eden, of course, was enraged at the way a major political and psychological advantage had been handed to the Soviets.

Throughout 20 April, which was a Friday, there were many secret meetings in Whitehall about the continuation of a cover-up. On MI5's advice – which proved to be counter-productive to say the least – the head of the Portsmouth CID, Detective Superintendent Stanley Lampert, was asked to visit the hotel on Saturday 21 April and remove all evidence of Crabb's stay there. He saw the hotel manager, Edward Richman, and on the basis of his identity card tore four pages from the visitors' book. Why he thought the removal of four pages was necessary has

Below: the Sally Port Hotel, Portsmouth, where Crabb stayed on the eve of his mission. After his disappearance, police removed all evidence of Crabb's stay here – including, inexplicably, *four* pages of the visitors' book in which he had signed his name

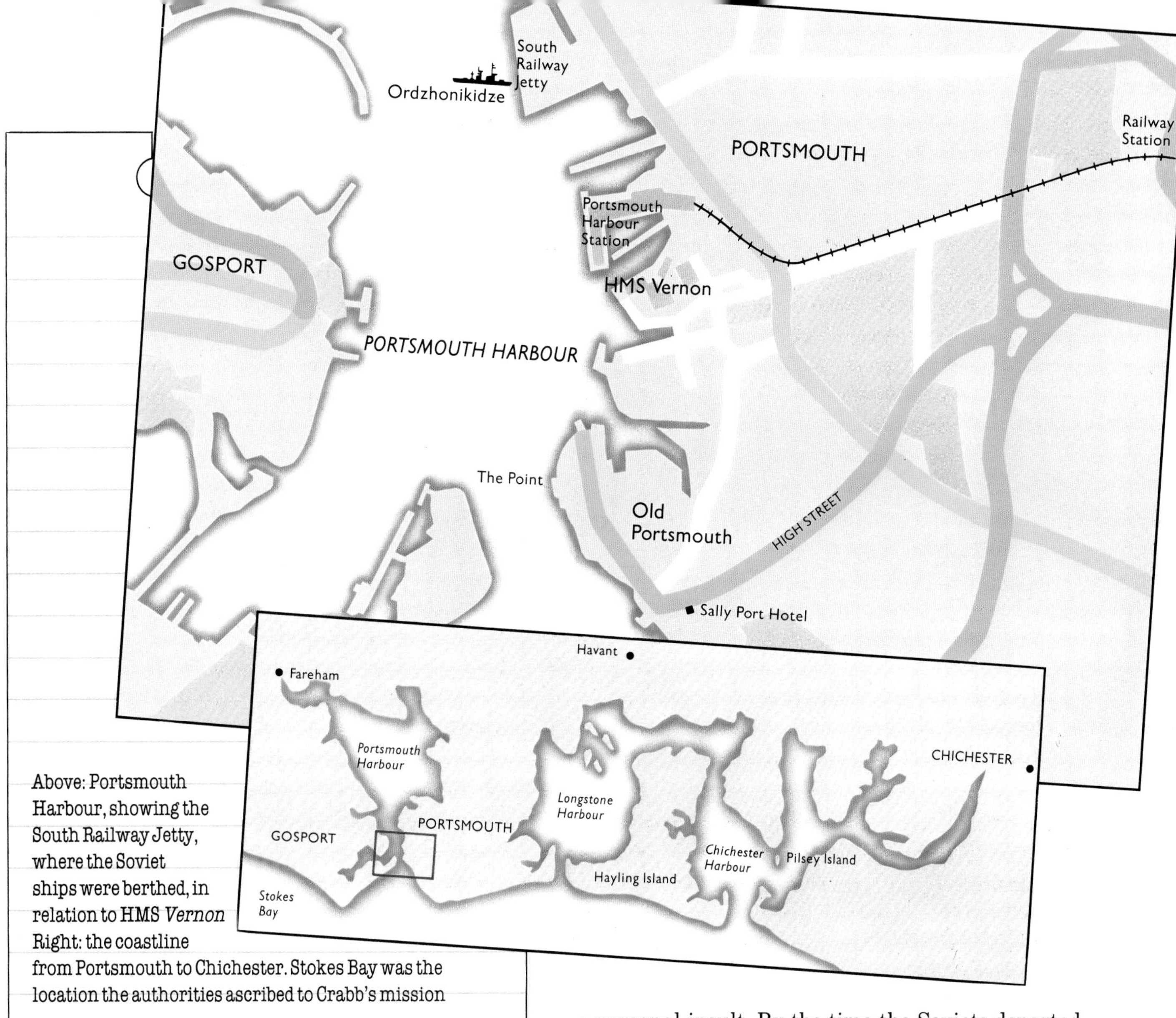

Above: Portsmouth Harbour, showing the South Railway Jetty, where the Soviet ships were berthed, in relation to HMS *Vernon*
Right: the coastline from Portsmouth to Chichester. Stokes Bay was the location the authorities ascribed to Crabb's mission

never been explained. When the manager objected Lampert threatened him with the Official Secrets Act if he told anybody what had happened. As was to be made clear in Parliament later, this was irregular, and the removal of the pages was illegal.

Unfortunate incident

The Soviets stayed their hand concerning any official complaint to the Foreign Office, or any leak to the media, and might have continued to do so but for an unfortunate political incident that occurred at a dinner at Claridge's on the evening of 23 April. Bulganin and Khrushchev were the guests of honour at a dinner given by the Labour Party Executive Committee and the two Labour leaders, Hugh Gaitskell and George Brown, were present. Brown (later Lord George-Brown) took the opportunity to make a plea for human rights in the Soviet Union and when Khrushchev brushed the request aside Brown cried, 'May God forgive you!' Khrushchev immediately asked for the remark to be translated and became extremely angry, seeing the criticism as a personal insult. By the time the Soviets departed with their warships the goodwill mission had been an all-round disaster, but while the row at Claridge's was widely publicised the public remained ignorant of the Crabb affair.

On Saturday 28 April, nine days after the commander was last seen, a naval officer from the Admiralty called on Pat Rose saying that he was missing. On the following day the Admiralty announced that Crabb was missing, presumed dead, having failed to return from 'a test-dive in connection with trials of certain underwater apparatus in Stokes Bay', 3 miles (5 kilometres) from Portsmouth.

As could be expected, the statement was not believed by many journalists, who speculated that Crabb had been spying on the Soviet warships, and drew attention to the extraordinary fact that no attempt at all had been made to find the body.

When inquiries revealed the removal of the pages from the Sally Port Hotel register and what had been in them, it quickly became clear to Parliament and the public alike that they had been the victims of an Admiralty and MI6 'disinformation' cover-up, and that lies had been told to spare embarrassment in Whitehall and Westminster.

Above: John Randall (right) and Ted Gilby, the two fishermen who found the headless, handless corpse of a frogman off Pilsey Island in June 1957 while fishing from their boat *Red Goose*
Top: the same body is buried with due ceremony – but was it really Crabb's? And if not, whose was it?

After deliberations with Kremlin colleagues, the Soviet leaders decided to make what political capital they could out of the situation, and the Soviet embassy in London sent a note to the Foreign Office claiming that Soviet sailors had seen a frogman near the *Ordzhonikidze*. The Whitehall authorities still hoped to keep the note secret but Soviet embassy officials, clearly acting on instructions from Moscow, leaked the fact that Soviet sailors had seen a frogman and that there could be little doubt that it was Commander Crabb.

This immediately led to a flurry of newspaper speculation about what might have happened. One theory claimed that Crabb had been captured and taken to the Soviet Union, another that he had been killed by the Soviets in the water and even that his body had been found by the British navy and secretly buried at midnight in a local cemetery, 'with full naval honours'. Realising that it had already made a monumental blunder by issuing its Stokes Bay statement, the Admiralty declined to confirm or deny any of the theories. The most exciting theory, and the one offering the biggest bonuses to the KGB, was that Crabb had been captured by Soviet frogmen, ever alert to any danger threatening a Soviet ship, and had been taken back to the Soviet Union for questioning. As will be seen, this theory was to be developed with a mass of detail that even cast doubt on Crabb's loyalty.

Meanwhile, the Foreign Office had secretly replied to the Soviet note admitting that Commander Crabb had carried out frogman tests and had, presumably, lost his life while performing them. It then went on to admit that: 'The frogman who, as reported in the Soviet note, was discovered from the Soviet ships swimming between the Soviet destroyers, was in all appearances Commander Crabb. His presence in the vicinity of the destroyers occurred without any permission whatever, and Her Majesty's Government express their regret for the incident.' This statement was false as both the Admiralty and MI6 had been intimately involved, and the Kremlin released the text of both notes, thereby making the matter more embarrassing for the British which, of course, was the objective.

As always happens, whatever the party in office, the opposition took advantage of the government's chagrin to make its own political capital. The publication of the notes forced the prime minister, Eden, to make a statement to Parliament on 9 May admitting that Crabb had been the frogman and had been near the Soviet warships. He insisted that the operation was 'without authority' or the knowledge of ministers and he added that 'appropriate disciplinary steps' were being taken. Otherwise he refused to be drawn, pleading the traditional respect for secrecy in such matters.

Eden had, in fact, ordered a secret inquiry by a group headed by Sir Edward Bridges, a very senior civil servant. Various officials who gave evidence were admonished and some were transferred. The chief punishment was reserved for the chief of MI6, Major General Sir John 'Sinbad' Sinclair, who was retired early and replaced by the man who was serving as director general of MI5, Sir Dick White.

The issue seemed to be dying away when, on Sunday 9 June 1957, fourteen months after Crabb's disappearance, a fisherman called John Randall saw a headless body in a frogman suit floating off Pilsey Island, a sandbank at the mouth of Chichester Harbour, about 10 miles (16 kilometres) from Portsmouth. The body was also without hands and it was impossible to identify it with any certainty.

Pat Rose, Crabb's fiancée, remains convinced that he was transported to the Soviet Union, and that he may still be alive, although she has never heard from him directly

Disinformation theory

An inquest was held on 11 June and it was revealed that there were signs of a scar on the body's left knee. Crabb's former colleague, Sidney Knowles, testified that the missing frogman had had such a scar, the result of an accident with barbed wire Crabb had suffered when they were diving together. The coroner recorded an open verdict but said he was satisfied that the remains were those of Crabb, who had died gallantly in the service of his country. This view received support from a newspaper report that the body of a frogman with the head attached had certainly been dredged up by a lone fisherman a few months previously. The fisherman was said to have told the local police that he had grabbed the head to haul the body aboard and it had come away in his hands, as it might well have done after it had been in the water for so long.

The convenient absence of the head and hands quickly gave rise to speculation that the body was not really Crabb's but that of another person from which the main identification features had been deliberately removed by the Soviets, who had then deposited the body from a submarine as part of a disinformation exercise. It appeared that three Soviet submarines had gone through the English Channel on their way to Egypt at the relevant time. Again, the Admiralty refused to comment, and Crabb's relatives issued a disclaimer, objecting to any suggestion that he had been taken to the Soviet Union and was working, disloyally to his own country, for the Red Navy.

The body was buried at Milton Cemetery, Portsmouth, on 5 July 1957. There were no navy representatives at the funeral and Pat Rose did not attend either, being in the south of France and remaining convinced that the body was not Crabb's. Mrs Rose returned to London the following year and a few months later received a telephone call, allegedly on behalf of Crabb, from someone who claimed to have met him in the Crimea in the Soviet Union. She was also approached on different occasions at Victoria Station, London, by strangers who said that they knew Crabb to be alive and that he hoped to be reunited with her. They refused to give their names or say any more. One of them showed her a rather poor photograph that, he said, showed Crabb in the Soviet Union, but he would not allow her to keep it. Later, in October 1959, she received another telephone call from an anonymous person who said that Crabb was alive in Vladivostok. Some of these occurrences could have been hoaxes, but they would also have been in keeping with the KGB's tactics.

The possibility that Crabb had been captured and was alive in the Soviet Union was developed and embellished by a middle European who wrote books under the name of J. Bernard Hutton. He claimed to have received a 'dossier' in November 1959 via the 'anti-communist' underground; it contained information said to prove that Crabb had been taken alive, drugged aboard the *Ordzhonikidze* and flown into the Soviet Union by a helicopter that landed on the cruiser when it was homeward-bound in the Skaggerak on 29 April 1956.

Information about Hutton's 'dossier' and his forthcoming book began to leak to the newspapers and CRABB IS ALIVE headlines appeared in the British newspapers in February 1960, being, of course, denied in Moscow which, however, took the opportunity of recalling Britain's perfidy. British security and intelligence authorities declined to comment but they privately dismissed the information as having no foundation in fact and that is still their opinion, or alleged opinion. They were careful, however, not to deny the existence of the 'dossier'.

Above: Lieutenant-Commander J.S. Kerans, who firmly believed that Crabb had been taken to the Soviet Union

In 1961 Hutton had a windfall in the form of a statement by Sir Percy Sillitoe, the former director general of MI5. He had been retired for eight years and had no contact with security affairs, but his name carried weight with the public when he claimed that a similar dossier had been obtained by British intelligence agents. He agreed with Hutton that the body buried in the Portsmouth cemetery was not Crabb's. Hutton also secured the support of a naval officer who had been much in the public eye, Commander J. S. Kerans, formerly of the warship *Amethyst*, which had run the gauntlet of a Chinese bombardment and escaped from the Yangtse river. Kerans, who had become an MP, said in writing that he was confident that Crabb had been taken to the Soviet Union. He also raised questions in Parliament about him but with no result.

Pat Rose, in some desperation, wrote to Khrushchev for information but received no reply. Little more was heard until 1964 when the late Colonel Marcus Lipton, a Labour MP who specialised in such causes, attempted to reopen the case in Parliament. He got small change from the prime minister, Harold Wilson who, like Eden before him, took the view that the Soviets had made more than enough political capital out of the episode. Indeed, Wilson may well have been advised by the security authorities that the Soviets were behind this new attempt to sow contentious disinformation. Though it may be coincidental, from the time of the Crabb affair the KGB had changed its general policy, deciding to concentrate more effort and resources on the use of disinformation as a way of confusing and discrediting Cold War adversaries such as Britain. The Crabb débâcle had certainly presented the KGB with a ready-made opportunity, and it is the view of MI6 officers that it was taken and pursued with a great deal of success.

According to Hutton, he continued to receive news from the Soviet Union about Crabb's career in the Red Navy, indicating that he had been promoted to commander and was enjoying life there so much that he had extended his 10-year contract. These titbits, which may have been deliberately fed by the KGB to keep the story going, were supported by others appearing in European papers indicating that Crabb was still alive.

The Crabb case seems destined to remain unsolved for all time. The only certainty is that to this day Whitehall, and the secret services in particular, remain extremely sensitive about the Crabb affair. Officials with inside knowledge of the case have been expressly forbidden to make any mention of it in their memoirs. This ban may simply be due to the desire to bury for good a deplorable and deeply embarrassing episode – or it may indicate that there are super-sensitive details that have still not been revealed to the public.

The tombstone at Milton Cemetery. The body in it has not been positively identified, and the grave could contain the skeleton of another body dumped by the Soviets

4
Who, what, where, why, how?

From time to time a serious crime is committed that the investigating authorities cannot solve because one or more vital pieces of the puzzle are missing – the place or time of death, the motive for murder or, in one fascinating case, the cause of death itself.

Death on a hillside

In November 1979, an Englishwoman, Jeannette May, and her Italian companion, Gabriella Guerin, disappeared in central Italy during the worst snowstorm for 35 years. Their bodies were found on a hillside more than a year later. Was May, formerly married to a Rothschild, abducted by Sardinian kidnappers? Why were the police so sure the deaths were accidental, when the evidence points to murder?

On Saturday 29 November 1980, two women visitors to the region of the Marche in central east Italy set out from their hotel for a drive in the Apennine mountains. They failed to return. There was a heavy snowstorm during that day and the first thought of their friends was that they had decided to shelter somewhere. But when they had still not shown up by Monday afternoon, a search party went out. The next day a more thorough search was made by 200 men – on foot, in jeeps, Sno-cats and helicopters. They found nothing. The women, Jeannette May and her friend Gabriella Guerin, had disappeared without trace.

Fourteen months later, a hunter came across their bodies in a mountain forest. Examination of the remains showed no evidence of trauma on the bones, no knife or gunshot wounds, and no fractures. The conclusion of the police was straightforward. The two women had gone up the mountain on a pleasure trip and had been caught in the storm. After spending two days in a shepherds' cottage, they had set out to walk to the nearest village. They had become disoriented in the snow and had wandered off the road. Exhausted, they had stretched out to rest and had died of exposure.

With this explanation, the police were prepared to close the file. But a team of British journalists, led by Phillip Knightley of *The Sunday Times*, was sure that there was more to it. They conducted their own, independent investigation. They carried out exhaustive cross-questioning of the witnesses, many of whom the police had failed to interrogate or whose evidence had been ignored. The results were highly disturbing. The evidence, they said, pointed to one conclusion: the two women had been brutally murdered, and the police – either through ineptitude or because of political pressure – had failed to investigate the crime.

Jeannette May was the wife of a British businessman, Stephen May, an executive with London's John Lewis department store. She dealt in art and antiques and ran a successful interior decorating business from an office in the basement of their Chelsea home. It was her second marriage; the first, to banker Evelyn de Rothschild, had ended in divorce in 1971 and she had married Stephen May in 1975. In 1979 they bought a 300-year-old farmhouse at Schito, a hamlet in the mountain region of the Marche, near the town of Sarnarno. After various trips to supervise renovations to the farmhouse, they knew the region very well.

Gabriella Guerin, a quiet, home-loving woman, came from a peasant family from Friuli in north-east Italy, from a village, between Venice and Trieste. She and her husband, Dante, had worked as domestic servants for Evelyn de Rothschild for sixteen years. He had been married to Jeannette for five years, and the two women got on very well together, Jeannette becoming godmother to the Guerins' first child. The Guerins returned to live in Italy in 1977. A year later Dante was killed in a car accident. Now a widow with two young children, Gabriella was about to settle again near to her parents in her home village of Ronchis. When Jeannette came to Italy, she stayed with her as a companion.

Jeannette with her husband, British businessman Stephen May. The couple had been married for five years before her disappearance

Two versions

Jeannette arrived at Sarnarno on Tuesday 25 November, and decided to stay at the Ai Pini, a small family hotel behind the market square. She registered, as she always did, as 'de Rothschild, Dorothy Jeannette Ellen'. This was the name in her passport, beside which was written 'now May', but there was no room in the hotel register for that amendment. She dined alone that evening and the next afternoon drove to Ancona in her car (a black Peugeot 104, registered in Siena) to collect Gabriella from the station. On Thursday and Friday the two women visited the farmhouse, went shopping, saw friends and relaxed. On Saturday they vanished.

There are two versions of what the women did on that last day they were seen alive. One is the official police account; the other has been constructed by the British team. What follows here is the police version.

The day began with a telephone call to the hotel from Jeannette's surveyor, Nazzareno Venanzi, at 9.45am. Informed that the women had not yet come down from their rooms, he left a message for them saying that, instead of meeting at 11.30 or noon, as they had previously arranged, they should now meet at 10.30. The women had breakfast in the hotel at 10am. At 10.30 they met Venanzi in the town square and went with him to Murra's, a builders' merchant's, to choose flooring materials for the farmhouse. At noon, the women had drinks with Venanzi and his wife and Jeannette mentioned their plan to go sightseeing. Venanzi drove the two women back to the square and left them. At 12.35 they were seen getting into their car, which was parked in the square, and driving off along the mountain road.

According to the police, they were not seen again until 4pm, when they called at Murra's. At 4.30pm they were seen in their hotel, and evidence was later found in Jeannette's room that she had changed her clothes. At 5pm the local dentist, who knew them well, saw the two women driving through the hotel

Below: the Mays' farmhouse in Schito, near Sarnano. It was in order to oversee building work on the house that Jeannette made the trip to Italy from which she never returned

gates. According to the police, they were never seen alive again.

At 10pm that night, a snowstorm hit the area – the worst for 35 years. By the following morning, drifts of up to 10 feet (3 metres) deep were blocking the roads. At 11am Venanzi, concerned that the women might not be equipped for such weather, called at the hotel and learned that they had not returned. By 6pm there had still been no word. Venanzi was by then getting alarmed, and went to the police to report them missing. But the police did not share his anxiety. Thinking that the women were up to some adventure, and sure that they would be taking shelter somewhere, the police were reluctant to organise a full-scale search in the face of such terrible weather conditions.

The next morning, Monday, still brought no news of the women. The police still refused to act, so Venanzi mobilised his own search party. With his cousin, the leader of the local Alpine rescue squad, he started off on skis soon after 1pm; two hours later the police joined them. But at 5pm a shop assistant from Murra's informed the police that the two women had called there at 4pm on Saturday. Sure that the women would not have set off for the mountains when it was already getting dark, the police called off the search.

Below: Elena Bolici, who ran the hotel where Jeannette and Gabriella Guerin stayed. The hotel register (bottom) contains the two women's names, and that of Stephen May, who went to Sarnano immediately he heard of his wife's disappearance

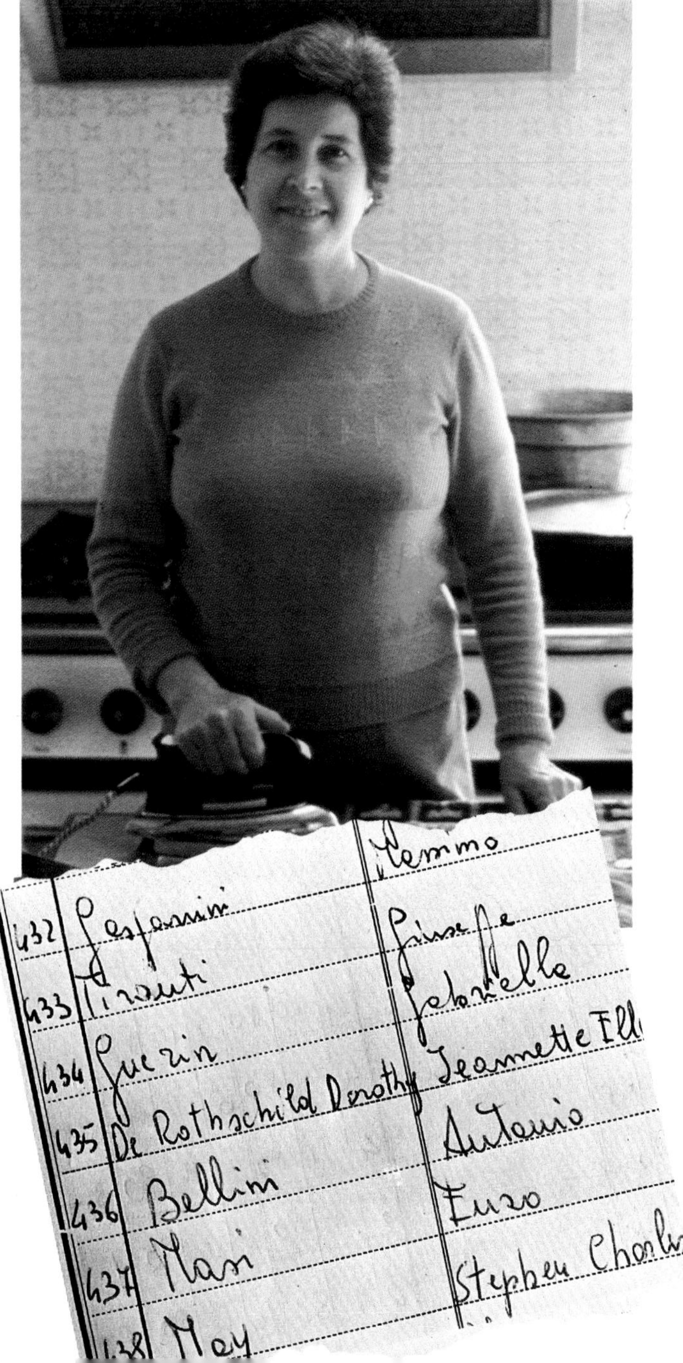

Casa Galloppa

Stephen May arrived from London that night. Next morning, Tuesday, the police mounted another search, this time on a large scale, but found nothing. Searching continued during the early part of December as hope for the women faded. Then, on Friday 19 December, a police helicopter spotted the top of the Peugeot just showing through the snow. The police were soon on the spot to dig it out. The women were not inside, but there were a number of clues available to the police.

There was no snow between the tyres and the road surface, indicating that the car had been driven to the spot *before* the snowstorm had started. It appeared to have been parked at the side of the road quite deliberately. The handbrake was on and the car started easily. Jeannette's driving shoes were on the floor by the front seat. Her wellington boots, which she kept in the car, were gone. Her tinted driving glasses were on the front seat. Gabriella's woollen scarf was on the back seat.

The police now searched the area. Just around the corner from the car, higher up the mountain, was a small cottage, the Casa Galloppa, which was used by shepherds during the summer. It had been closed for the winter on 11 October, the water turned off and the shutters closed.

The police found that the shutter on the front door was loose and had been propped shut by a heavy gas cylinder. The cottage had clearly been broken into. Inside, it was a shambles. A fire had been going in the fireplace and an enormous amount of wood had been burnt – about a quarter of a ton (250 kilograms) of logs along with some twenty wooden chairs, wine crates, the base of a sofa, the inside shutters from the windows and even some of the panelling from the living-room walls.

Whoever had been there had also eaten. A stack of plates had been taken from the kitchen to the living-room, and two of them had been used, as well as three forks and two glasses. The bathroom basin was full of blackened snow. In front of the house, on the balcony, was a tablecloth tied to the railings. In the

Above: Nazzareno Venanzi, who was in charge of the restoration of the Mays' farmhouse. When the women failed to return after the weekend, he and his cousin began to search for them
Above right: Stephen May is helped towards the snowbound Casa Galloppa, the shepherds' cottage in which the two women allegedly sheltered from the storm

corner of the balcony, someone had lit a fire, using plastic seats from deckchairs.

As far as the Italian police were concerned, the mystery was now solved. The women had driven up the mountain that Saturday evening and had been cut off by a snowdrift. They had left their car and broken into the cottage. They had lit a fire, dragged a sofa in front of it, spread a mattress to sleep on and made themselves a meal. The fire and the tablecloth on the balcony had been signals for help. When no one came, they had left on foot and had perished in the snow. Their bodies would doubtless be found in the spring.

But this explanation raised more questions than it answered. Why had the women gone sightseeing when it was getting dark? How could they have had a meal in the cottage when the shepherds had left no food there? Why would they light such a small fire on the balcony as an SOS signal when there was plenty of wood, and why hang out a tablecloth that could be seen only from the road, not from the air? And how long did the women wait before setting off? The amount of wood burnt suggested a stay of at least a week, but from Sunday morning onwards the cottage had been snowed in and the women could not have got out.

All these questions occurred to the British journalists who decided to take up the case in January 1981. They reviewed the evidence and the police investigation, and decided that there were two questions, in particular, that went to the core of the mystery. Why did the women drive up the mountain with darkness approaching on what was clearly going to be a bitter night? And why was the shepherds' cottage found in such a filthy state?

They began with the cottage, already closely examined by the Italian police, and quickly made an important discovery. The police had not investigated the stack of dishes properly. There were not two dirty plates, but *seven*. The top two were dirty, then there were four clean ones, then five more dirty ones underneath. There were not two used glasses but *nine* – the police had not noticed other used glasses scattered around the room. The evidence – suggesting as it did that more people had been in the cottage and over a longer period – confirmed the terrible suspicion that was already in the journalists' minds. Jeannette May, a former Rothschild, was an obvious victim for a kidnap attempt.

They urged the authorities to call in kidnapping experts from Rome and to ask Scotland Yard to look for a possible London link. But the police and the public prosecutor refused.

If the two women *had* been kidnapped, the reasons were obvious. Jeannette had a passport in the name of Rothschild – which had caused some anxiety to Gabriella. Her sister, Caterina, explained: 'In March 1980, when Gabriella had been to Sarnarno to help with the contract for the farm, all the papers had been full of the Schild kidnapping. On the way back my sister refused to stay with the *signora* in a hotel in Milan. She told the *signora* that it was stupid and dangerous to travel in Italy with Rothschild in her passport.'

In May 1981, six months after the women had disappeared, the Italian police were no closer to solving the mystery. The thaw had come but no bodies had been found. Then, suddenly, there appeared to be a breakthrough. A new witness came forward. Ortelio Valori, owner of the Sibilla Hotel at the ski-village of Sassotetto, had apparently seen the two women *twice* on the day they disappeared. The British journalists hurried back to Italy to interview him.

Valori said that the two women had first driven up to his hotel at about 10 on the Saturday morning. They sat for a while in the car park and then entered his bar and ordered hot drinks. 'The darker lady' (Gabriella) had made a local telephone call. Other people were in the bar at the time who could corroborate this. The second time he saw the women was at about 2pm. They had driven up again, this time in a light-coloured car driven by a man. Valori described him: 'He was tall, with chestnut hair; his face was a little podgy; he was 35ish, a distinguished-looking person. He wore a light-coloured wool suit, no overcoat, and he was smoking.' The three people spent about half an hour walking around in the hotel car park, Jeannette and the man talking together.

Stephen May now took matters into his own hands. He hired two private investigators, both former Scotland Yard detectives. They made two trips to Sarnarno and in July reported on what they had found. They had come across human hair in the bathroom of the shepherds' cottage, both in the washbasin and in the bath. Scientific examination of the hair in London revealed that some was definitely from Gabriella's head. It was not possible to identify the rest positively.

The detectives also found hair on two pieces of cloth in the bathroom, which matched that found in the bath and the washbasin. The obvious explanation was that the women had gone to the bathroom and had tried to dry their hair on the two pieces of cloth, and this was what the Italian police concluded. The detectives saw nothing sinister in their finds, and decided the women had died accidentally and the bodies would eventually be found. A search begun in August at Stephen May's urging, still found nothing.

Above: Domenico Panunti, who discovered the remains of the women's bodies on 27 January 1982, and claimed the reward offered by Stephen May

Ortelio Valori, who claimed to have told police that he had seen the women in his hotel car park. Why was such crucial evidence apparently disregarded?

Two bodies

May now waited five months, hoping against all the evidence that something would turn up. By January 1982, as a last resort, he announced two linked rewards. The larger, worth about £112,000, would be paid if both women were recovered alive. For information 'leading to a solution of the mystery', he would pay £45,000. Twelve days later, on 27 January 1982, Domenico Panunti, a boar hunter, found the remains of two bodies in a forest only 5 miles (8 kilometres) from where the car had been abandoned. Papers found nearby and dental evidence identified the bodies as those of Jeannette May and Gabriella Guerin.

The bodies were lying on the edge of a steeply sloping wood. That of Jeannette was found between two small trees; Gabriella's was in the open about 6 feet (2 metres) below her. Jeannette's remains were fully clothed. Her handbag was to her right and contained a document case, a purse with £400 in travellers' cheques and about £90 in lire. On the ground beside the handbag was a make-up bag and her sunglasses. Her car keys were in the pocket of her windcheater.

Gabriella's body had been unprotected by trees and her outer clothes were in ruins. Her handbag stood near her body and contained the gold earrings that she normally wore, two necklaces and, surprisingly, a metal fork, which was later identified as having come from the shepherds' cottage. The high heels of her boots were caked with mud but were otherwise undamaged. Oddly, both women's watches had stopped at different dates but both at exactly the same time – eight minutes to six.

Fresh snowstorm

According to the Italian police, the pathologist found no evidence of foul play, and all the indications were that the women had died naturally. They issued a revised reconstruction of events, taking into account the new evidence that had come to light. While in the shepherds' cottage, the women had dried their hair on the two pieces of cloth, then combed it out over the basin and the bath. Before they left, they had put out the fire with snow, and evidently had then placed the snow and ashes in the bathroom washbasin.

After leaving the cottage, they had come upon a signpost that indicated that the town of Acquacanina was only 5 miles (8 kilometres) away, and set off hoping to reach it. On their way, they had seen the lights of Podalla, a tiny mountain village, and had headed directly for it down a winding road. A fresh snowstorm had forced them off the road. They had stumbled over rocks and through ravines until, exhausted, they had stopped to rest and had died on the spot where their bodies were found.

This accidental death theory, convenient though it is, is riddled with contradictions. The couple were supposed to have gone up the mountain that night on a pleasure trip, yet Gabriella was known to have an obsessive fear of mountains, driving and the dark – a fear that was intensified by the circumstances of her husband's death. It is difficult to believe that she would have gone up the mountain that night for pleasure. The women were supposed to have left their car after being trapped in the snowstorm. But the examination of the car conducted by the police themselves showed that it had been parked *before* the snowstorm began. They broke into the cottage, say the police, and spent, perhaps, two days there. But in two days two women could hardly have burnt such an immense amount of wood. They dried their hair on the two pieces of cloth. But would two fastidious women have used filthy pieces of cloth for this purpose when they could have dried their hair before the fire?

The women were believed to have put out the fire with snow and then carried the snow and ashes to the basin in the bathroom. But it is difficult to put out a fire with snow and then carry away the snow and ashes. And why carry the mess to the basin, rather than throw it outside?

The women had struck out for Acquacanina, the police theory went. But they could not even have seen the signpost without walking about 200 yards (180 metres) on from the cottage through snow more than 6 feet (2 metres) deep. And why would they walk in that direction anyway? To do so they would be going *away* from Sassotetto, less than 2 miles (3.5 kilometres) back along a road they already knew. Then, said the police, the women had seen the lights of Podalla and had headed for them. But the electricity in Podalla had failed after the snowstorm on the previous night. They could not have seen lights, because there weren't any.

A new snowstorm had disoriented them, and they had wandered off the road and down the mountainside, according to the police. But all the local people insist that anyone who tried to get down the mountainside in deep snow would at best have been injured and would have been more likely to be killed by falling into a ravine.

There are other flaws in the police theory, more in the form of unanswered questions than actual

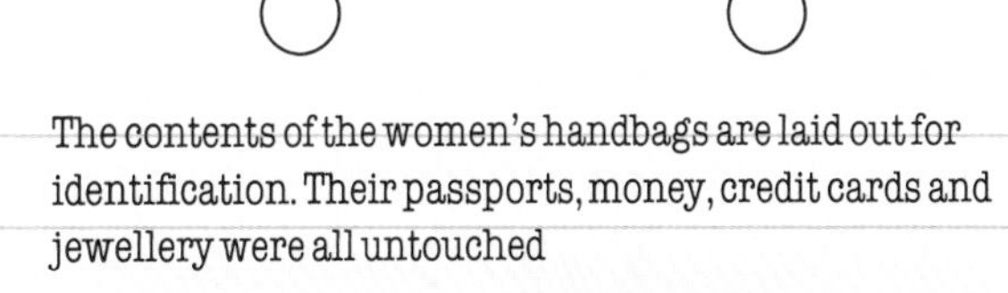

The contents of the women's handbags are laid out for identification. Their passports, money, credit cards and jewellery were all untouched

errors. If Gabriella Guerin had scrambled over deep snow, rocks and undergrowth to get to this spot, would it be likely that her high heels were not only undamaged but not even scratched? Why had she taken off the earrings that she habitually wore? Why was she carrying in her handbag a fork taken from the shepherds' cottage? And perhaps the oddest point of all, how could the women's watches, which stopped on quite different dates, have stopped at precisely the same *time*?

What does all this add up to? If the women did not die by accident, then the only answer seems to be that they were murdered. But why?

The British journalists are convinced that the women died as a result of an organised kidnap attempt that inexplicably went wrong.

Jeannette's business was in design and antiques: might she have arranged to buy or sell some valuable item of art during the course of her last, fateful, Italian trip?

News of her transactions in the art world could easily have reached the kidnappers. They could have made contact with Jeannette through an intermediary, who was to set up a sale or a purchase, and asked her to get in touch when she arrived in Italy.

The police have the women breakfasting at 10am on the Saturday, meeting Venanzi in the town square at 10.30, having drinks in his house at noon, and leaving in their car from the town square to take the mountain road at about 12.30pm. But the British journalists disputed this version. According to Venanzi and the Ai Pini owner, the women could have got the message and breakfasted by 9.00.

Left: the hillside above a ravine where the bodies of Jeannette May and Gabriella Guerin were found. The women's watches (above left) were found in their handbags; no one has been able to explain why they were not wearing them as usual. Both watches stopped at the same time, but on different days

'Sight-seeing'

The fact that the women left the town square in their car at 12.35 raises an interesting question. The previous night, Jeannette had put her car in the Ai Pini car park. So why should it have been in the town square at around 12.30, unless the two women had already used it that morning? If the police timetable is out by only an hour, the mysterious meetings the women had that morning can be accommodated. What follows here is the British team's reconstruction of the timetable. It departs significantly from the police version.

The two women had breakfast early enough to be at the deserted car park of the Sibilla Hotel at Sassotetto at 10am – a drive of about 25 minutes. They sat for about 10 minutes in the car park waiting for the intermediary to turn up. He failed to arrive, so they went into the Sibilla bar and Gabriella made a local telephone call, presumably to arrange a new meeting. All this is confirmed by the evidence of the owner of the Sibilla, Ortelio Valori. The women then returned to Sarnarno, where they met Venanzi at about 11am. (Venanzi's message had been that they should meet at any time 'from 10.30 onwards', not at 10.30 exactly.)

The women set off again from Sarnarno for their 'sight-seeing trip' at 12.35. At 1pm Primo Galiardi, the owner of a mountain restaurant about 4 miles (6 kilometres) beyond Sassotetto, saw a black Peugeot with a Siena licence plate, followed by a light-brown Autobianchi, also with a Siena plate, go past on the road to Ussita, which he knew was blocked by snow. He soon saw the two cars return and head back towards Sassotetto, where the meeting with the intermediary now took place at the original rendezvous, the Sibilla car park, at about 2pm. The time and place for finalising the deal was presumably fixed – it was to be that evening at one of the shepherds' cottages.

Above: Primo Galiardi with his family. On the day the women disappeared, he saw their car in convoy with another, which he believed belonged to a friend who was in jail – for kidnapping

The women drove up the mountain that night, Gabriella's fear probably outweighed by her unwillingness to allow Jeannette to go alone. Their car was seen three times. At 7pm a young magistrate, who knew it well, saw it in the centre of Sarnarno. At 7.30, the caretaker of the Hermitage Hotel at Sassotetto, driving home down the mountain, was waved down by a woman from a car who told him to drive slowly because further down the road two cars had stopped to put on snow-chains. The woman's description exactly fitted that of Gabriella. Later he saw two cars and three men. Valori of the Sibilla later saw three cars, one just like the black Peugeot he had seen earlier in his car park.

Seized and blindfolded

Before this convoy reached the cottages, the two women saw that the road had been partly blocked by a snowdrift. They stopped, parked and transferred to one of the cars behind them, which had chains. The three men probably did not know at which of the scattered cottages they were expected. The brief fire and the tablecloth on one of the balconies was a signal for them. The two women entered the cottage, expecting to conclude a business deal, and were seized by the kidnappers. They were blindfolded with the rags on which their hair was later found, tied up and put in the bathroom. When they were given a meal, Gabriella managed to take and hide a fork for possible use as a weapon. From the cottage the women were probably taken, within hours, to a mountain farm in the area.

In the course of the next few days, either Jeannette May succeeded in convincing the kidnappers that she was no longer a member of the Rothschild family, or the gang learned this for themselves. It is probable that the fate of the two women was inevitable anyway: they could identify at least three of the gang, including the intermediary. The women were murdered and their bodies dumped in the place where they were found – probably some days or even weeks later, when the weather had improved and the mountain spot was more easily accessible. Their watches were synchronised, presumably in the hope of making their deaths look like an accident, such as a fall, in which both watches might have broken at the same moment. But if this is the case, the murderers would seem to have made a very stupid mistake: they altered the watches to give the same time, but did not ensure that they gave the same date.

It must be emphasised that all this is theory, but it is the only explanation so far advanced that fits all the facts. What certainly is not theory, however, is that the Marche – far from being a crime-free area as everyone in the region, including the police, claimed – turns out to be a centre of Sardinian kidnapping and a favourite holding area for victims. But there are enough inexplicable angles to the affair to make it impossible to close the file. As one Italian police captain put it: 'Time and again, some of the stranger coincidences in this case led us to believe that we were on the verge of finding an answer. But every single time we have ended up with nothing but a handful of flies.'

The death of God's banker

Gian Roberto Calvi, president of Italy's largest private bank, was found hanging from Blackfriars Bridge in London on the morning of 18 June 1982. Police treated Calvi's death as suicide, but his family claimed he had been murdered. Was 'God's banker' the victim of a bizarre ritual killing?

In the early morning of 18 June 1982 the body of a man in a dark suit was found hanging by the neck from scaffolding under Blackfriars Bridge, over the Thames in the City of London.

The dead man had obviously been soaked in water and his legs were drenched below the knees. He was wearing a smart, well-cut suit that had been made in Milan, Italy. In the left-hand jacket pocket was half of a large brick. There were large stones in the right-hand trouser pocket, and a quarter of another brick in the left-hand trouser pocket. Inside the trousers, covering the genitals, was another brick, more than half the size of a house brick. In another inside pocket was an Italian passport registered in the name of Gian Roberto Calvini.

Suicide in the river Thames is common, and although there were some odd features about this body the police treated it as a routine case. Most people who commit suicide in the Thames do so by drowning. But Professor Keith Simpson, who began the autopsy at 2pm that afternoon, had known of people hanging themselves above the water, and had also encountered cases in which suicides had even hanged themselves after preparing to drown by stuffing their pockets with bricks and stones.

Professor Simpson's initial suspicions that the death was a suicide were confirmed as he continued the examination; he could find no marks on the body to suggest any struggle or rough handling, nor any signs of an injection. The man had obviously died from strangulation. Professor Simpson put the time of death at between 2am and 6am.

At this stage the man's real identity was unknown, but it soon became obvious that the Italian Embassy, which had been informed that an Italian citizen had been found dead, was treating the news more seriously than might have been expected. Before long, it became known that the dead man's passport was false.

He was Roberto Calvi, President of the Banco Ambrosiano of Milan, the biggest private bank in Italy. Until only a few days before, Calvi had been one of the most powerful men in Europe. But then the bank had collapsed.

On 23 July, less than five weeks after Calvi's death, the coroner for the City of London, Dr David Paul, presided over what was to be a controversial inquest. The hearing started at 10am and lasted until 10pm. Although the jury were told where Calvi stayed in the few days before his death, they did not hear evidence from a single witness who had seen or spoken to Calvi in that time, nor did they hear evidence from a single member of the Calvi family.

There were other omissions in the inquest. For instance, two watches found on the body had not been submitted for scientific tests, while evidence about the depth of the water around the scaffolding was hopelessly imprecise. After being warned against an open verdict by the coroner in a brief summary, the jury retired. They returned at 10pm and the foreman announced that Calvi had committed suicide.

The verdict was greeted with much sarcasm by the Italian media, but it was the Calvi family that was most outraged by the verdict. The banker's wife Clara Calvi, her son Carlo, and her student daughter Anna were all convinced that Roberto Calvi had been murdered. They felt they had important evidence concerning the death that had not been heard at the inquest.

In an attempt to get the verdict overturned, Sir David Napley – who had represented the Calvi family at the inquest – briefed one of Britain's top barristers, Mr George Carman QC. Nine months after the inquest, Carman rose in the High Court to ask Lord Chief Justice Lane, sitting with two other senior judges, to set aside the suicide verdict and order another inquest. On 24 March 1983 this was duly done.

Second inquest

A second inquest was arranged for 13 June 1983, under a new coroner, Dr Gordon Davies. This inquest was very different from the one-day inquest of the previous year. It lasted eleven days, but the chief difference was in the more detailed and precise evidence given to the jury. There was also more representation at this inquest. Mr George Carman QC appeared for the Calvi family, while Richard Du Cann QC represented Flavio Carboni, who had been with Calvi in the days before his death.

Professor Simpson maintained that Calvi died between 2am and 6am. Mr Roy Selzer, a police forensic scientist, examined the two watches taken from the body. He said that the self-winding watch Calvi had been wearing on his wrist, which was extremely rusty and had been severely damaged by water, had stopped at 1.52.5. A watch in the jacket pocket had also been affected by water. This watch, although waterproof, had a conventional winding and had wound down at 5.49.

The time it had stopped and other evidence indicated conclusively that Calvi had died shortly before 2am that Friday. At that time, the water was about level with what would have been the position of Calvi's shoulders as he hung from the scaffolding. This information was provided by Mr Laurence Ekblom, a senior hydrographic surveyor. He had studied the Thames' tidal waters for more than thirty years and was able to tell the court the exact height of the river water (to within an error margin of a few inches) at any time on the fatal night.

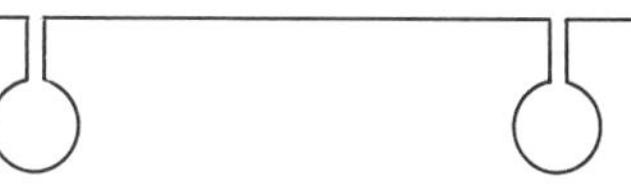

A police photograph of Roberto Calvi's corpse taken after he was found hanging at Blackfriars Bridge in the early hours of 18 June 1982. Calvi had fled to London from Milan only three days before, in a desperate attempt to escape the billion-dollar scandal surrounding his presidency of the largest private bank in Italy

Dr David Paul, coroner at the controversial first inquest in July 1982. Nine months later the High Court set aside the verdict of suicide and ordered a new inquest

From this evidence two startling points emerged. First, if Calvi had hanged himself, his fall would have been broken by the water long before the noose tightened on his neck. Second, Calvi's attempts to climb the scaffolding to get into a position from which he could hang himself would also have been impeded by the high water level. This new information about the water levels meant that at the most likely time of Calvi's death, the only way he could have approached the far side of the scaffolding would have been to step across from the ladder onto the upper poles themselves. This was a hazardous exercise even during daylight. The water-level evidence also dispelled the theory put forward in the first inquest to the effect that Calvi could have approached the scaffolding from the foreshore of the Thames. To do so he would have had to wade for some distance through waist-high water – and Calvi was a non-swimmer.

The second inquest heard of other difficulties Calvi would have faced in trying to commit suicide from the scaffolding. The stones and bricks in his pockets, which weighed about 12 pounds (5.5 kilograms), would have hindered what Carman called Calvi's 'bizarre manoeuvre' on the scaffolding.

The 62-year-old banker could hardly have walked 300 yards (275 metres) from the building site to the scaffolding with a brick in the flies of his trousers.

If the banker had not committed suicide, how had his body found its way under Blackfriars Bridge? If it was difficult for him voluntarily to climb down the ladder and over the scaffolding, it was surely more difficult for another man or group of men to carry him there, especially to do so without leaving any sign of struggle.

Mr Carman, the Calvi family's counsel, put forward one hypothesis. Could Calvi have been brought to the far side of the scaffolding by boat, been tied to it by his captors and left to hang? The Thames River police agreed that this was quite possible. They said it would not be a difficult task for an experienced boatman to carry out. Carman's hypothesis gained further support from the knowledge of the Thames water level at 2am on 18 June. The river was high enough to allow someone standing on the deck of a small boat to tie the rope to the second bar of the scaffold. Indeed, because of the timing of police patrols, it seemed likely that Calvi died at about 2am. The police boat left Blackfriars Bridge at 1am, and the next was not due until about 4am.

Boat theory

As the second inquest advanced, it became clear that the boat hypothesis seemed *more* probable than the suicide theory. So, if Calvi was taken to his death by boat, the next question was: how could he have submitted without a struggle? Extensive evidence was heard from toxicologists. They were asked about the possibility that drugs could have been used, either by injection or inhalation, to knock Calvi out for a time without leaving any trace. Mr Carman said that ethyl chloride and curare-type drugs could have been used without leaving any trace. All the medical witnesses agreed that a man can be rendered helpless by pressure on the neck that leaves no trace.

They also agreed that Roberto Calvi had at his disposal easier methods of taking his own life. In his flat police found a suitcase containing 28 types of

Mrs Clara Calvi, who missed the first inquest because she feared for her life, tells the world's press of her belief that her husband was murdered

Calvi's student daughter Anna, who was warned of the dangers to her life by her father in a telephone call hours before his death

drugs. Dr Roy Goulding, former director of the National Poisons Unit at Guys Hospital, said that had Calvi taken an overdose or a mixture of only a small number of these drugs he would have died quickly. Why, given this evidence, would he have chosen to walk 4½ miles (7 kilometres) across a strange city late at night, stuffed his pockets with bricks and clambered across a dark, slippery scaffolding to kill himself?

Next, the inquest began to reveal how Calvi had spent his last few days alive. The evidence, which was at times bizarre, was provided by the small group of people – two of whom were facing criminal charges abroad – who had been with Calvi in his final days. The chief of these, an Italian property millionaire called Flavio Carboni, could not give evidence because he was in prison in Switzerland awaiting extradition to Italy on serious fraud charges. However, he had given a statement to the Swiss police.

Since the Banco Ambrosiano scandal had emerged Carboni, whose businesses had prospered considerably from the bank's generosity, had become friendly with Calvi, the bank's president. On 7 June 1982, when a board meeting of the bank finally refused to support Calvi – in relation to a Bank of Italy inquiry about 1400 million dollars that had gone 'missing' – Carboni agreed to help Calvi escape from Italy. Two years previously Calvi had been convicted of exchange control offences, fined 16,000 million lire and given a 4-year prison sentence. He had been released on bail pending his appeal. His passport had been confiscated. Using Carboni's extensive underworld contacts, Calvi was provided with a new passport in the name of Gian Calvini. Also provided were two bodyguards, Emilio Pellicani, who accompanied Calvi by plane to Venice, and Sylvano Vittor, a small-time smuggler who, on 12 June, ferried Calvi on his boat from Trieste to a deserted quay in Yugoslavia, and from there took him to Klagenfurt in Austria. In Austria, the two men stayed at the home of Vittor's girlfriend, Manuela Kleinzig. (Manuela's sister Michaela was one of Flavio Carboni's many mistresses.)

On Monday 14 June, the group of five – Carboni, Vittor, Calvi and the Kleinzig sisters – met at Bregenz, on the Swiss-German border. They were joined by a business associate of Carboni – a 'fixer' called Hans Kunz. Kunz agreed to arrange for Calvi and Vittor to fly to London and to be accommodated in a flat there.

The group then broke up. On Tuesday 15 June, Calvi and Vittor flew by private plane from Innsbruck, Austria, to Gatwick Airport in Surrey, England. Carboni and the two girls went for a holiday in Amsterdam. Calvi passed through immigration at Gatwick without difficulty. He and Vittor then took a taxi to the London flat that had been arranged for them by Kunz. They went to Chelsea Cloisters, in Sloane Avenue, Chelsea, a block of small apartments.

Wanted man

Carboni and the Kleinzig sisters came to London on 16 June. They arrived at Heathrow in the afternoon and booked into the Hilton International Hotel in Park Lane. Calvi and Vittor came to meet them, but Calvi refused to go into the hotel for fear that he would be recognised. His sudden, illegal departure had been noticed and written about in papers throughout Europe. He was a wanted man.

Calvi spent the penultimate night of his life in Chelsea Cloisters, with Vittor in the next room. The following day, Vittor and the girls went first to a nearby restaurant, the Brasserie, and then to the Queen's Arms pub, while Calvi stayed in the flat telephoning. Although Vittor said that Calvi did not seem frightened, he agreed that the banker had insisted that Vittor ring him every 20 minutes while he was away from the flat, and that he knock three times when he wanted to come in. There was only one key to the flat, which was held continuously and tenaciously by Calvi.

At one stage, about 9pm according to the girls, Calvi himself came into the pub. It was the last time anyone admitted to seeing him alive. He seemed anxious and distraught, they said, and kept asking for Carboni. Still Carboni did not come. The sisters were fuming in the pub, and Vittor and Calvi were fuming in Chelsea Cloisters. Then at about 11pm

Property millionaire Flavio Carboni, who used his wide range of contacts in the underworld to organise Calvi's escape to London after the Banco Ambrosiano scandal

Carboni arrived in the foyer of Chelsea Cloisters and rang the flat on the house telephone. Vittor answered and Carboni told him he was in the foyer, and ordered him down. When Vittor passed this message to Calvi, he said, 'Calvi did not want to know and told me to tell Carboni to come up.'

But Carboni did not go up to the flat. Instead, Vittor went down, leaving Calvi alone. He met Carboni in the hall and the two men went off to see the girls. Carboni and the girls then took a taxi to the Sheraton Hotel, near Heathrow, where they spent the rest of the night.

Vittor, according to his evidence, turned back to Chelsea Cloisters and took the lift to the flat. He estimated it was about midnight and that he had been away for about three quarters of an hour. He knocked three times, but there was no reply. He knocked again and again, but there was still no answer. Thinking Calvi had gone out for something to eat, he went downstairs to get a duplicate key, which was eventually produced by a porter and a housekeeper. The housekeeper, who gave evidence, put the time of this rather later than did Vittor – at between 1am and 1.30am. If that time is right, there may be a crucial gap of an hour that Vittor has not explained. Vittor let himself in and found the flat in perfect order. He lay down to sleep and spent a fitful night. There were no telephone calls and he rang no one. Early next morning, when there had still been no word, Vittor panicked. Without leaving even a note for the porters, he left Chelsea Cloisters. He took a taxi to Heathrow and boarded the first flight bound for Vienna.

Meanwhile, as Roberto Calvi's body was being removed from the scaffolding, Carboni and the Kleinzig sisters were still in the Sheraton Hotel, Heathrow. The two women immediately flew home to Austria. Carboni's story was that he rang Chelsea Cloisters and was rather surprised to get no reply. He went to the Heston house of an English girl he knew, Odette Morris, and asked her to interpret for him for the day. They went to the Chelsea Hotel and Carboni made a lot of telephone calls.

Two notes

Carboni then asked Odette Morris to write a note to Sylvano Vittor and deliver it to him at Chelsea Cloisters. Miss Morris obligingly walked over to the block of flats and wrote two notes at the reception. One was left there, the other slipped under the door of Room 881, where Vittor and Calvi had been staying. The notes, with one or two minor discrepancies, read as follows:

> Dear Sylvano Vittor, I have telephoned many times but I have not heard from you or seen you. Tell me how I can find you and please telephone Aldi and Vitto immediately.

The notes were signed 'Odina'. There was no address or telephone number on he notes, and Odina was not Odette Morris' name. She could not explain to the inquest why she had written notes to someone she did not know or why she signed a name that was not her own. She simply said that Carboni had asked her to do so. 'It was obvious,' she said, 'that he did not want to go up there.'

Later that afternoon, Carboni returned to the Morrises' house, where he telephoned Laura Scanu-Concas, the 30-year-old niece of his hostess, who lives in Italy. Miss Scanu-Concas told him that Calvi's death had just been announced on television. Carboni said in his statement that he felt terrified. He spent a sleepless night at the Morrises' house and, accompanied by Odette, left early the next morning for Gatwick, where they boarded a plane for Edinburgh. After another night at another hotel

Two of the last people to have seen Calvi alive – Sylvano Vittor, a small-time smuggler from Trieste, and his Austrian girlfriend Manuela Kleinzig

Roberto Calvi – a family snapshot. According to the suicide theory, Calvi had been a desperate man when he fled Italy; removed from his office and position of power, he became depressed enough to kill himself

(the George in Edinburgh), Hans Kunz arrived on a private plane to take Carboni back to Switzerland. By the time Odette Morris woke up in her hotel room, Carboni had gone.

A strange meeting of the group of four, who were with Calvi in his final hours, was to follow in Switzerland. Their story, although credible, was to have some disturbing contradictions. The suicide theory that dominated the first inquest would, after the evidence of Calvi's wife and children, be replaced by a murder theory. But more than that, it was to expose an international scandal involving top politicians, the Vatican hierarchy, the Mafia and P-2 – an exclusive, secret Freemasonary sect also known as the 'black friars'.

When Roberto Calvi's last companions – millionaire Flavio Carboni, Sylvano Vittor and the two Kleinzig sisters – met in Switzerland after the banker's death, it is not improbable that they discussed in detail the events of his last day alive.

If so, their evidence was nevertheless not always consistent. For example, Carboni said that Calvi had shaved off his moustache when he met him on 16 June. Yet Vittor, who had shared the same tiny flat with Calvi, insisted that the moustache was shaved off on Calvi's last morning (17 June). Manuela Kleinzig was not sure when the moustache was shaved off, while her sister was not asked about it. These details may seem trivial, but they may be significant. When Mrs Clara Calvi heard that her husband's body had been found without a moustache, she was immediately suspicious. She and her advisors discovered that, if Calvi had been drugged with an anaesthetic held to his nose and mouth, the drug might have clung to a moustache and been traceable some hours later. The moustache might, therefore, have been shaved off by Calvi's killers.

The second, more important contradiction concerned Calvi's briefcase. The pilot of the plane that brought Calvi and Vittor to London thought that Calvi might have been carrying a briefcase. He never went anywhere without a combination-lock briefcase, and it seems inconceivable that he should not have carried one on his carefully planned flight. Even Vittor had said: 'He might have had something with some papers in it, but I'm not sure.' The Kleinzig sisters and Carboni were a little more certain that Calvi had not had a briefcase.

Certainly, if he was carrying a briefcase, it would weaken the suicide theory. No briefcase was found, either in the flat or in the Thames, and if the brief-case did vanish from the flat, and vital papers were taken, the only people who could have taken it were Vittor or others who may have been able to gain access to the apartment.

According to a statement by Sylvano Vittor, the final blow to Calvi's morale came on his last day alive, when the banker's secretary in Milan, Graziella Corrocher, apparently committed suicide by jumping out of a seventh-floor window of her office. On the same day, the Ambrosiano board formally suspended the missing Calvi as president of the bank and removed from him the considerable powers he had enjoyed.

But it was clear that Calvi's plight was not as black as Vittor had painted it. For instance, Calvi's currency crimes were not as serious as they appeared. Other directors of the same bank, charged with the same offences, had had their fines reduced and their prison sentences set aside on appeal. And when Calvi fled Italy he would have known that his action would result in loss of office. Kidnapping is commonplace in Italy, and Banco Ambrosiano, like all other major institutions, had special provisions for removing top executives from their responsibilities as soon as they went missing. Above all, as even Carboni's statement made clear, Calvi's flight was not sudden but carefully planned.

The picture of Calvi in his last days as a man with a definite mission was portrayed in stronger terms by Mrs Calvi and by her son. On 16 June, for instance, Mrs Calvi said that Calvi had telephoned her (as he did continually) at her flat in Washington. She said he told her: 'It is blowing up crazy, wonderful things for us which will change all our lives.' She said that her husband had hoped to make a bargain with Opus Dei, an organisation of right-wing Catholics that has 70,000 very rich supporters across Europe and South America. The Vatican, she suggested, had reneged on guarantees it had made for the money – about 1400 million dollars – which had 'gone missing', and that was the main cause of Banco Ambrosiano's problems. Calvi hoped to get the money from Opus Dei, and thus cause irrevocable damage to the ruling group in the Vatican.

In rapid, staccato language, Carlo Calvi, the 29-year-old son of the dead banker, told the jury of the intrigues of this complicated international financial scandal. Banco Ambrosiano, over a seven-year period, had made loans of about 1400 million dollars to Panamanian and other South American companies. The money had since disappeared. Carlo Calvi disclosed that the Panamanian company was owned by a Luxembourg holding company whose chief beneficiary was the Vatican bank, the IOR.

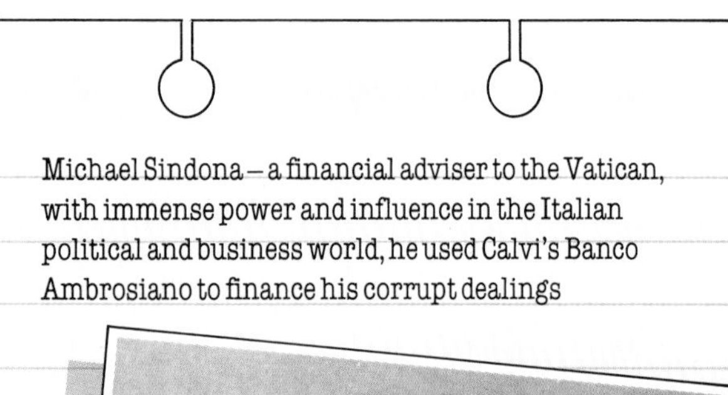

Michael Sindona – a financial adviser to the Vatican, with immense power and influence in the Italian political and business world, he used Calvi's Banco Ambrosiano to finance his corrupt dealings

Michele Sindona

One of the key advisors to the IOR was a Sicilian tax lawyer named Michele Sindona, who had had ties with both the American secret service and the Mafia.

In January 1979, Sindona had been sentenced to twenty years in prison.

Sindona had been a regular guest at the Tuscan villa of wealthy playboy and financier Licio Gelli. The police went to Gelli's house in Arezzo and found nothing. They then went to his office in a nearby town called Castiglion Fibocchi and found in a wall safe a set of documents that revealed a corrupt and exclusive sect called Propaganda 2, or P-2. This was a masonic lodge, strong on ritual but mainly devoted to twisting and corrupting Italian public life to the private advantage of its 962 members. They included three cabinet ministers, the heads of military and civilian intelligence, two former national chiefs of police, fifty generals and admirals, forty MPs and four judges.

It was Banco Ambrosiano that financed P-2's corrupt banking deals throughout the world. Its president, Roberto Calvi, was a high-ranking member of P-2. Among P-2 papers found in Gelli's safe was a special file of leaked documents from the highest political, administrative and judicial levels relating to the Bank of Italy inquiry into Banco Ambrosiano.

Banco Ambrosiano had inherited from Sindona a close relationship with the IOR. Together, the two banks had set up subsidiaries in countries – such as

Licio Gelli (born 1919), grandmaster of P-2, the secret Freemason's lodge of which Roberto Calvi was a member, had been a fascist enthusiast in Tuscany during the Mussolini years in Italy, but when Mussolini was killed in 1945 he became an anti-fascist. He had gained a reputation for torturing communist partisans in the region, but after the war he systematically betrayed his former fellow torturers to the authorities. He was rewarded with some fat business contracts and set up residence in the Excelsior Hotel in Rome's exclusive Via Veneto.

Gelli quickly discovered the importance of secret power, influence and money. These were the three main concerns of the masonic lodge Propaganda-2, or P-2, whose fortunes he revived during the Seventies. Gelli also travelled widely, using diplomatic credentials from the Rome government (which included several P-2 members) or from the Vatican. He gained considerable influence in Argentina, Malta and the United States.

After the sinister P-2 was uncovered and outlawed in 1981, Gelli was forced to leave Italy, where he was wanted by the police. But this did not halt his activities. During the Falklands War, for instance, he got into France illegally and tried to buy Exocet missiles on the black market for Argentina.

A few weeks after the second inquest into Roberto Calvi's death, Gelli was arrested in Switzerland as he tried to withdraw 55 million dollars from a Swiss bank. He was held in Switzerland's most secure prison on charges of fraud. But within weeks he disappeared – rescued or kidnapped. His whereabouts are not known, although he is said to have tried to get into Switzerland again in November 1983. The plane that took him there exploded on take-off the following day, but Licio Gelli was not on board.

Panama, Peru and Nicaragua – that were known for their lack of strictness in dealings with foreign banks. In June 1981, this Vatican link was formally (though privately) declared. In letters to two Ambrosiano subsidiaries, in Peru and Nicaragua, the IOR declared that it controlled the subsidiary companies, chiefly in Panama. These subsidiaries were receiving huge unsecured loans. Eventually, investigating officials realised that 1400 million dollars that had been lent to those so-called subsidiaries in Panama had vanished. Where the money went is still not known.

The final collapse faced Calvi in the spring of 1982. His failure to find financial support to cover the 'missing' 1400 million dollars placed him in deeper and deeper trouble. On Monday 7 June, the board of Banco Ambrosiano read a letter from the Bank of Italy stating the facts about the debts and asking for an explanation. There was no tolerable or credible explanation, and Calvi knew it.

In the days before his death, Calvi had not only an air of determination, but also of revenge. As Anna Calvi said at the inquest: 'He . . . told me the reason why he wanted to be out of Italy was that if anything was going wrong he was going to name names of the people who were responsible.'

This promise of retribution adds credence to the theory that Calvi was the victim of a ritual killing.

The manner of his death involved curious links with Masonic ritual: a noose around the neck is part of the initiation ceremony; rough bricks are a symbol of treacherous masons, and immersion 'by two tides' is the symbolic fate of any who break the rules. Furthermore, a black friar is the sign of the P-2, and Calvi was hanged under Blackfriars Bridge.

If Calvi was murdered by a gang who enticed him out of Chelsea Cloisters when Vittor and Carboni were out, who ordered the killing? The answer to that question is another question. Who received the 1400 million dollars that were suddenly 'lost' by the Panama companies who borrowed so much on so little security from Calvi's bank?

Then in 1986 there were two further twists to the mystery. Michele Sindona, serving his sentence in Volhera prison near Milan, was found dead in his cell on 22 March. The cause of death was cyanide poisoning, but whether he killed himself or was murdered remained an open question.

Two weeks later, the briefcase Calvi always carried with him, which vanished after his death, turned up – on an Italian television show. In it were 23 keys, mostly to safe deposit boxes. Did the boxes contain the missing money? Unfortunately, the keys were unlabelled and there were no other clues.

Death of a hero – birth of a legend

In May 1935, Thomas Edward Lawrence – 'Lawrence of Arabia' – was involved in a fatal motorcycle crash and the coroner's verdict was 'accidental death'. But the shock of the death, the surrounding security and the conflicting evidence gave rise to many rumours. Some thought Lawrence had committed suicide; others that he had been assassinated or that his death was staged

At 11.22am on Monday 13 May 1935, T. E. Lawrence, who found fame as 'Lawrence of Arabia', had a motorcycle accident. He was in a coma for six days and died the following Sunday, just after 8am. Within minutes of their learning of the accident, the government of the day took the most extraordinary security precautions. The War Office imposed a total ban on all information to the press, security guards ringed the hospital and special branch officers remained at his bedside until he died.

The evidence at the inquest was both inaccurate and conflicting. The only adult eyewitness stated that, from the sound of Lawrence's motorcycle, it was travelling between 50 and 60 miles per hour (80 and 100 kilometres per hour), when it was known to all concerned that the machine was recovered locked in second gear, which had a maximum at full revolutions of 38 miles per hour (61 kilometres per hour). The same witness attributed the accident to Lawrence swerving to avoid a large black car that appeared to crowd him off the road. Yet two young boys who were on their bicycles ahead of the accident denied having seen or heard a car of any sort.

The coroner advised the jury that the presence of a car was irrelevant. 'Lawrence,' he said, 'had either had an accident on his motorcycle or he had not.' Thus prompted, the jury recorded that 'Mr T. E. Lawrence had died from injuries received accidentally'. In a somewhat unseemly rush, the man who was the nation's hero was packed into his coffin and buried within two hours of the verdict.

The mysterious circumstances of the accident, the remarkable reactions of the authorities and the rushed funeral sparked off a spate of rumours that continue to this day. Many believed it was murder by either French, German or Arab agents.

It has also been suggested that Lawrence was killed because he had designs to become absolute ruler of England, a notion apparently encouraged by the author – and fascist – Henry Williamson, who advised Lawrence to 'seize power while' he was 'still a hero in the public eye'. One group of people believed that he was not killed at all, but that the secret service faked his death so as to allow him to undertake, incognito, important work in the Middle East during the approaching Second World War, and that he died of old age in Tangiers, Morocco, in 1968. Others suspect that Lawrence committed suicide because life no longer held any appeal for him. The most widely held belief of all is that he was victim of his love of speed and a personal death-wish, both of

The last picture of T.E. Lawrence, taken at his home at Clouds Hill. He is seated on the motorcycle, a Brough Superior, that he crashed, killing himself, on 13 May 1935. A witness to the accident stated that it had been caused by Lawrence swerving to avoid a large black car that was trying to push him off the road

which were expressed in a poem he wrote for a friend shortly before the accident:

In speed we hurl ourselves beyond the body.
Our bodies cannot scale the heavens, except in a fume of petrol.
Bones. Blood. Flesh. All pressed inward together.

It was a prophetic verse, almost matching the autopsy report, which reported a 9-inch (23-centimetre) gaping hole in the back of his head where his skull had been crushed.

Why, and how, did the accident happen?

Second son

Thomas Edward Lawrence was born at Tremadoc in Caernarvonshire, Wales, in the early hours of 16 August 1888. He was the second of four illegitimate sons sired by an Anglo-Irish country squire called Thomas Chapman. The young Lawrence was a loner. A former master described him as 'self-possessed, purposeful, inscrutable'. He took long, solitary cycle rides; he developed an interest in archaeology and military history, and spent holidays grubbing around Roman forts and battlegrounds. His contemporaries remember him as elusive, contrivedly enigmatic, yet generous with offers of reconciliation if his sarcasm cut too deep. In short, he acquired the classic defences of a shy, acutely intelligent and sensitive boy. At an age when most young men were discovering the sensual side of life, he deliberately withdrew himself from it. Any act of physical sex or of obtaining physical pleasure from food or drink disgusted him.

His peculiar talents had been recognised in Oxford, even before he went up to the university, by one of the most remarkable men of his time and one of the founders of the British intelligence service. This was D. G. Hogarth, who was then the Keeper of the Ashmolean Museum. He became Lawrence's mentor, father substitute and financial backer. Hogarth led a double life. Outwardly he was a respected archaeologist and orientalist, with an international reputation as a scholar. He was also the organiser of a private intelligence service that kept him remarkably close to successive foreign secretaries and prime ministers. Hogarth sought out 'dedicated men of special knowledge, in it for neither pay nor honour'. Outwardly, they would be academics or consuls, archaeologists or even businessmen, but secretly they would serve the British Empire by gathering and interpreting intelligence and manipulating people and events – Hogarth had a strong contempt for democracy. He was ever anxious to find such men to carry the torch, and it was to Lawrence that he handed it.

Lawrence's training as a new recruit to what Hogarth called 'the Great Game' was meticulous. He acquired a complete grounding in military history and was encouraged to develop supreme physical fitness. The final test of his endurance came in 1909. Ostensibly to prepare a thesis for his degree, Lawrence sailed for the Middle East. He arrived in Beirut and, 'living as an Arab', went on a 1000-mile (1600-kilometre) walk through Syria, which then included the countries known today as Israel, Jordan and the Lebanon.

On his return his thesis was accepted and he was awarded a first-class honours degree in history. However, the award he coveted most was Hogarth's acceptance of him as a fully fledged undercover agent. He was ready for his first mission, a 'dig', organised by Hogarth at Carchemish.

Hogarth's digs were usually something of a mystery. There were always excellent archaeological reasons for them, but they also often seemed to be in politically or militarily interesting areas. They were also often financed by such unlikely bodies as the War Office or Naval Intelligence.

It was a dangerous but thrilling time for Lawrence. He learned to speak numerous Arab dialects and managed to build up a network of agents and informers that not only produced the German plans for the Baghdad railway, but a series of accurate maps that were invaluable when war broke out.

At the outbreak of war Hogarth became head of the Arab Bureau intelligence agency, which Lawrence joined, being made a lieutenant and posted to Cairo.

Lawrence's wartime adventures were legion. On one occasion he was sent alone through the lines to try and ransom a British force besieged by the Turks. He had orders to bribe the Turkish general with up to £1,000,000. But the general refused – perhaps Lawrence's only major failure.

His organisation of the Arab Revolt, his guerrilla tactics, long overland forays into the desert by camel to blow up trains on the railways he had so patiently mapped, all paid a handsome dividend on Hogarth's investment. Although the Germans, Turks and Russians all put a price on his head, Lawrence was not really a military leader. He was a political strategist and adviser, specifically detailed to mislead the Arabs into believing that if they helped the British throw out the Turks and Germans, then they could have their own independent country. From the outset, Lawrence knew that this was not to be.

In reality the British plan was to divide the oil-rich territory into a series of protectorates, supervised by the victorious allied powers. The result was that Lawrence had bitter enemies amongst the French, Italian and German security services, and was blamed by many Arab nationalists for his part in double-crossing them.

The war and its aftermath took a heavy toll on Lawrence. In 1914 he had been described as a pocket Hercules, as muscularly strong as men twice his size. He came out of the war in a state of physical and mental exhaustion. He weighed under 6 stone (38 kilograms), and had had several traumatic personal experiences. He survived by immersing himself in the intrigues of the post-war peace conference and in two missions to the Middle East for Winston Churchill. Finally, he kept his disintegration at bay by setting down his experiences in print. His book *Seven Pillars of Wisdom,* which has become a classic, was eventually published in 1927, but by then Lawrence had organised a calculated obscurity.

On 28 August 1922 a physically and emotionally shattered Lawrence enlisted into the Royal Air Force (RAF), using the alias of John Hume Ross. The charade, for charade it was, angered many RAF officers, one of whom leaked the secret to the *Daily Express*. By the end of January 1923, however, Lawrence had been discharged and was on the run from Fleet Street. However, the Air Ministry and the War Office chose to ignore all rumours about Lawrence, and within six weeks he was allowed to repeat his performance. On 12 March 1923 he joined the Tank Corps at Bovington Camp, Dorset, as Private T. E. Shaw.

He spent two miserable years as a clerk in the camp stores, and then, after he had threatened that he would commit suicide if he could not get back into the RAF, he was allowed to transfer. He was posted to the cadet college at Cranwell, where he appeared to settle down to reasonable obscurity.

Lawrence's motive for this self-imposed misery from having betrayed the Arab cause during the war. This is only partially true. The real cause is more likely to have been his immensely repressed sexuality. His family background and his puritanical routine, largely self-imposed, had relegated his sexual desires to something wholly subservient, under rigorous control. Then, during his time on Hogarth's 'dig' at Carchemish, he fell in love with the donkey boy Dahoum. It was little more than an adolescent homosexual infatuation. His first championing of the Arab cause was not for love of the Arabs themselves, but for Dahoum alone. During the war Dahoum acted as an agent or courier for him, and died in Lawrence's arms of typhoid in September 1918.

Eventually Lawrence found the solitude and perhaps the solace he desired in the RAF, but not before his past record as a secret agent brought him into the headlines once more. He had been posted to an RAF station in northern India so that he would not be available at the time his masterpiece *Seven Pillars of Wisdom* was published. The station was Miranshah, a few miles from the Afghan border, and there was unrest among the neighbouring tribes. Predictably, Lawrence was implicated.

Civil war had broken out in Afghanistan, and newspaper stories linked Lawrence to it. The French, Russian and Turkish governments lost no time in encouraging and capitalising on this, and an embarrassed British cabinet shipped Lawrence home on the next boat. He was discreetly posted to

Left: Lawrence at Akaba. He captured this important Red Sea port from the Turks in July 1917 in collaboration with Auda, a renowned fighting sheikh Below: the triumphal entry into Akaba on 7 July 1917 Below right: Lawrence drives a Talbot car in the desert

RAF Cattewater, where he joined an experimental seaplane unit, with whom he was to spend the last five years of his time in the RAF. This was probably the happiest time of his life.

It was a tired but more fulfilled man who retired from the RAF on 16 February 1935 and motorcycled his way to his retirement cottage of Clouds Hill. He did not find the transition easy. The depressions returned and, sensing his loss of purpose, his friends began all sorts of manoeuvres to get him to occupy his mind and his talents. Mr Pat Knowles, his nearest Clouds Hill neighbour, believes – as a result of a conversation with Lawrence – that in March 1935, as the European political scene darkened, he was offered the job of reorganising home defence.

Retirement, therefore, was not as sweet and trouble-free as he had imagined, and the Lawrence of Arabia legend had returned to haunt him in the form of reporters who besieged Clouds Hill to see what the 'Kingmaker' would do next. Was he going to meet Hitler? Would he be prepared to become dictator of England? Lawrence refused to see them. Despite the constructive interest of influential friends, he seemed convinced that he was being 'laid aside before being worn out'.

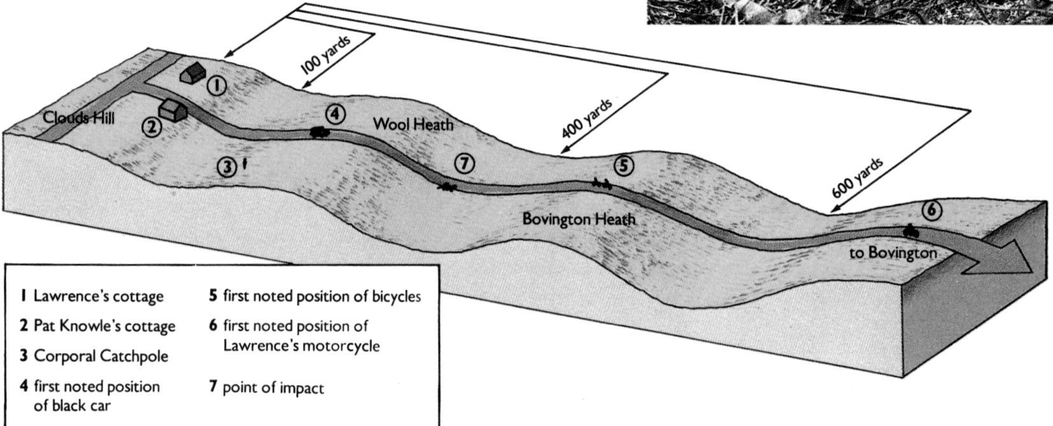

Above: a section of the road between Lawrence's home at Clouds Hill (top) and Bovington Camp, showing how the accident may have happened

The suddenness and manner of his death made it almost inevitable that a series of legends would grow up about it.

On the morning of the accident, Lawrence decided to go into Bovington to do some errands.

Clouds Hill is about 1½ miles (2.5 kilometres) from the few shops and the post office that serve Bovington Camp. The road between the cottage and the camp – much altered today – is straight and characterised by three dips at the Clouds Hill end. The dip furthest from Clouds Hill is the deepest, the second less deep and the third, just abreast of Lawrence's cottage, hardly perceptible. The first two, however, are both deep enough to hide approaching traffic from anyone who might be at the bottom of them.

The first dip is about 600 yards (550 metres) from Clouds Hill, the second 200 yards (180 metres) nearer and the third about 100 yards (90 metres) from a gate leading to the cottage itself. When Lawrence went to Bovington, he usually rode his Brough motorcycle. It was a noisy machine in first, second and third gears, but much quieter in top gear.

On the day of the accident Lawrence left for Bovington at about 10.30am. Knowles heard him start up the Brough and move off. Later, he heard Lawrence returning. He heard him change down the gears twice, then there was the usual silence that preceded his coasting into Clouds Hill. But he never arrived at the cottage.

At 11.10am Corporal Ernest Catchpole clocked out of the guardroom of Bovington Camp and began to walk his dog across the heath in the direction of Knowles' cottage.

At 11.13am two delivery boys on bicycles left the camp and also turned towards Clouds Hill. A few minutes later, shortly before 11.20am, Lawrence, having completed his errands, left Bovington for Clouds Hill. A few minutes after that, Catchpole heard the sound of a motorcyclist changing gear on approaching the first dip in the road. It was Lawrence, and as he entered the first dip, Catchpole saw, emerging from the third dip – the one near Clouds Hill – a black car travelling in the opposite direction. Catchpole also saw the two boys on the crest of the road between the first and second dips. Then he saw Lawrence enter the middle dip and for a moment Lawrence, the car and the two boys were all out of sight. Then the car emerged from the dip and went on towards Bovington. Almost simultaneously, Catchpole heard a crash, saw a riderless bicycle spinning along the road and discovered the motorcyclist lying on the ground, his face bloody.

Maximum security

At this moment an army lorry came along. Catchpole stopped it and told the driver to take Lawrence and one of the boys, who was injured but not seriously hurt, to Bovington Camp Hospital. Lawrence was unconscious when he arrived there and remained so until he died six days later.

As soon as his identity was discovered at the hospital, the War Office was told what had happened. Within an hour, the accident had become an affair of state. All ranks at Bovington were reminded that they were subject to the Official Secrets Act. Newspaper editors were told that all information about the accident and Lawrence's condition would be issued through the War Office. Even before the police had begun their investigations, an officer at the camp issued a statement saying that there had been no witnesses. Subsequently, the two delivery boys spent more time with the army authorities than with the police, and Corporal Catchpole was instructed by a superior officer that he was to make no statement to the press about the black car unless he had actually seen the collision, which he had not. To mention it otherwise would be misleading. A maximum security cordon was thrown round the hospital. The Home Office also took a hand in the arrangements and, until Lawrence's death six days later, one of two plain clothes men sat by his bedside, while the other slept on a cot outside his room. Newspaper reporters besieged the camp.

Lawrence's condition gradually grew worse and he died on Sunday 19 May, just after eight o'clock in the morning. On Tuesday 21 May an inquest was held at the hospital before the East Dorset coroner and a jury. It lasted two hours and was unsatisfactory in many ways. Corporal Catchpole, as the principal witness, estimated in his evidence that Lawrence had passed the black car safely. 'I heard a crash,' Catchpole said, 'and I saw a bicycle twisting and turning over and over along the road.'

The boys both said that they had heard the motorcycle behind them, so had moved into single file. They had ridden for about 100 yards (90 metres) when Lawrence crashed without warning into the boy riding in the rear. Both denied having seen or heard a car of any sort.

The coroner was unhappy about the black car and told the jury that this conflicting point in the evidence was rather unsatisfactory, but the existence of the black car would have to be regarded as an irrelevance. The jury's verdict was that Lawrence had died from injuries received accidentally.

It is not surprising that rumours of assassination and suicide should be fuelled by such mystery, but a careful reinvestigation of the occurrence suggests that it *was* an accident and that this is how it happened. It was quite possible that a black car was coming from the direction of Clouds Hill. Pat Knowles says a small black delivery van went past Clouds Hill at about this time every day, except Sundays. Seen from where Corporal Catchpole was standing, the black van could easily have been mistaken for a car. The two boys were mistaken about the time at which they changed from riding abreast to riding in single file. Lawrence would have been at least a quarter of a mile (0.4 kilometres) away from them when they claimed that they had heard him and moved one behind the other. This, added to the fact that the wind was carrying the sound away from the boys, suggests that they could not have heard Lawrence's machine behind them until just before the collision. At that moment he could not have been going faster than 38 miles per hour (61 kilometres per hour) because the Brough, which was badly damaged in the accident, was jammed in second gear, the top speed of which was 38 miles per hour, so the gear could not have been engaged if the machine had been going any faster.

It seems certain that Lawrence came upon the black van on the crown of the middle dip coming out of it as he was about to go into it. The road was narrow and they passed close to each other. Lawrence pulled nearer to the left-hand side of the road and, as he did so, came suddenly on the two boys directly in front of him. Knowles says: 'I heard his engine suddenly rev up and I thought he must have been stopping suddenly to speak to someone on the road.' Subsequent mystery about the death was due to the efforts of the authorities to avoid the hysterical publicity that any activity of Lawrence's inevitably attracted.

The wilder theories of how and why Lawrence died that have flourished during succeeding decades may seem more attractive and in keeping with the spirit of his Arabian career, but the facts do not bear them out. They point to a far more prosaic end for one of Britain's great heroes.

Who killed Janie Shepherd?

One Friday evening in February 1977 a young Australian woman, living and working in London, set off in her car to visit her boyfriend. She stopped to buy some groceries and then, apparently, vanished into thin air. Her car was found in a few days, covered in mud and scratches and cut on the inside with knife slashes. But it was not until eleven weeks later that her body was discovered, miles away in Hertfordshire. She had been brutally strangled, but how did it happen and who was responsible?

On the evening of Friday 4 February 1977, Janie Shepherd, a 24-year-old Australian living and working in London, left the luxury flat in St John's Wood where she lived with her cousin Camilla and Camilla's husband Alistair Sampson. She ran down the steps calling, 'I must dash, I'm frightfully late,' climbed into her dark blue Mini – and vanished.

Janie was heading for a quiet weekend with her boyfriend Roddy Kinkead-Weekes. It was 8.40pm, and Roddy was expecting her by 9pm. On the way to his flat – just 3½ miles (5.6 kilometres) away in Lennox Gardens, Knightsbridge – Janie was intending to call at a late-night supermarket to pick up groceries for their supper. When she had not arrived by 9.30pm, Roddy rang the Sampsons' flat to see if she had left on time or whether she was going to be late. Camilla and Alistair had gone to the cinema, but their maid informed him that Janie had left 50 minutes earlier.

When there was still no sign of Janie at 10pm, Roddy rang her home again, and then regularly at half-hour intervals. By the time the Sampsons returned home around midnight, all three felt real cause for alarm about Janie's whereabouts. Telephone calls to the main London hospitals produced no information and finally, at 3.15am on Saturday 5 February, Alistair Sampson officially reported Janie Shepherd missing at St John's Wood police station. Roddy Kinkead-Weekes went to Chelsea police station on the same mission.

Her description and the details of her car were circulated immediately, and the car was checked on the police computer to see if it had been stopped or seen anywhere. The police quickly established that Janie was not the sort of girl to drop into a pub or club on her own, and that if her car had broken down or if she had unexpectedly met friends she would have telephoned Roddy. A stable, happy girl, Janie would not have disappeared of her own volition. But she was the heiress to a considerable fortune (her stepfather was chairman of British Petroleum in Sydney) and the possibility that she had been kidnapped occurred immediately to her family and the police alike. Through a long, anxious weekend they waited for a ransom demand; it never came.

When she left the Sampsons' flat – at 103 Clifton Hill – at 8.40pm, she was wearing jeans tucked into Cossack boots, a man's check shirt over a thin, fawn polo-necked sweater, and a thick, white cardigan with a reindeer motif. Into her big red satchel bag she had put £40, some clean underwear, and a black sweater with a vivid red polo-neck and bright green cuffs. She also added a tapestry she was working on, along with some balls of coloured wool.

Detective Inspector Roger Lewis of St John's Wood CID was put in charge of investigating Janie's disappearance. By Monday he was already in serious doubt that she would ever be seen alive again. And the following day, Tuesday 8 February, there was a breakthrough in the case that seemed to confirm his worst fears. Janie's dark blue Mini was found in Elgin Crescent, Notting Hill. It was parked on a yellow line and there were two parking tickets on the windscreen, one dated Monday 7 February at 11.45am, the other Tuesday 8 February at 12 noon.

When Janie had left home on the Friday night, her car had been clean and shiny. A week earlier she had decided to sell it and had cleaned and polished it ready for potential buyers. She had placed an advertisement in the London *Evening Standard* for four consecutive days, and had put a large 'For Sale' notice in the rear window. But when it was found, the car was so covered in mud that several witnesses remembered seeing it as early as 1.10am on Saturday, barely five hours after Janie had disappeared. The 'For Sale' notice was still clearly displayed in the rear window.

Inside the car were Janie's Cossack boots and her red shoulder bag; the £40 in cash and her National Westminster cheque card were missing, as were her change of clothing, the tapestry and the balls of wool. In her red bag was a supermarket receipt and a receipt for £2.40 for petrol she had bought on Friday, an important clue for the police. This showed that she had topped up the 7½ gallon (34-litre) petrol tank with 3 gallons (13.6 litres) of four-star petrol at a self-service garage in Bayswater, and enabled the police to make a rough assessment of how far the car could have been driven. Given the amount of petrol left in the tank, it looked as though the Mini could have travelled about 75 miles (120 kilometres).

Chief Superintendent Henry Mooney of Scotland Yard's Murder Squad was called in to oversee the

Above: Janie with her boyfriend Roddy Kinkead-Weekes. On 4 February 1977, Janie set off to meet Roddy, but never arrived. Police found her dark blue Mini (below) four days later: it had two parking tickets on the windscreen and was covered with mud and scratches

investigation. One look at the interior of the car and he knew that 'something outlandish', as he put it, had happened. There were two parallel slash marks in the sun-roof and further forensic analysis revealed that a tremendous struggle had taken place inside the car. It had been driven deep into the country, since the mud splashed on the bodywork and embedded in the tyres showed traces of chalk and flint, also of oak and beech leaves. Further investigation of the tyres suggested that the car had actually been stuck in mud at some time, and fibres found in the tyres indicated that Janie's tapestry might have been propped under the wheels to give leverage. When analysis of the soil on the car showed it could have been driven to Oxfordshire, Hertfordshire, Wiltshire or Surrey, police from all those counties were alerted. The supermarket receipt was traced to Europa Foods in Queensway, where the till operator remembered Janie because 'she looked like a film star or model'. And a search in the vicinity of Queensway revealed the food that matched the receipt (smoked trout, yoghurt, tomatoes and chicory at a cost of £3.05) scattered around various back gardens.

Chief Superintendent Mooney also launched a direct appeal to the public. A full description of the clothes and jewellery Janie was last seen wearing was issued – her jewellery included a gold 'Woodstock' charm, a present from Roddy that she wore on a chain given to her by her mother; a Gucci digital watch on a grey leather wristband; a heavy gold bangle, and a traditional three-part gold Russian wedding ring.

Soil samples were examined by mineralogists from ICI, micro-palaeontologists from London University and other experts in an attempt to discover the exact spot where Janie might be found. Meanwhile, routine murder inquiries included interviews with all known sex offenders in the west London area. These inquiries resulted in many of what Detective Inspector Roger Lewis described as 'spin-off arrests': altogether, eighteen people were detained in connection with other offences as a result of the Janie Shepherd investigations.

Then, on Monday 18 April, there was another breakthrough. Two boys, schoolfriends and next-door neighbours, 11-year-old Dean James and 10-year-old Neil Gardner of Queen's Crescent, Marshalwick, St Albans, Hertfordshire, were out cycling during their Easter holidays on Nomansland Common when they spotted what they thought was a pile of rags half-hidden among gorse and hawthorn bushes. Curiosity soon gave way to fright, and the boys raced home. It was dusk by the time Dean James finally blurted out to his father, Peter James, that he thought he had seen a real body on the

Neil Gardner (left) and Dean James, who found a decomposed body while out on their bicycles. After their parents had informed the police, the boys went back with officers to the spot, where it was confirmed that the corpse was Janie Shepherd's

common. Peter James immediately contacted the police who came round to interview the boys.

Accompanied by their fathers, the boys led the police to the place; it was quickly established that they had indeed found a body. It was in a slight dip, a mere 25 yards (23 metres) from the B651 road from St Albans to Wheathampstead, in an area used extensively by motor-cyclists and model aircraft enthusiasts, known locally as Devil's Dyke. The Hertfordshire police were called in and the area cordoned off. An official call was put out to Professor James Cameron, a leading pathologist from the London Hospital, Whitechapel, and his colleague Bernard Sims, a forensic dentist. By now it was dark and raining quite heavily. After preliminary tests and the filming of the body on the spot, the corpse was removed to St Albans' mortuary.

The body was fully clothed in jeans, striped socks and a black sweater with a vivid red polo-neck and bright green cuffs. There were gold rings on two fingers of the right hand and on one finger of the left hand. Around the neck was a gold chain with a 'Woodstock' charm attached to it. Janie Shepherd's body had been found.

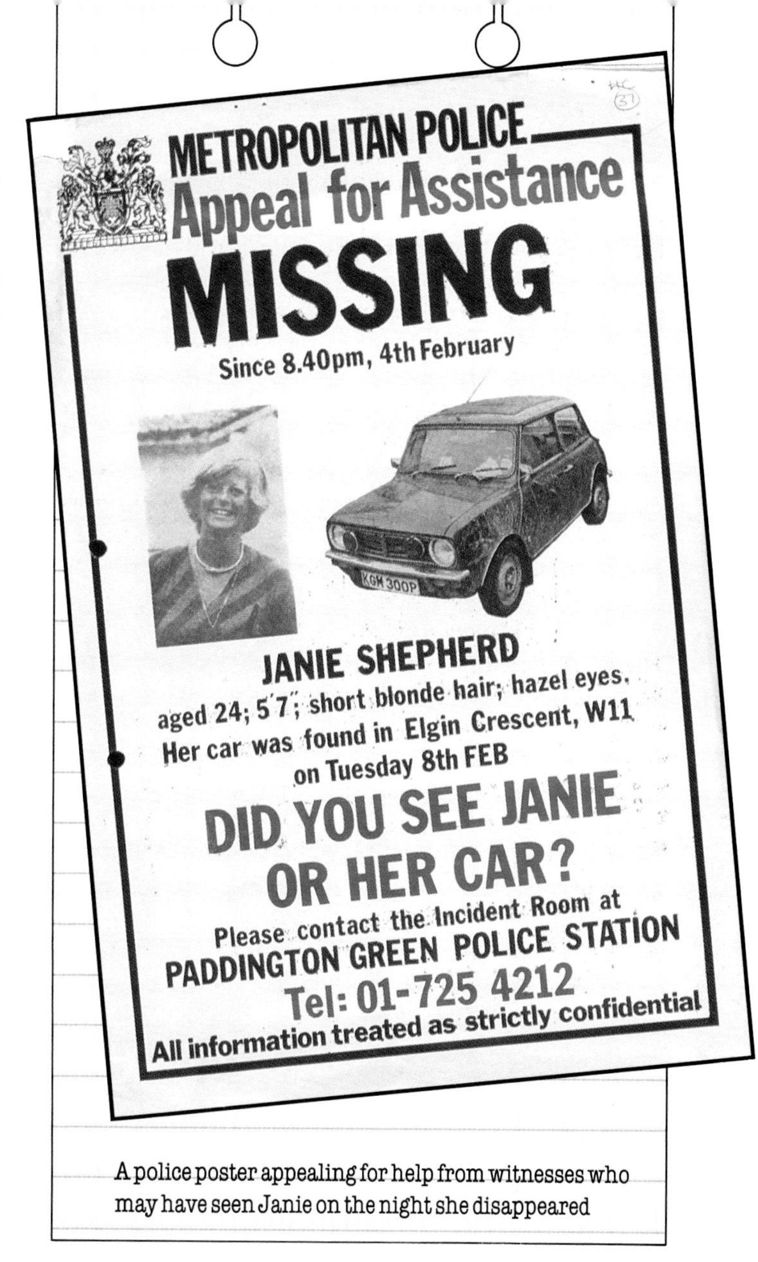

A police poster appealing for help from witnesses who may have seen Janie on the night she disappeared

Post mortem

It was 11.15pm by the time Professor Cameron and Bernard Sims began the post mortem examination, and it took four hours to complete. Cameron noted ligatures on the outside left ankle above the socks, indicating that the feet had been bound before death with the right leg placed in front. There were also ligatures on the upper arms, extensive bruising on the upper arms and chest and, possibly, fingernail marks on the breasts, along with additional bruising on the back of the left foot, the right shin, the right thigh and the left temple. There was no indication of fracture to the skull, but the lung and heart surface revealed elements of asphyxia. By 3.15am Sims had definitely identified Janie Shepherd's body by her dental charts, and Cameron had concluded that she died from compression of the neck. Death had apparently occurred about ten weeks previously.

Usually the finding of the body sheds some light on a mystery, but in Janie Shepherd's case it only confused the situation. When Janie had left the Sampsons' flat in Clifton Hill on 4 February she had been wearing a check shirt over a thin sweater, a thick white cardigan, jeans and boots. When her body was found it was clothed in the jeans, unzipped but buttoned at the waist, but in her other sweater, with the red neck and green cuffs, that she had been carrying in her bag. The pants Janie was wearing were the clean ones she had put in her bag. But her other clothes and her bra were missing. How, when and where had this change of clothes taken place, and where were the missing items?

The post mortem disclosed that Janie had been sitting upright before her death, but the degree of decomposition of the body made it impossible for the police to state whether or not she had been raped or indecently assaulted. The mystery deepened further when it was discovered that the soil in the area where the body was discovered did not match that on the tyres of the Mini. One explanation for this could be that Janie was abducted and attacked in her own car, but at some later time transferred to another car and driven to Hertfordshire, where her body was dumped. If that was the case, then where was the Mini driven to for it to become so splashed with mud? The police became convinced that if they could only find the place with soil that matched the soil on the car, then they might also find Janie's missing clothes and tapestry, and possibly other evidence as well. But no witnesses have ever come forward to say that they saw the Mini anywhere except when it was parked in Elgin Crescent.

Detective Chief Superintendent Ronald Harvey of the Hertfordshire CID took over the investigation on 18 April but was unable to find any trace of the missing clothes, or the tapestry, in the area around Nomansland Common. To this day, they have never turned up. Are they still half-buried somewhere in the countryside around London? Or did Janie's killer destroy them? The police – who had hoped and even hinted that the finding of the body would lead them to one man – were confounded.

The Mini had revealed frustratingly few clues – and none that led the police to any particular suspect. There were some traces of semen, but semen is a bio-destruct enzyme that disintegrates very quickly: after four days it is difficult to learn anything conclusive from it, not even whether it has come from one man or several different men. There were no fingerprints inside the car either from Janie or her attacker or attackers, since only certain types of surface attract and retain fingerprints. The forensic experts found no identifiable pubic hairs or clothes fibres.

The Hertfordshire police believed that the killer may have driven, or forced Janie to drive, out of London on the M1 from Hendon, left the motorway at junction six, then gone via the A405 to St Albans and turned on to the B651 to Wheathampstead. But this was not necessarily in the Mini – it could have been in another car, perhaps the killer's. Or Janie and her killer could have driven in convoy – but that would presuppose that she knew her attacker and went willingly with him, without telephoning Roddy to let him know, and there has never been any evidence to support such a theory. And it is also a distinct possibility that Janie was raped and killed far from St Albans – maybe even in London – and that her body was kept hidden for several days before the killer eventually felt safe enough to drive out to Hertfordshire and dump it. The police were still unable to estimate or examine the number of places where the killer may have stopped, and no witnesses have come forward to help.

The inquest on Janie Shepherd was opened on 22 April 1977 at the Coroner's Court, St Albans, where the coroner, Dr Arnold Mendoza, heard formal identification from Bernard Sims and Ronald Harvey that the body found on Nomansland Common was indeed that of Janie Shepherd. The inquest was then adjourned for further forensic tests.

The hunt for Janie Shepherd's murderer continued and on 24 October 1977 the inquest was reopened before a jury. Professor James Cameron told the jury that Janie Shepherd had died of compression of the neck, but he was unable to say whether it was manual or caused by a hard object. She had been bound hand and foot and extensive bruising suggested a desperate struggle or a beating.

Open file

Her cousin Camilla's husband, Alistair Sampson, gave evidence of her good health and high spirits when he saw her last, and confirmed her plans for the evening of 4 February. Roddy Kinkead-Weekes told the court how she had failed to arrive at his flat for supper. The jury then heard that despite taking 825 statements the police had still failed to identify her killer. An inch-by-inch examination of the area surrounding the spot where the body was found had failed to produce the garments Janie was last seen wearing, or the tapestry or wool she had with her. The jury returned a verdict of murder by a person or persons unknown. Later that day, Janie Shepherd's remains were cremated at Garston Crematorium near Watford.

By the end of the year, the police admitted they were still no nearer to finding the killer of Janie Shepherd. Detective Inspector Lewis said that he thought the Janie Shepherd inquiry would go on forever.

The file on Janie Shepherd remains open – and many questions about the events of the night on

A briefing for police officers searching for Janie's body near Beaconsfield along the A40 out of London

which she died remain unanswered. How did Janie meet her killer? She was last seen alive in the crowded Europa Foods supermarket in Queensway. Tall, blonde and beautiful, she would stand out in any crowd – and she was alone and concentrating on her shopping. Did her killer spot her in the supermarket and follow her, in the expectation that she lived nearby? Or did he act on impulse, using the 'For Sale' sign so prominently displayed in the rear window of her Mini as an excuse to strike up a conversation? Janie was anxious to sell the car in order to buy a new one: could she have accepted an on-the-spot offer and invited her killer in for a run around the block? Janie was an independent girl who had travelled the world alone – perhaps the very idea of danger from someone, even a stranger, in the middle of London simply never occurred to her.

For three consecutive Fridays after her appearance the police staged a repeat-action operation at the supermarket, on the principle that most people are creatures of habit and that many of the shoppers in the area on 4 February would be regular shoppers there. Some 6000 people were questioned but nothing of importance emerged.

Country lane

Perhaps, when the killer entered the car, murder was not on his mind; it is possible that he intended only to drive Janie to some darkened back street in order to rape or assault her. Then he may have noticed the full petrol-gauge and decided on a safer area, such as a little-used country lane. There is no evidence to show who drove the Mini that night, only enough to prove the killer possessed a knife.

But exactly where Janie was attacked and murdered remains a mystery. The spot with soil exactly matching the mud and debris found on the car and tyres has never been identified. The night of 4 February was rainy and many of the mud-splashes adhering to the bodywork of the car could have come from the banks or puddles of narrow country lanes. The problem is made more difficult because of modern farming methods. With scientific fertilising to balance the structure of the soil, it is almost impossible to pinpoint an area where the soil analysis might be crucially different between one side of a hedge and the other. The only thing that is known for certain is that the soil in the place where the body was found did not match the soil on the car.

Did the killer change Janie's top clothes – if so, was it before or after her death? Of the likelihood that rape took place inside the car the police are in little doubt, and it is probable that Janie's clothes were ripped during the struggle. Perhaps her attacker then persuaded Janie to change her clothes herself with the promise of letting her go in exchange for her guaranteeing not to go to the police.

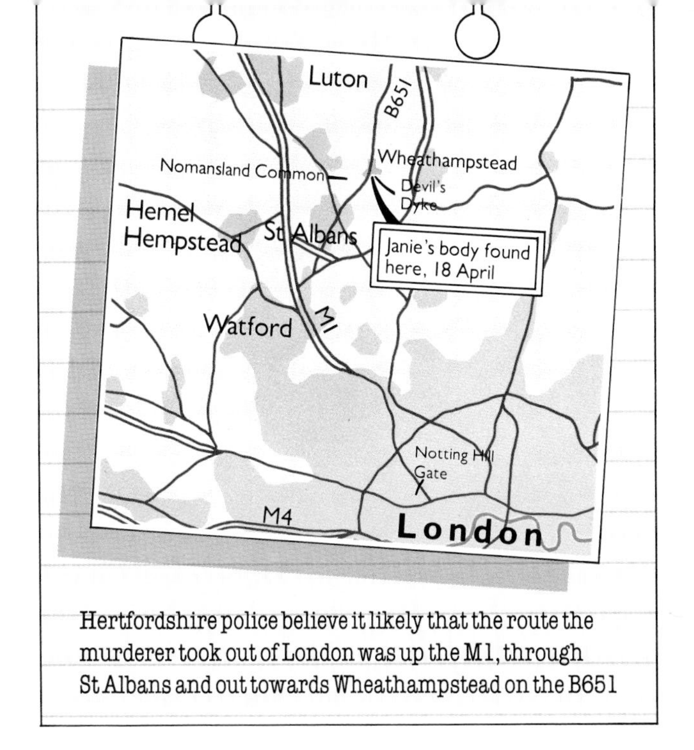

Hertfordshire police believe it likely that the route the murderer took out of London was up the M1, through St Albans and out towards Wheathampstead on the B651

The changing of Janie's pants could mean one of two things. If she had simply been raped, and not murdered by her rapist, he may have been knowledgeable enough about semen tests to demand that she change her pants – a woman reporting rape would be examined immediately by a police doctor for traces of semen because it is known to disintegrate quickly. It could be possible that she was then murdered by someone else. But equally, her killer may have changed her pants after death to suggest this very idea – that the man who had raped her had not killed her. He could not have been sure that the body would remain undetected for so long, and was obviously taking no chances.

That the killer was cunning is certainly in no doubt. Janie's gold jewellery was worth several hundred pounds, but the selling of it openly would eventually have been traced. Most of it was left on her body – but her £40 in cash was stolen. It is difficult to tell whether the killer knew the area where Janie's body was found for, although the spot he chose on Nomansland Common was in a slight dip and he covered the body with branches and leaves, it was an area frequently used by local people. That the body was not discovered for ten weeks, when it was only a few paces from a major road, can only be put down to chance.

It is perhaps useless to hope that any further information will come to the surface to throw light on the mysteries surrounding the disappearance and death of Janie Shepherd. Roddy Kinkead-Weekes, now married with a family of his own, summed up everyone's feelings when he said: 'You cannot forget the past but I believe the future is more important. Of course I sometimes think of Janie. It took me a long time to adjust to life. The months following Janie's murder were without doubt the worst in my life . . . Even now it is worrying that her killer has not been charged.'

Anastasia - the sole surviving Romanov?

The entire Romanov family – Tsar Nicholas II, his wife, their four daughters and one son – disappeared while being held captive by the Bolsheviks in 1918. The official view is that they were all killed, but one woman – Anna Anderson – steadfastly maintained that she was Anastasia, the youngest of the Grand Duchesses, and that she had escaped her captors

In July 1918 anti-communist White Russian investigators moved in to Ekaterinburg in the Ural Mountains and announced to the world that the imperial family had been massacred there by the Bolsheviks. As proof they pointed to the bloodstains and bullet holes at the scene of the crime and to charred scraps of imperial clothing and fragments of jewellery found in a mine shaft nearby. One witness claimed to have seen the bodies – but none were ever found.

Despite the startling lack of evidence, history has accepted the story of the massacre. After all, none of the family was ever seen again, though scores of impostors have been unmasked. Even Anna Anderson, who claimed for over 60 years that she was the Tsar's youngest daughter Anastasia, and that she had escaped the bullets and the bayonets, was not able to prove her identity, though her court case was the longest this century.

In 1971 two BBC journalists, Anthony Summers and Tom Mangold, took a fresh look at the mystery. For five years they pursued tantalising loose ends and subjected all the existing evidence to rigorous scientific analysis. Their investigations showed that much of the original evidence had been forged or planted and that vital documents were missing. Eventually the trail led to America where they discovered the dossiers of the first White Russian investigators, which had been lost to view for over half a century.

Tsar Nicholas II had ascended the throne in 1894. He was an uncomplicated, gentle and affectionate man, totally unprepared to rule an already disaffected Russia. Nicholas was easily swayed by his forceful and highly strung wife, the Tsarina Alexandra; and his rule was dogged by violent incidents, made worse by the couple's obtuseness in public affairs. He acquired the nickname 'Nicholas the Bloody'.

Nicholas always found refuge in the heart of his family. After bearing four daughters Alexandra produced the desired heir, but the Tsarevich Alexei suffered from the painful disease haemophilia. Conventional medicine could not help, and the Tsarina turned to Rasputin, a disreputable Siberian 'holy man'. Soon she managed to convince the Tsar that Rasputin's political advice was equally valuable. This association with a debauched drunkard brought the Romanovs to their lowest point in the esteem of their subjects.

Although Rasputin was murdered in 1916, it was already too late for the Tsar. The war with Germany was devastating Russia and revolutionary fervour could no longer be held back. In March 1917, as Nicholas travelled to St Petersburg, the imperial train was ambushed by dissident troops and he was forced to abdicate. A provisional government was set up and the imperial family were confined at Tsarskoe Selo. In August the Romanovs were moved for their own safety to Tobolsk in Siberia; and in

Above: the Romanovs – the Russian Imperial family – before their downfall. The Grand Duchess Anastasia is seated on the left of the Tsar Nicholas II

Grand Duchesses Olga and Tatiana carry turf in the park at Tsarkoe Selo, which the family cultivated during their imprisonment there during the spring and summer of 1917

April 1918 they were transferred to the remote city of Ekaterinburg, where their last privileges were removed and their imprisonment began in earnest in the confines of the heavily guarded and barricaded Ipatiev House.

By 14 July White Russian troops had surrounded the city and the fall of Ekaterinburg was imminent. The fate of the Romanovs had to be decided.

One theory was that the family had been taken towards Perm, the next Bolshevik stronghold. The other was that they had been murdered in a most brutal fashion by the revolutionaries.

The White Russians preferred to believe that the imperial family were alive – it was the rallying cry for their cause – but as the months went by and the Tsar did not reappear, it became expedient to prove that the Romanovs had been martyred at the hands of the Bolsheviks. A massacre was good propaganda.

When the Ipatiev House was examined, it struck Investigator Nametkin of the local justice department that no clothes or shoes had been left behind by the imperial family.

The 'murder cellar', a semi-basement room on the side of the house, measured only 17 by 14 feet (5 by 4 metres). Into this room 23 people were supposed to have crowded – 12 killers and 11 victims (four members of staff were alleged to have died). If a massacre really had been carried out in those cramped conditions, the *killers* would have been severely at risk. Nametkin's successor, Judge Sergeyev, did find evidence of violence in the 'murder cellar'. He counted 27 bullet holes and noted bloodstains on the floor that someone had attempted to wash away. Nevertheless, he did not see evidence of a massacre. 'I do not believe that all the people, the Tsar, his family, and those with them, were shot there,' he wrote. It was his opinion that only the Tsar and possibly Alexei had been killed, and that the rest of the family had been smuggled out of the house in disguise and sent to safety.

Tsar Nicholas and his children on the conservatory roof of the Governor's House in Tobolsk, Siberia, to which they were moved, for their own safety, in August 1917

In February 1919 the Whites appointed their own investigator, Nikolai Sokolov, to take over the case. It became his life's work. He gradually collected seven volumes of evidence.

After lengthy detective work, Summers and Mangold tracked down the original seven volumes in Houghton Library at Harvard University, and were able to reconstruct the truth.

Their conclusion was that the Tsarina and the four Grand Duchesses had left the Ipatiev House alive and had been taken west on the Bolsheviks' line of retreat to Perm.

Alexander Kirsta, a White investigator who diligently followed up leads in Perm, made a startling breakthrough when he interrogated a nurse called Natalya Mutnykh. The nurse's brother was deputy to Beloborodov, the man in charge of 'important prisoners' at Ekaterinburg. She testified on three separate occasions, without contradicting herself.

In April 1918, the Romanovs were transferred to Ipatiev House (left) in Ekaterinburg in the Ural Mountains. It was here, in a semi-basement room (above), that they were all allegedly murdered. The evidence left in the room seemed to increase with each investigation: first there were three bullet holes and no blood; then 27 holes and some blood; later bullet holes and blood everywhere

She claimed, convincingly, to have seen the Tsarina and her four daughters lying on mattresses in a squalid basement under heavy guard. Another witness claimed that one of the Grand Duchesses, Anastasia, had tried to escape along a railway track and had been shot and wounded by Red Army soldiers in the course of her flight.

A Perm doctor, Pavel Utkin, recorded his own dealings with the escaper. In late September he had been called by the chairman of the Cheka, the secret police, to their headquarters to tend a young woman:

> I started to examine the woman lying on the couch. I remember well that under one eye, the left one I think, she had a large bruise. . . . The corresponding corner of the left lip had been cut. . . . The general impression was that the sick person had been beaten; she . . . was in an unconscious state. She was shaking violently. When I started my examination . . . all the men left the room; one woman remained. . . . A little while after . . . the sick woman regained consciousness and looked at me. I asked her: 'Who are you?' In a trembling voice, but quite distinctly, she answered me: 'I am the daughter of the ruler Anastasia.'

Dr Utkin spoke of the girl's plump figure – puppy fat had been a trait of Anastasia's – and her lovely hands – a well-known trait of Romanov women.

Important prisoner

But the fact that it was thought necessary to call in a doctor to tend the 'sick woman' indicates that the escaped and recaptured prisoner was obviously a person of great importance.

A further indication that the fugitive was Anastasia comes from the Swedish Red Cross delegate, who was travelling through Perm Province at the time by train:

> In my capacity as the chief of the Swedish Red Cross mission in Siberia in 1918, I travelled in a private railway car. At some place, the name of which has escaped my memory, the train was stopped and searched in order to find the Grand Duchess Anastasia, daughter of Tsar Nicholas II. The Grand Duchess was, however, not aboard the train. Nobody knew where she had gone.

According to the original, unpublished evidence, the women were held in Perm until the end of November 1918, when they were evacuated to Glazov. After this they were moved towards Kazan, in the direction of Moscow, in the early months of 1919. And it is here that the trail finally peters out. Lenin may have had them shot, or just left them to their fate at the hands of his soldiers.

On 17 February 1920 a young woman about 20 years old was hauled out of the Landwehr Canal in Berlin by the police and taken to hospital. It was assumed that she had tried to commit suicide, but she refused to answer any questions or to reveal her identity. After she had remained silent for six weeks her doctors sent her, in exasperation, to Dalldorf Insane Asylum, where she spent the next two years.

'Fräulein Unbekannt' ('Miss Unknown') spoke German with a Russian accent. An examination revealed that her body was covered in scars and that she was no longer a virgin. She suffered from toothache and had had several teeth extracted – she even asked for healthy teeth to be removed in an attempt to change her appearance. She was obsessed with not being recognised and plucked her hair out to alter her hairline.

In March 1922 a fellow inmate called Clara Peuthert, who had managed to get closer than anyone else to the patient, was discharged from the asylum. On her own initiative she informed a former tsarist officer that 'Miss Unknown' was the Grand Duchess *Tatiana*. The news caused a furore of excitement in White Russian circles in Berlin. But when Baroness Buxhoeveden, a former lady-in-waiting who had shared the Romanov captivity until Ekaterinburg, was persuaded to visit the asylum, the patient hid under the bedclothes and refused to speak to her. Naturally, the Baroness could only draw one conclusion – that she was an imposter.

Support for the mystery woman came from Baron Arthur von Kleist, who offered her a home in his family. Gradually, the Baron and his wife gained the confidence of 'Miss Unknown' until she told them that she was not Tatiana but Anastasia, and her story was coaxed out of her. It was a fantastic tale and, though the loyal émigrés believed it, it always remained a stumbling block in her fight for recognition. The latest evidence for the family's survival

Below: the Landwehr Canal in Berlin where 'Miss Unknown's' suicide attempt was thwarted on 18 February 1920. The young woman refused to reveal her identity or answer any questions, and was eventually committed to Dalldorf Insane Asylum

beyond Ekaterinburg also contradicts the story – but there is reason to believe that, even as she told it, 'Anastasia' knew it was pure invention.

Baron Kleist lost no time in making 'the story' public, and, though he and his wife revelled in the reflected glory of having a grand duchess in the house, 'Anastasia' deeply resented the stream of visitors who came to stare at her. Under the strain, her health deteriorated, and she ran away. Now began a period of restlessness. She became the object of a tug-of-war between the émigrés, staying with different families, her visits interrupted by periods spent in hospital.

But interest in the patient was not confined to tsarist sympathisers – the royal families of Europe began to make inquiries about her. In 1922, while she was convalescing in the country home of Police Inspector Grünberg, she was visited incognito by Princess Irene of Prussia, the tsarina's sister. The princess did not recognize her but admitted it was ten years since she had seen the imperial family.

A 1955 press photograph of the 'Anastasia' claimant, by then known as Anna Anderson. She habitually held a handkerchief to her face, to hide her missing teeth

Royal visitors

'Aunt Irene' was to become one of 'Anastasia's' most vehement opponents, yet the meeting upset her so dreadfully that the subject became taboo in her house. When she was approached later she protested: 'I could not have made a mistake!' Suddenly she began to cry and in tones of anguish burst out: 'She *is* similar, she *is* similar, but what does that mean if it is not she?'

As for 'Anastasia', she was 'humiliated' and 'bewildered' when she realised that her aunt had come to her pretending to be a stranger.

Crown Princess Cecile of Prussia, daughter-in-law of the now exiled Kaiser, was the next royal visitor. She was 'struck at first glance by the young person's resemblance to the Tsar's mother and to the Tsar himself, but I could see nothing of the Tsarina in her'. But Cecile later told her brother: 'I almost believe it must be she.'

In 1925 'Anastasia' was visited in hospital by her former nursemaid, 'Shura', and her husband, Pierre Gilliard, who had previously been the Romanov children's tutor. Shura had been sent by the Tsar's sister, the Grand Duchess Olga. Though 'Anastasia' was delirious, they were sure enough of her identity to urge the Grand Duchess to visit the invalid herself. As with Shura, when 'Anastasia' recovered, there was an instant and positive response on both sides. 'My reason cannot grasp it,' said Olga, 'but my heart tells me that the little one is Anastasia. And because I have been raised in a faith which teaches me to follow my heart before my reason, I must believe that she is.' Yet when 'Anastasia's' case came to court, neither Olga nor Gilliard stood by their original conviction that this was she.

In the same year 'Anastasia's' friends made overtures to the Tsarina's brother, 'Uncle Ernie', the Grand Duke Ernst Ludwig of Hesse. As they were preparing a dossier to show the Duke, they asked the patient where she had last seen him, and she astounded them by saying: 'In the war, with us at home.' This was surely impossible, her friends argued, since Russia and Germany had been enemies. But 'Anastasia' insisted that her uncle had travelled incognito to the Russian court on a secret peace mission from her father's cousin, the Kaiser.

The claimant's supporters realised the potency of this remark if it could be proved to be true, but naturally enough 'Uncle Ernie' did not want his wartime secrets made public, and, as soon as he heard what she had said, he refused to have anything to do with 'Anastasia'. When she came to trial he was her chief opponent, pouring thousands of pounds into the fight against her recognition. However, other members of the family testified that the Grand Duke had been on a secret, though failed, mission to the Tsar, and the evidence today suggests that 'Anastasia's' remark was indeed accurate. She was also the first person known to speak of the Grand Duke's unsuccessful Russian mission in public.

A very important step forward for the claimant came in summer 1926 when she was recognised by Tatiana Botkin, a childhood playmate and daughter of the imperial family's physician, who said: 'It is Grand Duchess Anastasia Nikolayevna. I have recognised her. It is the same person I knew before. Only the lower part of the face, the mouth, has changed. Otherwise nothing.'

Tatiana has never withdrawn her support for the claimant, and her brother Gleb Botkin, who had settled in America as a journalist, arranged for

'Anastasia' to go and stay on Long Island as the guest of her second cousin Princess Xenia.

After this, 'Anastasia's' financial affairs became increasingly muddled, and she grew more and more distraught. Always an autocratic and demanding guest, her presence was putting undue strain on Princess Xenia's marriage. Gleb removed her and, under the patronage of the pianist Rachmaninov, she took up residence in a hotel in the name of 'Anna Anderson' – a name that stuck for the rest of her life.

In 1930, after again having been handed round a circle of society hostesses, none of whom wanted to keep her for very long, Anna Anderson was nearly taken over by a professional adventuress, Jill Cossley-Batt. Cossley-Batt claimed to be a friend of the Queen of England and the Prince of Wales and, when she was unmasked as an opportunist fraud, the shock to Anna Anderson was so great that she had a fit of hysteria that lasted all night, during which she accidentally trod on and killed one of her beloved pet birds.

This was the last straw for her hosts, and they had her committed to a mental home. The men who came to fetch her broke down the door of her room with an axe.

Within a year Anna Anderson was back in Germany in another mental home, Ilten, where the fees were cheaper than in America. Though she was comfortable in the home, the doctors eventually persuaded her to leave because: 'From our observations there can be no question of insanity.'

Anna Anderson in 1981. She died in a mental home in Charlottesville, Virginia, on 13 February 1984

On her release from Ilten, Anna Anderson embarked upon thirteen years as the guest of various aristocratic houses. Her life took on a more peaceful aspect, but behind the scenes her supporters were pressing harder than ever her claim for recognition, though it is worth noting that Anna Anderson never pushed her own case.

Vast fortunes

Her friends got their opportunity in 1933, when a Berlin court ruled that all the Tsar's children were dead, and that all his collateral heirs should divide between them what was left of his assets in Germany. Although the sum of money involved was insignificant, the Tsar had been one of the richest men in the world, and this case would no doubt set a precedent for others that might follow. With the possibility of vast fortunes at stake, it was no wonder that the collateral heirs – among them 'Uncle Ernie', 'Aunt Olga', 'Aunt Irene', and the Tsarina's other sister, Victoria, Marchioness of Milford Haven and mother of the late Lord Mountbatten – presented a united front against the claimant. The longest court case this century had begun.

As the trial progressed, Anna Anderson settled into a house in the Black Forest. She lived there until July 1968 when she flew to Charlottesville, Virginia, in the USA, to take up the invitation of a history professor, Dr John Manahan, who had offered her marriage and a home.

Summers and Mangold visited the Manahans in 1974. Anna Anderson-Manahan told them: 'There was no massacre there . . . but I cannot tell the rest.'

Anna Anderson-Manahan spent the last years of her life in a mental home. She had lost her chance to 'tell the rest'. The file on the Tsar – and his daughter – remains open.

Who murdered the Sydney scientist?

The deaths of Dr Gilbert Bogle and Mrs Margaret Chandler have been called 'the mystery of the century'. Their bodies were found half-naked in a country park near Sydney, Australia, but police and pathologists were completely baffled – it looked like murder yet, despite intensive investigation, no cause of death was ever found. Did they accidentally overdose on LSD or were they killed in cold blood

Unlike most Australian parties, the one at the home of Kenneth Nash at Chatswood, Sydney on New Year's Eve 1962 was a quiet and sober affair. Nash, a photographer based at the Commonwealth Scientific and Industrial Research Organisation (CSIRO), and his wife Ruth had a reputation as good hosts who relied more on fine food, sparkling conversation and little gimmicks to make their parties swing rather than a heavy supply of alcohol.

The gimmick that night was to be an exhibition of modern art. The 22 guests, mostly Nash's colleagues from CSIRO, plus a sprinkling of men and women from Sydney's professional and arts world, had all been told to bring a painting of their own. As each guest produced his work, the others were to act as critics and at the end of the evening the best artist and the best critic would win prizes.

If the game sounds naïve, it was not when played by Nash's guests. Although this was suburban Australia, the sexual revolution that had stirred Britain and the United States in the early Sixties had also penetrated here, and under the surface of conformist respectability on this quiet and sober evening there simmered dangerous passions. These mature, well-educated and articulate people, and the 'Push' or set to which they belonged, were capable of combining innocent art criticism with barbed innuendos about the others' foibles and amorous liaisons.

So, on what was to be the last night of his life, Dr Gilbert Bogle, 38, a CSIRO scientist, arrived at the party with his clarinet in his car, and carrying his art entry, a Picasso-style drawing. He came alone. His wife, Vivienne, was at home looking after their four children, one of whom was ill. Margaret Chandler, 29, arrived at the party with her husband Geoffrey, also a CSIRO scientist.

Bogle and Mrs Chandler had met ten days earlier at the CSIRO Christmas party. Mrs Chandler had two children and was, according to what her husband said later, 'fed up with a closed-in, domestic existence'. She had apparently found Bogle attractive at that first meeting because – again according to her husband – she raised the possibility on the way to the Nash party of having an affair with Bogle: 'It would be an interesting experience.' Chandler said later that he had replied, 'If you want to have Gib as a lover, if it would make you happy, you do it.'

Mrs Chandler, as we shall see, was not the only woman drawn to Bogle. He was a brilliant scientist, an accomplished musician, a linguist, and widely travelled. Born in New Zealand, he had been a Rhodes scholar and went on to get his doctorate at Oxford, researching atom crystal structure. He also had a master's degree in arts and science. His dark good looks and easy social manner had made him many sexual conquests. But he had a reputation for being insensitive and uncaring when he decided to break off a relationship.

Margaret Chandler had been a nurse before she married. She was a vivacious and attractive woman with an extrovert personality. There is hardly a picture of her in the family album that does not show her smile. She was a good mother, had many friends and, to all external appearances, was happy in her marriage with Geoffrey Chandler. The only slight shadow in their relationship that their friends could discern was that Margaret missed the excitement of her nursing days and found her domestic existence boring.

Car parked

At the party she and Bogle spent several hours together. Geoffrey Chandler took no notice of this and after an hour or so announced that he was going out to buy some cigarettes. After doing so, he drove to Balmain to the party of a friend, Ken Buckley, a prominent member of the Sydney Push. There he joined a girlfriend, Pamela Logan, a secretary he had known for some time. Shortly after midnight, Pamela Logan and Chandler drove to Logan's flat.

At about 2.30am Geoffrey Chandler was back at the Nash party. He joined his wife and Bogle and chatted with them until nearly 4am. He then said goodnight to his hosts and drove off. A few minutes later Bogle and Margaret Chandler also said goodbye. They were seen by other guests getting into Bogle's car. Fifteen minutes later a motorist saw them driving into Lane Cove River Park.

Geoffrey Chandler, Margaret's husband. His appearance was unusual for the time, and his unpopular ideas about sex, marriage and politics created considerable antipathy towards him from the general public. Sydney split into two camps: those who believed that he was the murderer, and those who believed he was a suspect simply because of his unconventional life style

Margaret Chandler – she and Gilbert Bogle (above left) had first met only 10 days before their bizarre deaths

At 5am a passer-by saw them in the car, which was parked by the river bank. It was already sufficiently light for the man to notice that Bogle looked quite pale. That was the last time the couple was seen alive for, when another man passed the car a few minutes later, it was empty.

At 8am two youths, Michael McCormick and Dennis Wheway, arrived at the park to search for golf balls lost from the adjoining golf course. They wandered slowly along the tracks by the river bank, occasionally breaking off to search in clumps of bushes and undergrowth. On one of these forays, McCormick saw the figure of a man lying near the river bank. He took little notice, deciding that it was probably a drunk sleeping off the excesses of the previous evening. But an hour later, when he passed the spot again and saw that the man had not moved, he called Wheway and the two youths went closer to see if the man was all right.

The first thing they noticed was that the man's face was purple and that there was a small trickle of blood from his nose and from the corner of his mouth. Wheway thought the man was dead and that they

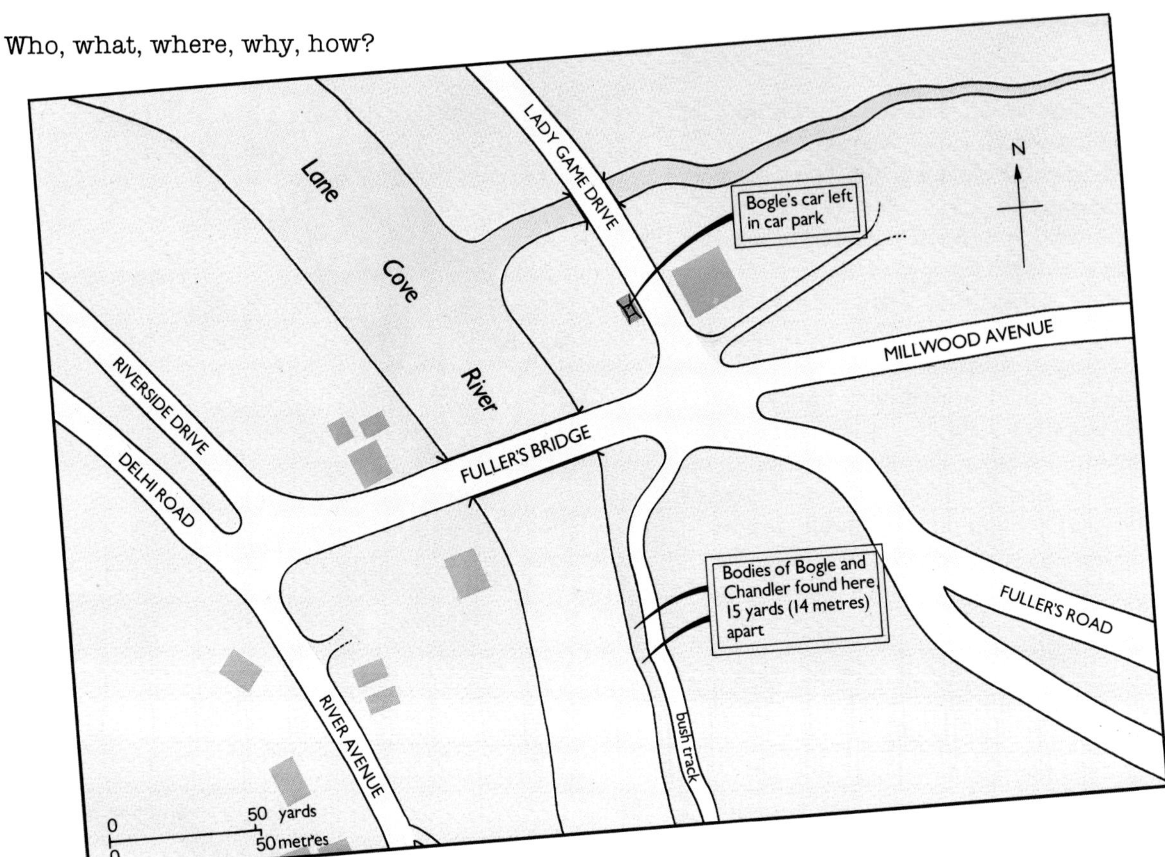

Map of Lane Cove River Park, showing where the bodies of Gilbert Bogle and Margaret Chandler were found on New Year's Day 1963. When the police arrived on the scene, they were struck by the bizarre arrangement of the bodies. Both were partially naked, and some attempt had been made to cover them, which led the investigating officers to believe that there had been a third party at the death scene. But there was not a shred of evidence to substantiate such a belief

should call the police as soon as possible.

The local police were on the scene before 10am. Sergeant 'Andy' Andrews said later that he was immediately struck by the bizarre arrangement of the body and made detailed notes on this even before attempting to identify it. The man was wearing his shirt and tie and his shoes and socks. He was not wearing his underpants, his trousers, or his coat. He was lying flat on his stomach with his legs fully stretched out.

The strange thing was that the body was covered from the neck to the buttocks with a piece of carpet about 3 feet (90 centimetres) long and 2 feet (60 centimetres) wide. Over the top of this carpet the man's suit coat and trousers had been draped in a very neat fashion, giving the impression to a casual observer that the man was fully dressed.

The sergeant noted that the man's face was discoloured to a deep purple shade and that rigor mortis was well advanced. The man's shoes were partly covered with mud, and this led the sergeant to look further down the river bank where the ground was soft. There he found fresh human excreta. Returning to the body he noticed a small amount of vomit. Having noted all this, the sergeant then identified the body from papers in a wallet in the suit coat pocket. The man was Dr Gilbert Bogle.

By this time the Sydney Criminal Investigation Bureau (CIB) had been notified, and Bureau detectives arrived soon afterwards. At 10.55am they discovered Margaret Chandler's body in a small depression about 15 yards (14 metres) from that of Bogle. She was lying full length on her back. She was wearing a dress with a floral pattern, but this had been pulled down, together with her brassiere, to expose her breasts, and the bottom part of the dress had been pushed up around her waist. She had no underwear on, but a pair of men's underpants was bundled up between her ankles. On a dry part of the river bed below the high water mark, police found her white underwear and brown shoes, and Bogle's trouser belt. The underwear was wet, as if it had been washed out in the river.

Margaret Chandler's knees were slightly stained with mud. Her body was still warm and rigor mortis only just beginning. And – another bizarre touch – over the top of Mrs Chandler, covering her completely from sight, were three flattened cardboard beer cartons. The CIB officers at first thought that one of the local policemen on the scene had done this to preserve Mrs Chandler's dignity, but soon established that this was not so.

Officers from the scientific squad had by now arrived and they took photographs, fingerprints, soil samples and measurements. It was afternoon before they had finished and the bodies could be removed to the Sydney morgue, then located in out-of-date premises near Sydney Harbour Bridge.

At this stage Detective Inspector Ron Watson, who was in charge of the case, was puzzled by the strange way the bodies had been covered, but still thought he was dealing with a reasonably straightforward investigation; it was either murder and then a suicide, a double suicide, or accidental death from a drug or alcohol overdose. So what happened next, if inexcusable, is at least understandable.

New Year's Day is a holiday in Australia. And when a holiday falls on a Sunday, it is a local custom to make the next day, the Monday, the official holiday. With all Sydney enjoying a four-day break, the morgue was staffed only on a stand-by basis – a pathologist was available to be called for emergencies, but was not in attendance. This was not considered an emergency, so it was not until Bogle and Mrs Chandler had been dead at least thirty hours that the autopsies were carried out. Up to this moment the pathologists expected to be able to give the police the answer they anticipated within hours. Instead, it was the beginning of a real mystery.

No injuries

The two bodies were without any obvious signs of injury. The pathologists quickly ruled out shooting, stabbing, bludgeoning and strangling. Bogle had a few cuts and abrasions to his right hip and thigh and Mrs Chandler had abrasions and scratches on her knees and feet. But there was no other sign of external injury.

Equally, there was no evidence of internal injury in either body. Bogle's body showed signs of faeces in the region of the anus and buttocks, consistent with a bowel evacuation shortly before his death. There were some haemorrhages on the surface of the lungs and on the lining of the windpipe. The lung tissues were full of fluid. The heart was of normal size and shape with no signs of disease. The arteries showed no disease and neither did any organ. The stomach contained eight ounces (225 grams) of food, all of it well-digested. The examination of Margaret Chandler's body produced much the same result.

Faced with a clinical picture of two healthy people who had apparently suffered no violence but who had nevertheless died in suspicious circumstances, the pathologists took the next logical step as dictated by their training: they took specimens of all the vital organs and sent them to the government analyst. The results were astounding. To begin with neither body showed any indication of alcohol. As the then director of the New South Wales Department of Forensic Science, Dr John Laing, said later: 'So help me, a New Year's party and no alcohol. That was the moment we realised that we were up the original gum tree.'

For, as well as showing no alcohol, the analysts' tests showed no poisons either. The pathologists went back and searched the bodies for signs of injection, pinpricks, or bites – and found nothing. They initiated further tests, which ruled out snake and spider bites, ruptured ear drums from high frequency sound waves, and radiation poisoning – residual radioactivity levels in the bodies were found to be normal.

In the hope that they had overlooked something, the officers of the police scientific squad went to the Nash house and took away samples of every remaining item of food, every bottle of drink, everything Bogle or Mrs Chandler may have touched at the party, and tested them all. Every result was negative. Bogle's car was examined, dust from the pockets of his clothing analysed, and the clothing itself checked. All that emerged from these extensive investigations however, were traces of semen on his suit jacket.

At bay, their confidence in their professional skill shaken, the pathologists reluctantly put down the cause of death for both Bogle and Margaret Chandler as 'acute cardiac failure associated with anoxia and pulmonary oedema'. Cardiac failure means that the heart stopped beating; anoxia means that the blood was starved of oxygen; and pulmonary oedema means that the lungs filled with fluid. But

Detective Inspector Ron Watson, who headed the investigation. He was convinced that he was dealing with a straightforward case – and his lack of urgency delayed the autopsy

the order in which these events occurred is left open. In other words, Bogle and Margaret Chandler died either because they stopped breathing and then their hearts failed, or their hearts failed and so they stopped breathing.

The police had learnt very little that was positive from the autopsies except that whatever killed one also killed the other, and that Mrs Chandler probably died as much as an hour later than Bogle. So, although she could have lived long enough to cover Bogle in the manner already described, it was highly unlikely that she then covered herself with the flattened beer cartons. First, she must have been too ill to do so – the abrasions and mud stains were consistent with her having crawled or stumbled around, evidently in a state of some distress. And, even if she had found the strength in her last minutes to cover her partial nakedness, wouldn't it have been easier and more logical for her simply to adjust her clothing, rather than search for the empty beer cartons, flatten them, and then pull them over herself? If she had the strength to do this, wouldn't she also have removed Bogle's underpants from between her ankles?

The pathologists and the police agreed privately that everything pointed to there having been a third party at the death scene. The problem was that there was not a shred of evidence of any sort to prove it. No one had been seen there, no footprints had been found that could not be accounted for, and what would have been the person's motives for covering the bodies in such an elaborate manner?

Between the autopsies and the formal inquest, the police stepped up their inquiries. Detective Sergeant Jack Bateman, one of the best CIB detectives in the New South Wales police force, joined the team. He, and other detectives, spent the next six weeks interviewing Bogle and Mrs Chandler's relatives,

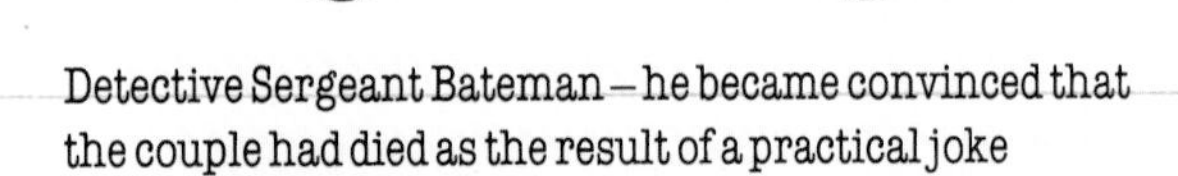

Detective Sergeant Bateman – he became convinced that the couple had died as the result of a practical joke

J.J. Loomes, the coroner of the inquest, which opened on 21 March 1963. His refusal to consider certain evidence fuelled speculation about the deaths

friends and colleagues. They were looking for a motive, and found more than one person who had one, but discovered no clearly incriminating evidence.

Poison theory

The climax of public interest came with the opening of the inquest on 21 March 1963. The coroner was J. J. Loomes. There were two principal scientific witnesses: the Director of Forensic Science, Dr Laing, and the Professor of Pharmacology at Sydney University, Roland Thorpe, an Englishman. Laing described the autopsy procedures and all the tests made to try to detect a poison. He said: 'We could not help the analysts by naming any one particular poison suspected to be the cause of death.' To head off possible criticism he made a point of telling the coroner that every facility known to modern science for determining the cause of death was available when the investigation began.

Professor Thorpe's opinion was that the cause of death was poisoning – although all tests had proved negative. He suggested that the poison might have dissipated, or have been an unusual one available only to research workers.

But the real interest at the inquest centred on three people – Geoffrey Chandler, his friend Pamela Logan, and a mystery witness called Margaret Fowler. If reporters had hoped that the mysterious Mrs Fowler's evidence would provide the key to the mystery, then they were soon disappointed. She

Left: Margaret Fowler, the witness whose evidence was excluded by the coroner. Information that came to light after her death in 1977 revealed that she had had an affair with Bogle and that they had been planning to live together – until his encounter with Margaret Chandler

The police file remains open: Case unsolved

No poison was detected on the bodies...'

Officially Dr Gilbert Bogle and Margaret Chandler died from acute circulatory failure on the New Year's morning of 1963.

That was the brief non-emotive finding of the then Coroner, Mr J.J. Loomes.

He summed up the feelings of a bewildered nation when he said he found it "hard to believe" that he was no more able on that day to determine the manner and cause of their death than when the inquest opened.

Dr Bogle was 38. Margaret Chandler was 29. The hearing in May 1963 lasted 14 days and at that time was the long[illegible] in Australia's history.

Fifty witnesses called

Dr BOGLE, SCIENTIST

Each of the 22 guests

The inconclusive results of the inquiry produced a rash of indignant newspaper articles. Some criticised the delay in carrying out the autopsies, perhaps allowing any poison present to dissipate

stepped into the witness box and took the oath. But before she could give her evidence, her own counsel, counsel for the Bogle family, and counsel for the Chandler family, all objected to her evidence being heard. The coroner adjourned the hearing to hear submissions in private. When he resumed he said that Mrs Fowler would not have to appear. 'I feel that her evidence would not now help in any way. . . .' In retrospect, it seems that this decision may have been mistaken both in terms of solving the case and satisfying the public.

The inquest ended on 29 May. There had been 15 days of hearings. Over 50 witnesses had been called, 63 exhibits presented, and a quarter of a million words spoken in evidence (762 typed pages). And it had all come to nothing. Loomes said that the enquiry had been as exhaustive as it could have been. 'Every person who I felt could give any information as to the deaths of these unfortunate persons has been summonsed to appear. . . . One would like to feel that no stone has been left unturned to have all the available evidence that could assist in any way placed before this inquest. . . . I think that not only my hopes but the hopes of everyone engaged in these proceedings were that at some stage some insignificant fact, dropped perhaps at random, might be the key to unlock this mystery. . . . It gives me no satisfaction to sit here and tell you that all we know about this is that the two people died from acute circulatory failure, the cause of which is still unknown.'

But had the inquiry been as exhaustive as he claimed? Information that has since come to light demonstrates that Loomes failed to consider certain evidence. He did not pursue inquiries into motives any of Bogle's associates might have for wanting him dead, or whether the military significance of his research might shed light on the mystery; he did not deal with the fact that semen was found on Bogle's coat; he excluded evidence that Margaret Chandler had a former lover; and, probably most serious of all, he excluded Margaret Fowler's evidence.

The inquest thus succeeded in fuelling speculation about the deaths. The first story to go around Sydney was that Bogle had been working on some sort of 'death ray' and had been killed by enemy agents. (Mrs Chandler had been killed simply because she was with him when the murderer struck.) The story had its origins in Bogle's work background, his imminent departure to work at Bell Laboratories in

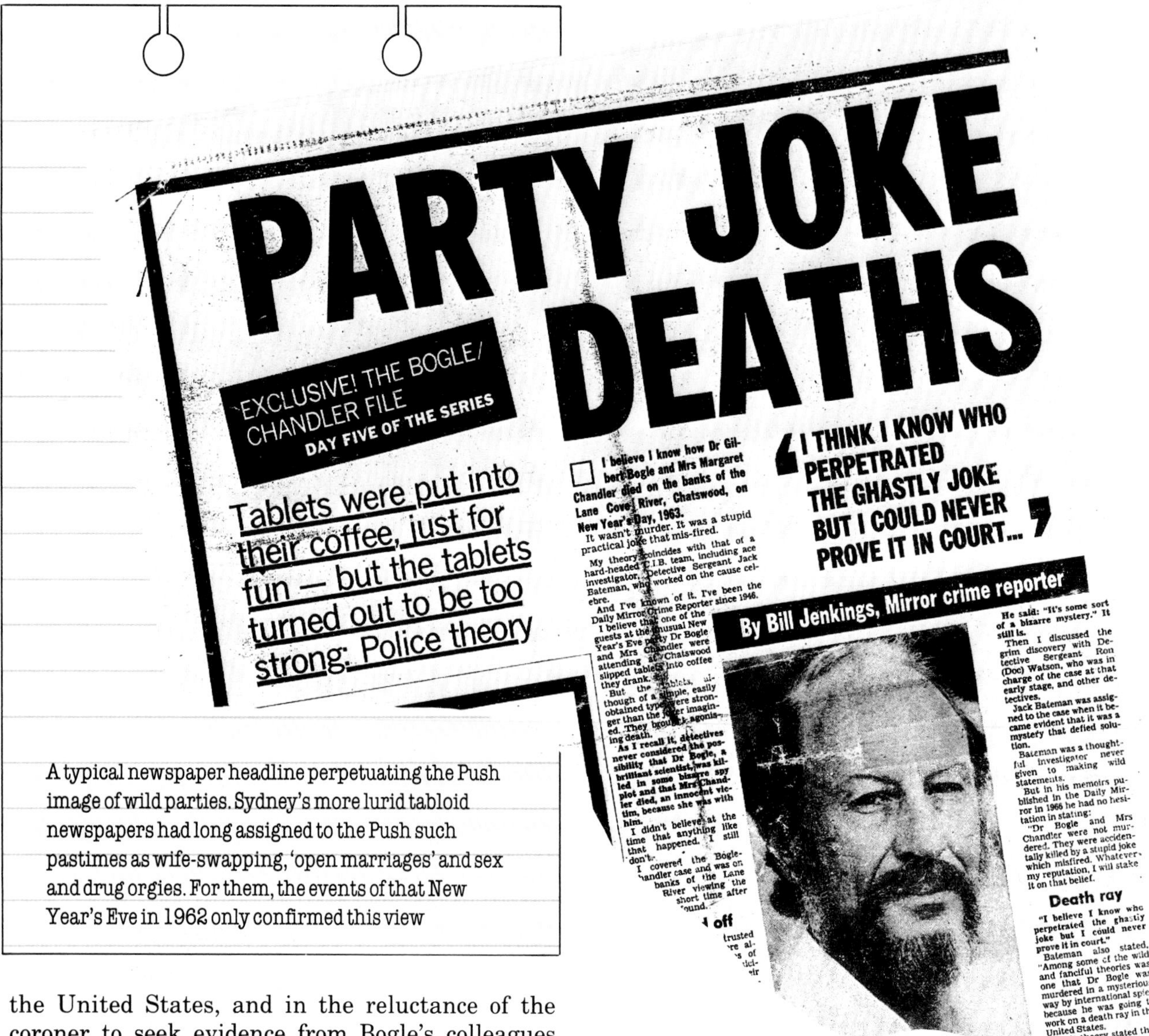

PARTY JOKE DEATHS

EXCLUSIVE! THE BOGLE/ CHANDLER FILE
DAY FIVE OF THE SERIES

Tablets were put into their coffee, just for fun — but the tablets turned out to be too strong: Police theory

'I THINK I KNOW WHO PERPETRATED THE GHASTLY JOKE BUT I COULD NEVER PROVE IT IN COURT...'

By Bill Jenkings, Mirror crime reporter

I believe I know how Dr Gilbert Bogle and Mrs Margaret Chandler died on the banks of the Lane Cove River, Chatswood, on New Year's Day, 1963.

It wasn't murder. It was a stupid practical joke that mis-fired.

My theory coincides with that of a hard-headed C.I.B. team, including ace investigator, Detective Sergeant Jack Bateman, who worked on the cause celebre.

And I've known of it. I've been the Daily Mirror Crime Reporter since 1946.

I believe that one of the guests at the unusual New Year's Eve party Dr Bogle and Mrs Chandler were attending at Chatswood slipped tablets into coffee they drank.

But the tablets, although of a simple, easily obtained type, were stronger than the joker imagined. They brought agonising death.

As I recall it, detectives never considered the possibility that Dr Bogle, a brilliant scientist, was killed in some bizarre spy plot and that Mrs Chandler died, an innocent victim, because she was with him.

I didn't believe at the time that anything like that happened. I still don't.

I covered the Bogle-Chandler case and was on banks of the Lane River viewing the short time after found.

off

trusted re al- s of tici- eir

He said: "It's some sort of a bizarre mystery." It still is.

Then I discussed the grim discovery with Detective Sergeant Ron (Doc) Watson, who was in charge of the case at that early stage, and other detectives.

Jack Bateman was assigned to the case when it became evident that it was a mystery that defied solution.

Bateman was a thoughtful investigator never given to making wild statements.

But in his memoirs published in the Daily Mirror in 1966 he had no hesitation in stating:

"Dr Bogle and Mrs Chandler were not murdered. They were accidentally killed by a stupid joke which misfired. Whatever my reputation, I will stake it on that belief.

Death ray

"I believe I know who perpetrated the ghastly joke but I could never prove it in court."

Bateman also stated, "Among some of the wild and fanciful theories was one that Dr Bogle was murdered in a mysterious way by international spies because he was going to work on a death ray in the United States.

"This theory stated that

A typical newspaper headline perpetuating the Push image of wild parties. Sydney's more lurid tabloid newspapers had long assigned to the Push such pastimes as wife-swapping, 'open marriages' and sex and drug orgies. For them, the events of that New Year's Eve in 1962 only confirmed this view

the United States, and in the reluctance of the coroner to seek evidence from Bogle's colleagues about this work.

The coroner had been told that there was no security aspect to Bogle's work at the CSIRO, but in his new job Bogle was about to become involved in expensive, highly complex scientific research of great military importance vital to the defence of the United States. There is further evidence of this. In 1980, the *National Times,* a Sydney-based weekly magazine with a reputation for thoroughly researched investigations, made vigorous efforts to obtain from the FBI in Washington any information it might have in its files about the Bogle-Chandler deaths. It had decided to do this because it had learnt from New South Wales police sources that Bell Laboratories had wanted a security clearance for Bogle and had asked the FBI to give him a positive vetting on their behalf.

On 27 March 1980, the US Department of Justice replied to the request from the *National Times* enclosing some copies of documents relating to Bogle, but adding that 18 pages were being withheld in their entirety. The reason given for this was section 552 (b) (1) of the Freedom of Information Act. Under this section, a US Government department can withhold information from the public if it is currently and properly classified, 'in the interest of the national defense or foreign policy, for example, information involving intelligence sources and methods'.

The *National Times,* as was its right, immediately appealed against this decision, but learned on 25 April 1980 that the appeal had been dismissed. The Associate Attorney General of the United States wrote that 'none of the information being withheld is appropriate for discretionary release', and gave again as the reason 'national security'.

The Sydney police discounted any suggestion that Bogle's death had anything to do with his work. One of them, Detective Sergeant Jack Bateman, was convinced that the couple had died as the result of a stupid practical joke. He believed that one of the guests at the Nash party had slipped something into the coffee that Bogle and Mrs Chandler had drunk. 'I believe that I know who perpetrated the ghastly joke,' he wrote in his memoirs in 1966, 'but I could never prove it in court.'

The theorists now recalled that the government analyst, E. S. Ogg, had said privately that he believed that Bogle and Margaret Chandler had died from an overdose of LSD. So was it possible that someone at the Nash party who had access to LSD – not difficult for people in the scientific and medical world – had slipped some into the coffee that the couple had drunk? And since little was known about LSD at that time, had he or she accidentally given them an overdose? And was the LSD not discovered at the autopsies because it had dissipated from the corpse within 24 hours, and the autopsies did not take place until long after that? This theory was the most popular in Sydney and probably would have been accepted even in police circles if it had not been for an event in a London hospital in 1977.

On 18 June of that year Margaret Fowler, the mysterious witness at the inquest, died in London after an illness. Her death freed journalists from the very severe libel laws in New South Wales, and Marian Wilkinson of the *National Times,* a brilliant reporter who had always been interested in the Bogle-Chandler case, was able to investigate Margaret Fowler's role in the mystery and to publish her findings.

Turbulent affair

They were sensational. In brief, Fowler and Bogle had had an affair; Fowler had become obsessed with Bogle; Bogle had treated her callously and dumped her; Fowler learned of his interest in Margaret Chandler; Fowler had told friends that Bogle and Chandler were 'going to cop it'; Fowler had been interviewed by the police; and at least one senior detective was convinced that she was the murderess.

During the course of their turbulent affair Fowler had made efforts to keep away from Bogle. She took a new job in north Sydney, but still managed to get news of Bogle from a friend of the family, Jenny Newbold. Newbold told the *National Times* that when Fowler heard that Bogle was leaving Australia she became hysterical. She said that she was in love with him and had been for a long time. She added, 'I should have taken the poison I had. I can't live without him.' Fowler later told police: 'He called on me after he had been to the American Consulate about his trip to America. He said to me, "We'll have a flat together in London." I had told him that I could not live without him. It was generally agreed that we would share a flat together in London.'

Then came the CSIRO Christmas party at which Bogle first met Margaret Chandler. Fowler was at the party and noticed Bogle's reaction to Chandler. She later told her husband, 'I pity that Bogle if he's going to get mixed up with the Chandlers.'

Detectives investigating the Bogle-Chandler deaths interviewed Margaret Fowler on 7 January 1963 and on four further occasions. She also wrote them two letters. She told the police that she had not gone to the Nash party and had been at another party in Turramurra with her husband. They had left that party at 3.45am and had gone home. Fowler later told Newbold: 'The police asked me if I had wanted to do away with myself and I told them that I had on dozens of occasions. Anyway it was only phenobarb that I had. I had an alibi that night. I was at another party.' In what may have been a highly significant remark, overlooked at the time, Fowler speculated that Bogle could have taken a 'sex drug'.

About that time, Graham Carlton, a colleague, found Fowler in a state of great distress. He told the *National Times* that Fowler kept repeating the phrase, 'It's all going to come out.' When he asked what she meant, she replied, 'You'll soon know.' Fowler than began talking about the deaths of Bogle and Chandler. She said that she had been having an affair with Bogle and had planned to meet him overseas. She said, 'My life is ruined.' She implied that

Margaret Chandler – was she killed simply because she happened to be with Bogle when the murderer struck?

she was involved in the deaths. Carlton remembers Fowler remarking, 'They were going to cop it.' On another occasion Fowler discussed poisoning someone on a dance floor by pressing a ring containing a toxic substance into the victim's back. At the time Carlton did not believe anything that Fowler had said. He thought that she was a very bright woman, but that she had problems, and was 'very scatty'.

One former senior detective who worked on the case said later that he had not wanted Fowler to leave the country after the inquest but there was no evidence to hold her on, nothing that a court would accept. Other detectives felt that she was innocent but neurotic.

Police ceased to work on the case years ago; the file is still open, but there are no more leads to follow. However, the following theory fits the facts.

GEOFFREY CHANDLER
A fresh theory

MARGARET CHANDLER
An innocent victim

GILBERT BOGLE
Target for murder

International conspiracy!

A FRIGHTENED MAN ACCUSES SECRET AGENTS

two people who could be responsible."

He told me that the organisation was part of an unholy alliance formed by Russian Jews, the American Central Intelligence Agency, and helped by security forces in various countries.

Bogle was assassinated to prevent his impending departure for America where he was to work for the Bell Telephone Laboratory on further extensions of his Maser research.' The Maser is a device for producing large quantities of power at very high frequencies.

That, simplified, was wh
man with the guttur
lieved w

will not accept certain things that defy traditional thinking.

We know something of the undercover activities of the CIA and our own security services. But we do not know into what vast areas they reach.

Prominent Americans have referred to the CIA as the "real world government." I believe this.

Similar allegations have been made by Mrs Catherine Dalton, daughter of Robert Gr
English poet.

Her husband

theory that she went to considerable trouble and expense to publish a book recently, Without Hardware, so that her beliefs could be aired.

Many other people take it seriously.

Right now, the Attorney-General, Mr Hughes, is inquiring into Mrs Dalton's allegations.

He revealed this in Federal Parliament last Wednesday after a question from an NSW Labor politician, Mr L. R. Johnson.

I have my own beliefs. They lie somewhere between those of Mrs Dalton and the man with the guttural voice on the telep..one.

Gilbert Bogle, you must understand, was more than a brilliant CSIRO scientist with a happy-go-lucky approach to social lif

An article by Geoffrey Chandler in the Sydney *Daily Mirror* revealed his chilling theory that Bogle died as the result of an international conspiracy

Lethal dose

Bogle, despite his reputation as a lady-killer, had sexual problems. In fact, his constant search for new partners may have been a symptom of this problem. Some psychiatrists regard LSD as a true aphrodisiac, and if anyone in Sydney could have obtained a supply of LSD it would have been Bogle. Bogle had been experimenting with LSD as a cure for his impotence. He may well have used it with Margaret Fowler. She speculated to her friend, Jenny Newbold, that Bogle may have taken 'a sex drug', a strange remark to make without some evidence of previous use of such a drug.

Bogle took the LSD in his coffee at the Nash party, deciding to slip some to Mrs Chandler as well. At that stage of the drug's development, no one knew what constituted a lethal dose. The usual dose, about 600 micrograms, hardly covers a pinhead. Either Bogle accidentally overdosed himself and Mrs Chandler, or, in keeping with Detective Sergeant Bateman's theory, another guest knew what Bogle was doing, and, for a joke, added to it.

Bogle and Mrs Chandler went to Lane Cove River Park. They had sexual intercourse. During or immediately after it they became violently ill with vomiting and diarrhoea. Margaret Chandler took her own and Bogle's underwear to the river to wash it. Bogle, who was too ill to move, died while she was away. Chandler died before she got back to Bogle.

At this stage, Margaret Fowler came on the scene. (One report to the police early in their investigations was that Fowler had been seen outside the Nash house some time after midnight.) She had followed Bogle's car to the park, waited, and then had gone to confront her lover and his new woman. She found them unconscious or already dead. She then arranged the bodies in the manner in which they were found shortly afterwards. Backing for this part of the theory comes from Sydney psychiatrists. The arrangement of Bogle's body suggested to them that whoever had done it wanted to give Bogle a semblance of dignity. The dressing of a corpse had been beyond the person, but the draping of the clothes to make him look as if he were clad suggested that the person felt sorry for Bogle and cared about him. On the other hand, the indecent way in which Mrs Chandler's body had been arranged suggested disapproval and contempt. The psychiatrists said that everything pointed to the fact that whoever had done this to the two bodies was a woman who knew them both. Margaret Fowler's worry that 'It's all going to come out' was not that she had killed Bogle and Chandler, but that she had been on the scene and would be a prime suspect in the police investigation.

Unfortunately, this theory, if a little more credible than others, founders in the end because of one inescapable fact. More than two decades after Bogle's death, his FBI file is classified. Even today something in it constitutes a danger to U.S. security.

We would all prefer the human solution: Bogle and Chandler died as a result of passions that got out of control. But there are sufficient facts about their lives and deaths that make it impossible to rule out the theory that they were victims of a conspiracy with international security implications. The chances are that we will never know what happened.

5
Missing, presumed dead

An English aristocrat allegedly commits a brutal murder and disappears without trace. An experienced American flier is lost somewhere over the Pacific. This chapter looks at two famous examples of one of the most intriguing of all mysteries – people who vanish into thin air.

Lost in the Pacific

In July 1937, Amelia Earhart disappeared during a flight around the equator. Were she and her navigator claimed by the ocean, or did they make a forced landing and become prisoners of the Japanese?

Pioneer airwoman Amelia Earhart carefully taxied her Lockheed Electra 10-E twin-engined aircraft to the take-off stand at the runway at Lae, New Guinea. Behind the cockpit in the main cabin was seated Captain Frederick Noonan, her navigator. He had secured all loose items and cinched tight the safety belts attached to his seat.

It was 2 July 1937. Earhart was embarking on the first ever attempt at a flight around the world by the longest route – the equator, a distance of 27,000 miles (43,500 kilometres). Already she had become the first woman to fly solo across the Atlantic and the first pilot ever to fly alone from Hawaii to California.

The round-the-world attempt had begun on 17 March when Earhart and two navigators flew the 2410 miles (3880 kilometres) from San Francisco to Honolulu. But bad luck struck almost immediately. As the Lockheed Electra was taking off from Honolulu, it crashed and the landing gear collapsed.

On 1 June, Earhart started again. She had changed her plans, and set off from west to east, this time with only one navigator, Fred Noonan. (Captain Harry Manning, the other navigator, decided after the crash that he had risked his life enough in the interests of Amelia Earhart and returned to his sea command.) Earhart and Noonan flew successfully over South America, Africa, Asia and Australia and then made the short hop from Darwin to Lae.

They had publicly acknowledged that the forthcoming stretch would be the most difficult and dangerous part of their well-publicised flight. Their course would take them over an expanse of Pacific Ocean never flown before – 2556 miles (4113 kilometres), mostly over open water – to tiny Howland Island, a fleck of land ¾ mile (1.2 kilometres) long by ½ mile (0.8 kilometres) wide, just north of the equator, where the US Navy, Army Air Corps and Department of the Interior had recently scratched out a rudimentary airfield.

The US Navy and Coast Guard had each provided a guard vessel to keep watch on the flight. The Navy's USS *Ontario* would be stationed in the open sea at the flight's mid-point and the Coast Guard Cutter USS *Itasca* would anchor near Howland Island. Both vessels would try to assist with communications and both could serve as rescue ships should Earhart and Noonan have to attempt an emergency landing on the ocean.

Perhaps the most dangerous and difficult aspect of the endeavour would be the take-off. The aircraft was grossly overloaded with 1050 US gallons (3980 litres) of 86-octane fuel, together with 50 US gallons (190 litres) of 100-octane petrol to provide extra power for the initial lift. The take-off went well. A few minutes after the Electra disappeared from sight, radio operator Harry Balfour in Lae received the long-awaited weather forecast for the Earhart flight from the US Navy Fleet Air Base at Pearl Harbor. The message had been routed through American Samoa and Suva, Fiji, which is why it took so long to arrive. To Earhart and Noonan it was navigationally vital to know wind directions.

No cause for alarm

At 10.22am, 11.22am and 12.22pm, Balfour transmitted the information by radiophone on Earhart's daytime frequency, 6210 kilocycles.

Balfour heard no acknowledgement from Earhart, but supposed she had got the message and had simply been too busy at the time to reply to it.

Then, at approximately 3pm Lae time, Earhart's voice came through Balfour's receiver, clear and unhurried. All seemed to be going well. At 5.20pm, Earhart broke through again. Both calls indicated that she was losing height and speed because of weather conditions, but there was no immediate cause for alarm.

To US Navy Lieutenant Horace Blakeslee, the assignment as commanding officer and navigator of USS *Ontario* was both fascinating and frustrating. The *Ontario* was the US Navy's only remaining coal-burning vessel and serving as a guard ship for the Earhart flight stretched her capabilities to the maximum extent.

Blakeslee had no illusions that two-way communication between Earhart and the *Ontario* would be easy to establish. The Electra had a low-frequency receiver, but no broadcast capability, and the *Ontario* had no high-frequency equipment.

From Earhart's 5.20pm reported position and speed, the Electra was due over the *Ontario* at approximately 10pm. One of the officers believed he

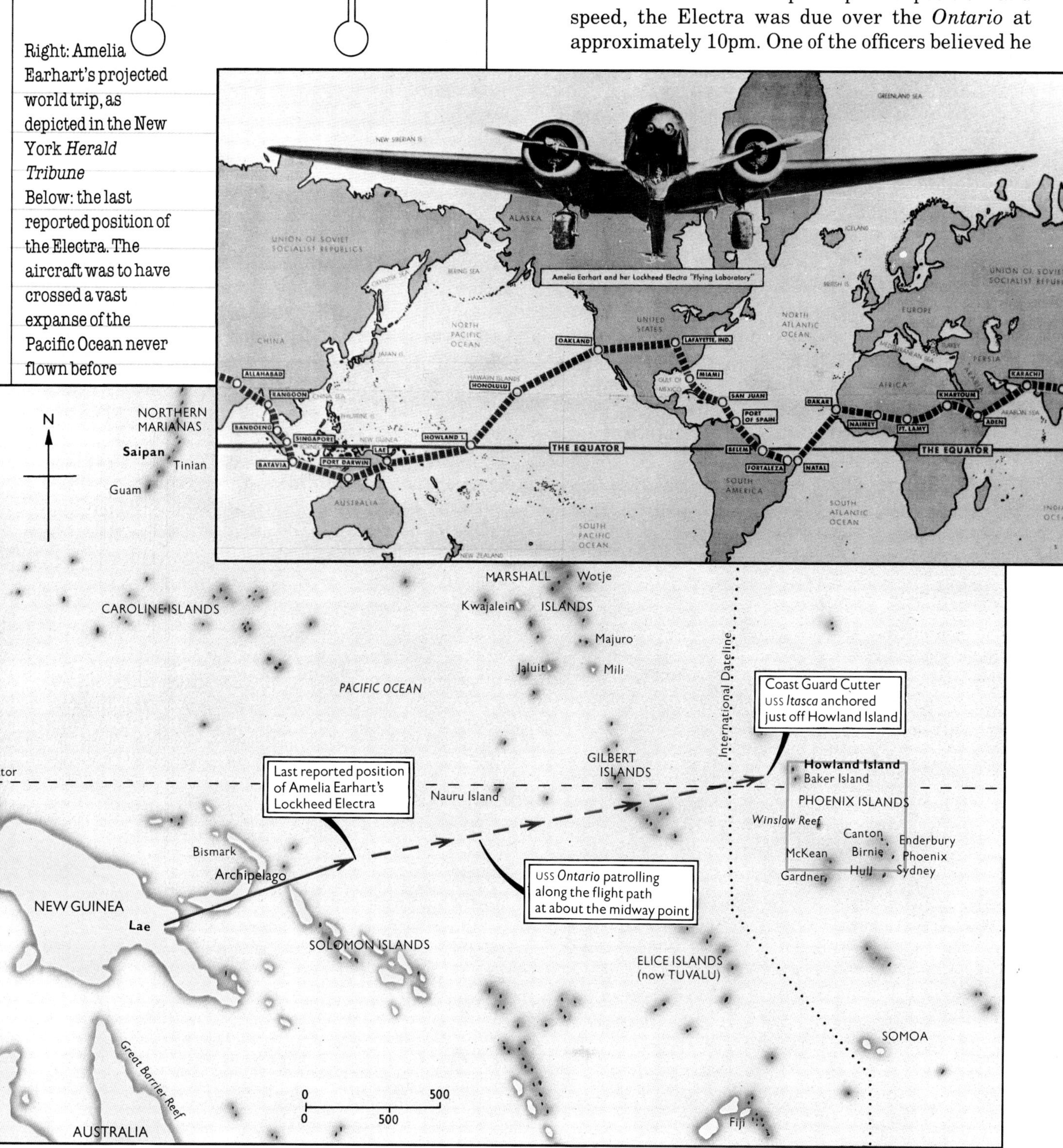

Right: Amelia Earhart's projected world trip, as depicted in the New York *Herald Tribune*
Below: the last reported position of the Electra. The aircraft was to have crossed a vast expanse of the Pacific Ocean never flown before

had heard the sound of an approaching aircraft a few minutes after 10pm. The *Ontario* searchlight swept the sky but nothing could be seen for cloud.

By 1am the overcast had become complete and heavy rain squalls were buffeting the ship. Blakeslee radioed, asking for permission to return to base, which he received. The old ship had difficulty making it, 'scraping the bottoms of the coal bunkers'.

At the same time as the men of the *Ontario* believed the Earhart aeroplane to be passing overhead, the radio operator of the Nauru Island station to the north copied Amelia saying, 'A ship in sight ahead.'

The 250-foot (76-metre) Coast Guard Cutter USS *Itasca* steamed slowly by Howland Island, barely keeping way. The radio room was fully manned, and a satellite station ashore on Howland housing a new and top secret high-frequency radio direction finder was ready for action as well.

By midnight, the *Itasca* radio-room was crowded. The wire service correspondents jockeyed for position with the Army men. William Galten and Thomas O'Hare, two Coast Guard radiomen, along with chief radioman Leo Bellarts, hovered over the transmitters and receivers. It was a long wait. Earhart's voice did not break through the static on 3105 kilocycles – her night frequency – until 2.45am, and then all that could be clearly understood was 'Cloudy weather ... cloudy'. An hour later, at 3.45, her voice was heard again, saying: '*Itasca* from Earhart. *Itasca* broadcast on 3105 kilocycles on hour and half-hour – repeat – broadcast on 3105 kilocycles on hour and half-hour. Overcast.'

The *Itasca* operators then transmitted on 3105, asking Earhart to send on 500 kilocycles so that the ship's low frequency direction finder could get a fix on her. Obviously no one on the *Itasca* knew that Earhart did not have the equipment to broadcast on 500 kilocycles.

Then, after another long wait, at 4.53am Amelia's voice was recognised again, but her signals were unreadable. The first real sense of worry began to permeate the radio room. At 5.12am, Earhart's voice came through again, and for three and a half hours afterwards fractured, frustrating calls were received from her. Frustration etched every face. As one of the operators said later: 'It was like not being able to reach a friend who was falling over a cliff.'

At 8.43am, Earhart's voice, which some later described as frantic, blurted: 'We are on the line of position 157-337. Will repeat this message on 6210 kilocycles. We are now running north and south.' Earhart was switching to her regular daytime frequency of 6210 kilocycles. The *Itasca*'s radio operators immediately monitored 6210 kilocycles but only got static. At 10.30am the *Itasca* radioed Honolulu that it was going to begin a search.

Headline news

Search, indeed. But where? What did '157-337' mean? It was probably a sun line that Noonan had been able to get a bearing on just before Earhart's last radio transmission. But a sun line was no good without a reference point. The aircraft could be anywhere along 2000 miles (3200 kilometres) of that sun line. On a compass reciprocal, '157-337' could represent a south-east to north-west line through Howland Island itself. Thompson reasoned that since the weather front to the north-west might have

stopped Earhart and Noonan from seeing Howland Island, he would search in the area immediately around the island first.

The disappearance of the world's most famous flier was headline news in America and in most of the rest of the world. President Franklin D. Roosevelt, who had arranged for US government co-operation with the flight, and whose wife had flown with Earhart during Roosevelt's presidential campaign, immediately ordered the battleship USS *Colorado*, which was on a reserve training cruise near the Hawaiian Islands, to proceed at top speed to the Howland Island area to assist with the search. The *Colorado* carried three catapult observation aircraft that could cover wide areas of ocean. And on the evening of 3 July 1937, the president ordered the aircraft carrier USS *Lexington* and three destroyers to proceed from the west coast of America to the vicinity of Howland Island to augment the search.

It was clear it would take at least 10 days for the *Lexington* and the accompanying destroyers to reach the scene, and there was considerable grumbling in Navy circles and in Congress about 'spending millions of dollars and disrupting Navy training schedules to search for a couple of stunt fliers'.

In the first days following the disappearance, many sources reported radio distress signals received from what was believed to be the downed Earhart aeroplane. Two amateur radio operators in Los Angeles claimed to have heard two SOS calls followed by Earhart's call letters, 'KHAQQ'. On 4 July, three radio operators at the Wailupe Naval Radio Station in Honolulu, Hawaii, took the message: '281 . . . north . . . Howland . . . KHAQQ . . . beyond north . . . don't hold with us much longer . . . above water . . . shut off.' At the same time, an amateur radio operator in Oakland, California, heard: '281 . . . north . . . Howland . . . can't hold out much longer . . . above water . . . shut off.'

Far left: Amelia Earhart with her first flying instructor, Neta Snook, in 1920, when she was 22
Left: the Fokker seaplane *Friendship*, after completing the flight from Newfoundland to Burry Port in Wales in 21 hours. The date was 17 June 1928 and Amelia Earhart had become the first woman to fly the Atlantic

On the strength of the two specified messages, the Navy and Coast Guard asked the *Itasca* and a passing freighter, SS *Morby*, to search the area 280 miles (450 kilometres) to the north of Howland Island. The effort was futile.

The next day in Los Angeles, Paul Mantz, who had been technical advisor for Earhart's first attempt at the round-the-world flight, dropped a small bombshell. He told the press that he had learnt from sources at Lockheed Aircraft that Earhart's aeroplane was incapable of broadcasting from the surface of the water. This statement had immediate and disastrous effects. All the messages so far received were discounted as hoaxes, the cruel work of charlatans and damnable publicity seekers.

Radio signals

But Mantz, in fact, did not know the state of Earhart's radio equipment, and neither did the people at Lockheed Aircraft. Mantz had been dropped from the flight team after the Honolulu crash, and was not even in California when the second attempt at the flight began.

There was only one man who knew for certain about the Electra's radio gear – Joseph Gurr, who had been assigned, alone, to the task of adapting a Bendix-built US Navy high-frequency direction finder for Earhart's flight and making sure the rest of her equipment would function properly. Gurr believed it possible that signals from the downed Electra in the vicinity of Howland Island could have been heard 3750 miles (6030 kilometres) away in the United States. 'Signals can skip great distances and play some crazy tricks,' he said.

On 5 July 1937, most newspapers carried a brief story alluding to possible signals from the Earhart aeroplane being received at Honolulu, on Midway Island and on Wake Island by high-frequency direction finders owned by Pan American Airways. The bearings from those signals indicated that the aircraft might be down in an area several hundred miles south-east of Howland in the vicinity of the Phoenix Islands. But this story was quickly discounted by the US Navy and Coast Guard for security reasons. One of the most important aspects of military intelligence communications was strategic direction finding, particularly in the high-frequency range. America did not want the rest of the world, particularly Japan, knowing what her capabilities in that area were. The disguise concealed grave weakness. The US Navy would later learn as the Second World War got under way that Britain, Germany and even Japan were far more advanced in direction finding development; indeed, as early as 1937 the Japanese had a string of direction finding stations in the Marshall Islands to the north of Earhart's flight path. They could track her aeroplane better than the Americans could.

Pan American Airways and US Navy communications, which had become partners in the Pacific, were still relying on the Adcock direction finder, which was of British origin. Pan Am provided an excuse for developments on strategic islands in the Pacific that could, and did, have military application. So, in the interests of security, the Navy quashed the story of Pan Am's direction finding bearings on possible signals from the Earhart aeroplane. The records of those bearings were later picked up by Navy intelligence officers at the Pan Am communications headquarters in Alameda, California, but they remained sequestered from the public until the early Seventies.

Above: the new, all-metal Lockheed Electra, designed by Clarence 'Kelly' Johnson. The aircraft was stripped of its eight passenger seats to make room for the extra fuel tanks necessary for the flight, but it was still grossly overloaded

Phoenix Islands

But George Palmer Putnam, Earhart's husband, had seen the reports, and when the direction finding base on Howland Island reported on 6 July that it had got a bearing on 'KHAQQ', which could either be south-east or north-west, he begged the Navy to instruct USS *Colorado* to begin its search to the south-east of Howland and extend it to a group of eight small coral atolls known as the Phoenix Islands. He urged that a particular effort be made to locate several small coral reefs plotted on the hydrographic charts as being approximately 165 miles (265 kilometres) south-east of Howland.

The 14th Naval District at Honolulu agreed, and so did Captain Wilhelm Friedell, the commanding officer of the *Colorado*. He made a rendezvous with Captain Thompson and the *Itasca* at 6am on 7 July, and the Navy then took charge of the search. By mid-morning the *Colorado* was on course for the general area of the reefs. At 2.30pm three young pilots were launched from the ship in their open-cockpit bi-planes. They returned just after 5pm, having found nothing but open ocean.

After debriefing his fliers, Captain Friedell came to the conclusion that the charted reefs probably did not exist at all, and a decision was made to begin searching the Phoenix Islands themselves the following day.

During the following five days, the *Colorado* aviators averaged four flights of three aircraft each day. Each aircraft flew for more than 21 hours and together they covered an area of more than 25,000 square miles (65,000 square kilometres). They searched Enderbury, Phoenix, Birnie, Sydney, McKean, Gardner and Hull Islands, and then finally Canton, the northernmost island in the Phoenix group. All were uninhabited, save Hull Island where Lambrecht landed in the lagoon and was greeted by the British resident commissioner and a boatload of natives who had paddled out to get a close view of this wonder. None of them had even heard of Amelia Earhart, let alone seen her.

Friedell and his men might have contemplated another search of the area had they known that amateur radio operators in northern California had picked up two more messages on the night of 7 July. One read: 'Plane on reef ... 200 miles [320 kilometres] south ... Howland ... both OK.' The other was: 'SOS ... KHAQQ ... east ... Howland ... lights tonight ... can't hold...'

At 7am on 12 July 1937, the *Colorado* met and refuelled the destroyers that were leading the aircraft carrier USS *Lexington* to the search scene. After refuelling, the *Colorado* was detached from the search and returned to port.

The carrier USS *Lexington*, with 60 aircraft, began its search to the north and north-west of Howland Island on 13 July. Ocean currents in the area are generally to the north-west and the reasoning was that a drifting aeroplane could now be hundreds of miles from the place where it originally went down.

Japan had serious cause for concern about United States intentions in the search for Amelia Earhart. Japan had occupied the Marshall, Caroline and Mariana Islands during the First World War, and had maintained control of the area under a League of Nations mandate after the war. But, beginning in 1934, Japan had gradually sealed off the islands from the rest of the world. It was believed that the Japanese were building airfields, fuel depots and expanded harbour and communications facilities in preparation for a Pacific war with the United States, in total contravention of the conditions of the League of Nations mandate.

The Japanese surprise attack on Pearl Harbor on 7 December 1941 was the climax of years of secret preparation in the mandated Pacific Islands. Japan's military headquarters in the islands was on Saipan

The Japanese-mandated Marshall Islands lie only 550 miles (880 kilometres) north and west of Howland Island, and the construction of an American airfield on Howland was most disconcerting to the Japanese. They had repeatedly sent surveillance vessels to Howland to try to determine from offshore the extent and progress of the construction of the strip.

By 18 July, the *Lexington*'s aeroplanes were searching areas almost touching the Marshalls, and over the years there have been allegations that some of the *Lexington* pilots made deliberate detours over selected Japanese-held islands to take illicit photographs. The *Lexington*'s official log and search report, however, do not support such contentions, nor do the recollections of officers who participated in the search.

After the air search on 18 July, the *Lexington* set a course for San Diego, California, while the destroyers *Drayton*, *Lamson* and *Cushing* headed for Pearl Harbor, Hawaii. Aircraft from the *Lexington* had covered 151,556 square miles (392,530 square kilometres) of ocean without finding any trace of Earhart or Noonan or any wreckage.

Straightaway, the rumours began to spread. One had it that Earhart had been working for the United States government at the time of her disappearance. Another was that she had purposely lost herself so the US Navy could search the Japanese-controlled islands. The most dramatic speculation – not taken seriously by the American public – was that she and Fred Noonan had been forced to land on or near one of the islands and that they were being held prisoner by the Japanese.

The cell in the ruined prison at Garapon on Saipan where Amelia Earhart was reportedly held until she died, possibly of dysentry

The *Oakland Tribune* in May 1938 began a series of articles about the Earhart disappearance by reporter Alfred Reck. Somehow, Reck had managed to gain access to the then highly classified Coast Guard files. In the first article he alleged that Earhart and Noonan had been lost because of the failure of the US Navy direction finder on Howland Island, and that Richard Black, the US Department of Interior representative who had brought the Navy direction finder aboard the *Itasca*, had supplied the wrong kind of batteries, so that the equipment failed at the very moment it was needed most. Immediately the Navy, Coast Guard and Black brought their full authority to bear on the *Oakland Tribune* and reporter Reck. The remaining articles were censored and suppressed.

Also in 1938, the popular *Smith's Weekly* newspaper, published in Sydney, Australia, printed a lengthy article alleging that the United States had used the Earhart disappearance as a pretext to fly over the Japanese-held islands and that Australia's defence establishment had been informed of the plan and of its results: 'So when Amelia Earhart went down and her faint distress signals located her aeroplane around the Phoenix Islands, the search gave the needed excuse. Sentiment comes second to secret service.' One Republican senator felt that the primary motive of the article 'may have been to stimulate ill feeling between Japan and the United States'. But the Japanese sinking of the American gunboat USS *Panay* in the Yangtze River two months later effectively buried his concern. Ill-feeling had now become outright hostility. By the time of the attack on Pearl Harbor on 7 December 1941, Amelia Earhart was virtually forgotten.

Unmarked graves

Rumours about the fliers' disappearance continued to circulate, however. In 1944, on Majuro Atoll during the invasion of the Marshall Islands, Vice Admiral Edgar A. Cruise learned from a native interpreter that two American fliers, a man and a woman, had been picked up and brought to the Marshalls in 1937. At almost the same time, Eugene F. Bogan, the senior military government officer at Majuro, interviewed a Marshallese native who told the same story.

Four other Marine Corps and Navy officers turned up similar information: an American man and woman, fliers according to the Japanese, had been brought into Jaluit in the Marshalls, then transported to Majuro and Kwajalein, also in the Marshalls, and finally taken to Saipan in the Marianas. Saipan was Japan's military headquarters in the Pacific islands before and during the Second World War. The woman had died of dysentery, and the man reportedly had been executed some time after her death. They had been buried in unmarked graves outside a native cemetery.

In 1964 two former US Marines, Everett Henson Jr and Bill G. Burks, came forward to say they were part of a group of Marines who recovered the remains of Amelia Earhart and Frederick Noonan on Saipan in July 1944. They had found remains, they said, in an unmarked grave outside a small graveyard and placed them in metal canisters for transport to the United States. To this day, the US Marine Corps will neither confirm nor deny such an event ever occurred.

It was not until 1960 that a real investigation began, and that investigation was civilian. The Columbia Broadcasting System in San Francisco sponsored four expeditions to Saipan Island in the Marianas and two more to Majuro Atoll in the Marshalls to try to find answers to the Earhart mystery. Several hundred natives on Saipan were questioned and more than 30 individuals told stories that supported the theory that two American fliers, a man and a woman, had lived and died on Saipan before the war.

When the Freedom of Information Act became law in the United States in 1966 a number of files began to appear, and since the 'streamlining' of the Act in 1974, more and more pertinent material has been found and declassified. From 1968 to the present day, well over 20,000 pages of records concerning the flight from seven departments of the US government and the military have been released, and there is certainly more to be revealed.

One revelation is the close involvement of the government in the preparations for the flight. The idea for a round-the-world flight had begun at the Purdue Research Foundation at Purdue University in Lafayette, Indiana. Amelia Earhart had served the university for brief periods as a lecturer and counsellor to women students. The foundation, formed to seek 'new knowledge in the field of aviation, with particular reference to National Defense', was in close communication with the US War Department, Army Air Corps and Naval Aviation. The foundation provided the funds for the purchase of Earhart's Lockheed Electra on the understanding that the aeroplane would be used 'for the purpose of improving radio direction finding equipment'.

Earhart first planned to fly the Pacific from east to west and refuel in flight over Midway Island with the assistance of a specially equipped US Navy aircraft. Techniques such as mid-air refuelling were then in their infancy and extremely risky. Then the pilot's needs and those of the military coincided. Earhart needed a safer method for crossing the Pacific, and the Navy and Army Air Corps needed an excuse to build an airfield on an island near the equator. America had agreed with Japan at the Naval Treaty Conference in Washington in 1923 that military construction on most of the Pacific islands controlled by each nation would be prohibited. The United States had long believed that Japan was violating that treaty in the mandated islands, but could not prove it. America had played the same game on Midway and Wake Islands through co-operation with Pan American Airways. Now, Earhart provided a purely civilian reason for building an airstrip on Howland.

From the records that have now been released, Earhart does not seem to have been conducting an overt spy mission during the world flight, though, at one time, that did look possible. There is, however, evidence and testimony that she and Noonan were gathering what is called 'white intelligence'. As civilians they were quite legitimately going to visit and fly in and out of places seldom, if ever, visited by the US military, and observation of these areas would be valuable.

Strong testimony

Nothing in the records released so far proves that the Japanese captured Earhart and Noonan, though the testimony gathered from Marshallese and Saipanese native witnesses is very strong. Nor is there anything documentary to substantiate the claim that the remains of Earhart and Noonan were recovered on Saipan in 1944 by US Marines.

After 23 years of research, 12 trips to Saipan and four to Majuro Atoll, the author has arrived at certain conclusions that might offer a solution to the mystery. Namely, at the time of their disappearance, Earhart and Noonan *were* co-operating with their government, and there is strong testimony that two American fliers were picked up by the Japanese military units somewhere in the Pacific and taken to the Marshalls and then to Saipan.

But just where the Electra landed is very much a matter for conjecture. If the Japanese know, they have said nothing. If Earhart and Noonan were off course considerably to the south (which could have happened if they did not receive the weather forecast predicting significant winds from the north-east), the Phoenix Islands would surely have been their choice. Until the mysterious and uncharted reefs lying between Howland and the Phoenix Islands are thoroughly searched and the lagoons of those islands are plumbed, the possibility remains that the wreckage of the Electra could still be found.

THE WEATHER
Saturday and Sunday generally fair and warmer

Columbus Evening Dispatch

OHIO'S GREATEST HOME DAILY

VOL. 67, NO. 3. Telephone—MAin 1234

SATURDAY, JULY 3, 1937.

14 PAGES

Wirephotos Associated Press International News Service

AMELIA'S VOICE, CALLING S-O-S, IS HEARD BY LOS ANGELES RADIO MAN; SIGNALS SPUR SEARCH

FLYER'S OWN STORY WRITTEN BEFORE LAST TAKEOFF

By Amelia Earhart

NEW GUINEA, JULY 2. — "Denmark's a prison" and Lae, as rare and unusual as it is, appears to be just as confining. The Lockheed is poised for our longest trip.

It is weighted with gasoline and oil to capacity. There is only one runway and a parallel is needed to take off. However, the wind is blowing the wrong way and threatening clouds conspired to keep her on the ground today.

In addition Frederick Noonan, my navigator, has been unable, because of radio difficulties, to set his chronometers. Any lack of knowledge of their fastness or slowness would defeat the accuracy of celestial navigation. Howland is such a small spot in the mid Pacific that every aid to locating it must be available. Despite our restlessness and disappointment in not getting off yesterday morning, we still retained enough enthusiasm to do some exploring of native villages a few miles from Lae.

We commandeered a truck from the manager of the hotel and with Fred Noonan at the wheel because the native driver was ill with fever we set out along a dirt road. We forded a sparkling little river, which after a heavy rain so common in the tropics, can be turned into a veritable torrent, and drove through a lane of grass taller than the truck. We turned into a beautiful cocoanut grove before a village entrance. The natives grow the cocoanuts mostly for their

CONTINUED ON PAGE 2, COL. TWO

... Earhart Is Lost ... on Pacific Flight to ... Such a Tiny Island

IN THE EXPANSE INDICATED HERE MISS EARHART IS LOST

Operator Sure He Heard Flyer

Planes and Ships Rush to Hunt For Aviatrix, Down at Sea After Futile Attempt to Reach Howland Island.

LOS ANGELES, JULY 3.—(INS).—Amelia Earhart's voice came crackling over the Pacific today from her big airship drifting helplessly in mid-Pacific.

The voice was heard by a Los Angeles amateur radio operator.

"S O S. KHAQQ. . . S O S. KHAQQ . . ." she repeated. The rest of the message, probably giving her position, faded away.

The message was picked up here by Walter McMenamy, an amateur operator. It was the same message received earlier in dot-dash form by McMenamy and other radio operators on the west coast.

"I have been in radio touch with Miss Earhart on other flights, and I know it was her voice," McMenamy said.

HONOLULU, JULY 3.—Distress signals signed with the call letters of Amelia Earhart's monoplane flashed over the Pacific today in the midst of a feverish sea and sky hunt for the famed aviatrix missing in equatorial waters surrounding tiny Howland Island.

Amateur radio operators in Los Angeles heard repeated calls of "S O S—KHAQQ" shortly before 1:30 a. m., Pacific time (4:30 a. m., Eastern Standard ...) was more than 14 hours ...

The saga was widely reported in the press. In the end, all the hopes raised by reports of signals from the aircraft were cruelly dashed and, after 16 days of the largest air-sea rescue operation in history, the search was called off

The case of the vanishing Earl

Immediately after his children's nanny was killed and his estranged wife brutally assaulted in November 1974, the Earl of Lucan, the gambling aristocrat known as 'Lucky', disappeared. A coroner's jury found him guilty of murder, and his mysterious behaviour supports this allegation, yet he has never been traced

It was a cold, wet Thursday night in November when Lady Veronica Lucan ran from her Belgravia home to tell the assembled drinkers at The Plumbers' Arms of the murder she had just discovered. Wearing a rain-soaked dress, no shoes and with blood pouring from a deep wound above her face, she burst into the small pub lounge shouting: 'Help me, help me ... I've just escaped from a murderer ... my children, my children ... he's in the house ... he's murdered the nanny ...' Head barman Arthur Whitehouse helped her to a bench seat and laid her down while his wife brought damp towels to help stop the bleeding. The landlord telephoned for the police. They arrived within minutes and an ambulance took Lady Lucan to St George's Hospital at Hyde Park Corner. Two officers had meanwhile forced entry to the Lucan family home, an expensive five-storey Georgian house at 46 Lower Belgrave Street.

The lower half of the house was silent and in darkness. Police Sergeant Donald Baker shone his flashlight down the narrow hallway and discovered, at the far end by the stairs leading to the basement, what appeared to be bloodstains on the wallpaper. Cautiously, the two policemen made their way along the passage until they reached the top of the stairs, which led to a half-landing. There, beside a door leading to a breakfast room, they saw a pool of blood in which two or three footprints were evident. The officers began a search of the other floors. On the second floor they found the first light burning in the house, and in one of the bedrooms, on the pillow of a double bed, lay a bloodstained towel. On the top floor Baker found two children, a boy aged seven and a girl aged four, asleep in a nursery. He opened another door and saw 10-year-old Lady Frances Lucan, dressed in pyjamas and looking wide awake and bewildered. After comforting the child, he returned to the basement. There, on the floor, he discovered a large canvas mailbag. Inside it was the battered body of the children's dead nanny, a young woman called Sandra Rivett.

Baker had uncovered the victim of a murder that was to become one of the most curious mysteries in British criminal history. No one has stood trial for the nanny's murder and the seventh Earl of Lucan, Richard John Bingham, has not been seen since that fateful night.

Thirty minutes after the alarm was raised, Detective Sergeant Graham Forsythe, who was eventually to become Lady Lucan's bodyguard, found the bloodstained murder weapon on the half-landing. It was a 9-inch (23-centimetre) piece of lead piping, weighing 2¼ pounds (1 kilogram) and wrapped in adhesive medical tape.

With Lady Lucan now lying unconscious in hospital Forsythe needed, above all, to talk to Lord Lucan. The peer owned a mews house at 5 Eaton Row, near the rear of the Lucan family home. Just after 11pm Forsythe checked the two-storey house,

Above: the Lucan family home in London's Belgravia, where the nanny was killed

Above: the innocent victim, Sandra Rivett, nanny to the Lucans' three children. She might not have died had she taken her usual Thursday night off

Above: Lord Lucan's mews house in Eaton Row; a police search revealed no trace of him

but found it empty. Then, he returned to Lower Belgrave Street. At the family house forensic scientists had begun their work. Lucan's mother, the Dowager Countess of Lucan, had arrived too. After Forsythe had explained the night's events to her, the Dowager Countess said that Lucan had just telephoned and asked her to go to the house.

She said that Lucan had told her that there had been a 'terrible catastrophe' at the house and that his wife Veronica was hurt and the nanny injured. He had asked her to collect the children. She told Forsythe that her son had said he was passing the house when he spotted someone attacking his wife. He had gone into the house, where his wife was screaming and shouting. Her son sounded shocked, said the Dowager Countess, and rang off without saying from where he was calling. The call came neither from a call-box nor through an operator.

Lucan's mother then told Forsythe that her son was separated from his wife – he did not live at the family house – and the children were wards of court.

Second call

Next, Forsythe checked Lucan's flat at 72a Elizabeth Street, just 300 yards (250 metres) from the family home. Parked outside was the earl's two-year-old Mercedes. Inside, there were signs that Lucan had expected to return that evening. A suit was carefully laid out on the bed, and on a bedside table were his spectacles, the contents of his pockets, cheque book, small change and car keys. His passport was in a drawer.

Shortly after midnight Lucan again telephoned his mother; he asked about the children, and she told him they were safe. Then she said, 'Well, look, the police are here. Do you want to speak to them?' Lucan replied, 'I will ring them in the morning. And I will ring you.' But before the police officer standing next to the Dowager Countess could take the receiver from her hand, Lucan rang off.

Meanwhile, Detective Chief Superintendent Roy Ranson, head of A Division CID, which covers the Belgravia area, was contacted by his deputy, Detective Chief Inspector David Gerring, who informed him of the details of the nanny's death. Ranson had no reason, then, to suspect that Lord Lucan would not contact him. The suspicion that Lucan was the murderer had not yet formed in his mind. At this stage, the police were still treating seriously the story that Lucan had told his mother, that he had interrupted a fight. As a precaution, an alert was sent to ports and airports that Lucan should be stopped if he tried to leave the country.

Lady Lucan told the police that when she had gone to look for the nanny, she found the half-landing above the kitchen in darkness. She called out Sandra's name, but there was no reply. Then she heard a sound in the cloakroom behind her, and a man leapt out, striking her with a heavy weapon. She screamed and they fought, but her attacker tried to thrust gloved fingers down her throat and gouge out her eyes. After he had forced her to the ground, she grabbed him by the genitals and he let go. Her attacker, she said, was her husband. She had recognised his voice in the dark. According to Lady Lucan,

he told her he had killed the nanny in mistake for her. Lady Lucan told detectives that she calmed her husband by offering to help him. They went upstairs to the bedroom where she lay on the bed and her husband went to soak some towels in the bathroom to bathe her wounds. When she heard the taps running she ran from the bedroom, down the stairs and out to the public house.

Ranson realised that without the testimony of the earl, the scientific evidence would be vital. The autopsy on Sandra Rivett, conducted by the distinguished pathologist Professor Keith Simpson, found she had been struck with a blunt instrument – almost certainly the lead pipe. Lady Lucan's injuries were probably caused by the same weapon.

Vivacious girl

In the meantime Ranson began gathering information about the victims and the possible killer. He discovered that Sandra Rivett came from a working-class background in Basingstoke, Hampshire. She was the 29-year-old mother of a small child and had separated from her husband, Roger, a security guard at Gatwick airport, in April the year before. Sandra was described by her family as a 'vivacious girl, always laughing', who had loved her job. She had worked for Lady Lucan for only five weeks, living in and being paid £25 a week to look after the three children. Ranson could discover no motive for her murder and wondered whether her death could have been a case of mistaken identity.

He learned that Sandra, although plumper, was the same height – 5 feet 2 inches (1.58 metres) – as Lady Lucan. More significantly, he discovered that she had a boyfriend, John Haskins, who was a relief barman at The Plumbers' Arms, where Lady Lucan had first sought help. Sandra's night off each week was usually Thursday, but that week she had taken Wednesday off instead to go out with Haskins. Perhaps, Ranson reasoned, Sandra's killer had gone to the house expecting only Lady Lucan to be there on a Thursday night. When he discovered that Lord Lucan had questioned his daughter Camilla about the nanny's night off, the suspicion grew in Ranson's mind that Lucan was the killer.

Ranson found his suspect's background full of surprises. On the face of it the family was comfortably off, with a grand house in Belgravia, a second home, a live-in nanny, a Mercedes and all the other trappings of wealth. Gradually Ranson was to discover that Lord and Lady Lucan were far from happy, and that there had been an acrimonious court battle over the custody of the children. The wealth was an illusion, too, as the house was owned by a family trust, Lucan's flat was rented and rent was owing.

Veronica Duncan first met Lucan when she was bridesmaid for her sister, Christina, at her wedding to Lucan's friend, the millionaire amateur jockey Bill Shand Kydd, at Holy Trinity, Brompton, London, in January 1963. In the spring of that year, Veronica stayed with her sister and new brother-in-law at their country estate in Bedfordshire. There Veronica again met the dashing Lord Lucan. A brief courtship ensued that summer, and by the autumn Lucan had bought a ring from Cartier's and announced their engagement in *The Times* of 14 October 1963.

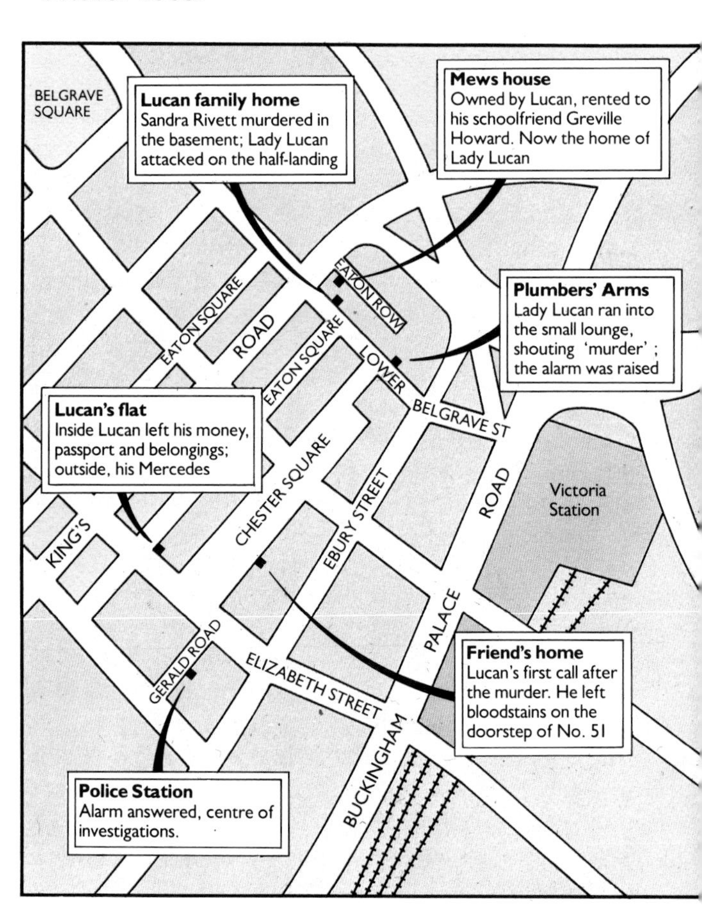

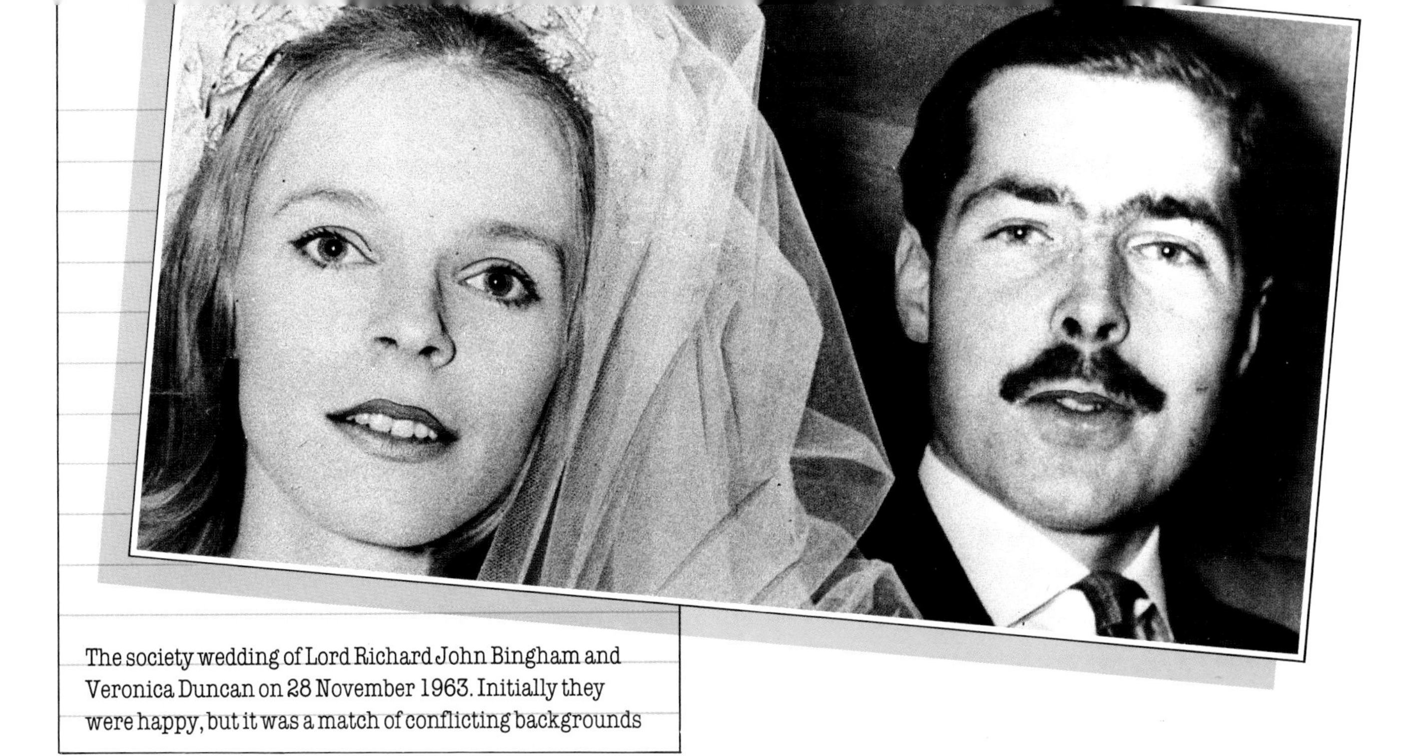

The society wedding of Lord Richard John Bingham and Veronica Duncan on 28 November 1963. Initially they were happy, but it was a match of conflicting backgrounds

On 28 November Veronica returned to Holy Trinity for her own wedding. In January 1964, Lucan's father died; he succeeded to the title and inherited a fortune, estimated at £250,000, which included family estates in Ireland, land in England and the family silver. Veronica became the Countess of Lucan. The couple bought 46 Lower Belgrave Street for £19,000 and moved in to begin a smart life of society parties and touring holidays. In October Veronica gave birth to their first daughter, Frances. Lord George Bingham was born in 1967, and three years later a second daughter, Camilla, was born.

In the early years of his marriage Lucan was known as a perfectly charming English gentleman. His friends, however, noticed that, in the months leading up to the murder, he became increasingly depressed. Ranson realised that after Lucan had separated from his wife in January 1973, he had become obsessed with the welfare of his children. Two months after the separation, he had snatched two of them as they walked in a park with a nanny. He kept them at his Elizabeth Street flat while he fought and lost a case to gain custody.

The case cost him £40,000 and left him feeling bitter and angry about the legal system. He was already paying for the upkeep of the family home, a £40-a-week allowance to his wife, £25 a week – ordered by a High Court judge – to the nanny and the £50 a week rent and upkeep of his flat. At one stage it is estimated that Lucan was also paying up to £400 a week on employing a private detective to watch his wife's home.

His debts were accumulating and his only income – fixed at £7000 a year – was from a family trust. The financial and emotional pressure affected his habitual gambling at the Clermont Club, Berkeley Square, and he started losing heavily and borrowing to make ends meet.

Lucan's decline became more rapid as he faced mounting debts. He owed rent and payments on his car. A £10,000 cheque to the Clermont bounced and the club denied him credit facilities for a time.

Lucan's movements

By the evening of Friday 8 November, detectives had begun tracing Lucan's movements in the hours immediately before the killing. At 8.30pm on 7 November he had telephoned the Clermont, spoken to the assistant manager, Andrew Demetrio, and booked a table for four people for dinner at 10.30pm. About 15 minutes later he arrived at the Clermont in person. He spoke to the doorman, Billy Edgson, for a few minutes, inquiring whether his friends had arrived, and then drove away. Edgson noticed Lucan was driving his Mercedes. The drive from the Clermont back to Lower Belgrave Street at that time of evening takes about 10 minutes. The timing, Ranson reasoned, was perfect if Lucan had been trying to establish an alibi. When Greville Howard and three friends arrived at the Clermont at 10.45pm they told the assistant manager, Demetrio, that Lord Lucan was to be their host. A fifth chair was brought and another place laid for the host, who was never to arrive.

On the morning of Saturday 9 November police searched Belgravia and discovered that Lucan had called on a family friend, Mrs Madeleine Florman, in Chester Square. Her daughter attended the same school as the Lucan girls, and Lucan may have called to ask her to look after his children. She, however, had not answered the door to him. Forensic scientists later found blood on her doorstep. Later that morning, Ranson received a telephone call from Bill Shand Kydd, Lucan's friend, who said that two letters had arrived at his London home. Both of them

Police frogmen searched Newhaven docks for Lucan's body after the car he borrowed had been found in the town

were postmarked Uckfield, Sussex; Lucan's handwriting was on the envelopes. There was also what appeared to be blood on them. The first letter read as follows:

> Dear Bill, The most ghastly circumstances arose tonight, which I have described briefly to my mother, when I interrupted the fight at Lower Belgrave Street and the man left.
>
> V. [Veronica] accused me of having hired him. I took her upstairs and sent Frances to bed and tried to clean her up. She lay doggo for a bit. I went into the bathroom and she left the house.
>
> The circumstantial evidence against me is strong in that V. will say it was all my doing and I will lie doggo for a while, but I am only concerned about the children. If you can manage it I would like them to live with you.
>
> V. has demonstrated her hatred for me in the past and would do anything to see me accused.
>
> For George and Frances to go through life knowing their father had been in the dock accused of attempted murder would be too much for them.
>
> When they are old enough to understand explain to them the dream of paranoia and look after them.

The letter was signed 'Lucky'. The second letter was headed 'Financial matters' and again it began 'Dear Bill'. It went as follows:

> There is going to be a sale at Christie's which will rectify the bank overdraft. Please agree reserves herein.

Lucan was referring to the sale of family silver; he then made a list of its estimated value, concluding: 'Proceeds to go to Lloyds, Coutts and National Westminster . . . and the other creditors can get lost for the time being.' This, too, was signed 'Lucky'.

This was the first indication Ranson had had of the seriousness of Lucan's financial debts. And the letters exposed the deep animosity between Lucan and his wife. But one line that particularly interested Ranson was Lucan's fear of his son seeing him in the dock accused of 'attempted murder' – not murder. Perhaps Lucan did not know the nanny had been murdered? Perhaps, after all, he was not the killer they were looking for?

Ian Maxwell Scott, a cousin of the late Duke of Norfolk, had helped John Aspinall establish the Clermont Club and he, like Lucan, whom he had known 20 years, was a compulsive gambler. His winnings had paid for their seven-bedroomed Victorian mansion, Grants Hill House, on the outskirts of the East Sussex village of Uckfield. The house had three acres of grounds, a croquet lawn, tennis court and swimming pool. Maxwell Scott's wife Susan, a trained barrister, was the daughter of Sir Andrew Clark, QC. The couple were devout Roman Catholics and had six children. In happier times the Lucans had been frequent weekend visitors to Grants Hill House. Ranson knew that Mrs Maxwell Scott would be a vital witness in the case.

Mrs Maxwell Scott told Ranson that on the night of the murder her husband had telephoned at around 10pm to say he was staying in London. She had gone to bed at 11pm and was dozing a little later when the doorbell rang. She looked out of a window and saw Lucan standing below. After letting him in she gave

Ian and Susan Maxwell Scott at their home in Uckfield. Lord Lucan was last seen leaving this doorstep after speaking to Mrs Maxwell Scott on the night of the murder

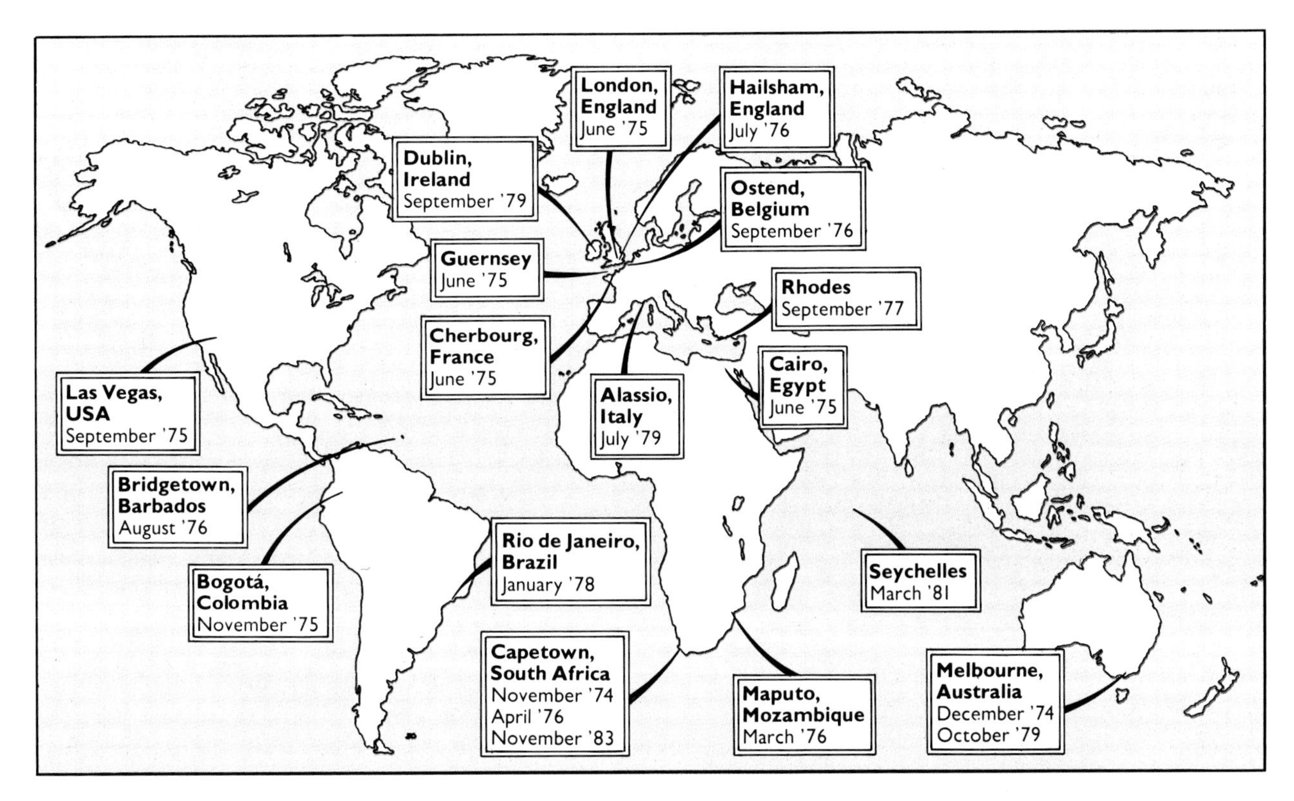

Map of the major sightings of Lord Lucan since the murder of Sandra Rivett, based on reports received by Scotland Yard

him a scotch and water. Lucan, she said, had looked a little dishevelled and was wearing a light blue silk polo-neck shirt, brown sleeveless pullover and grey flannels with a dark patch on his trousers at the right hip. He told her he had been passing his home on his way to his flat to change for dinner, when he had looked through the venetian blinds of the kitchen window and seen a man attacking his wife. He had entered the house using his key, and as he went down to the basement he had slipped in a pool of blood. The man who had been attacking his wife ran off. Mrs Maxwell Scott said Lucan had said he had not chased the man but had gone to his wife, who was covered in blood and very hysterical. Despite Mrs Maxwell Scott's appeals to him to stay the night, Lucan said he had to 'get back' to clear things up, although he did not mention London specifically. She told police that Lucan drove away from her house at around 1.15am in a dark saloon car.

Escape car

At about 3pm on Sunday 10 November Ranson heard from police at Newhaven, on the East Sussex coast, that the escape car used by Lord Lucan had been traced to Norman Road, a quiet street away from the seafront and harbour. The car, a battered old Ford Corsair, had been borrowed by Lucan two weeks before from his friend Michael Stoop, a backgammon player and retired company director.

The abandoned Corsair had bloodstains on the inside of the driver's door, on the dashboard and on the steering wheel. Also inside was a full bottle of vodka, and in the boot was a length of lead pipe wrapped in adhesive medical tape, which seemed identical to the murder weapon. The car had been parked in the street on the morning of Friday 8 November, some time between 5am and 8am according to observant residents. The mystery facing Ranson was that if Lucan had left the Maxwell Scott house at 1.15am, where had he gone in the hours before the car was parked? The 16-mile (26-kilometre) drive from Uckfield to the coast could not have taken as long as 3¾ hours, let alone 7.

Two trawlermen told police that on the Friday morning they had spotted a distinguished-looking man walking along the jetty where their boats were moored. Perhaps Lucan had taken one of the many boats moored in the area or had boarded a cross-Channel ferry. One ferry had left Newhaven at 11am that day. It was also possible that Lucan, an accomplished boatman, had taken a boat out, although a force eight gale was blowing throughout the night of the murder. Detectives began the huge task of checking the thousands of boats moored at Newhaven, but none were found to be missing. Lucan, Ranson knew, had left his passport in London, but he could have obtained a 60-hour travel permit on the quayside at Newhaven, for which no proof of identity is required. But there was no record of this. Detectives travelled to Dieppe to check with immigration officials, but no one recalled anyone resembling Lucan. Boarding houses and hotels in the area were checked but produced nothing. Ranson drew up plans to search Beachy Head, the South

Lady Lucan, after being discharged from hospital. The countess had never managed to become part of her husband's social circle, and it certainly offered her no friendship after the tragic events of November 1974

Downs above Newhaven, and the waters in the harbour in case Lucan was hiding out or had committed suicide.

On Monday 11 November, Ranson decided he now had enough evidence against Lucan to seek warrants alleging murder and attempted murder. He dictated a report to Sir Norman Skelhorne, Director of Public Prosecutions.

At 5pm on Monday 11 November, Ranson received a telephone call from Michael Stoop, the friend who had lent Lucan the Corsair. He was at the St James's Club, and he told Ranson that he had just received a letter there from Lord Lucan.

Police did not see this letter until 3am the next day; and by then they had discovered that Stoop had thrown away a vital clue – the envelope with its revealing postmark. A police search of rubbish containers at the club failed to uncover the envelope. The letter read as follows:

> My dear Michael, I have had a traumatic night of unbelievable coincidence. However, I won't bore you with anything to involve you except to say that when you come across my children, which I hope you will, please tell them you knew me and that all I cared about was them. I gave Bill Shand Kydd an account of what actually happened, but judging by my last effort in court no one, let alone a 67-year-old judge, would believe me – and I no longer care, except that my children should be protected. Yours ever, John.

Ranson thought the tone of this letter was more desperate than that of the other two that had been received from Lucan since his disappearance, and judged that it might be a farewell letter. It was probably written by Lucan as he sat alone in the Corsair; if he had written it while with Mrs Maxwell Scott, he would surely have asked her to post it.

Later that Tuesday morning Bow Street magistrates' court issued two warrants for the arrest of Lord Lucan. One alleged he had killed Sandra Rivett, the other that he had attempted to kill his wife. It was the first time in 200 years that a peer of the realm had been a major murder suspect. The previous case was that of the sixth Lord Byron, accused and cleared of murder in April 1765.

Police began a more wide-ranging search for Lucan, allowing for the possibilities of his suicide or escape. Frogmen went into the waters around Newhaven, while police with dogs searched the South Downs. No clues emerged. The search was spread to country estates but nothing was found.

Unconfirmed sightings

On Saturday 30 November in Johannesburg, South Africa, the first of many unconfirmed sightings of Lucan overseas was reported. The new year of 1975 brought hundreds of other sightings, none of them confirmed, and Ranson became convinced that the earl was dead. He hoped that, as spring came, Lucan's body might be found, perhaps by walkers on the South Downs. In early May, police launched another major search using an auto-gyro fitted with an infra-red camera, but again they found nothing.

The new year had also brought the first steps to declare Lucan bankrupt. Police had already sought a court order in November to open up the earl's bank accounts. But instead of finding, as they had hoped, information about withdrawals of cash that Lucan might have made since his disappearance, they discovered that, in addition to other debts, in four British accounts he owed a total of £14,477. To help pay these debts the Lucan family silver had been sold at Christie's for £17,410 on 27 November. Ranson had, however, discovered a deposit of 20,000 Rhodesian dollars (approximately £9000) in a bank in Bulawayo. But access to it was barred by the foreign exchange freeze imposed after Rhodesia's Unilateral Declaration of Independence in 1965.

By this time Lady Lucan, who had spent a quiet Christmas at home with her children, had come to agree with Ranson about the fate of her husband: 'My husband was always a very honourable man. So I am sure he would have thought the only honourable thing to do was not to go through the embarrassment of returning. . . . If he had access to a gun I think he might have used it on himself.'

The only conclusive act in the unsolved Lucan mystery was the long-delayed inquest into the death of Sandra Rivett, which opened at the coroner's court in Horseferry Road, Westminster, on 16 June 1975.

It was designed to investigate the nanny's death, but began to resemble a murder trial with the defendant, Lord Lucan, absent. In view of the legal difficulties relating to the naming of a killer not in custody, the Westminster coroner, Dr Gavin Thurston, decided that Lady Lucan should give her evidence only 'in connection with part of the matters'.

After speaking for 90 minutes Dr Thurston sent the three women and six men of the jury out of the court to consider their verdict. After 31 minutes they returned. Their verdict on the death of Sandra Rivett was murder by Lord Lucan.

The coroner said: 'It is very rare for a coroner's court that a person is named as you have done. It is my duty to commit that person to trial at the Central Criminal Court. In this case there is nobody I can commit for trial because we don't know where Lord Lucan is. There is no doubt that if he turns up he will be charged with the offence.'

Lucan's family, shocked by the verdict, vowed to take legal steps to try and clear his name. For Roy Ranson, the inquest was the culmination of a long, difficult inquiry, the most baffling in his career. He believes that Lucan is dead and will never stand trial for murder.

Scotland Yard's file on the case is still open and the mystery of Lucan's whereabouts remains.

Lady Lucan shows the strain as she is driven by detectives from Westminster Coroner's Court on 18 June 1975, day three of the inquest into the death of Sandra Rivett

Detective Chief Superintendent Roy Ranson – haunted by the face of Lucan. Later made head of investigation into breaches of security at the BBC, he keeps this Lucan gallery at his London office – and speculates on how the earl may look now

Index

Main entries are in **bold**.
Picture references are in *italic*.